Alastair Scott was born in Edinburgh in 1954. He now lives with his wife, Sheena, on Skye (with occasional bouts of vagrancy), working as a photographer, writer and broadcaster. He is the author of *Scot Free*, *A Scot Goes South*, *A Scot Returns* and *Tracks Across Alaska*.

Also by Alastair Scott

Non-Fiction:

SCOT FREE – A Journey from the Arctic to New Mexico

A SCOT GOES SOUTH – A Journey from Mexico to Ayers Rock

A SCOT RETURNS – A Journey from Bali to Skye

WANDERLUST – An Anthology of 'Best' Extracts from the Trilogy *Scot Free, A Scot Goes South & A Scot Returns*

TRACKS ACROSS ALASKA – A Dog Sled Journey

SALT AND EMERALD – A Hesitant Solo Voyage Round Ireland

ECCENTRIC WEALTH – The Bulloughs of Rum

TOP TEN SCOTLAND (Eyewitness Travel Guide)

Fiction:

STUFFED LIVES

DEGREES OF ILLUSION

NATIVE STRANGER

*A Journey in Familiar
and Foreign Scotland*

ॐ

ALASTAIR SCOTT

sphere

SPHERE

First published in Great Britain in 1995
by Little, Brown and Company
Published in 1996 by Warner Books
This edition published in 2013 by Sphere

A CIP catalogue record for this book
is available from the British Library.

ISBN 978–0–7515–5318–5

Typeset in Times by
Palimpsest Book Production Limited,
Falkirk, Stirlingshire
Printed and bound in Great Britain by
Clays Ltd, St Ives plc

Papers used by Sphere are from well-managed forests and other
responsible sources.

MIX
Paper from

To Tom Barry

Who saw my first book seven years before it was written, and has urged me on ever since.

Acknowledgements

My thanks to:

Sheena, above all, for contrary and complementary points of view which helped shape my own; and for editing which tidied up many loose ends and added sense where it was lacking.

Barbara Boote of Little, Brown and Clare Roberts of Rogers, Coleridge & White, for faith, hope and a contract.

My father for compiling a meticulous list of all things likely to attract or repel me along the route.

The many whose lives, opinions and stories form the basis of this book (in some cases, under fictitious names), and those who provided assistance during my journey. Especially: Nigel Hall, Doug Kearney, Hamish and Maggie Moore, Maxwell MacLeod, Duncan and Jan Sandison, Andy and Audrey Sturgess, the Scottish Women's Rural Institute, HM Prison Perth, HM Coastguard (Lerwick), Alan & Ker (Ullapool), Gulf Offshore N.S. Ltd, and the crews of 'Oscar Charlie' and *Highland Pride*. Vango (Scotland) Ltd generously provided a tent and outdoor clothing, and kept me storm-resistant.

Every effort has been made to contact the holders of

copyright material quoted in the text. The following have kindly granted me permission to quote:

Chapter

 1 Pan Books Ltd, from Jonathan Raban, *Hunting Mr Heartbreak*, 1991.

 9 Sabhal Mor Ostaig, from the 1992 Sabhal Mor Ostaig lecture; John Goodlad, 'Shaping the Future'.

15 George Mackay Brown and *The Orcadian*, from his weekly column 'Under Brinkie's Brae'.

18/87 Mainstream Publishing, from James Hunter, *Scottish Highlanders, A People and Their Place*, 1992.

21 Random House UK Ltd, from 'A Man In Assynt'; Norman MacCaig, *Collected Poems*, Chatto & Windus.

26 Western Isles Education Business Partnership, from the *Western Isles School Leaver – 1993*.

30 Raghnall MacilleDhuibh, and the *West Highland Free Press*, from his column 'The Quern-Dust Calendar' (to be published as a book in 1997; Ronald Black, *The Gaelic Calendar, Vol 1*, The Tuckwell Press).

35 Carcanet Press Ltd, from 'The Cuillin' and 'Heroes'; Sorley MacLean, *From Wood to Ridge*, 1991.

36 Jarrold Publishing Ltd, from Rev J A Carruth, *The Bonnie Prince Charlie Country*, 1971.

37 Dr George Hendry, from his *Midges in Scotland*, Aberdeen University Press, 1983.

44 Lawrence Edwards, *The Vortex of Life*, Floris Books, 1993.

50 Scotia Bar, Glasgow, from *The Scotia Folk & The Clutha Clipe*.

53 Mainstream Publishing, from James Mackay, *Burns – A Biography of Robert Burns*, 1992

58 Peter Russell, from his article 'New Age Religion', in 'The Holy Island Project Newsletter 1993'.

60 Oxford University Press, from A N Wilson, *The Laird of Abbotsford*, 1980.

62/83 Chambers Harrap Publishers Ltd, from *The Chambers Dictionary*.

65 *The Scotsman*, from the column of Dr Anne Smith.
Constable & Co Ltd, from Iain Finlayson, *The Scots*, 1987.
Canongate Publishing Ltd, from Alasdair Gray, *Why Scots Should Rule Scotland*, 1992.

77 *Kingdom By The Sea: A Journey Around the Coast of Great Britain* by Paul Theroux (Hamish Hamilton, 1983), copyright (c) Paul Theroux, 1983. Reproduced by permission of Hamish Hamilton Ltd.

79 Constable & Co Ltd, from Andrew Birkin, *Barrie And The Lost Boys*, 1979.

79/88 Scottish National Party Publications, from the Donaldson Lectures: William McIlvanney, 'Stands Scotland Where It Did?', 1987; Professor Neil MacCormick, 'Constitutionalism and Democracy', 1988; Joy Hendry, 'Flourishing Under the Burden of Nationhood', 1992.

80 Jonathan Cape, from Tom Cullen, *The Empress Brown – The Story of a Royal Friendship*, Bodley Head, 1969.

86 Hugh Dan MacLennan, from his *Shinty*, Balnain Books, 1993.

87 Edinburgh University Press, from Grant Jarvie, *The Highland Games – The Making of the Myth*, 1991.

88 Richard Drew Publishers, from Nigel Tranter, *Nigel Tranter's Scotland*, 1983.

MACDUFF   Stands Scotland where it did?

ROSS   Alas, poor country. Almost afraid to know
                 itself.

Shakespeare, Macbeth

The happiest lot on earth is to be born a Scotsman. You must pay for it in many ways, as for all other advantages, on earth. You have to learn the Paraphrases and shorter Catechism; you generally take to drink; your youth, as far as I can find out, is a time of louder war against society, of more outcry and tears and turmoil, than if you had been born, for instance, in England. But . . .

R.L. Stevenson, A Scot Abroad

. . . But?

∞

Contents

Glossary

Ashet	large serving plate
Birkie	smart, conceited man
Brae	hill, slope
Brogues	heavy leather shoes
Brose	oatmeal and boiling water/milk
Canty	cheerful, merry, brisk, lively
Chap	hit, strike, knock
Clarty	dirty, muddy, sticky
Close	entry to a tenement, alley
Connacht	spoiled, destroyed
Coof	rogue, fool, useless person
Corbie	crow
Couthie	agreeable, pleasant, homely
Crabbit	cross, bad-tempered
Crack	gossip, banter, chat, news
Cromag, crummock	shepherd's crook
Dominie	schoolmaster
Dirl	shake, vibrate, quiver
Dour	sullen, dull, sluggish
Dreich	dreary, tiresome, bleak
Dwam	stupor, daydream
Fank	sheepfold, sheep sorting yard
Fankle	tangle

Fly	tea, supper
Gaidhealtachd	Gaelic-speaking Scotland
Gloaming	evening twilight, or dawn
Haar	cold mist or fog
Harled	roughcast
Hirple	walk lamely, limp, hobble
Howff	favourite haunt, (freq) pub
Hurdies	buttocks, hips
Keek	peep, watch surreptitiously
Kenspeckle	conspicuous, easily recognisable
Lallans	Lowland Scots
Ma-tha	'Well, then'
Mercat	market
Muir	moor
Nappy	ale
Neuk	corner, lurking-place
Piece	snack, (freq) packed lunch
Pecking	panting, out of breath
Piobaireachd,	– usu. *ceol mor*, the 'great music'
piobroch	of the bagpipes
Quaich	drinking cup
Scalpaich	native of Isle of Scalpay
Sgitheanach	native of Isle of Skye
Slàinte	health, a toast
Stank	grating in a gutter
Swee	movable iron bar over a fire
Targe	hand-held shield
Teri	native/inhabitant of Hawick
Thangka	Buddhist painted scrolls
Thrawn	obstinate
Thole	suffer, endure

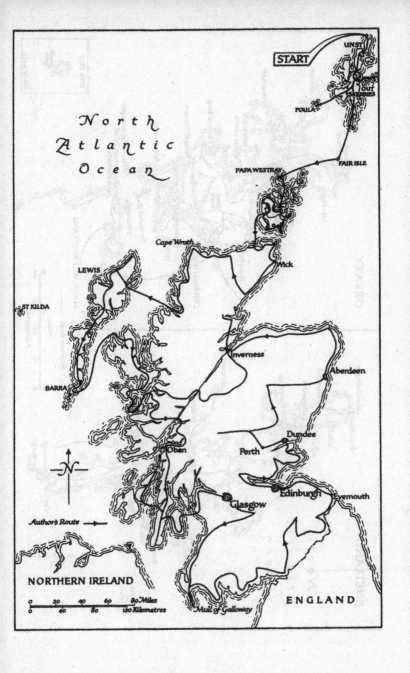

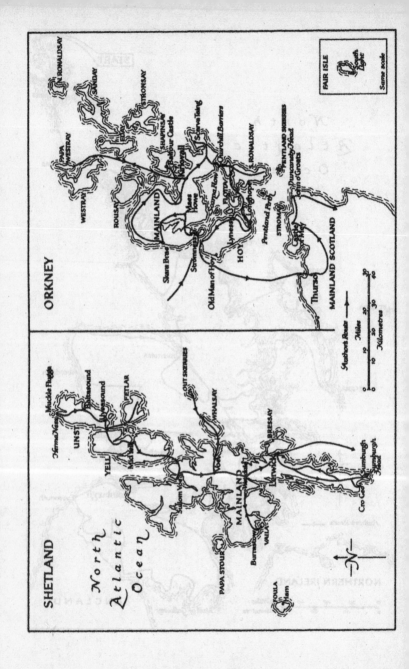

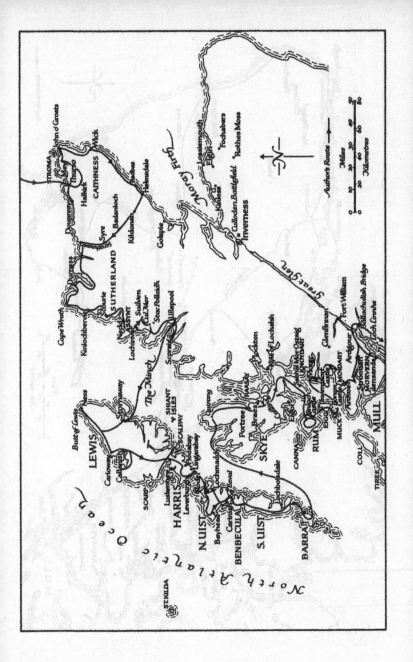

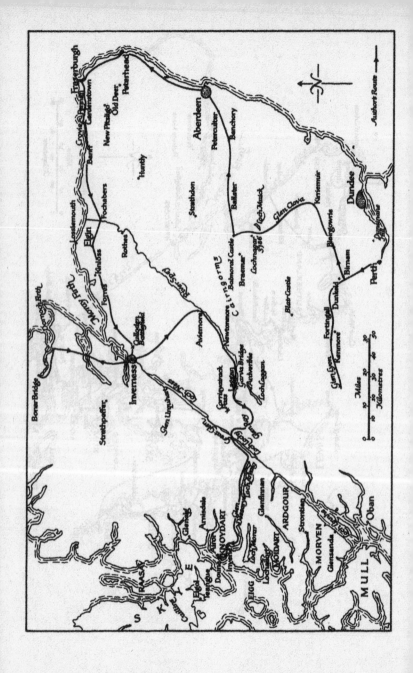

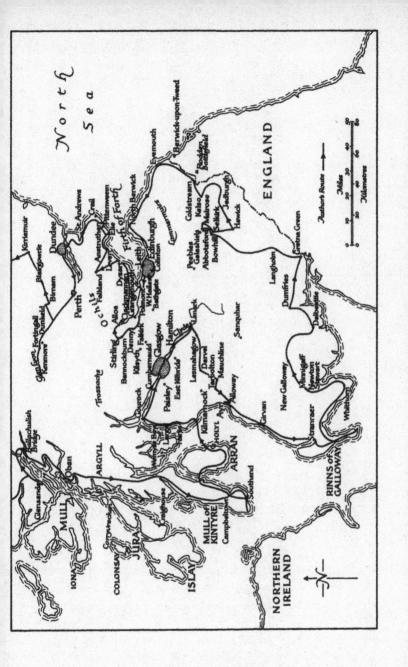

1

⚭

Arthur Caldback's Shop, Shetland

Hunch-backed crows perched on posts, scouring the land with a matronly eye for disorder. They would have found it nearby in the shop of Arthur H. Caldback. He owned the most northerly emporium in the British Isles and he stood behind its counter, an elderly man untroubled by mildew or mould and neatly dressed in a suit as he presided over a world in imminent collapse. His thin frame had been bent under a lifetime's struggle with Shetland's wind, roof leaks, handbags, Snoopy Annuals (1976) and Royal Wedding plasticware; but neither adverse climate nor immovable stock had crushed his faith. Arthur H. Caldback just knew that one day the door would open and a figure would step in and say, 'I'd like two pounds of onions, one of those trays and a nineteen-seventy-six Snoopy Annual, please.'

It had been a long wait. His face had oxidised to a crusty frown as a result of this and years of exposure to tourists' facile remarks about weather, beauty and loneliness. He was capable of two expressions: this frown and, to local people, a hearty smile, and he switched from face to face with the abruptness of a swivelling tragi-comedy mask. Currently the mask was set on frown for he had before him a tourist of the most inquisitive kind.

'There's not much you *haven't* got here!' remarked the tourist, having already unsuccessfully touched on gales and isolation. This was certainly true. Mr Caldback's shop occupied two adjoining cottages. Its internal labyrinth extended through seven rooms on two floors and they were chock-a-block with all the needs of humanity: fishing rods, mousetraps, postcards, framed pictures of Lassie, wellies, and boxes of Christmas decorations (in June); the contents of *Glassware* had been on show for so long they were now a bewildering assortment of mausoleums for moths, earwigs and spiders; 'Kenneth McKellar sings Robert Burns' announced a bowed LP cover whose glue had lost its grip and it gaped like a gin trap; shelves rose ten feet up the walls with bulging squadrons of jars and tins, many so old they had begun to leak and their labels were bacteriological showpieces; but if time appeared to stand still here, a tub of 'fruit fragrant pencils' showed Mr Caldback was smack up to date with children's fads.

You could go left and right and left again and upstairs, flicking switches as you went, inhaling wonder as naked lightbulbs revealed another Tutankhamun chamber of knick-knackery. Below five layers of wallpaper peeling from the ceiling, brand-new handbags were piled on the floor; shoes displaying the styles and pricetags of previous decades were heaped in disarray, and clothes could only be located by burrowing and tugging. Generations of cobwebs festooned the windows and reduced them to peepholes. Mr Caldback did not believe in vacuum cleaners or the art of presentation but he did believe in security. Each room lay under the eyes of Sony closed-circuit cameras.

'Aren't you worried about the damp?' the tourist asked, pointing to a motorway of white rot which traversed the ceiling.

'Naw. Allus been like that.' Mr Caldback's business had been supplying the community of Uyeasound since 1700.

The tourist bought a tin of mould-free tuna and two postcards. Mr Caldback looked him over critically while he tried to extricate his money from a plump daypack. He was a man of around forty, with curly fair hair which clearly had little experience of combs and was receding above the temples. His ruddy complexion and ginger beard looked Highland but his accent placed him elsewhere, in the Borders maybe, or even south of them. He wore a thermal jacket and tracksuit trousers stained with oil around the ankles. Mr Caldback straightened his tie and looked disapproving.

'Where da belong ta?' he asked. The Shetland dialect broadened certain consonants and pinched certain vowels. English words passed through this linguistic mill and emerged mutilated, plumped up or strangled but in the soothing singsong lilt of the Scandinavian influence.

The tourist hesitated. It was obviously a question that made him uncomfortable. 'Edinburgh, originally.'

'Aw, Scotland! I ance hid ma haldays i Scotland.'

The tourist looked at him in confusion. He was referring to the place as if it were a foreign land. 'To Scotland? But we're in . . .' he began. He let it drop. Mr Caldback had produced a third mask. Very Severe Frown. The tourist realised he'd asked too many questions, thanked the proprietor and left.

As travel writers constitute the eyes, ears and thought-processors of the selective experiences they offer, and as travel writing inevitably carries autobiography in its baggage, it is a courtesy of such writers – if not actually incumbent on them – to reveal something of their background and nature. This is particularly the case where the subject is Scotland: home, or a parody of one, to so many.

I am a Scot. My home has always been in Scotland. My ancestry is Scottish as far back as family records go, and in so far as they are honest; if any gene invasion has occurred, the conviction remains among the family that it must have failed dismally. Like Stevenson, we have always regarded a Scottish birth as a reasonably happy lot, and the historical image of Scot and Scott to be reasonably clean. I was brought up in Moray, and attended schools there, and in Aberdeenshire and Yorkshire. I went to Stirling University where lectures in German and Economics interrupted a life of running and canoeing. Then followed eighteen months as a trainee studio photographer in Edinburgh. These are simply the circumstances of my life, in which I have neither pride nor shame.

The smallprint of this undistinguished CV reveals a flibbertigibbet's restlessness. Two holiday seasons were spent in service to the Loch Ness Investigation Bureau, armed with a leviathan of a camera and looking out for strange ripples. I herded reindeer in the Cairngorms. For months, as black as mourning, I worked as a peat cutter on Rothes Moss, earning 25 pence for every cubic yard raised and being enthralled by the poetry recited by my equally black companions. Then my lot turned to window-cleaning. All the thousands of panes of glass at RAF Kinloss and Lossiemouth have witnessed my swirling chamois. A North Sea oil platform took me offshore for a year, and then I spent seven of the next ten years working and travelling round the world. For much of the journey I wore a kilt.

This sojourn left me feeling that I knew more about politics in Nicaragua and problems in China than I knew about life in my homeland. My 'Scottishness' was instinctive but I felt it represented a desire to belong rather than a belief that I actually did belong. Claiming allegiance to the whole, or even half or a quarter of the country, was suspect, unconvincingly loose. Scotland was far too big and varied to authenticate intimate and personal relationships with its entirety. No, specific parochial attachments were required. 'Belonging' meant where your family had its roots, where your neighbours had known your granny for half a century.

This could be Unst or Wester Hailes or Kirriemuir or Govan, but it couldn't be East Scotland or *Long*itude 3°W, *Lat*itudes 55°55′ to 57°40′ (which would have suited me just fine, encompassing Edinburgh and Elgin); and this is where I became unstuck.

My grannies were known in Colinton and North Berwick, but I wasn't. My father was a distiller (a legal one) and we moved around Edinburgh a bit. We moved to Fochabers, then to Elgin. This last move covered only eight miles but to a primary school kid it was half a hemisphere away. In Elgin home stayed put, but my schools near Huntly and Kendal continued to enforce the nomadic life. I suffered no trauma from this – at least, it hasn't manifested itself yet – just, years later, the discomfort of being asked, not 'Where are you from?' but 'Where do you belong to?'

Orphans of mobility are a caste apart.

I was sent to school in England because my father and his father had been sent there. Why my great-grandfather set this process in motion remains unexplained. Perhaps he launched his son into that drift to England, that fantasy of southern superiority, which has persisted since the Union of the Crowns, and especially since Culloden. Perhaps he adhered to the Victorian code of toughening your children by sending them as far from home as possible. Whatever the original reasons, at thirteen, too immature to ponder the ethics of education, I made my trek south, viewing the experience as a glimpse into another race, as if I were being sent, for example, to Amritsar or Tierra del Fuego.

At school in England I held on tenaciously to my Scottishness, being one of seven (of 450 boys) who wore a kilt on Sundays. I knew nothing about kilts and cared less; this was all about symbols, and identity. In spare time at university I immersed myself in the elements of my culture which were most conspicuously missing, taking up Gaelic and the Highland pipes, but my degree of application was no match for other distractions. At the peats and at the

windows I even tried to recast my public school accent
into a semblance of the Doric, and threw in as many swear
words as were necessary to establish credibility with my
workmates. Learning to be myself is taking longer.

By the end of my university days I was familiar with
much of Scotland in terms of its physical character but my
knowledge was otherwise superficial. Scottish history had
never been on my school agendas. I could not have filled
a paragraph on the Scottish Reformation or explained the
significance of the 1886 Crofting Act. I had read Chaucer,
Austen and Golding but not Scott, MacDiarmid or Grassic
Gibbon. Raised in the generous space that exists between
an atheist (possibly agnostic) and an ecumenical Episcopalian, I had a mild flirtation with the Scripture Union at the
age of twelve, and faithfully (in its secular sense) read my
Bible before bed. The phase fizzled out in a disappointing
lack of understanding, blinding lights or angels. And five
years later, even to save my soul, I could not have
differentiated what set me, a nominal Episcopalian, apart
from a Presbyterian or a Free Presbyterian. I was still,
however, of open mind.

And politically I was naive. I had read up more about
the Sandinistas than I had about the Scottish National
Party. It was easier to dabble in the affairs of foreign lands
where there was no requirement for personal investment
or responsibility. Politics, appearing more the science of
squabbling than of governing, had never held a fascination
for me. Through apathy, therefore, I contributed to the
rot of a democracy which I saw as flawed and restricted,
but preferable to anything else I had encountered. In
my naivety and apathy I suspected I was not alone,
but like many who, either through complacency or the
dogged acceptance of inherited values, remained in a back-
water of outmoded beliefs. We had ceased to plumb their
depths, or question them in the context of contemporary
change.

This journey was to redress the deficit of being one of

Scotland's cultural and political waifs; to learn about Scotland's past where it happened and to see what was happening here today. The route would embrace the whole country: its interior, its coastline and its islands, from Shetland to the Rinns of Galloway, from Lewis to Eyemouth. Inevitably it would be Scotland through peepholes, a series of vignettes drawn by those I met on a random journey of chance, and some prearranged, encounters.

This was the plan. First, I read all about us.

We were reported as being heroic, hospitable, romantic, maudlin, dour, thrawn, thrifty, and downright bloody mean.

We ate too much red meat, overdosed on chips, smoked too many cigarettes and inclined towards alcoholism.

Our race was a byword for ingenuity, for inventors, for engineers, for a few writers, fewer poets, and a scarcity of composers and artists.

Politically, we were all over the place, never able to agree amongst ourselves let alone get an act together to strive for mutual benefit. We felt isolated through the geography of power which divorced our politicians from us: a situation some of us liked, others resented.

Only sport had ever united us, briefly.

There were four times as many of us living out of our country as in it, but those of us lucky enough to be in this *Land o' Cakes* inhabited a natural theatre, if the brochures were to be believed, where kilts and shaggy cattle were as plentiful as our blue skies.

We were oddities. If anything was unusual we wore it, ate it or arranged contests to throw it. If it was mundane we wrapped it in tartan and sold it at twice its value.

The diversity of our parts was much more complex than the composition of the mythical Chinese dragon, but, unlike the dragon, **we** were given credibility. Others not only believed we existed in this form, they also believed they knew us intimately. Like James.

James was consumed by the sense of his own 'dispossession'; it made him ache for 'the luxury of some such
close and sweet and *whole* national consciousness as
that of the Switzer and the Scot'. (Henry James (1904),
quoted by Jonathan Raban in *Hunting Mr Heartbreak*.)

The Scots are the inheritors of a national image that,
typically, stems from a confusion of history and myth, but
which is remarkable for the breadth of its popularity. We
inherited this image but we also created it and perpetuate
it. To what extent do we believe it? Do we see ourselves
as others see us? Who are the Scots today? How do we
live? What gives us a national consciousness? How 'close
and sweet and *whole*' is it? What value do we place upon
it now?

The tourist in Mr Caldback's shop felt a deep affinity
for this land which he wished to explore and perhaps
explain. He travelled by bicycle. This was not because
he was a bicycle fanatic; he was *not* of that ethereal world
where people talk models and specifications, give their
conveyances personal names to create surrogate travelling
companions and exchange records of achievements and
punctures. He travelled by bicycle because it came close
to the perfect form of transport: silent, slow enough to
look and think, fast enough to cover distance, and exposed
enough to encourage interaction with those he met along
the way. This last attribute was important. His interest,
above all, was in people. To him, people were the soul
of a landscape.

So his was a nameless old machine with ten gears. He
fed it generously on oil (which transferred to his trousers),
loaded it with panniers, flung on a tent, sleeping bag and
cooker, and set off confidently in possession of a puncture
repair kit and the intention of ditching the bike for other
means of transport wherever the fancy took him.

He headed for Shetland in search of Scotland and the
Scots, and found neither.

2

∽

Unst

Over the last six centuries Shetland has cut loose, drifted
off the map and found independence. Of its one hundred
islands, fifteen are inhabited by 22,000 people and 330,000
sheep. The most northerly of these is Unst where it rains
on 253 days of the year and blows a gale on 42 of them. If
the people only painted their houses red, blue or yellow,
the land would be indistinguishable from the Faroes. If the
Norn dialect of their litter bins ('DUNNA CHUK BRUK')
was spoken by more than one-third of the population, then
linguistically they would be Norwegian, for over 10,000 of
their words are Old Norse. Culturally the Shetland Islands
are bobbing about 200 miles north of their present position
but the current is steadily drawing them south.

In 1850 a woman stood on the cliffs at Hermaness and
looked out to sea, to the horizon beyond the craggy islet of
Muckle Flugga where today a lighthouse stands and marks
the official beginning of Scotland. Those who were with
her said 'she stood for some minutes on the sombre rock,
quite silent, tears falling slowly, and her hands stretched
out towards the north'. She had come to 'send love on the
wings of prayer' to her missing husband and to come as
close as physically possible to him. That woman was Lady
Jane Franklin, wife of the Arctic explorer, and, unaware

that her husband had died two years earlier and that her quest to find him would continue for another six, she had made the arduous journey from London to Shetland to raise men for another expedition to look for him. She had no difficulty. Shetlanders were used to the short haul to the top of the world.

Unst gathered its heather, grass and bogs into one last flurry of lumps before ending abruptly at the sheer cliffs of Hermaness. I wondered if Lady Jane had been harassed by great skuas, or 'bonxies' as they were called here. These large brown birds, the terrorists and pirates of seagulls, came swooping out of the sky with a terrifying rush and only aborted their attacks when a few feet from my head. Their assault was relentless and my nerves were frayed by the time I reached the end of the land.

Muckle Flugga lighthouse looked like a tall extension of the guano which covered the rock around it, and the three keepers who still lived there must have had it well stocked with videos and jigsaws. In January 1992 the storm which demolished houses and sent boats tumbling across fields picked Muckle Flugga as the venue for Britain's all-time wind speed record. It pushed the anemometer's needle to 150 knots (173 mph), where the scale ended, and then on to an estimated 194 mph. Muckle Flugga looked a place for the birds, and a shortcut to insanity.

On this particular day the weather was balmy and thoughts of gales and Arctic hardship clashed with the placid view. A gentle breeze tugged at loose hanks of fleece – hentilaggeds – caught in the grass. As the Vikings had found, Shetland on a good day was as good a place as any to postpone an expedition. I found a safe spot and peered over the cliff.

Puffins crowded the ledges. They wore evening dress and carnival faces. Their wings seemed too short and slender to support their dumpy bodies, and the uncertainty of flight was only overcome by frantic flapping. Down they dived, faster and faster. They entered the airborne mêlée of fulmars, gannets and guillemots as artlessly as missiles, ricocheted off the cliffs, shot up skywards on the laws of momentum and somehow returned to their ledges without ever having gained control. Each flight exhausted the maximum potential out of what was a kamikaze design.

I was bonxied again as I returned to my bike and the start of the road. Names on the map warned me of a mythological landscape ahead and to be on my guard against the sort of nasty surprises you might expect to have ridden in on the back of a gale: Willa-mina Hoga, Birries Houlla Komba, Trollakeldas Houlla, Hoo Stack, Hogg of Papa . . . I could imagine Shetlanders learning to eat their rice puddings under threat of the evil Willa-mina, or almost any of their child-devouring names. But I looked forward to experiencing Sodom, Funzie and a Hawaiian-Rice Krispyish assortment of islands called Rumble, Snap, Vongs and Mooa.

The first surprise, a ewe in woman's clothing, appeared early. Among a flock of ordinary sheep was one wearing a Shetland jersey. While the others chomped away in their whites, this one paraded a jazzy Fair Isle pattern of purple and pink.

'Well, she wis losin' ha fleece so ah jist sewn her up i an old sweater,' explained the farmer when I tracked him down. 'It's whit we allus did, an she's nae sheddin' the hentilaggeds noo.'

Everything I cycled past was Britain's 'most-northerly' this'n'that: golf course, transvestite sheep, post office, rugby pitch, RAF base, public lavatory, gnomery. But these tags are important only for the purposes of tourism and commerce. And there were precious few tourists about. Recession, isolation and the bad press of the wreck of the *Braer* were all being blamed for the poor showing. So I was one of only a handful of visitors who responded to a noticeboard invitation to attend a meeting of Baltasound Fiddle Club.

The fiddlers ranged in age from those not long out of

rompers to those not far from zimmers. They were led by a retired teacher, Tom Polson, who wore a home-knit sweater and stomped his Hush Puppies so loudly on the floor it almost drowned the music. His mouth worked as if spitting out abuse as he sawed notes off the strings. The evening was part recital, part history lesson, and structured on the flight pattern of a puffin. Tom would be talking away when a word reminded him of a tune and he'd launch into it without telling the others, but one by one they picked it up and joined in.

Tom talked of Vikings and the brutal lairds introduced to the islands by Mary, Queen of Scots; of necromancy, the 'gentleman's witchcraft' they practised, and that reminded him of a tune. He talked of the fishing, of sixareens out in the far haaf (deep sea) and of the steam drifters. 'Hears du me?' he asked, to illustrate the familiar form of address still in use, and that ignited another tune. Then he related how Shetland was a nation of sealers, whalers, fishermen, merchant seamen; they were travellers and the travelled upon; Vikings, war convoys, oil – they were used to invasions and incomers. Twenty thousand of them arrived in uniform during the last war, and in the 1950s so frequently did Scandowegian boats mob Lerwick that krona and krone were common currencies along the length of Commercial Street. Experience had imbued confidence in Shetlanders, and they could afford to be friendly without fear . . .

'Fear . . . at remainds me o' "Da Faded Cabbage".'

The connection between this tune and fear escaped me, but 'The Faded Cabbage' set Tom's Hush Puppy off once more.

The remainder of Unst unfurled as I rode south, heading for Yell and a ferry to Out Skerries, one of Shetland's most remote communities. Sunlight picked out wild flowers field by field, moving its late-evening spotlight across the array of mottled hills and bogs. Unst had poor-grade peat; cows grazed its bogs; fertility was confined to the odd rig of potatoes and the gardens of the ubiquitous kithouse; you saw at once the narrow margin that had let Unst scrape a living in the eye of the Atlantic's hostility.

A keen wind buffered my progress and bent me low over the handlebars. Its influence in shaping the character of the people was not to be underestimated. They had learned to read its moods and intentions. It sharpened their guile and resilience, and tested their tolerance. Racing through the hummocky landscape and coastal crags with the sound of ripping Velcro, it terrorised them. One afternoon in July 1881 it wrecked six sixareens and drowned 58 fishermen. But it also taught them music. Tom had said the people here were not poetic, but musical. The wind wrought tunes out of fences, blew notes from heather and rocks, and this permeated the people. Everywhere fiddle music drifted out of open windows. You saw children practising, and being respected for it, in school playgrounds. The Hardanger fiddle music of Norway could not have found a more nurturing medium.

Uyeasound and Arthur Caldback's shop fell by. The hunch-backed crows continued to stare with a scrutiny more impeccable than Arthur's Sony cameras. So sinister and relentless was their watch over the island, it seemed, that only when they slept could Unst sleep. I camped that night by the road and expected to wake up with my eyes missing.

From Yell ('YELL FOR LIGHT FOR YELL' had been the campaign slogan for bringing electricity to the island) I caught a ferry to Out Skerries. Judging by their size and remoteness, they would be quaint and primitive; and according to repute, an ideal sort of place for social anthropologists, drop-outs and travel writers.

3

Out Skerries

'You know, I was halfway up a mountain in New Zealand when I got talking to this man and, as one does in such circumstances, we got onto where we would end up. And I said I wanted to be a dotty old woman in some isolated place with a houseful of cats. And here I am! I've done it!' She leaned closer and winked a mascara-laden eye. 'And not many people can say that!'

I met Miss Adrienne Rankin on my way to the Out Skerries dance. She was in her sixties and certainly not part of the scenery you'd ever have expected to find on a New Zealand mountain. Her face was a mixture of the shocking and powdery hues of an apothecary's window. Her thick blonde hair was swept back into a pony tail and she wore dark glasses, a woolly hat and a jacket in bullfighter red. *American . . . on an ancestor hunt . . .*, flashed a mental warning at first sight of her, but Miss Rankin was English, a retired teacher. She injected her conversation with sugary enthusiasm – 'wonderful! . . . marvellous! . . . terrific!' – in affected tones and I wondered if she were trying to convince herself. It was wonderful here. Ebsolutely turrrifick.

We met on the rubble airstrip because the island was small and to make a decent walk out of it you had to walk everywhere. Within five minutes Miss Rankin had lightened herself of the salient points of her life. She had made a conscious decision not to marry because she knew she 'couldn't stand the suffocating presence of a partner'. Cats were marvellous companions. The *Sunday Times* had always exerted a major influence on her life. Its advertisements had taken her to jobs around the world, but always she had taken her holidays in places like Out Skerries. Then, seven years ago, a cottage here was advertised for sale: £18,000. She'd come up to see it. Turr-rifick! She'd offered £14,000 and got it. Wonderful! At first she kept six cats but the *Shetland News* kept advertising homeless kittens, and now she had eleven. 'I really think I'm going to have to stop reading that column.'

Miss Rankin's utopia of cats, *Sunday Times* and dottiness was blemished only by the degree of isolation: it wasn't isolated enough. She wrinkled her nose and said, 'To be honest, I can actually do without people.' I saw at once how ebsolutely perfect she would have found the Muckle Flugga Light.

Thus far the wider world's preconception of Out Skerries was firming up nicely.

The dance took place in the community hall, a modern state-of-the-art facility; the artificial grass for indoor bowling had been rolled away as had the mobile theatre stage. Trade at the bar was patchy and modest, for a dance in this community clearly meant a dance, embracing all ages. Everyone was on the floor. Some fishing boats were still at sea and this resulted in a shortage of men, which, almost anywhere else in the country, would have left an array of frustrated wallflowers around the room but here women danced unabashed with each other.

I had never seen a dance like it. Coyness was not a Skerries hang-up. Their fine stylish footwork read the music. They tapped heels and kicked, launched themselves into figures of eight and blurred with their partners in a dozen locked-arm spins . . . Quadrilles, The Lancers, Paul

Jones, Faroese Ring Dance, Strip-the-Willow and a host of others from that far-off, foreign land of Scotland. In the interval, tea, homemade mutton sandwiches, bannocks and cakes were served. Then they danced again, and ate again. In common with every Shetland dance I was to attend, it was a matter of pride for the musicians to play on until the last dancers shuffled off the floor, and in this case that happened five hours later at 3.30 am. Apart from the bar, it was an evening untouched by money.

While supping tea and munching mutton, I fell into conversation with another man who had two left feet and had been trying to avoid the dance floor. Johnnie Graham had never been a good sailor, and was as thin as the lighthouses in which he'd worked as a relief keeper. Beach-combing had been his hobby. One day he'd come across a balloon which was almost deflated. By stretching it taut he managed to decipher a cartoon character called 'Hairy', the words 'Howdy from me', and the Philadelphia address of someone called Sharon Singer. He wrote to her. She was thirteen and had released the balloon on her birthday. It had taken three weeks to cross the Atlantic. They struck up a correspondence and on her twenty-first birthday Sharon and a friend came to visit Johnnie. He met them at Lerwick, and the story made it into the *Sunday Times* (Adrienne would have seen it). The American girls stayed a week and cried when they left.

'This really got me going,' Johnnie explained. He began throwing message bottles into the sea like mad. 'Nah, no good. Few replies. But they wis glass. I swapped to yon plastic fizzy drink boattles. They wirk richt fine.'

He had thrown two hundred into the sea and received replies from about fifty. The bottles had a habit of stranding themselves in Denmark and Norway, and Number 83, he cited with distinction, had made it round the North Cape.

Johnnie's shyness was acute. Undoubtedly he would have preferred our conversation to be taking place in one of those old-fashioned stores like Jenners, where we could have shot messages in brass canisters back and forth along pneumatic tubes. Notes and bottles were his medium. When the Royal Mail brought him no letters, he combed Out Skerries' high tide line to check the North Sea Mail. Over the years he had found six messages: one Portuguese (no reply), one Russian (which he sent to Lerwick High School for a translation; a eulogy of love to some girl – no address), two from oilrigs and two from yachts. For several years now he'd given up throwing out messages as he felt guilty about the pollution, but he had half a mind to start up again. 'I love da excitement o gettin replies, but, awww, da writing amost kills me.'

When he left the dance Johnnie had a few empty fizzies under his arm. I left with an invitation to visit the community fish farm.

Out Skerries consisted of three main islands. The third island was Grunnay, privately owned by an absentee Double-Barrell who had flown in a few times with enough tinned food to last months, and flown out again the next day. Grunnay's 54 acres, lighthouse keeper's cottage, walled garden and remains of a nine-hole golf course were currently on the market for £40,000. The local shopkeeper considered it a bargain, if not for the island, at least for the mountain of tinned food.

Out Skerries' two main islands, almost touching and connected by a bridge, were owned by Cussons (soap). A drain encircled the largest hillock and channelled water into the community's precious reservoir. As on Unst, Yell, Fair Isle, Foula, Fetlar, Whalsay and Papa Stour, no MOTs were required for cars and no more than provisional licences were required of their drivers. Bashed and rust-ridden, cars came to these islands to die. They were thrawn these wrecks. Exhausts fell off, doors blew away and windscreens shattered but it took a major stroke to end their noisy lives. Out Skerries was more exceptional in this respect. It had a greater proportion of Audis and

Volvos in pristine condition, because Out Skerries was
relatively rich.

Eighty-six people lived on this rocky outcrop and they
administered an island economy with £2 million's worth
of assets. Theirs was a 'sub-sidey-wise society'. They
had worked a generous system of grants to maximum
advantage and founded their existence on fish farming
and four large trawlers. They had amongst them a Blues
writer/reviewer, a treasure-trove diver working a Dutch
wreck, two teachers, two shopkeepers, a minister and a
postman. Out Skerries was, as Mark Twain might have
put it, 'smiling with the calm confidence of a Christian
with four acres'.

Dave Williamson, the manager of the fish farm, ran me
out to the flotilla of wooden walkways and submerged nets
which covered about six acres of the bay. Here 120,000
silvery shapes swam in confined shoals, contributing to
Scotland's ranking as the world's second largest producer
of salmon. 'When the smolts arrive here they weigh forty-
eight grams, and when we harvest them fifteen months
later, they weigh three or four kilos,' Dave explained as
we walked on the undulating pavements. I had visited
a salmon farm before and watched oilskinned figures
endlessly refilling demand-feeders and scattering pellets
into the cages like proverbial sowers. But they didn't work
like that here.

We entered a floating office wallpapered with warm
flesh. Out Skerries might have been dealing in escorts,
with nets full of Cindies, Tracies, Susies and Misses
Rubberclads. An operator sat before a computer screen,
against a backdrop of *Mayfairs, Penthouses* and *Fiestas*.

'We were about the first in the country to go onto this
system. We used to dry feed the fish but now we buy a
special food from Norway. It looks like sand and has oil
mixed in. A machine here squeezes it into tubes of different
diameters depending on the size of the fish, and serves it to
them through water pipes.'

He made it sound like silver service.

'We've cut our food bills by a third, reduced waste in the cages, and produce healthier fish and a cleaner seabed. A computer monitors the entire system and even checks the water temperature. Warmer water, more food. It sends the right size of food in the right quantities to the right cage at the right time. By pressing a button we can change the schedule of every cage or any particular one. And we don't even have to go outside and get wet.'

In 1974, Dave explained, the Zetland County Council Act was passed to allow the Shetland Isles Council (SIC) (as it subsequently became) to control oil-related developments within the islands. As an unforeseen consequence of this Act, when fish farming appeared on the scene some years later the SIC found itself with the power to grant or refuse seabed leases – the sole prerogative of the Crown Estates Commission in the rest of Scotland. 'The council made it a policy that, as far as possible, fish farms were to be locally owned – and today almost all of them are.'

'With what particular advantage?'

'That communities own and manage one of their largest employers. We'll run this farm even if it does nothing more than break even because it provides an income for nine full-time and twelve part-time employees. An outside owner would probably only be interested in profit. In actual fact, we've done really well.'

The farm had started with one cage and 5,000 smolt. Shareholders had each put in £2,000, and their shares were now worth £30,000. The annual turnover exceeded £1 million. No wonder they could afford such expensive wallpaper.

I camped near the reservoir. After three days on the island I felt I knew everyone. Morag the Mallet, as I called her, stopped at my tent each morning for a chat. She carried her huge weapon for banging in stakes to tether sheep. Out Skerries had vegetable plots and few fences and it was a by-law that sheep had to be tethered. Morag let her sheep devour a circle of grass and then moved them to a new radius. 'We still hae the auld runrig system here,' she laughed, as she went off to tend her potatoes and oats.

Runrig, a system of grazing and cultivation under which agricultural plots were reallocated each year to ensure that the good ground was shared equally throughout the community, went into decline in the rest of the country in the early part of the nineteenth century.

Morag the Mallet confided in me more of the islands' secrets. They hadn't enough sheep to keep the pasture down. The dogs here were all bitches. Ancient driftwood rights were still upheld; wood piled above the high water mark became the property of the finder. Burials were free except, 'Ya hae to pie da gravedigger'. (With the amount of rock about that couldn't have been cheap.) And in a community where the men were too often at sea, the islands' fire brigade had an all-woman crew.

The ferry *Filla* carried me west towards an appointment at Sullom Voe. I noted with dismay that *Filla* had not been born in the Clyde but in a Norwegian fjord flush with government aid. The crew handed out 10-gallon black bin-liners as sick bags. I prepared for a rough crossing. Through a porthole, beside which a Gideon Bible rested in its own stand instead of the more usual hammer labelled 'IN CASE OF EMERGENCY . . .', Out Skerries could be seen swimming steadily eastwards in a choppy grey sea. I was to travel many more miles before I fully appreciated how right Adrienne had been. Out Skerries were worth travelling the world to find. They held the ideal size of community: big enough to gang together and achieve, small enough to have to bury the hatchets and pull together.

They had found a viable strategy for survival. They could dance. They had runrig and the most modern fish farm in Europe.

4

Sullom Voe

On 5 January 1993, the Very Large Crude Carrier *Braer* was steaming into a gale in the Fair Isle channel, to the south of the Shetland mainland, *en route* from Norway to Quebec. She was registered in Liberia – and so-called 'flags of convenience' immediately suggest 'inconvenience' to everyone else – with a mixed crew of Filipinos, Greeks and Poles, and her cargo was 20 million gallons of North Sea crude. The cause of her engines failing was later alleged to have been a consequence of faulty welding and pipes rolling around deck, smashing air vents which allowed water to enter and contaminate her fuel tanks. Captain Alexandros Gelis was alleged to have delayed excessively before calling for assistance, and to have abandoned the ship too early. The *Braer* was pinned against the rocks of Cro Geo where she slowly broke up, releasing more than twice the quantity of oil spilt by the *Exxon Valdez* when she smothered the Alaskan coastline. The memory still made Captain Anderson sombre and fey.

'It could happen again tomorrow,' he warned. 'Here at Sullom Voe we've got no less than five tugs capable of towing the world's largest ships, but they couldn't get to the *Braer* in time. So what do we have to do? Have standby tugs at strategic places around the coast? Fine, but that's big bucks. Who'll foot the bill? The Government could, the oil industry could, the motorist could . . . but none of them *will* unless forced to. The bottom line is that *you* . . ,' he pointed an accusing finger, ' . . . me, we're going to have to pay more for our gallon of petrol. We're living in a fantasy of artificial prices. The day's coming when we're going to have to pay the real price . . . but don't worry, there'll need to be a good few disasters of a particularly horrendous scale before that day comes.'

Captain Anderson was a master mariner who had given up the bridges of VLCCs and taken the top office in Shetland's Harbour and Port Authority. From his window he overlooked a headland of silver drums, complexes of interwoven pipes which hissed steam and smoke, and three tall flare stacks whose 40-foot flames always danced above Sullom Voe, the largest oil and liquified gas terminal in Europe. Hundreds of miles of pipeline connected Sullom Voe with the North Sea rigs and 75 per cent of Britain's oil production arrived here. Oil flowed in at a rate of 800,000 tons per week and it would take exactly one week to swamp Sullom Voe unless a regular fleet of tankers came to carry the oil off. It was Captain Anderson's job to ensure that the 500 VLCCs that visited the base each year did not hit each other or run amok within six miles of his office.

He was small and serious and his shirt looked very clean compared to mine. 'Things are OK here. We keep a tight control over the ships. But, beyond six miles our authority ends. We can do nothing. Take the Fair Isle channel for example. God knows how much oil passes through there each year. We ask ships to advise the coastguard who they are and what they're carrying each time they pass through, but few do. We've no radar surveillance. We've no idea what's going on there. If we knew the movements of old or potentially dangerous vessels, we could put emergency services on alert. But we can't change the rules. Shipping's an international trade and the Rules must be globally recognised. Currently the

Right of Innocent Passage allows ships to go where they please.'

A more practical solution, he suggested, was to attack the problem at the shipping end. Twin hulls could be fitted to every ship, but that wouldn't have saved the *Braer*. Nothing could have withstood the pounding she took, Captain Anderson admitted. No, better would be to fit them with a second engine and prop. 'But what would it cost to redesign and refit all the world's oil fleet? Both oil and shipping are now marginal industries. Oil companies are cutting back and gearing themselves to another ten years of low prices and low returns. The world currently has twenty-five per cent excess tankers. As I speak, there are fifty-eight VLCCs tied up in the Arabian Gulf waiting on spec for a cargo. One got a load last week. And it costs the owners forty-nine thousand dollars a day to run a VLCC. So they bid each other down. The ones who perhaps have cut their maintenance costs and gone for a cheaper untrained crew – usually the older and least seaworthy ships – tend to offer the cheapest price and so get the load.'

'What about the Donaldson Report?' I asked. This was the government enquiry into shipping regulations and safety in the aftermath of the *Braer*. 'Won't it do something?'

Captain Anderson snorted a derisory laugh. 'My guess would be nothing. *There's no political will*. If the Braer had happened on the edge of London, then some urgent action might have resulted. But Shetland? That's too far away.'

'Are you saying that the real tragedy of the *Braer* is that it wasn't serious enough?'

'No, I'm not saying that. That was the view of Greenpeace and I disagree. That would simply have meant more destruction and more mess here. No, Shetland is just too far away to count. I don't expect anything to change for ten to twenty years.'

His computer screen bleeped. 'I'm afraid you'll have

to excuse me. The *Bloom Lake*'s ready to leave.' With a capacity of three *Braers* she was heading for the US Gulf with a massive 267,095 tons of black viscous oil.

'You seem to have a perfect record here,' I remarked, reading a wall chart of safe shipments.

Captain Anderson glowered and touched wood. 'It's only as good as your last consignment.'

5

❦

Vaila Island

Shetland with a tailwind is a gift for the cyclist. My wheels purred contentedly. Thrift saturated the air with the fragrance of its pollen. A torpid seal, bent over a rock like a black banana, yawned and groaned. The land rose and fell in a uniformity of muddy browns and greens, and some creature had laid across it long turds of extruded peat. It had also frightened off the people. The world seemed uncomfortably stripped of clutter. I inhaled the scent and tried not to notice my shadow which the sun contrived to project in front of me at every turn of the road. It showed a thin figure on an elephant. My bicycle was dangerously overloaded.

The Weisdale Valley cut a shockingly luxuriant passage. Green-ness burst from its slopes in the forms of rich grass and Shetland's only trees. In that valley I cycled through Buchan, Dorset and Montana but at the far end it was just plain old Shetland again. It is contrast that injects vitality into a landscape: contrast of colour, texture and shape. But Shetland has little contrast. All too often it is bland and monotonous, wearied by its ravishings, reduced to cold comforts for sheep and the usefulness of something solid against which to tie your boat. Only its cliffs and weather lend it a sense of drama or beauty, but they are loans invested with a fearful unpredictability.

I felt more at home here than in any cityscape. I liked the way oystercatchers brazenly saw me off their territory with crabbity piping, and the way successions of little ringed plovers played games of dare, landing in front of me and running at such speed their legs seemed sure to trip, until discretion forced them into flight, and boldness into a repeat performance. I liked the way Shetland bus stops were fitted with gates to prevent sheep from taking them over, and the way community noticeboards kept me abreast of world affairs: North Nesting Public Hall was holding a meeting, Happyhansel School was starting a new term, and 'Diane's' was offering 'Cuts, Bobs, Trims, Spiral Perms, Blow-waving, Tinting, Highlighting, Lowlighting, Clippering, Demi-waving and Razoring.' This, to someone who seldom dared to look in a mirror, was truly unexplored territory.

I was on the Shetland mainland, drifting west, courting chance encounters and the unpredictable. It was what I loved about travelling, gambling on hearsay and direction: character and compass roulette. I was addicted.

The start of this particular day provided no inkling that it would end in a baronial hall on a private island.

Vaila Island was first mentioned to me in Burrastow House, a hotel where I stopped for coffee when the mainland came to a sudden end. Both Burrastow and Vaila, the waitress said, had been left to Henry Anderton but the upkeep of both had proved too costly and, reluctantly, Henry had decided to part with the island. It had been on the market for eleven years and only recently been sold.

'Who's bought it?'

'A Polish woman.'

I phoned her to ask if I could visit. 'Sure! I'll send the booat over.'

A few days earlier I had visited Brough House on Fetlar, the home of another island laird. I had arrived there late, about twenty years too late. A dead seagull occupied the chair where Lady Nicolson once sat. Her high-heeled shoes were still piled in a cupboard, *Burke's Peerage 1937* dominated shelves of books, and belongings were strewn about, but the house was a deserted wreck. Those who had once been cleared from the island to make way for the Nicolsons' sheep doubtless would have viewed the scene with satisfaction and a sense of justice. Lady Nicolson had passed on. No longer would the council Housing Director have to entreat the obstructive old bat to sell land for needed housing, and no longer, it was rumoured, would he feel obliged to accept her invitation to a game of draughts in which she used Smarties instead of counters.

So I was feeling wary of eccentric island lairds when Freddy delivered me to the new owner of Vaila.

If I was late at Brough House, I was a little early at Vaila Hall. A delay of twenty years might have seen it finished. The hall was a solid blockish building standing pompously on 700 acres of moor and rough grazing. Its builders seemed to have been at odds with each other. One had thought a small castle with an arched entrance was about right. Another had sandwiched this between two corbie-stepped gables, and another had thrown a round tower on one corner. Freddy led me to the back door.

'Hi! So you'f made it! How d'you take your coffee?' Dorotta was 32 and spoke with a thick Polish accent. Her brown hair was pulled tightly back and pinned behind her head, revealing a round, pretty face with eyes that were sharp and alert. Over a robust build she wore a long, loose cardigan and an ankle-length skirt. She was calm and relaxed but when she moved she conveyed an air of unstoppable momentum.

'D'you know how haard it is to find a twel-elf century building to buy?' Dorotta asked. I said I didn't. 'Well it's almost eempossible. Richard . . . that's my partner in this venture . . . and I, we were looking *ev-verywhere* for something very old and very run down, you know, to restore. But the National Trust have almost *ev-verything*. Then we heard about Vaila and came to see. And at once we knew our search was over. It's so *ugly*, so *romantic* . . . we just love it.' She used a smile in careful measures but frequently spoke in italics.

They had bought it for a quarter of a million. Henry had thrown in half-tester beds, tables, and even family portraits that he had no room for at Burrastow. 'Some of them are quite fun but none are any good, and all of them say *new money*.' Dorotta was qualified to judge. She was an art dealer in London.

The whole place was *nouveau riche*, she said, but it was fun. What she found particularly refreshing was the consistency of its vulgarity. It had been built as a place for parties by a Yorkshire mill-owner, and Dorotta seemed intent on continuing the tradition. Seventy-five guests were about to fly up from London. 'It has the smell of textiles about it. Textile millionaires always have the same smell, same taste.'

Dorotta had known that smell in Poland. Latterly she had lived in Wooj ('That's Poland's second largest city, next to Chicago.'). Like Bradford, Wooj was industrial, in textiles. Her story then became fragmented and I picked up what pieces I could. Her grandfather had been an aristocrat in Belorussia. Her mother was a Communist. Dorotta had joined the young Solidarity movement and been blacklisted. She came to Britain to improve her English and let things cool down but shortly afterwards martial law was declared and a return to Poland would have meant imprisonment or, at least, no hope of employment. Britain refused her refugee status on the grounds that she was too young to have been politically active. She smiled wrily. 'And yet I was old enough to be blacklisted in Poland!'

The story fragmented again. She had married. Her husband had died. It was logical to assume her marriage had provided her with the right to stay in Britain, and

perhaps some money. Then she had met Richard who was
a solicitor and a widower.

'But what are you going to do with this place?'

'We just want to restore the island and hall into a home
again. It's a project, an ambition, a fun venture.'

And what fun it was proving to be. The stove had
blown up.

'Henry was very upset . . . oh, we *adore* him but he
does want to be involved in *ev-verything* we do. I think
he still regards this as his home . . . we do have to do
things, um, tactfully. So the stove blew up. It was an old
stove. It died. But Henry took it personally. He thought we
might blame him for selling us shoddy goods. And the roof
leaked. Henry said it couldn't possibly leak. He'd repaired
it twenty-three years ago. We needed a large gas fridge.
Henry said they didn't make them any more. I found one
in Harrods. It's a *wonderful* store. I don't shop for the
name but the fact is that Harrods has . . . or can get . . .
most things. So I get the fridge. When Henry sees it, he's
miffed. And now when I ask him where's the best place to
go for something like galvanised wire, he just says, "Why
not try Harrods?" But we do *adore* him.'

She was ripping out the polystyrene tiles Henry had
put on the kitchen ceiling. She was replacing a fireplace
he'd installed. She'd just bought an Aga, and then the
generator had packed in. That was another £5,000 away.
They were repairing two other houses on the island but it
was almost impossible to get workers here. Shetland had
full employment. She'd had to wait months to get the JCB
driver to come and mend their private roads. She'd had to
import interior decorators from London. It was all *terribly*
difficult.

It must have also been *terribly* expensive. But cost was
never mentioned. That would have been unacceptably
vulgar.

'I don't think it'll ever be finished. I think this project's
for life.' This, and a monstrous jigsaw she'd scattered over

a side-table. In this dark home Dorotta was bright and
warm and utterly herself. I hoped the romance wouldn't
fade before the ambition was realised. Shetland's long
winters were hard to stomach on diets of jigsaws great
and small.

She swept me on a tour. The main dining hall occupied
almost one-third of the building. Stained-glass lancet
windows rose the full height of the walls. A balcony
ran round the upper reaches on three sides, with a stone
balustrade and cloister-like arches. It was here that the
band would play for Dorotta's parties. Dark heavy furniture brooded around the central table, a monolith of carved
mahogany. Fake weapons encrusted the walls and Dorotta
had installed a suit of armour bought from a stage-prop
company ('Oh, it's going rusty! That's *much* better.') She
flung open the hall's main doors and let in a Force Six.

'The hall was aligned on that castle. You see?'

And there in the distance, perfectly framed in the
doorway for the delight of the head of the table, was
Mucklabery Castle, a little one-up, one-down folly perched
on the horizon.

We went from room to room, along corridors, through
a conservatory of silk bay trees and silicon-injected bonsai
from China, passing half-tester beds and twenty-three
cases of stuffed birds. Glass-eyed owls, golden eagles,
sea eagles, king eiders and a dusty flock of others stared
at us. They had all been shot on Vaila and, not surprisingly,
many of the species represented were now rare, or had
vanished.

It was all typically Victorian, as Dorotta admitted, and
so vulgar. But what struck me most was how un-Wooj it
had to be. Perhaps this was its appeal, a counter-reaction
to communism, a nostalgia for lost days in Belarus.

As Freddy and I walked down to the boat, a large fawn
otter loped in a leisurely undulating rhythm from the sea
towards the Hall. Perhaps it was just curiosity, or the novelty of London money, but life was returning to Vaila.

6

❧

Bobby

I met Bobby on my way to Cro Geo. He was 44, a fish-farm worker. The night the *Braer* came ashore, Bobby went out for a stroll before bed. He smelled oil in the air and feared the worst. Back in the house, the phone rang. It was a friend who owned a fish farm.

'It's all over,' the friend said. His voice was limp with emotion. 'This place is fucked.'

'What d'you mean?'

'Can you not smell the oil? . . . . it's coming in here. I tell you, this coast's fucked.'

Bobby said he sat down and cried. 'Everything I grew up with . . . the beach, the sea, the birds, the fishing . . . everything I held dear, I saw finished.'

He was afraid to look out the next morning.

7

❦

Braer

Cro Geo was awash with the pink and yellow heads of thrift and buttercups. Its grass looked verdant but, six months after *Braer* Day, cows were still banished from grazing there. Below the crags the green and white bow of the wreck protruded above the water and trailed a broken rope which swayed in the tide. Like any corpse, the sight of it sent a shiver down the spine of the living.

A unique feature of this spill was the way the wind lifted the oil from the water and carried it across the land. Houses were coated, fields turned slimy and roads had to be sanded. The smell of oil was oppressive. People developed sore throats and for days no one could open their windows. Worst of all were the uncertainty, and the rumours: that the sheep would be poisoned, the birds smothered, the grass choked, the wild flowers destroyed.

Before the Second World War, Shetland (along with Norway) was one of the poorest and most neglected men in Europe. The realisation that Shetland was of strategic importance initiated the first phase of modernisation. The discovery of the Brent field by Shell/Esso in 1972 heralded the second and more important phase of material benefit.

If the oil companies hoped the forerunner of the
Shetland Isles Council would prove a soft bargaining
partner, they were confounded by the County Clerk.
So skilful a negotiator did Mr Ian Clark turn out to be
that SIC did very nicely out of the deal, and Mr Clark
was subsequently snapped up by the oil industry and his
talents employed on its behalf in future.

Today the SIC has £300 million in its Trust Fund, and
£7 million is added annually from revenues levied at
Sullom Voe. It is the second smallest local council in
Britain, but easily the richest. Poll Tax was charged at
a flat rate of £1. Pensioners travel free on SIC transport
and receive a Christmas bonus of £200. Every community
on the three main islands is within easy reach of a
multi-million-pound leisure centre, complete with real
palm tree growing by the pool. But there had been
hidden costs.

'Oil has made us greedy,' admitted Bobby. 'Lerwick's
wanting a bigger and better pool. It'll cost twelve million,
but so what? . . . what's twelve million to SIC! Piece
o'piss! That's what we think. You see brand new halls all
over the place. Many are hardly used. The novelty's worn
off. We've got better roads but now more people use them
to go to Lerwick to shop and work. Oil brought sixteen
hundred jobs, but we had full employment before, so it's
the traditional fishing, farming and knitting that've lost
out. The woollen industry's crying out for knitters . . .'.
And there was the cost of oil spills.

The *Braer* disaster proved much less dire than had
been feared. Just a quarter of a mile from an asphalt
road and less than six miles from Sumburgh Airport
where the rescue helicopter was based, the ship could
scarcely have found a more convenient location to wreck
itself. The oil was a light crude, and the storm which drove
the ship ashore raged for a further five days and proved
the most effective dispersant. Rain gradually washed
the slime from the fields. Contaminated birds counted

remarkably few. The grass grew, wild flowers returned and sheep failed to perish.

But there were casualties. Approximately 600,000 tainted salmon were slaughtered and the fate of 2 million more still hung in the balance. The real cost of the *Braer* is the lost trade to the tourist, shellfish and salmon-farming industries through the erroneous perception that Shetland no longer represents 'clean water, fresh food'.

I left Cro Geo and cycled to the southern tip of the Shetland archipelago, to Sumburgh, where I hoped to accompany Oscar Charlie on one of his rescue sorties. Above the cliffs at Sumburgh Head I came across a girl knitting in a Land Rover. From her seat she could peer into a powerful telescope and operate the controls of a rotating antenna. She was knitting one, purling one, and prying into the lives of razorbills, or cooter-nebs as Shetlanders called them. A select group had been fitted with transmitters which fed back to her their personal details. By chance, she said, a comprehensive three-year study of this area's birdlife had been completed shortly before the *Braer* sank. She was part of a team from Glasgow University's Department of Zoology undertaking a follow-up study. To everyone's surprise there appeared to be no ill-effects resulting from the oil spill. Even the sand eels, which three years earlier had been scarce, were more plentiful. Her cooter-nebs were doing just fine.

A large tanker crawled across the horizon, bringing back the image of Captain Anderson touching wood. And another image followed, a picture Bobby had stuck in his album. 'I love this picture,' he said. It was a press shot of the first eider ducks being released after their clean-up, their wings outstretched as they ran to the sea. 'I know that sense of relief.'

8

Oscar Charlie

Oscar Charlie weighed 10 tons and looked the sort of creature that might have been responsible for excreting peat across the land. He was 20 years old but all his parts were replaceable, and indeed, had been replaced, and he was expected to have an indefinite lifespan. Wanting nothing but vast amounts of paraffin, he could fly on his own, bristled with acronyms of clever equipment and enjoyed a prestigious replacement value of £5 million.

Oscar Charlie was the call sign of Bristow's dedicated Search And Rescue helicopter which was under contract to HM Coastguard. Sumburgh, Stornoway and the Solent were the three places in the British Isles where such contracts operated, for these were gaps in the network of cover provided by the RAF. Each day, where possible, the crews were required to complete an hour of training to keep their skills honed, and I had been told they were always on the look-out for rescue guinea pigs.

My informant spoke from personal experience. He was a surgeon in Lerwick, performing everything from major operations to routine prostates, and picking glass out of backsides (this, he elaborated, was the common Hogmanay malaise, caused by unintentional collapse with a whisky bottle in a rear trouser pocket). Occasionally

Oscar Charlie took him out on simulated rescues. On one such practice he had been put in a survival suit and deposited somewhere in the North Sea. The helicopter had flown off out of sight and then returned to look for him.

The point of the exercise had been to test Oscar Charlie's FLIR, one of the cleverest gadgets aboard. An eyeball under the helicopter's fuselage was the all-seeing camera of the Forward Looking Infra Red system. Irrespective of lightness or darkness, it could detect the heat of a human head bobbing on the surface of the sea up to a quarter of a mile away. Seal heads, seagulls, cooter-nebs . . . all were discernible to FLIR, and as long as an object was at least half a degree centigrade warmer than the sea, it could reproduce its shape on a VDU inside Oscar Charlie.

Surgeons, it transpired, were expendable, but writers were not. The Chief Coastguard apologised but said that if they lost the surgeon, at least the Civil Aviation Authority might accept the justification for involving a medical expert in the training programme, but they'd never accept the casual immersion, let alone the loss, of a mere writer. No, he could only sanction the helicopter crew to do something innocent with me. I signed the bit of paper absolving everyone of responsibility for my life, and reported for duty.

It took me ten minutes to manoeuvre through the chest and into the arms, legs and feet of a rubber survival suit.

'Too slow!' remarked the winchman. 'If this had been an emergency, we'd have left without you three minutes ago. Three minutes to get into your gear, four minutes to start the chopper, away in seven. That's what we aim for.'

My intended response never emerged. Like the rest of me it was trapped inside an orange Michelin man. 'How the hell am I meant to move in this?'

Richard showed me how to squat down and purge the air from the suit. The suit spluttered indecently as it reduced me to a vacuum-packed joint of meat, but at least it was more comfortable than the alternative. I felt my face ripening to the shade of the rubber as Richard ran through the safety procedure. 'In the event of a non-recoverable situation, you're not to panic . . .'

I made a mental note to force a smile if a rotor blade happened to go zinging off on its own or if my orange feet tripped as I was passing the open hatch, but this was not what Richard had in mind. 'Non-recoverable situations' excluded imminent death and assumed the craft had safely ditched in the sea. Oscar Charlie was designed to float but not to take off from water. Emergency striplights would self-activate on contact with salt water and, even with a dead generator, his skeleton would glow. We would have to stay inside until the blades stopped turning.

We were joined by the three other crew members – the Captain, First Officer and Winch Operator – and boarded the Sikorsky 561N. The huge blades, 60 feet in diameter, hung flaccidly. They were filled with pressurised nitrogen and electronically monitored for any change which might indicate a crack. The interior was spacious with seating for nineteen, but 'as many as can find a hand-hold' could be taken aboard in an emergency. I was handed a set of earphones and microphone and seated at the captain's shoulder within an arc of liability for ranks of buttons and switches. I was scared to move.

Captain Norman Leask was in his late forties and he had a near perfect set of teeth. (Precious little else is visible in a survival suit.) He carried with him the aura of calm efficiency to be expected of a pilot who had once experienced a non-recoverable situation and sat inside his ditched craft for three hours until the fuel ran dry, the risk of an explosion was eliminated and the blades stopped turning. It sank shortly after he managed to get out.

'The blades are not actually powered mechanically,'

he explained. 'We've two ruddy great jet engines which blast air at them. We move by redirecting the airstream.' His gloved hand ran over levers and dials as he checked their settings. 'And don't believe what you see in films. A jet doesn't stutter or slow down – it's either fully on, or it's off.'

The blades began to move and as their speed increased, so did the vibration until everything became a noisy, rattling din. When a dial showed the blades had reached 2,000 revolutions per minute, this whirling cacophony, costing an average of £2,500 an hour to run, gently lifted off. Oscar Charlie roared and trembled.

Within minutes I was summoned to the open hatch and inserted into a sling.

'OK?' Richard asked, nodding. I copied the nod. My mind was numb. As the winch hoisted me off my feet and hands swung me out over the void, I could already see the headlines: 'MAN IN SHOCK PLUNGE FROM HELICOPTER! . . . A VALID MEDICAL EXPERIMENT, CLAIMS CAA.'

Sumburgh spun slowly round me and then I found myself gently grounded on tarmac. It was an uncanny sensation, impersonal, as if I had just teletransferred somewhere like a fax. But I wasn't allowed to enjoy it, or terra firma, for long. The next moment I was a dangling bundle rising up 50 feet towards 10 tons of hovering metal. Hands pulled me aboard, a consignment of bewilderment with fear strangely anaesthetised.

Safely back in my seat, I began to develop some of the confidence of a survivor. 'What frightens *you*?' I asked Richard.

'A lot . . . we're human too, you know . . .'

It was easy to elevate these men to a plain beyond normal emotion. Because of their professionalism, their daily dicing with a greatly enhanced possibility of death, their record of success, we tended to ascribe to them a heroic, even child-like insensibility to fear.

'Why do you do it then?'

'For the money.' Richard grinned insincerity. 'No, not for that, though it's nice. I suppose I like the job because it makes me feel useful . . . it's a good feeling saving someone's life.'

'Don't you think of "Non-Recoverable Situations" every time you come up?'

Certain subjects were taboo aboard, and this was one of them. 'I wish you hadn't asked that . . . there's no wood about.' Like Captain Anderson, helicopter crews held faith in wood. I changed tack. 'What load can that winch take?' 'About enough for three very, very fat people.' The cable was three hundred feet long and could be guillotined by an explosive charge, if, say, the three people snagged on the way up and the safety of the helicopter was jeopardised. Winching was fraught with danger. Once Richard was being lowered onto the deck of a stricken ship when the wind suddenly swung him towards the funnel just as the ship rolled. 'I left an imprint, Tom and Jerry style, on that funnel like you wouldn't believe, and Brother! . . . did it hurt. Yeah . . . that one sank . . . though not as a result of my collision, you understand.'

We moseyed off to look for a ship on which, Norman said, I could do a *real* practice. Passing ships were evidently very obliging. My confidence took a battering.

Shetland diminished below us and my journey of three weeks was suddenly, and unfairly, compressed into thirty minutes with the reappearance of Muckle Flugga. We didn't find any ships to hand so Dave threw out a buoy for us to recover. We flew on and gave it a chance to become lost and then returned to hunt for it.

'Let's pretend that it's almost dark. We're looking for a man overboard and we spot him. Now, forget all the other gadgets we've got on board for locating him and watch this.' Norman pressed a button as we passed over the buoy. He then took his hands and feet off the controls. 'Now it's over to Oscar and R-NAV.' The helicopter was flying itself. It had logged a satellite fix on the target, now it was slowly turning, looking for the wind direction, assessing its speed and our drift. It would approach the target into the wind. We swung round in a long arc. The buoy had disappeared. A minute later the helicopter stopped and hovered at 200 feet. The buoy was slightly ahead of us and at one o'clock, the best position in the pilot's restricted area of vision.

Norman resumed control. To move this heavy hulk a foot to the left, the joystick had to move a foot to the left and then be quickly corrected. We descended with the winchman leaning through the hatch and talking the pilot through lefts and rights that were measured in feet; once over the scene of action, a pilot was blind. The downdraught squashed the water and snakes of surf dispersed in all directions as the buoy was retrieved.

'What are most of your call-outs for? Yachts and such like . . . ?'

'No, most of the yachts which get as far as Shetland are in good hands. The majority of our cases are injured fishermen. We get about sixty to eighty call-outs a year.'

Recently they'd been called to a Russian ship to medivac a crewman who'd suffered a heart attack. 'The ship was pretty close to our 180-mile limit so it put us at risk. Anyway, we got the guy on board and thought it strange as he was covered in blood. Back at hospital they had to drain sea water from his lungs. Some "heart attack"! We heard later that the ship's doctor had attacked the guy with a marlin spike and thrown him overboard. The Russians aren't always totally honest about their "accidents".'

They must, I remarked, receive many touching letters of gratitude. No, they said, very few. Six years ago a Dutchman on holiday dropped his backpack over a cliff. He gave it up for lost, but they somehow heard about it and retrieved the pack. He wrote them the longest letter of thanks and every year sent them a Christmas card. But he was the exception. Over nine years and 500 missions, Norman could recall about twenty letters of thanks being delivered to the base.

The view remained empty. 'That's a shame,' Norman remarked. 'There just don't seem to be any ships around today. Looks like we'll have to forget the winch drill.'

'Pity,' I replied, and immediately began to enjoy the trip.

9

෨

Ferry to Orkney

In the company of a spraggle of other Sooth Moothers I took passage, as they say, for Orkney. The *St Sunniva* rumbled away from Lerwick's hill of grey stone houses, its harbour of recuperating yachts and rusting fishing boats, past a warehouse with the unlikely name MALAKOFF which dissolved into a sprawl of wharves and yards laden with the bits and bobs of drilling for oil. Like all Shetland's invaders, we aliens left as we had arrived, through the South Mouth, where the channel yawns widest between the Mainland and Bressay.

I felt comfortable playing the part of Sooth Moother because I knew it was just a game. I claimed spiritual, if not national, rights to Shetland citizenship. We understood each other, its air of harmless pretence. Shetland pretends not to be Scottish, that oil doesn't really matter, that oil hasn't changed it, that its annual Viking festival – Up Helly Aa – is authentic and ancient. As for the latter, it isn't. It's a wholly contrived late-Victorian piece of fun with no Viking links whatsoever. That's what appeals to me about Shetlanders. They can act, but they know who they are.

The ship's PA system crackled to life. 'EVENIN,

LADIES UN GUNTLEMEN . . . FUR YUR ENT-TER-TAIN-MENT TI'NITE IN THA PENTLAND FURTH GRULL",' announced a gluey Aberdonian voice, 'THA FUL-UM WULL BE . . .'

The fulum was to be a thruller. Rup, Van and Wunkel were playing in the Bar Suite. The voice announced the programme of happenings as if they were verdicts and places of execution. It was obviously some time since he personally had experienced a thrull.

I read my copy of the *Shetland Times*. Dinghy racing was given equal coverage to football. A red-flanked bluetail (*tarsiger cyanurus*) had mistaken Fetlar for Siberia and was hot news among twitchers. And page two contained the following admission: 'The SIC has taken action to end a recent insensitive practice where bereaved relatives inquiring about burial arrangements were referred to the "Refuse" section of the council . . .'

Rip, Van and Winkel finally drove me to seek peace at the stern where I found a discarded magazine. It contained a speech by John Goodlad, Secretary of the Shetland Fisherman's Association and Vice-Chairman of the Shetland Movement. Written in the vernacular and entitled, 'Shapin Wir Future', it concluded:

> Hoosumever, whin I look ahead, I'm braaly hoopfil at wir communities could be on da aidge o a time o economic growth an excitin new developments at wir never kent o afore. But dis'll only happen if we hae an awaarness o wir ain identity an a confidence i wir ain abilities. An forbye dat, we maun hae mair say in decisions aboot wir ain future.'

These were words and sentiments which were to have a long and frequent echo.

10

Maes Howe and Miss Harcus, Papa Wesy

In 1150 a band of flaxen-haired louts were caught short by a snowstorm on Orkney's mainland. They broke into a 4,000–year-old burial tomb, sheltered there for three days, vandalised the place and scribbled graffiti on the walls. Some years later another gang lodged in the tomb on their way back from a crusade in the Holy Land, and they too wrote on the walls. Their messages, predictably, concern sex, money, and the Viking equivalent of 'Kilroy was here' ('Haermund Hardaxe reist runar'). Their graffiti now represents the most important collection of runes in Europe, and the vandalised Maes Howe is considered one of the finest architectural achievements of pre-history.

On the outside it was no more than a green wart on the fields, on the inside it was pitch black, and Norrie Slater held the only torch. He was a gruff, no-nonsense man in a flat cap and he had been a guide there since shortly after Haermund Hardaxe had vacated the place. Over the years foreigners had taught him odd words and he could now give the tour in French, German, Spanish, Italian and Dutch, and say 'walrus' in Japanese ('*sey-oochi*'). But he would retire soon, he said, before he became an ancient monument himself.

If the presenter of the Pentland Grill entertainment

ever wanted a break, Norrie was the *St Sunniva*'s man. He delivered the tour in a single no-frills no-thrulls sentence.

'Well welcome to Maes Howe this tomb is five thousand years old and was built by a sophisticated farming community the three burial chambers are (*torch on*) here, here and here and if you look at the floor and ceiling of each you'll see a single stone slab weighing thirty tons and if you look along the entrance tunnel you'll see a stone slab thirty feet long the tunnel faces the winter solstice so we know they were astronomers the Vikings broke in here now repaired and left a carving of a walrus, *sey-oochi*, and many runes . . .' His beam lit up rows of incised figures like stick insects in various postures of crucifixion.

HE IS A VIKING . . . COME HERE UNDER THE BARROW . . . IS TO ME SAID THAT TREASURE IS HERE HIDDEN VERY WELL . . . TRYGGR CARVED THESE RUNES . . . THORNI BEDDED, HELGI CARVED . . . INGIGERTH IS THE MOST BEAUTIFUL OF WOMEN. And next to the last observation was carved the head of a slavering dog.

The first inhabitants of Orkney were the primitive farmer-gatherers who left these islands with a full inheritance of houses, tombs and standing stones. The mysterious Picts spent time here and left little beside such names as the Pentland (Pictland) Firth. Hardaxe and the invading Norsemen followed and established their headquarters in Orkney. The last Norwegian earl died in 1231 and Scottish earls took over, swearing allegiance first to Norway, then to Denmark; but through an oversight they neglected to pay the rent for two centuries.

In 1469 Denmark ordered the Scottish earls to settle the debt. They refused. Charles VII of France was invited to arbitrate and he put forward the inspired suggestion (for the Scots) that Margaret of Denmark should marry James III of Scotland. Margaret was offered with a dowry of 60,000 florins, and was accepted. Quite why such a handsome dowry was proposed remains a mystery because Denmark managed to raise only 12,000 and went broke, and the Danes agreed to forfeit both Orkney and Shetland.

The Scottish earls who ruled after this were rogues with a penchant for greed and cruelty; they were by no means unusual in these characteristics, but Orkney's misfortune was in attracting the worst. This is why Orcadians regard the Pentland Firth as an ocean, the Fair Isle channel as a sea, and theirs as a land apart.

On a map Orkney's islands appear to have been shredded and they lie scattered as nibbled, twisted fragments. Through a wide-angle lens they almost disappear, so low and flat are their outlines at sea-level; through a telephoto lens the reason for Orkney's vanity is justified, and immediately apparent. Grass. Lushness and fertility exude from sixty-nine of these seventy islands.

The seventieth island is Hoy, the southernmost and the exception. It is mountainous, covered in moor and peat, and should by virtue of its composition belong to Shetland. The others consist of Middle Old Red Sandstone which, I'm told, erodes into rich soil, but Hoy is made of sterner stuff, Upper Old Red, and is all the poorer for it.

Cows, *Burnt Mound*, cows, farm, *Tumuli*, cows, cows, Standing Stones, farm, *Tumulus*, *Tumuli*, cows, *Chambered Cairn* . . . the view from two feet above my handlebars was of a soft, gently undulating, agricultural graveyard. Plenty for the beef-leg'n'teats enthusiast, for the archae-bio-ornith-ologists, and heaps for the morbidly inclined. I stopped at every opportunity and crawled into dark damp tunnels. I gazed disappointedly at grassy hump after grassy hump which my map promulgated as *Wheel House* and *Styes of Aikerness* in the full evocation of gothic script. At Skara Brae, while crawling through the kitchen of a Bronze Age dwarf, past a stone sideboard and dresser, I overdosed. My stamina parched, I was tombed out.

My bicycle carried me towards a ferry and Papa Westray, one of the outer-lying islands, and the address of a Miss Harcus. She came to represent for me the concept of 'belonging' in its deepest sense.

By the time I reached Orkney, which I had once regarded as my own Scottish soil, I had ceased to be a Soothmoother and metamorphosed into a Ferrylouper. And once on Papa Westray, I had to learn that, to those in the know, I was actually on Papay. But after that I was in the club, especially with my local contact.

Before embarking on this journey it had been one of my rare touches of inspiration – I thought – to write to that venerable organisation, the Scottish Rural Women's Institute, for a list of branch secretaries around the country who might be able to put me in touch with *unusual* characters in each locality. Miss Harcus had written back to say she could certainly give me some names, but when I met her I realised I need look no further.

Two children were playing ping-pong in Papay's hall under the distant and slightly myopic gaze of Miss Harcus. She sat alone at a table at the far end, watching, occasionally extending a hand towards a stray ball as it approached, with good and eager intention but to less effect. Black ankle boots with very pointed toes protruded from flared trousers, and a slate greatcoat enveloped her up to a floral neckerchief. Her woolly hat was pulled down low to her glasses and these magnified confident, determined eyes through glass as thick as ships' portholes. She was 71, thin, frail and saintly.

'So you're the man who wrote to me . . .' I admitted I was. She nodded thoughtfully. 'Do you play pool?'

Her question caught me off guard. I said I had played but was hopeless. This pleased her. There was a pool table in the hall. Did she want a game? No, she answered, but she also played. The schoolteacher had shown her, and had beaten her. Last week some children had taught her how to hold the cue, and she had been practising for the return match. Miss Harcus obviously did not like being beaten. She came here to help. The young children needed supervision. You had to do your bit, didn't you?

Miss Harcus had always done her bit. She was a stalwart of fundraising for the RNLI, and had recently been presented with an award by the Duke of Kent. 'Oh I wis right proud o'it,' she said, glowing, while I tried to disseminate the Orcadian accent. It was hard to pin down for it had its lyrical moments and then went haywire, careering off into thick gutturals. The Coastguard was the Costgairt, and a goat was a got. 'The ferryloupers from England all got gots. They seem tae think that wi' a handful o' gots they kin come tae Orkney an' survive.' Nine times out of ten, she said, if you saw a goat, the owners would be English. 'If you see a got outside, you can bet there's a got inside,' she added.

Miss Harcus knew a lot about gots, cows, crops and silage. 'Abody makes the silage now. Naebody makes hay any mair. Soon there'll be nane left fer the chair-muckers.' And later others repeated that straw was, indeed, in short supply for Orkney's distinctive chairs; straw was bound into tight faggots which were then bound together into the rigid, high-backed chairs with their characteristic drawer under the seat.

Pollution was to blame, she said. Pollution had changed the weather and now Orkney no longer had guaranteed sunshine for making straw. 'Pittin' men on the moon wis ah very weel, but whit good's come o'it? And such a cost!' She paused, and I visualised her visualising herself handing over a cheque for a hundred billion pounds to the RNLI. 'An now we canna pit the world's ane problems to right.' You could rarely buy fish any more, ragwort had become such a menace . . .

At nine o'clock the children smacked a last ball into the net, the hall closed and Miss Harcus invited me to her home for a coffee. She picked up a dainty little handbag on a long strap and hung it from one shoulder as she locked the door. I walked to my bicycle while the fragile figure of my companion limped to her 29-year-old, blue, Super Dexta Ford Tractor which was parked in a corner of the yard. She hauled herself over the rear cluster of hydraulics and up into the seat, adjusted her woolly hat, and a moment later the engine whooped to life. She set off with a fair jolt, took the entrance gate severely off centre but without mishap, left her turn too late – a wheel caused fence wire to screech – found the true line of the lane, and settled down to a comfortable four miles an hour.

She lived on the farm where she'd been born, and which she'd run on her own for half her life. She'd ploughed, harrowed and sown. A nephew worked the place now, but she still did a bit of ploughing, a few drills of potatoes. She thought soon the European Union would not allow dung to be spread on fields – bad smell, bad for people – and it would have to be *pumped* into the ground. She scoffed. I guessed Miss Harcus would gladly have submerged the EU in her dung pit.

We sat drinking coffee in an immaculate kitchen painted in rainbow greens and yellow but which otherwise could have changed little in a century. A rare box-bed was recessed into one wall and seven cats snuggled against the solid fuel stove. Her only sister lived three miles away at the far end of the island and their only brother was ten miles away on the adjacent island of Westray. The scheduled flight between Papay and Westray was the shortest in the world, lasting two minutes, and it cost £3 for a pensioner on standby. But Miss Harcus didn't travel much. She went to Kirkwall, had been to Shetland once and Edinburgh four times. That was all. She didn't take holidays. Her world was Papay and she was content in it. I envied her that sense of being a part of the island's history, and of finding fulfilment in the familiar without need for distance or far horizons.

Hers was the only blue tractor on Papay. I met it

everywhere. It was parked outside the shop when I went
to restock on tuna and spaghetti, for Miss Harcus used it
when collecting her groceries. When I was waiting for
the Sunday service to begin, it came chugging along, for
Miss Harcus always drove it to church. She waved from it
while I was looking for *primula scotica*, the rare Scottish
primrose which exists almost exclusively on six Orcadian
islands, and she parked it nearby when I was looking over
a cliff, wondering how it felt to be the very last of your
kind. 'Here lived one of the world's last great auks. It was
shot in 1813', read a small memorial.

'Have you ever had a car?' I asked.

'Niver. Niver driven one – weel, that's nae quite true.
Once we had tae tau a car that broke tae the ferry, an' I
steered. I niver had the need o' a car. Whit kin a car do
that a tractor canna?'

She cranked the blue Super Dexta into life and,
smiling, set off to travel Papay once more at the speed
of the plough.

11

❦

Camping near the Crown

My life on and off a hard, narrow saddle had fallen into the loosest definition of a routine. Depending on where my tent was pitched, I would be woken early from a night of only two or three hours of darkness by skitterbrolties, tammy norries, scootie allans, pickieternos, whaups, or, most commonly, mallimacks. (The Northern Isles had given corn buntings, puffins, arctic skuas, arctic terns, curlews, fulmars and all their birds such runcible Lear-like names.)

Mallimacks thronged every cliff and would view my breakfast of brose and dried fruit with disinterest. These stiff-winged seagulls, the supreme exponents of effortless flight, are the bird success story of the twentieth century. Prior to 1878 they were only found on remote St Kilda, the closest lump of Scotland to America. Then, inexplicably, they colonised Shetland's Foula. Today they are found all over our coastline. A sign by one of my wild campsites advised that 90,000 pairs were breeding on this little patch of Orkney alone. As a unit, this population outnumbered Orcadians eight times.

By eight o'clock my dew-soaked tent would be rolled up and my pedals turning. I'd cycle all day, stopping at every opportunity to talk to people over garden walls, visit prearranged contacts and sidetrack at signs of curiosity. Lunchtime would see me turn Viking, invading a grocer and pillaging milk, pies, cheese, bananas and Mars Bars; and stocking up with Cup a soups, tuna and spaghetti for the evening. My diet seldom varied. Since I began travelling the taste of food has ceased to have much importance and my tolerance for monotony usually lasts a journey.

By eight in the evening, I would be seriously looking for a place to camp. If a wild spot with no clues of ownership was available then this would be my first choice, and if not, I would seek permission at the nearest house or farm, and was never refused.

Chilling, with the evening fall in temperature and the sudden end of my exertions at the pedals, I would get my stove going and supper cooked. Then I would retire to the nearest or seediest looking pub, not for the beer but for the pearls of gossip, wisdom and bias that writers make it their business to collect. Then back to my tent where I'd write my diary by the light of a candle for the hour it always took; wondering how Raban, Thubron, Theroux and the others I admired went about it on their travels.

One of my campsites (mallimacks and scootie allans) was close to the rocks of Scarvataing, near Kirkwall, and a tall memorial to the victims of the *Crown*. The Northern Isles have a long history of being inconveniently in the way. Several ships of the Spanish Armada foundered here (the survivors of one of them, legend has it, taught the inhabitants of Fair Isle the art of dyeing which made them famous and their sheep fashionable) and over the centuries hundreds more like the *Crown* have come to sudden grief.

Having refused to heed a warning to anchor in Deer Sound before an approaching storm, the captain of the *Crown* found himself caught in a violent sea off the Scarvataing rocks on the night of 10 December 1679. In the hold he had a cargo of covenanters bound for the colonies of the New World to be sold as slaves, 257 of them confined in a space that would have been cramped for a hundred. They had been taken prisoner at Bothwell Bridge where they had fought for religious freedom – specifically for the right to be Presbyterian and to choose their own ministers – against the turncoat Charles II who had promised all they wanted in order to win their support and the crown, and then imposed Episcopacy and his hated bishops.

Unable to resist the force of the wind, the *Crown* broke her anchor and was driven onto rocks. It is said that the terrified prisoners pleaded to be released, promised they would peacefully go to any prison of the captain's choice if he would open the hatches. Not only did he refuse but he ordered the crew to secure the hatches with chains. They then cut down the masts and constructed a bridge by which all officers and crew safely reached the shore. As the ship broke up and some prisoners managed to escape, the captain had his crew lined up along the beach with orders to drive them back into the sea. Over 200 covenanters perished and the survivors were later recaptured and sent to the slave markets of Jamaica and New Jersey.

When I asked the nearest farmer if I could camp near the memorial, he interrupted his meal and let it go cold while he chatted. He told me a different version of the story: the *Crown* was a ramshackle tub, the captain feared it would never survive an Atlantic crossing and he had no intention of trying. He deliberately ran the ship aground. Then, the farmer maintained, he spread word among the locals that the prisoners who escaped were dangerous convicts and should be given neither food nor quarter, and the covenanters died of cold and starvation.

This all seemed to weigh heavily on the man.

'Of course, you can camp anywhere. It was nice meeting you. We're always very glad to help strangers here.'

Balfour Castle, on the Isle of Shapinsay, had a more consistent history of hospitality.

12

❧

Castle Balfour, Shapinsay

In outline Shapinsay resembles an emaciated Australia. A neat gridwork of lanes indicates that its farms did not grow up by chance but by the design of a feudal lord, and some – Balaclava, Inkerman, Lucknow – reveal his dates. Like stains spilled carelessly over a patchwork of sulphur and olive fields, the island possesses a few lochs, the odd marsh and one of Orkney's three woods. Where you would expect to find the city of Perth, or maybe Kalgoorlie, stands Balfour Castle.

'Come in a bit closer . . . Goodness, you're a nervous group today. I must've got my wrong teeth in.'

Mention of the word 'tour' once conjured up for me the sequential images of buses, sweat, chatter, yawns, blockages, deafness, drought, euthanasia, and guides in the final stages of adrenaline deficiency. But the only way to visit the castle was on an official tour, unless you wanted to part with £60 and spend the night there. I braced myself for two hours of emotional degeneration.

'Good morning, my name's Catherine and I'm your guide.' Tall, 60-ish and forbidding, she challenged everyone with her eyes which brought to mind bayonets and Toledo steel. I realised we'd met before on several occasions, only then she'd held a sickle in her hand or stood by a conveyor belt. All over the old Soviet Union, her robust, classical features had looked down on me from murals whose themes were Patriotism and Productivity.

'The castle in its present form was built by the Balfours, a Fife family who had interests in mining, and did rather well in India. In 1847 David Balfour decided to turn the existing house into a castle for his shooting holidays. It was to have three hundred and sixty-five windows, fifty-two rooms, twelve entrance doors and seven turrets.' I jotted down these figures because Catherine had a schoolmistressly way of intimating that notes should be taken.

'An Edinburgh architect, David Bryce, drew up the plans and oversaw the work which took thirty men just two years to complete. He had quoted Balfour a figure of six thousand, seven hundred and thirty-eight pounds and seventeen shillings for the job, including the importation of all the stone. He was just two pounds under when the final reckoning was made. The Balfours, as of course one did in those days, took themselves off to Italy for the duration of the work, and sent back craftsmen to see to the marble and plasterwork. The last Balfour died thirty-three years ago. He had four wives and no children. He drank heavily and left the estate to his mistress. She sold the house and contents intact, lock, stock and staircase.'

'Who owns it now?'

'I do.'

The castle was a repository of a rich man's toys and curios. 'I'm told I must put up ropes and DO NOT TOUCH notices, but I refuse.' Catherine Zawadski spoke with the accent I would have expected the Balfours to have used. 'It's impossible to REALLY experience a thing by looking at it. You need to TOUCH it. FEEL it.' She swelled with the emphasis. 'And I haven't had a single thing stolen. I don't think those sort of people make it as far as Orkney.'

Zawadski was not a surname common to Vikings or Orcadians. Unlikely as it may seem, the two northernmost baronial homes in Scotland are owned by unrelated families with Polish connections.

Every door was of solid oak, made from the packing cases used by the Balfours to transport their souvenirs back from Italy. We were encouraged to stroke busts and run a hand over 'half a marble table' from the Vatican (its matching half was still there) – Catherine had no idea how Balfour had come by it, or why a Pope should agree to slice up his furniture.

Enigmatic, and undoubtedly paternalistic, Balfour was nevertheless considered a fair and generous landlord in his day. When the Clearances were in full swing in the rest of the country, he subdivided farms to let more people work the land. Whenever a vacancy for a maid arose, the island girls queued in the hope of being chosen for the salary of £30, plus board, and two shirts, skirts and pairs of boots per annum.

At half-time we tourists were ushered into the old servants' room for tea (and to revise our notes) before the garden section. Three local women served home baking as timidly as if one word from us and their £30 and free boots would be terminated.

'This is the walled garden and the Victorian Walled Garden was the first high-tech agricultural development. It was perfection. It will never be surpassed. Those who worked here were technicians, serving a twenty-five-year apprenticeship.'

The voice was much the same but the owner was different. Andrew had taken over from his mother-in-law. He didn't have her eyes but the same knack of making attention appear compulsory. A frustrated Victorian, he was clearly out of his century, and he had me right in there with him, hooked on his enthusiasm for the garden.

'The gardeners started at the bottom. Two years as a pot boy, two as an "improver", and then they became a journeyman, in charge of one section of the garden. Every five years they usually moved on to another property and repeated the process. To become a head gardener you had to have worked at five different gardens – twenty-five years.'

We were among two acres of vegetables bursting out of the ground with Zawadski energy. One of our group peered at a vine of blue pods. 'What are these?'

'Peas. The Victorians grew two hundred and fifty varieties of peas in various colours. Today, Britain produces twenty-five . . . and they're all green. We're losing it . . . we're regressing.' This garden was one of only three remaining in the country still used for its original purpose – to provide the big house with fresh vegetables all year round. Continuity meant successful planting for nine months and, Andrew emphasised, *traditional* varieties of vegetables. 'Modern varieties have been genetically engineered to create a machine-friendly homogenous crop once a year. The Walled Garden was the last direct and constant interchange between producer and consumer. If the product wasn't good, it wasn't grown any more. Gardeners were always experimenting, always pushing back the frontiers. Taste and quality were everything.'

We entered a glasshouse and passed through thirty paces of Cyprus: peaches, apricots, figs, plums and grapes.

'The tourist brochure claims Orkney gets the same amount of sun as the south of England. In fact, we get thirty per cent more. The maturation of fruit depends on the hours of sunlight. It's a clock that counts and can't be cheated. When enough sunlight has been absorbed, a chemical process takes place in the fruit's sugar, turning lactose to fructose. This is what creates the fragrance and taste.'

By this time we were all eager students, ardently Victorian.

'Ripening is simply a function of temperature and

water. You'll know that commercial fruit growers usually pick their crops before they're ripe, and they ripen during storage or in transit to the market. But this cheats the maturation process, so the fruit is tasteless.'

Guests at Balfour Castle underwent the fruit bowl test over dinner and fell into two groups according to their reaction to the fragrance which emanated from the crystal bowl. One group, those over forty, invariably went into raptures and recalled childhood memories of 'real' fruit. The other group invariably asked, 'What's that funny smell?'

It was an exceptional tour, ending at Balfour's sea-flush public lavatory (seating for three), which was listed as of World Architectural Importance. Experts, we were told, came from all over the world to measure and examine it.

Then the ferry arrived to take us back to Kirkwall, across a deep, deep pea blue sea.

13

❧

Kirkwall Show

In mid-August ferries shuttle back and forth through Orkney's firths and flows with increased regularity, emptying the islands and transferring their populations to Kirkwall. One thousand farms and an annual production of 130,000 head of cattle collude to put dung in the treads of most Orcadians' wellies, and few people are prepared to miss the County Show. Crowds are disgorged from the harbour and they filter through the town's streets to sounds of lager cans being kicked and crushed, past the soaring, muddied red and white cathedral, and the ruined Earl's Palace, to a street which leads steeply to Bignold Park.

Here I found animals in sections according to breed. The Suffolk rams had drawn the lot next to the Waltzers where teenagers screamed in a holocaust of Heavy Metal. The pigs had done better and commanded a fine view of bungee jumpers yo-yoing from the jib of a crane. A man in white overalls grinned stoically as the children of a potential customer bounced on the seat, wrenched the gears and played tug-of-war with the door of the John Deere 7700 tractor he was trying to sell. My gaze scanned the faces, hopefully, for Miss Harcus, but she was not to be seen.

I avoided the horse section where long-nosed women in swaggering riding gear brushed and fussed, looking murderously competitive, and sat down on a bale of straw next to a woman knocking back Bacardis. Mrs Flett was almost as large as her bull.

'What type is he?'

'Limousin.' She lingered on the last syllable, as if he had four wheels.

'Are you selling him?'

'Nah. We're jist here fer fun.' She got up and rubbed faces with two tons of muscle and breeding equipment. 'He's done all right. Best in Breed.'

I looked about. There wasn't another Limousin to be seen.

'Ah'm jist aboot tae pit him oot fer overall champion.'

But she didn't fancy his chances. 'Sea-mentals,' she complained. 'Tae many good sea-mentals here the day.'

Further on were the gots. The moment I saw the gots, I heard the English accents. I asked one man how his Toggenburg billy had done.

'Nae bad, Jimmy. Done better, done worse, know whit I mean?'

I had picked the exception. Angus Craig was a Glaswegian Jew. As was not uncommon among Glaswegians he not only declared his city but also his religion, unprompted. He had come to Orkney to retire but his wife, Maggie, had always wanted a goat. They got a goat. One day a request arrived for all the cheese they could supply. They bought another twenty-two. Fourteen goats in milk, twenty gallons a day, twenty pounds of cheese.

'He says, "I'd like a fag now, Jimmy".'

Angus had that habit among pet owners of putting words into animals' mouths and believing they were being original, even amusing. He broke the filter off a cigarette and gave it to Thorfinn who devoured it and waggled his beard.

'Ah dinnae gie im mair than three a day.'

Thorfinn had other strange habits. Maggie used to sing Danny O'Donovan ('Ye've surely heard o' Danny O'Donovan, pal?') songs to the nannies while milking, and Thorfinn used to listen. One Christmas Angus was dozing in his chair feeling life was wonderful, when Maggie said she'd just go and get Thorfinn and let him watch the O'Donovan video. 'Ah thought . . . this isnae real. This is Christmas, an she's bringin' a goat in . . . jist haud oan a minute, pal.' But Thorfinn had eaten two fags, a bowl of peanuts and calmly watched an hour of Danny O'Donovan.

Where there's a got outside, I thought . . .

Kirkwall Show was said to mark the beginning of winter, and the afternoon fizzled into rain. I hadn't seen a single kilt and was admonishing myself for even looking for them – after all, this wasn't Scotland – when Kirkwall Pipe Band came marching in and blew my theory. The tannoy announced the winners of endless categories . . . 'In the Two-Year-Old-Heifer-in-Calf-or-Milk-and-Not-Showing-More-Than-Four-Teeth section, the winner is . . .' The overall champion was also announced and Mrs Flett was right. A Sea-mental won. This triggered a general dispersal, with drunken farmers staggering behind sedately swinging cows heading for their floats and the peaceful fields of home.

Back in town the wet flagstones had a bright sheen from the street lights as throngs of figures made the traditional pub pilgrimage. Puddles were prodded by the rain until they were a confusion of ripples. Underfoot came the brittle crunch of plastic glasses which other feet had already crushed. The Bothy Bar was impenetrable. In Queens I ended up pinned against a fruit machine. The pressure of people forced me into their conversations.

'Three-one. Westray played like a bunch of wankers.'

'Got a second fer the Charolais.'

'John, this is Doreen – we were at school the'gither, an' her Dad was my Dad's best man at the weedin.'

'Wan I looked doon from yon cage and they wis sayin "Jump!", I nearly shat myself.'

'Have ye met Doreen? She an I were at school the'gither, and her Dad was my Dad's . . .' She interrupted this statement just as I was awaiting confirmation of *the weedin*, suddenly spotting a busty friend clamped in the crowd nearby. '. . . HELEN! PUT YOUR TITS AWAY, YOU LITTLE SLUT! Ohh! I jist loves ye.'

It was, by all accounts, a good show.

14

Scapa Flow, Longhope and Hoy

The morning sun declared that winter had been postponed by painting the land in primary colours. The Alps had moved in during the night and now stood aloof on the horizon, cold and crusty, but closer inspection revealed them to be clouds using Orkney as a layby. Cattle, wide-eyed and steaming, outlined in silver by the infusion of rays, poked wet noses through fences and gaped at me; sometimes they took fright, snorted and went blundering into backward stampedes. Not a tractor in the land was idle that morning, as the road led me south in the direction of Hoy. They were turning fields into pretty arrangements of stripes, lemon on lavender, cutting swaths in the stuff that makes silage, and, where the land was yellowest, impaling bales with nasty spikes like lumbering medieval jousters. Scapa Flow spread out to my right as a great cobalt pond, looking so benign that it was hard to imagine it had ever witnessed the spluttering horrors of mass drownings and the death of a fleet.

By the outbreak of the First World War, the Admiralty had sent the Grand Fleet to Scapa Flow for safe-keeping, despite being aware that U-boats could penetrate this natural haven formed by a ring of islands. Block ships were sunk in some of the narrow access channels, booms and nets were rigged up and the defences gradually improved. In May 1916 the Home Fleet steamed out to confront the German High Seas Fleet at the indecisive, muscle-testing Battle of Jutland, an engagement involving no less than 249 ships. A week later Scapa Flow saw Lord Kitchener make his fateful departure.

Lord (Horatio Herbert) Kitchener of Khartoum was then 66 and at the peak of an illustrious career; scourge of the Dervishes at Omdurman; Commander-in-Chief of, variously, the Egyptian Army, Indian Army and British Army in the Boer War; and Minister for War, whose moustached face and pointing finger ('wants *YOU*') sent more men to their graves than any other recruitment poster. Kitchener was on a secret mission to the Tsar of Russia. He left Scapa Flow on HMS *Hampshire* the same day he arrived, 5 June, heading for Archangel. Kitchener decided to take the unusual west coast route past Orkney in the hope of gaining shelter from the filthy weather, unaware that seven days earlier *U-475* had laid 22 mines along that route. HMS *Hampshire* sank that evening in less than fifteen minutes, drowning 653 men. Twelve survived, but Kitchener was not one of them and his body was never recovered.

At the end of the war the majority of the German High Seas Fleet was escorted to Scapa Flow for internment while the Allies decided its future under the terms of the Armistice. *Friedrich der Grosse, Emden, Derfflinger, Seydlitz, Hindenberg* . . . the might of the German Navy steamed in, numbering 74 vessels in all. For eight months depressed and frequently mutinous German crews were confined to the ships under the command of Admiral von Reuter. On 21 June 1917 a group of schoolchildren were on a sightseeing trip in the Flow when they noticed that the ships were looking 'a bit funny'. They were listing severely. Realising that the German Navy was about to be disbanded, von Reuter had given the order to scuttle the fleet. By evening half a million tons of shipping lay on the seabed.

Only Truk Lagoon in the Pacific Ocean could claim a greater concentration of wrecks, but today three battleships and eight lesser ships of the German Fleet remain. The rest have all been salvaged over the years. What makes the remaining wrecks particularly valuable today is the excepionally low level of radioactivity found in the metal. They were constructed of steel uncontaminated by the radioactive fallout of the nuclear age which makes it an ideal material for specialised medical equipment.

But the most tragic wreck had yet to settle below the waters of Scapa Flow. Just six weeks into the Second World War, *U-47* slipped past a blockship in Kirk Sound and fired six torpedoes at HMS *Royal Oak*. The battleship sank in thirteen minutes with the loss of 833 men out of a complement of 1,200. *U-47* made good her escape and returned to an heroic reception in Germany. HMS *Royal Oak* remains an official war grave and a protected wreck, and, fifty years on, oil still seeps from her fuel bunkers and forms a visible slick on the surface.

Despite being a case of bolting the stable door too late, the War Office decided to secure the western approach to Scapa Flow once and for all. The construction of the Churchill Barriers, four causeways linking South Ronaldsay with the mainland, lasted the duration of the war and involved the dumping of a million cubic metres of rock to block the channels. (The secret codename for the operation, 'ROCKWORKS', was a masterpiece of deception.) Without the arrival of 1,700 Italians captured in North Africa, the project would never have progressed.

I cycled along the barriers later that day. People were fishing from the long jumble of rocks, and the odd blockship was parked nearby as if it too were just checking out the scene. A few cars were drawn up outside the famous Italian Chapel, a couple of nissan huts disguised on the outside to look like an old Sicilian church, and on the inside to appear as stuccowork in an extravagance of baroque relief when the reality was a flat plasterboard wall under a thin layer of paint. The deception was perfectly fitting. All Scapa Flow looked nothing more than a pleasant afternoon out.

At St Margaret's Hope, a fishing boat gave me a lift to Hoy.

I was fifteen at the time and can vividly recall the black headlines, the swingeing sense of shock, of injustice, and, days later, the photograph of the coffins and the crowded cemetery in an empty landscape. Until then few people had ever heard of Hoy and even fewer of the small village of Longhope, but after 17 March 1969, the nation knew exactly where they were.

On that day the Longhope lifeboat, *TGB*, was called out to the assistance of the Liberian-registered SS *Irene* which had run aground on South Ronaldsay in a strong south-easterly gale. *TGB* capsized and all eight of her crew drowned. One woman lost her husband and two sons in the accident. Ironically, the *Irene* survived the storm and was successfully refloated.

Ian MacFadean eased back the throttle and *Lord Saltoun* dropped at the stern, reared at the bow and churned the sea into a turmoil of white. With 840 horsepower below us – twin engines, twin turbos, twin props, twin anti-fouling blades; everything doubled for safety – we cut through the Pentland Firth at eighteen knots. *Lord Saltoun*, only six years old, had already been superseded by a faster (25 knots) and more expensive (£1.5 million) class of lifeboat, but she was pretty representative of the state of the art.

'Yeah, she can cope with most weather.' There was doubt to be read here, the inference that one can never be sure, that arrogance is only a shade away from confidence and has no place on board ship. Ian had been a member of the crew at the time of the *Irene* but happened to be away on that particular day. But he had lost his brother in the accident.

'It was a wild night, yon. Kirkwall lifeboat was also out, on another call, and the cox said the boat was falling sixty feet off wave crests.'

'What was *TGB* like as a boat?'

'OK for those days but she could only do eight-and-a-half knots at best. That made life tricky. Under certain conditions there's a twelve-knot current at the Pentland Skerries, and we often get call-outs there. If *TGB* got too close to that current, she couldn't get out. She wasn't self-righting. We could've had that type but we chose not to.'

'You chose *not* to have a self-righting boat?'

''Cos they weren't like these, they were an old design and really rolled about. But maybe an S-R would've saved them. I dunno. It was just a huge sea.'

Lord Saltoun glowed like a muscular, blue and orange bullet. Below the non-slip deck was an open-plan hold on two levels; the lower level was a 'survivors' room', complete with benches (one of the seats being the heads, no privacy), cooker and self-heating cans of Irish stew; the upper level contained the controls, tables, and chairs for cox, radar and radio operators, and navigator.

'We've all the usual gear, and yon's a radio signal locator. If we can't see the target we'll ask it to speak to us every five minutes – and yon'll get a fix on the signal and give us a bearing.' What I took to be hand torches were rocket launchers capable of sending a line 250 metres, and beside them were smaller torches, white flares which would descend by parachute and light up the search area. In this stash of 007 gadgetry, even the cox's coffee mug looked multi-functional.

We passed Kirk Hope (*bay, inlet*) where *U-47* sneaked into Scapa Flow, and entered Aith Hope where *Lord Saltoun* lived in a royal-mail-red house on stilts. She reversed into the ramp, slotted her keels into grooves, took a loan of a winch and was hauled home backside first. Once snuggled safely in she formed the centrepiece of an

arena of black boards elegantly scripted in gold. They took
me back to school, to the dining room, where those same
funereal boards hung over us, intimidating, glorifying the
achievements of those who had 'shaped up splendidly' as
Heads of House, School Prefects, Captains of Rugby and
daring any of us to fail their gilded example.

Only these boards were less brash and their testimonials
immeasurably more profound. They listed the dates and
names of stricken vessels, the nature of the assistance
rendered, and the number of people rescued. Since their
inception in 1874, Longhope lifeboats had notched a tally
of 623 lives saved.

I joined some of the crew for a pint at the Royal Hotel,
an infamous hostelry whose erstwhile charm had been
replaced by a layer of Evo-stik and formica. At a corner
table I fell into conversation with a tall burly man who
looked like an inflated version of myself with slightly
more hair. Billy Budge was the current cox of the lifeboat
and he was two pints into an evening of scrupulously
rationed drink.

'I don't go out on every exercise. Best if others get a
shot in the hot seat from time to time.' He'd been cox for
the last six years. You could never *really* relax, he said.
Call-outs happened any time, but that didn't bother him.
Other things did, however.

'I'm a bit disillusioned at the moment.' He lowered
his voice. 'Not wi' the service, the boat, the job . . .
not wi' things like that, it's still the best . . . but wi'
the RNLI. Almost all I do is fundraising. You wouldn't
believe the amount of time taken up wi' endless tours and
promotions.'

He disliked being paraded as the 'Cox of the Longhope
Lifeboat'. He envied the Coastguard who had no need to
go to clubs and galas, to force a smile and be friendly to
everyone.

'I just want to get on wi' the job of training and rescuing.
I've no regrets about the past, but it's got to change in

future. Aye, the government's going to have to fund it.'
He then regretted he had been so candid. 'Hell, I shouldn't
have said that, but that's how I feel. Jackie Groat . . . now
there's a man . . . Jackie'll give you another opinion.'

Jackie Groat was the longest-serving RNLI secretary
in Britain, and I found him less than a mile away at
his home.

He was 70, a quietly spoken man, his words deliberate
and measured, and he'd held his voluntary post for 32
years. Without mentioning Billy, I brought up the subject
of a government takeover.

Jackie stiffened but his voice remained calm. 'We don't
want it, and neither do we need it. At the moment it costs
£50 million a year to run the RNLI. If the government took
over it would probably cost double that. Men would want
pay, and overtime. It would be more paperwork, more
restrictions, more indecision, more waste. Money changes
everything. No, I don't think it would work. As long as it's
voluntary – it's cheaper, more efficient, and much more a
team effort.'

Legacies were the major source of income but women's
guilds were the backbone of the fundraising effort. All
over the country people like Miss Harcus rattled cans,
played whist, drank coffee, baked and sold the contents
of their car boots (those who had them) and raised enough
money to buy, equip and maintain lifeboats along 100,000
miles of coastline. And in each area branch secretaries
kept the machinery moving, people like Jackie Groat who
had given his time freely to the cause for half his life.

Had he not thought of giving up in the aftermath of the
disaster?

'Yes. Yes, I did. I'd had enough. I wanted no more to
do with lifeboats. Eight good strong men out of our little
community . . . it was a tragedy. But then I thought . . .
their sacrifice will be wasted if it ends here. I knew we
had to go on. At the funeral people came up to me and
whispered, "Bear me in mind when you next want a crew."'

The new boat arrived within nine months. Four years later eleven men were rescued from almost certain death on a trawler. 'The *Ross Tern* it was. Yes, we were right to go on. We've seventeen on the waiting list for crew now.'

He fell silent for a moment. 'Have you ever looked into the eyes of a man pulled alive from the sea when he thought he was going to die? No? . . . no . . . I suppose not. Eight lives lost . . . but so many won.'

Hoy had pumped itself up into mountains. Small, lumpish affairs in reality, but compared to the view in any other direction they appeared lofty and wild, coloured with the same shades soldiers wear to look like swamp. Colditz Castle, formerly the Signals and Communications HQ for Scapa Flow and now an eerie concrete catacomb inhabited by thirteen pigeons, sat high on a shoulder coldly unaware of its dispossession. Out at sea Flotta held a tall candle to the evening sky, suckling a tanker through a slender proboscis with oil from the distant Piper and Claymore Fields. Between Flotta and Colditz, on flat land by the sea, the few inhabitants of Lyness moved about the razed ghost town of brick where 12,000 personnel were once stationed.

With the victims of *Royal Oak, Hampshire* and others behind me in the naval cemetery at Lyness, I thought – and hoped – that I could turn to more cheerful topics in what had become a mortuary tour of my favourite Orcadian island. Seven miles of waltzing coastal road sustained this hope until a white slat fence caught my eye, alone in an expanse of moor, and led me to the grave and story of Betty Corrigall.

A young country girl, she lived sometime last century, and fell in love with a sailor who soon deserted her. When she discovered she was carrying their child, the shame and trauma of her position overwhelmed her and she tried to drown herself in the sea. But she was pulled out in time. Shortly afterwards her body was found hanging in a barn. Because she had committed the sin of taking her own life, her body was not permitted to be buried on consecrated ground. The two landowners, the lairds of Hoy and Melsetter, refused to allow her burial on their lands. The only solution was to bury her on the parish boundary. So a pathetic and distressed group of relatives carried her seven miles from her home in Lyness to this line of no-man's-land and put her in an unmarked grave.

The grave was lost for almost a century but discovered by peat cutters in the 1930s. Twenty years later an American visitor became interested in the story and erected a fence round the grave. He asked a local man, Mr Berry, if he would put up a headstone and Mr Berry said he would, when he could find the time. He found it twenty-seven years later and because the peat was too soft to support a stone, he made a memorial out of fibreglass. 'Here lies Betty Corrigall', reads the inscription, though more apt would be the epitaph written for her some years later by an anonymous hand.

> So sweet
> So small
> Here lies
> Betty Corrigall
> Outwith the bounds of kin
> They buried her
> And not within
> The burn beside
> The brae above
> Keep her with more
> Abundant love

From Hoy I caught a ferry to Stromness, Orkney's second town, where I had arranged to meet one of Scotland's great Men of Letters.

15

George Mackay Brown

LOST: A three-legged dog, blind in the left eye, right ear missing, large scar across throat, tail broken in 3 places, recently castrated. Answers to the name of 'Lucky'. No reward. Ring AR AAP, Queensland, Australia.'

The notice was the humorous exception among a miscellany of typed notes whose themes were vitriolic 'exposés' ('Local councillor should be shot', 'The Pirates of Finance') pasted to the inside of a derelict café window on Stromness' main street. My obvious bewilderment produced an explanation from a passer-by. This window represented the shoulder chips of one Hugh Yorston, a local who'd done good in Australian mining and who returned each year to add to his quaint Orcadian scrapbook. The guy was a loony, I was told. Lucky was the wounded psyche of Mr Yorston himself, they said.

Anyone who could generate such a bad press and afford to spend six months each year trafficking scandal rather than more normal commodities like drugs, arms or double vanilla 99s, had to be just the sort of person I was after; controversial, outspoken, that almost-fictional character that is the raw material of non-fiction. The SWRI certainly wasn't throwing up too many like him.

I tried to locate Mr Yorston but every avenue led to a blank. He seemed to be in hiding. So did the rest of Stromness's population. I caught sight of legs disappearing round corners, and figures slipping from one doorway to the next. It was probably just the rain but a Kafkaesque sense of barriers prevailed.

The streets of Stromness are cut off from the sea by a front of houses whose walls drop into the water on either side of private piers. Flagstones pave each lane and a central strand of cobbles survives from the times when horses' hooves sought their roughness for grip. Stepped closes branch off uphill, looking slippery and algae-grown in the drizzle. But in sunlight Stromness chameleons into Orkney's postcard town: the neat harbour, the squiggly lines of streets (Hellihole Road, Khyber Pass), tiers of greystone houses on the slope of Brinkie's Brae; you feel at any moment the rusty old cannon on the point will *boom* the time-honoured announcement that a whaler or Hudson's Bay ship is coming in for water, supplies and crew.

I found the address I'd been given, a first-floor council flat a book's throw from the main street.

'I really don't know, I've never counted . . .' George Mackay Brown, author, poet, and die-hard Stromnessian, had lost count of how many books he had written. He reached for his latest and totted up the titles listed. 'Good Lord! . . . thirty-two! It's really rather a lot. Too many, far too many.'

'Why d'you say that?'

'Half of them make me cringe. Wish I'd never written them. The rest are OK.' Some bits were even good, he admitted reluctantly. 'I don't know of any finer feeling than the glow that comes from having expressed something just right, exactly right.'

He swung his legs onto a footstool and sank back into a cramped armchair, hoping it would absorb him, but instead it blocked his retreat and held him upright, looking stiff and uncomfortably vulnerable. His lean, frail body was the product of grappling with words rather than boxes of ling, and suggested frugality, even austerity; not as virtues but as irrelevant incidentals to the *raison d'être* of expressing himself just right. Pleasantries and light conversation passed easily enough, but opinion, in the company of a stranger, made sparing and quick sorties from beneath a veil of shyness.

Connected by a loose fisherman's pullover were a pair of enormous hands and an extraordinarily long face. His eyes were deep-sunken, his jaw very angular. Below a handsome wave of white hair bulged a forehead befitting a man who had lived so much of his life in his mind. It was an academic forehead, I thought, and used the word. That parted the veil. 'I dislike academics. I'm much happier talking to fishermen on the pier.'

In his weekly column 'Under Brinkies Brae' in *The Orcadian*, he had recently written about his disappointment over the disappearance of a certain institution from his youth.

That day, I caught a bad cold. It can't have been the weather – for, as I say, it was a beautiful summer day. I think the ailment was what they call nowadays, 'psycho-somatic', caused by a victory of prose over poetry.

Make no mistake: Prose versus Poetry, that constitutes the great war of our times.

Be sure that you enrol in the armies of light.

'So you'll enrol on the side of Poetry?'
'Oh, yes, I like poetry better. It's something you've either got in you, or you haven't.' What neither of us knew at that moment was that his thirty-third book, *Beside the Ocean of Time* – prose – was just about to be short-listed for the Booker Prize. ('Booker prize – Nobel prize – what a song and dance about such baubles!' he had written ten years earlier. 'What does it matter, the opinion of a

few contemporary judges, compared to the near-infallible verdict that time sends down its long corridors?')

Born in Stromness in 1921 to a father who was a tailor and postman, and to a mother from Caithness who had Gaelic, George was one of five children, and from his earliest memories all he wanted to do was write. 'I was first published relatively late, in my thirties, and before that I was a burden on the state, on Social Security . . . or Welfare Allowance, as it was then.'

'By choice?'

'Well, I couldn't earn enough to live off . . .' He threw his head back and mimed a laugh that was almost silent. 'You see, it's the only thing I can do . . .'

His name, he stressed, was not double-barrelled. He disliked double-barrels intensely. 'I wanted to be different from just *any* George Brown, and there was a parliamentary minister of that name at the time with whom I certainly did *not* want to be associated. Mackay was my middle name, from my mother's side, and I wanted to include a Scottish touch. So I had the Mackay put in when my name was first published.'

Brought up a Presbyterian, he had 'thought things out' for himself, and converted to Catholicism. He lived alone in this simple flat whose only extravagances were an abundance of paintings and half a wall of some of his favourite writers: Yeats, Keats, Brecht, Thomas Mann and E.M. Forster. He had never driven a car ('And I'm not going to start at my age!'), didn't cook, type, word process or travel, and had never married ('And I'm not going to start *that* either!'), and didn't know where the Tartan Army had gone.

'Do you know the Duke of Sutherland memorial, overlooking Golspie? It even has the impudence to say "erected by a grateful tenantry". I can't understand why it hasn't been blown up. Now, if it was in Ireland it wouldn't have stood for long. I don't know, the Tartan Army seems to have lost its vim.'

'Do you say that with regret?'

'No, of course not. I'm against violence and acts of destruction . . . though I wouldn't mind if that monument went.'

His day began at 8.20 am. Egg and toast. 'I do that myself,' he remarked in jovial defence. He was at work by nine, writing the previous day's entry in his diary for ten minutes. It warmed him up for the morning's work. He only worked mornings and hated being disturbed. He made his bed at twelve, and then usually went out to 'bum his lunch off someone'. He said he was invited out a tremendous amount.

'Does that please you or does it become bothersome?'

'Oh no, I love it . . . but I do choose my hosts very carefully.'

'Why don't you like travelling?'

Again the toss of the head and the breathy laugh. 'I spent six years at university in Edinburgh. That was enough. Oh, I've had invitations to lecture in Canada and Australia . . . nothing doing. I like it here. I don't even go around Orkney much now. No, my country is between Ness Road and the pierhead.'

It was a slightly smaller country than that of Miss Harcus. It was Scotland, yes, it was Orkney, yes, but it was specifically Stromness. It was half a mile long, quarter of a mile wide and occupied by people who remained invisible to me. Yet George Mackay Brown knew them, and their history. The slim margin of this country provided all he needed to fill thirty-three books and an unbroken sequence of weekly columns spanning thirty years.

That week, in 'Under Brinkie's Brae', he wrote: 'I am too old and lazy to travel myself. I do regret the laziness of my youth that kept me from learning Gaelic and Norse. I wander about in a no-man's land between two cultures.'

He wanders that land well.

My need for space was greater and I set out the next day

to invade mainland Scotland. Orkney, I felt, had got it right. Everything was in moderation: people, oil, church, sobriety, indulgence. They were all there but scattered, and no one produced a dominant effect. Only tombs and cows ran to excess but the former were dead and harmless and the latter, green and allowable.

Orkney had hidden itself in mist, and even the Old Man of Hoy was reluctant to show itself to those clutching binoculars on the deck of the *St Ola*. In the beer-stained saloon my nearest fellow invaders were an oafish oilrig worker called Ralph and two elderly ladies trying to grasp the nature of the industry.

'You're a *what*, dear?'

'A mud-logger . . . 'scuse me!' Ralph had burped and rather spoiled the dignity which would have otherwise accompanied his reply. He had been drinking heavily.

'A mud-logger . . . I see . . . but I thought you said you worked in oil?'

Ralph rolled his eyes, then smiled. 'Yah, I work in oil. Look, we drill a hole, the drill don't like it, we pump down a lubricant, we call it mud, I measure the mud . . . MUD . . . LOGGER. OK?' He must then have felt he'd been a bit hard on them for he changed tone and offered them something more cheery, leaning close and resting his paunch on the table. 'Had a bit of a heavy night last night. Thought I was lookin' a bit rough this morning but when I went into ma mate's cabin . . . well, if you'll 'scuse th'expression . . . I've seen prettier creaturs in a brothel.'

The ladies managed a hint of polite smile. One returned to her knitting, the other to her paper. Ralph provided some of the laugh he had expected and slumped back in his chair. Soon he was snoring.

He awoke some time later, yawned, stretched and looked out of the window. The mist had lifted. 'Oh, aye, there's hard stuff, all right.'

The hard stuff was the coastline of Caithness. The invasion was about to begin.

16

∽

The Winstons' B&B

The invasion was, in fact, over. Admittedly incomplete, it was nevertheless all over, bar the tailenders and the bandwagons. The vanguard had conquered and dug themselves in. There had been casualties, of course, as in any long, drawn-out campaign; those whose 'bargains' now hung as millstones from the neck, and unhappy bands of deserters who had found the climate ghastly and the people awful and fled back home – but not the Winstons.

Caithness had risen half an inch since my arrival. My wheels lifted a gallon of rain off the road with each revolution and sprayed it over my feet. I had let the miles pass and the light fade in the vague hope that, round the next corner, Caithness would conveniently rearrange itself into the Mediterranean cover of its brochure which was stuffed into my left pannier. It remained tundra in a monsoon and eventually I chanced upon a phone box with the Winstons' business card tucked into a crack. Shalimar B&B. The name rang a warning but it was too foul to be picky. I phoned. Yes, they had a room. Take this road, then that, and they'd be watching out for me.

I tied my torch to the handlebars, followed the instructions and gazed at a choice of three lights in a panorama of night. Suddenly one triggered a chain reaction of brilliance and Shalimar was floodlit in a message of six flashes. I pedalled on and there was a smiling John holding open the gate and waving me through into the corner of Cornwall he'd imported. Shalimar, under 2,000 watts, had the appearance of a traditional cottage with a modern extension but in fact was the Grand Hotel Truro. There was Janet waving by the Enquiries sign, and beyond was the Car Park with three delineated spaces each with a P in a circle painted in true Highway Code colours. The proprietors of the Grand Hotel Truro clearly had too much time and too few customers.

Inside, Shalimar shrank into the Tongue 'n' Groove department of B&Q. John and Janet mothered me with a concern that was touching, but excessive, and made me fear that after the welcome cup of coffee a fatted calf would be dragged in on a silver platter. Within five minutes they had unburdened themselves.

'We're not English, we're Cornish. We're Celts.'

'We couldn't afford a house in Cornwall because the English pushed up the prices to a hundred and twenty grand.'

'Look, I'm wearing my Cornish rugger shirt to prove it.'

'This is our local friend, Iain.' I shook hands with Iain, wondering if he'd suddenly blow a stopper and go spiralling around the room.

'Got this house for eight thousand quid – real bargain.'

When John, large and gnomishly merry, began the story of how he'd been a fireman in the Midlands until he'd got injured, and compensation, and a pension, and it was the 'best thing'd ever happened to him' . . . I said I was tired and excused myself. He hung on, offering a tour of the renovations he'd done but I didn't need a guide. They were obvious, open wounds looking savagely raw. Wherever straight edge met curve was a copybook illustration of incompetence with a fretsaw. ('Not like this, but . . .')

I was so glad to escape I didn't mind the room which had recently been fumigated with car freshener. Sofa, bedspread and wallpaper were clashes of floral warfare, and the carpet, a bilious turbulence of pink, mauve and blue; an entire showcase of cats, in every substance known to man, occupied the walls along with brass tigers, glass porpoises and three sets of Plate Offers (Myth and Fairyland, British Wildlife, Chinese Emperors), and any spare spaces were filled with Janet's 'Unique' design machine-knit sweaters . . .

I wrote my diary till late, thinking, you couldn't get away with Shalimar if this were fiction.

17

❧

Dounreay and the Swelkie

Not far from where a large golf ball breaks the Caithness horizon is a sea whirlpool called the Swelkie. Legend has it that below the water lies the magic mill of King Frodi which would produce anything to order: food, gold, money, B&Q Tongue 'n' Groove, anything. It was stolen by another king, Mysing, and carried away in his ship. Finding that he'd run out of salt, he ordered the mill to provide it, which it did, and only then did Mysing realise he'd started something he didn't know how to stop. The ship filled with salt and sank, Mysing drowned, the world's oceans became salty, and the mill is still churning away, as the whirlpool bears witness. For an old parable, the Swelkie is found disconcertingly close to Dounreay, Britain's prototype fast-breeder reactor.

With a workforce of 1,600, the Atomic Energy Authority is the largest employer in the top one-third of Scotland and at 4.30 pm each day the only traffic jam north of Inverness takes place as Dounreay empties and the town of Thurso fills. On a day of Black Alert security – normal – I was one of a group of visitors who entered Dounreay and the slick, carefree world of Public Relations. We were issued with our kit. Dressed in white overalls and yellow hard hats and looking like free gifts from Kellogg's, we sat down to our physics lesson.

My understanding of the process was limited by a sad career in science. A missed lesson in long-division scuppered an already flawed ability at maths, and physics tumbled in its wake. Chemistry (good entertainment, bad smell) unravelled few of life's mysteries for me, and a biology based on baiting woodlice and eviscerating earthworms was never destined to appeal to an obsessed animal-lover. However, at Dounreay I struggled manfully with the splitting of the atom.

Simplistically, if you fire a cannonball, called a neutron, at a bit of uranium, the impact causes a microscopic explosion which breaks the uranium into two pieces and triggers off more cannonballs which hit more bits of uranium, and so it goes on. Instead of this happening all at once and producing a Hiroshima (that's another lesson), it appears to be a continuous scuttle of activity for several years until insufficient targets and sources of cannonballs remain and the whole thing fizzles out. This chain reaction, which if necessary can be dampened until it stops, is effectively the element of a large kettle. It boils water to make steam to drive a generator to produce electricity. The process has, of course, two disadvantages: it gives off radiation and leaves a dangerous waste product that no one wants or knows where, or how best, to store.

To have risked a Kellogg free gift gaining unsupervised access to the works would have been as unthinkable as it could have been disastrous, and our tour was a paragon of security which took me back to a pre-*glasnost* visit to Moscow: sealed bus, continual headcounts, camera restrictions and an official interpretation of the view which dwelt on its virtues, successes and advanced state of well-being.

'Sixty per cent of Scotland's electricity is produced by nuclear power and this ranks us fourth in the world behind France, Belgium and Hungary,' we were told by a sparkling Caroline, as we were driven through the complex. We looked from her face, to her trim AEA uniform, to a block landscape of glass and steel interspersed with grass where a vigorous group of scientists and technicians were engaged in lunchtime football.

'Britain leads the world in its expertise on fast-breeder technology but unfortunately the Government has decided to abandon the programme and concentrate on Advanced Gas Cooled Reactors.'

Caroline lost me here on technical matters but there was no mistaking her indignation. Clearly she believed the Government was wrong, it was making a big mistake – and worse – it was treachery, going for these uppity AGRs and abandoning her fast-breeder, her Dounreay. I read in her expression the redundancy notice, the quarter-full supermarket trolley, the ordeal by depression at Thurso Job Centre.

But Caroline was a professional. 'Dounreay began in 1971 and it's taught us all we know about fast-breeder technology. Our brief has always been research but we've been allowed to sell the electricity which our prototype reactors produce, and currently we can supply all the Highlands and Islands. The large white dome you see there is the obsolete second experimental reactor. It has now been decommissioned and its run-down process will take ten years. We, the nuclear industry, get a bad press despite our exemplary safety records.' (Several Kelloggs yawned.) 'But you must consider this: a single large coal power station emits ten million tons of carbon dioxide into the atmosphere each year and this contributes greatly to the so-called 'greenhouse effect', *and* 200,000 tons of acidic gases associated with acid rain. The entire nuclear industry produces no carbon dioxide, no acidic gases and no more high-level waste than will fill a double-decker bus.'

'How about your low and intermediate levels of waste?'

'The middle range would fill an average house, the low

level an eight-storey housing block. But it would be unfair to single us out; Britain produces four million cubic metres of toxic waste each year, and eighty million of a non-toxic nature. They're enough to fill Central London to a depth of one metre.'

'It's already been filled,' a Kellogg chipped in. 'I live there.'

We disembarked at a door and Caroline swiped her security card through a slot. The Kelloggs each swiped their cards and somewhere a computer checked details and opened the door. Caroline could not proceed without every one of us, and we could not proceed without her. At each swiping point our progress through the building was logged.

Air-lock doors closed around us and the atmospheric pressure was lowered before we entered the main building; work here went on in a slight vacuum so that the only leaks would be into the building and not out. The atmosphere was heavy, hot and stifling, and explained why fresh air with exercise was the favourite lunchtime menu. A couple of self-op geiger counters were positioned by the door for workers to check their reading before leaving. Caroline ran the machine over the resident of London's refuse but he failed to register. She had once done the same to another visitor who was carrying a First World War compass with luminous paint.

'He went off the scale. No way would we tolerate that level of radiation among our workforce.' Luminous fishing lures also scored highly, though I failed to see who would bring a bag of tackle into the place. What Shalimar was to bed and breakfast establishments, this building was to science-fiction sets. Pipes, cranes, stop-cocks, dials, flashing lights, levers; it was all to Hollywood excess. We strolled four and a half metres above the nuclear reaction. Around us were 3,000 sensors producing 400 pages of readings every day. We learned that the fuel came in rods and the rods sat in flasks and the flasks were examined in the Post

Radial Fuel Inspection Area, also known, more sensibly, as 'the caves'.

We watched a caveman peering through lead glass four feet thick as he operated a pair of mechanical hands and dismantled the lethal rods inside. When they were deactivated, when the cannonballs' fuses were dampened, it still took *six months* for them to cool down from their working temperature of 600°C to 200°C. It was then that I began to appreciate more fully the power of the beast.

'Both at Three Mile Island and at Chernobyl,' I read later in AEA leaflets, 'operators turned off safety systems designed to prevent overheating. They acted for different reasons, but both sets of operators made the situation worse than it need have become.'

'The people of Thurso have faith in Dounreay and want Dounreay,' Caroline stressed. When, the following day, I saw 300 people queuing outside the AEA recruitment office in Thurso for one temporary job, that need was obvious, but it didn't necessarily imply faith, just trust or desperation.

'We, the nuclear industry, have an exemplary safety record,' Caroline repeated. 'Our waste storage is secure and under control.'

'We, the peoples of the Soviet Union, want no more war,' echoed a government voice from the past.

A month later I heard a Radio Scotland news bulletin: 'An enquiry into the storage facilities of radioactive waste at Dounreay has revealed "a legacy of inadequate measures" and that "management has been operated in a hand-to-mouth fashion."'

18

∽

Jack Green, Halkirk

Scotland yielded before my bicycle with surprising passivity. Here she had run out of mountains and energy and flopped into a state of apathy, though every now and then weak arguments of rucks and wrinkles were raised; they were gestures of assertiveness and carried little conviction. Two miles of flat, featureless white may pass on a Caithness map without the intrusion of a single brown contour. Pasture, bog and plantation are this land's lot, and 'fences' of upright slabs. As far as the eye could see fields were boxed by impenetrable rows of tombstones, unengraved, mottled with lichens.

For a hundred years, from 1820 to the 1920s when the use of cement became widespread and killed the market, Caithness worked a flourishing trade in flagstones. Durable and weather-resistant, these flagstones were shipped to England, Europe, the Americas and Australia to pave their streets and roof their houses. At the turn of the century the industry ranked with farming and herring fishing in importance as an employer, but today only a few quarrymen work the flags, used mainly for the renovation of historic properties, and one such quarryman is Jack Green.

I spotted him easily on a white patch on the map near

Halkirk. Calder Quarry was a one-man show, a slight dent among fields and shallow enough to fit between 10-metre contours. A fair proportion of Britain's 80 million cubic metres of rubbish had blown into the hollow and I would have dismissed the place as a tip had it not been for a *tap, tap, tap* and the sight of a hunched figure chapping away in clockwork rhythm.

The constituents of his seat had changed, but for forty years Jack Green had sat on an oil can and cushion and used a heavy blade to guillotine slates into shape. Thin flags were used for slates, thick ones were machine cut for paving slabs. Jack was working on an order for five thousand slates.

'Three, maybe four months, that should see it. Aye, then I think I'll pack in. Too old for this caper.' He suddenly grimaced in pain and punched the small of his back with both fists working in unison. 'Arthritis. It's a horrible thing. Only hit me these last six months and only when I stand.'

He was a handsome man with tufted eyebrows and a warm smile. At 78 he still worked a six-day week, using the techniques of last century, for modern machines were too rough and damaging. With a hammer and wedges he prised slabs from the quarry walls, transported them to his oilcan seat where they were split, cut and trimmed to size.

'D'you find many fossils here?' The area was famous for them.

'Oh, yes, all the time. Plants and fish, I get them all the time. I'll show you if you like.' He got to his feet and another shot of pain, so intense the agony was transmitted to my spine too, sent him into another spasm of back-punching. We searched the floor and walls and found several plants, black curlicues clearly imprinted on the grey stone.

''Bout five years ago I raised this slab and there were footprints of a lizard,' – excitement animated his face – 'a very rare lizard. He was only a small fella, maybe twelve inches end to end, but he's believed to be the first creature that ever came out of the sea.'

The lizard was walking, not running, dragging its tail and, Jack hopes, dying. 'If I can find that lizard, Edinburgh University say he'll be worth three, maybe four hundred thousand pounds.'

'That much? How do they put a price tag on something like that?'

'Don't ask me, but that's what they say. Four hundred thousand . . . Ahh! I hope I can find that lizard,' he said, and chuckled.

'What would you do with four hundred thousand pounds?'

'I dunno – ach! . . . . it's a bit late for the money now. I may be in a box next year. But I like looking for that lizard. I'd just love to find him. I'm sure he's here.'

Just yesterday he had come across the lizard's tracks again, 'going that way,' he said, pointing in the direction of Wick.

But it worried me to see that Jack's quarry was only about 400 yards square. What were the chances of the lizard choosing this spot for the last paces of its fatal journey – a journey that might have covered scores of miles – and of kicking the bucket before Jack's parked car and his perimeter fence?

'Aye, he's here somewhere. You want to know more, you talk to Professor Baird. He'll tell you.'

Later, with some difficulty, I located Professor Baird at the Royal Museum of Scotland in Edinburgh, and spoke to him over the phone.

'Jack Green? . . . Ah! Yes! Marvellous man . . . The lizard? No, I can't give you its scientific name because it doesn't have one. It'll certainly be worth a lot of money if he finds it, a *huge* amount of money. But if he's still looking, there'd appear to be some misunderstanding. He won't find a lizard. It doesn't exist. I'm afraid he's sixty-two million years too early.'

Like Hoy, Caithness was largely composed of Middle Red Sandstone. This was laid down approximately 400 million years ago, Professor Baird explained, and although this was a relatively late deposit, it pre-dated the evolution of reptiles. Plants and fish were abundant at the time and readily subjected themselves to fossilisation in its layers, but reptiles were creatures of the future.

'So if Jack does find it, it would be a pretty shattering world-first?'

'It doesn't exist. Finish. The earliest reptile found in Scotland, near Bathgate, dates back to the Lower Carboniferous era, that's 338 million years ago. Jack's quarry is just too old.'

Nevertheless, I still hold out hope that Jack might be right after all, and I picture him now on the trail of his elusive quarry, an old man pummelling arthritis with his fists, prising open segments of Caithness, peering at the dusty stone, his eyes alight for a little lizard, 62 million years ahead of its time, plodding wearily towards Wick.

19

❧

Wick, Badbea and The Clearances

A thick haar smothered the dawn. Every so often Stroma's foghorn rumbled the air with two, low, quivering exhalations which followed me along the 400-million-year-old lizard trail to Wick. The lizard would have done well to have avoided John o'Groats, despite being assured of a warm welcome by the sign of De Savary's hotel. In my case this consisted of a foghornish 'Mornin'' in a Derbyshire accent, and I didn't wait for more. John o'Groats is neither the most northerly point on the mainland, nor is it the most distant from Land's End, but for commercial purposes it's near enough to bestow upon it the groundless designation of Milepost 0, or 876. Existing without a function except as a boast, a label to collect, this vacuous cluster of tourist tat, faintly Disneyesque but without the charm, is the ultimate Tea Shoppe on the Northern Tour.

To the south, green fields of lambs sandwiched the road which carried little traffic besides the odd lorry and 'Groats or Bust' voyagers. Lapwings spiralled madly about, uttering their kazoo-sounding calls. Keiss Castle came into view, looking smutty and in need of a good dose of Imperial Leather, which the owners could well afford, considering this was another possession of the Cussons family. Then downhill into Wick.

Once the greatest herring port in Europe, the town's fortunes had since dwindled. There was still evidence of money about, though, but opportunities and values had changed, from clinkers to curlers. Formerly home to a dozen boatbuilders, now all but one had been replaced by hairdressers. Wick blew glass and built refrigerators.

R.L. Stevenson, whose father engineered the harbour improvements, called it 'the meanest of man's towns, situated certainly on the baldest of God's bays', but an impression of meanness no longer remained. Despite the locked doors and dirt-plastered windows of the streets of Lower Pulteneytown, the harbour area, Wick exuded a quiet confidence, a mysterious affluence, and a high regard for stylish hair.

I pedalled on, keen to reach the cliffs and ruins of Badbea and spend the night with its ghosts. At the end of each range of hills the road corkscrewed down into deep glens and then forced me to regain my height. My gaze had time to alight on roadside litter, fuelling thoughts of indignation but also enabling me to piece together fragments of people's lives. Those who had passed before me seemed depressingly indulgent: voracious consumers; they drank more lager than soft drinks and quenched their thirst every ten feet; by first choice they smoked B&H or Silk Cut and emptied a packet every fifteen feet; they devoured sweets continuously, used the odd condom in quiet lay-bys, and, weirdest of all, they frequently collected their litter, put it in bags, carefully knotted the tops and then hurled it into the countryside.

How, I wondered, did Scandinavia achieve such cleanliness in its countries and a no-litter mentality? Education had to be the key, but how to change the practice of a nation?

The roadside was a disheartening catalogue of hard-luck stories: broken glass and a dead roe deer told explicitly of extinction, while a vodka bottle and a Tammy Wynette tape, a suicidal combination, simply hinted at it.

Badbea, I knew, would provide little to cheer me. It was a bad choice for a campsite but I went because it was a pilgrimage of sorts, to pay homage. I had to push my bike over a hill and through quarter of a mile of bog to reach the ruins.

Badbea was a Clearance village. It occupied a thin strip of pasture between barren moor and cliffs which plummeted to the sea. So frequently and so intensely did gales scour this inhospitable spot that sheep, and even children, had to be tethered to the ground in case of sudden changes in the weather. At its peak, about eighty people lived here, comprising the dozen or so families who were evicted from Ousdale and the Strath of Kildonan in 1813, and their descendants. The last of them emigrated to New Zealand in 1911.

The man responsible for burning their homes in the more fertile glens and sending them to this most marginal of existences, and to whom they paid rent for the privilege, was, according to the inscription on his memorial, 'a judicious, kind and liberal landlord, who identified the improvement of his vast estates with the prosperity of all who cultivated them' . . . [a man who would] 'open his hands to the distress of the widow, the sick and the traveller'.

Today the effigy of the first Duke of Sutherland stands thirty feet tall on a column on Beinn a' Bhragaidh, overlooking Golspie. This is the statue that George Mackay Brown would not be averse to seeing blown up, should the Tartan Army recover its vim. And, as he remarked, the inscription to one of the most hated men of his time, continues, in deep cut capitals, 'A MOURNING AND GRATEFUL TENANTRY UNITING WITH THE INHABITANTS OF THE NEIGHBOURHOOD, ERECTED THIS PILLAR, AD 1834.'

Accusations are frequently levelled at the Highland mentality that it dwells too much on the past and that it suffers a persecution complex. This is undoubtedly true, but what those accusers fail to appreciate is the wonder that anything has survived at all, that so much of the Highland language, culture and identity has survived what, until remarkably recently, has continued to be overt or covert oppression.

It is impossible to understand the Highland psyche and the Highland landscape without understanding the nature of that oppression, and one of its principal factors was The Clearances, 'The Evictions'. Their story has been told often, and has been distorted or romanticised equally often, so it is worth summarising the facts and placing them in the context of history.

The eighteenth century was the climacteric epoch in the history of the Highlands. A region once outwith the bounds of government jurisdiction became, after 1746, the focus of punitive measures designed to disempower and subjugate a people, and change irreversibly its social and political structure.

Highland life within the so-called 'clan system' was never halcyon or utopian, as is frequently implied, but a constant struggle against weather, famine and internecine feuds. Yet central, and unique (at least in Britain), to this system was an extraordinary sense of community, a relationship between leader and people which commanded mutual respect, and responsibilities accountable to all. It was a life geared to communal farming, albeit not as efficient as it might have been, a spot of reiving and the maintenance of an ever-ready fighting force. A feudal system of landholding in which the clan chief held private title to the land did exist in the Highlands, but it was less prevalent than the patriarchal system, whose essential difference was that the land of the Highland clans was *not* the private property of their chiefs but the public property of the clansfolk.

After 1746 Highlanders were prohibited from carrying arms, and the judicial powers of the chiefs were abolished. With their patriarchal responsibilities removed, those chiefs lacking title to estates assumed ownership of the land once held in common by their people and, like the feudal chiefs adopted the lifestyles and roles of southern, commercial landlords. Inevitably their orbits moved to the political and social centres of the south and their need for hard cash increased accordingly.

Their Highland properties provided miserable rents. Black cattle were the mainstay of these primitive economies, supplemented by goats and sheep; but these were small sheep, often as small as dogs, weighing between 11 and 16 kilograms, with straight horns. Lowlanders grazed the larger and more productive Cheviot and Blackface breeds, and these were now seen as being the means of 'improving' – and this was strictly a landlord's term – the Highlands. Sheep would bring in an average fourfold increase in revenues. The unfortunate people who happened to occupy the best grazing, the inland glens, would have to be moved to the poorest lands and the coasts.

The first clearances took place in Perthshire in the 1760s but it was twenty years later that the practice was pursued with more widespread vigour. By 1800 sheep, not cattle, dominated the land south of the Great Glen, and experiments to introduce them to the far north had proved successful. The White Plague of *na caorich mora*, the 'big sheep', or the 'four-footed clansmen' as the Highlanders dubbed them, was set to invade the north. Soon there would be 300,000 in Sutherland alone.

The Sutherland clearances achieved the most enduring notoriety but they contain few features which were not matched in terms of cruelty and violence in hundreds of other instances across the Highlands and Islands. Not all landowners instigated evictions but those who did not were the exceptions. Occasionally with the assistance of armed militia and usually with the voiced or mute sanction of a Church tied to the purse of the landlord, factors and their henchmen cleared the land; dragging the obdurate, old and infirm from their homes, firing the thatch and ensuring the destruction of the roof timbers, a householder's most valuable possession and his sole means of beginning again on that spot. That 'judicious, kind and liberal' Duke of Sutherland (or the Marquis of Stafford, as he was at the time), and after him the Duchess, evicted 15,000 of their tenants with the help of their evil factor Patrick Sellar.

The first quarter of the nineteenth century witnessed clearances at an unprecedented rate, spurred on by the gains to be made in a market starved of imports by the Napoleonic wars; soaring wool prices and a thriving kelp industry (for the production of alkali), which not only employed a displaced population but justified displacing it, added hugely to the landowners' revenues.

In the shadow of the Clearances came the waves of emigration which flowed when the population was clearly redundant (and too costly to feed during the years of famine), and ebbed when it could be put to work and when laws were enacted making emigration either impossible or impossibly expensive. Usually the fittest, most able and enterprising went first. Aboard such ships as the *Dove of Harmony* and *Highland Lad* they went – for irony could add nothing to their bitterness – and sailed to the Carolinas, Nova Scotia, Lord Selkirk's prairie settlements along the Red River in Manitoba, and the unknown. By 1850 the Clearances – the forced evictions – were effectively over, for the collapse of wool prices had removed their profitability. The émigrés still departed in their thousands, and rent-racking, insecurity of tenure and famine continued the work of the clearers but on a greatly decreased scale.

Some revisionist historians assert that the Clearances were necessary, that landlords merely precipitated an action that would have occurred anyway, for the land simply could not support its population. Changes undoubtedly would have taken place but never on such a drastic scale and never involving so much suffering. The land had supported the population for centuries before this;

the potato, with its vastly superior nutritional properties, had replaced cereal as the basic foodstuff around this time; the archaic system of agriculture could have been reformed by making more land available to the local population, by allowing it to manage smaller numbers of the big sheep rather than clearing them and importing Lowland farmers. And if emigration was seen as a genuine expediency, how different it is to call for a volunteer and offer assistance rather than burn his house and leave him little alternative.

The Clearances were profoundly selfish acts of greed, and it is this sense of injustice that still scars the Highland psyche, and its empty landscape. 'You can try,' wrote James Hunter in *Scottish Highlanders, A People and Their Place*, 'on looking at the desolation which has taken the place of community – to take such comfort as you can from the reflection that, where there was once considered to be nothing but barbarity, there is now civilisation.'

The next morning, eager to leave the emptiness of Badbea, I set off early and reached Helmsdale three miles later. It was an unlikely place to meet Dame Barbara Cartland. I rolled into the town and found her reclining on a chaise-longue, powdered, made-up, waxy-yellow and looking frighteningly immortal, but this was evidently the price you paid for holidaying in the area and being a benefactor of the local exhibition centre. I rolled out again, noting Helmsdale Castle (Avery, scales) and followed the Strath of Kildonan. When the last field and farm was squeezed out by the narrowing of the glen, community ended and 'civilisation' began.

I lunched beside a trio of Range Rovers whose owners were tipping flasks beside an arsenal of rods.

'Too bright,' moaned one, shaking his jowls, and I frowned suitably, wondering if he meant the weather or the fish. Further on, at the junction of the Suisgill Burn, things were bright enough for a family panning for gold and trying to relive the rush of 1868 which attracted 3,000 prospectors to this spot.

After that I cut a lone figure crossing the blanket peat bogs of the Flow Country. Grouse would cackle unseen from the drab expanse of heather, and once a short-eared owl cut across my bow, its wings stroking the air noiselessly. The horizon seemed interminably distant under a big blue sky. The five buildings of Badanloch Lodge (Lord Leverhulme) appeared as a metropolis with a wood the size of the Schwarzwald, but then they too shrank behind me.

At Syre Lodge (formerly Patrick Sellar, now Lord Liffey, *Birmingham Post*) the road turned into Strathnaver and then skirted round the flanks of Ben Loyal and Ben Hope – names that could never have been given by those who lived here – and then headed vaguely towards my next destination, Cape Wrath.

Alone again in one of the loveliest glens in the country, I found myself at the mercy – and it wasn't a region well-known for mercy – of the region's most abundant passers-by. Low-flying jets seared the air and my ears, the only ones left celebrating, and making the most of, the Clearances.

20

∽

Cape Wrath

Beside the small ferry which runs foot-passengers across the Kyle of Durness, a sea loch, to the private road leading to Scotland's north-west corner stands the following sign: 'CAPE WRATH BOMBARDMENT RANGE: The road across the range IS/IS NOT subject to delays today. Any delays or inconvenience is regretted.'

It's hard to see how being bombed can be anything other than an 'inconvenience' but I was relieved to see the sliding cover was concealing IS. I had decided to dump my bicycle and walk thirty miles round the coast, taking in a lighthouse and a bombsite. The hill Fashven, my map informed me, was out of bounds, for it had been so inundated with explosives that had failed to go off that it was effectively one large minefield. The wisdom of bombing bogland seems as suspect as the Ministry of Defence's concept of 'inconvenience'.

The Kyle of Durness was draining, leaving kaleido-scopic patterns in the sand and a dozen seals looking like old beanbags in need of a good plump and shake up. The road climbed and dipped, passed a house with windows and doors bricked up, and once allowed a glimpse of a bay with gigantic white horses rolling in from Iceland. Mother Earth looked ancient and tired, wearing bleached canvas heavily stained with chocolate, and yet with all the appeal of forbidden fruits. She often tempted me to trespass, but my desire to remain intact was stronger. I noticed miles of felled telephone posts and an uncommonly large number of dead sheep – only to be expected among the illiterate, I supposed – but the real wonder was that sheep were allowed to graze a simulated war zone in the first place.

Eight miles later I reached the lighthouse.

'Well, suppose you'd better come in.' Mr Matlock didn't like visitors. He was sick of them. Ten thousand arrived each year. Two minibuses a day carted them along the road in summer. They knocked on the door, dirtied and wet the steps, asked if they could see the light or use the toilet ('We dinnae hae enough water fer abody') and then, as often as not, after they'd gone, you'd find they'd crapped behind the wall. No, they were a curse. But then the whole job had gone to the dogs.

'It's nae the job I joined thirty years ago. Onybody could dee it noo,' he said, adding with disconcerting directness, '*you* could even dee it.' He'd worked all over . . . Stroma, Shillay, Hyskeir, Skerryvore . . . he reeled off names sounding like great victories in a personal Crimea. But there were no more battles for Mr Matlock, not *real* battles.

'Just press a button noo, that's all. Aye, *you* could dee it.'

I made a note of this spare career to keep up my sleeve, and later wrote to the Northern Lighthouse Board for a Job Description.

Not every man is suitable to be a lightkeeper. The good lightkeeper has or acquires the temperament so necessary for this job which involves residence close to the sea and which has much loneliness and isolation in its composition. While primary duty is to keep watch at night, to ensure that his light flashes correctly to character, and to keep a fog watch throughout each 24 hours . . ., a lightkeeper must be a man of parts. He will acquire a good working knowledge of engines; . . . he will know about Radio Telephones; from his study of the sea he will respect its immense power; he will be a handyman of varying proficiency but mostly of a high standard; he will be a useful cook and a good companion. Lightkeepers are expected to serve at any Station and the good lightkeeper makes the best of each and every Station to which he is sent. A lightkeeper will not make a fortune but the odds are he will be at peace with himself and with the world.

Mr Matlock had obviously once passed muster, and so had the job. 'What did it used to be like?'

He seemed to emit a burst of candlewatts. 'We hid *clockwurk* engines turning the light in those days.' Clearly an object of reverence, he voiced the word with full military honours. 'Wis beautiful the *clockwurk* – hid a huge chain of brass teeth an these great weights which hid tae be wound up ivery thirty minutes. Ivery Monday morning we hid tae clean the burner – paraffin it wis – an ivery mornin we hid to clean the elements an top up the paraffin. An ivery fortnight we hid tae scrub the place doon frae top tae bottom.'

'It sounds nothing but bloody hard work.'

'No, no. There wis pride in the job then. There's none noo.' He tossed a scornful glance at the battery of Gardiner water-cooled engines in the background which, for all their fanciness, had failed to convince Mr Matlock they could be a patch on the clockwurk. The problem was, they didn't need his love. They didn't need his meticulous cleaning, fiddling and fussing. But at least they needed some. In three years they would be replaced by air-cooled models, virtually maintenance-free, and Cape Wrath would be fully automated. Mr Matlock would be out of a job.

'Nah, I'm gettin oot next year onyway. Sixty-two.

Retirin.' He was worm-thin; his grey beard as neatly in order as I imagined the light's elements had once been. 'Ma wife loved it too in the old days. Raised oor family at South Light, Fair Isle. Aye, we were all family in those days. Nae noo.' His two colleagues ignored us, sitting reading by a window. Two clocks ticked away, seemed to be ticking life away. The quarters here were for single men only. I wondered where Mrs Matlock had gone and guessed she had cracked under the boredom when the children had grown up.

'Suppose you'd like tae see the light?'

'If it's not too much trouble.' I hadn't dared to ask.

The place was immaculate. You could have safely performed surgery on its floor. The walls were Wedgwood blue and the steps a ripe strawberry with white borders. I made a prolonged show of wiping my feet, and followed apprehensively in case I clouded brass, dulled chrome or in some way sullied pride.

'Sometimes when you went tae a new post you'd ken there wis something wrang but you couldnae pit your finger on it. Then one day you'd be climbin up an you'd realise it wis the spiral, it was *anti-clockwise* and fer the last five years ye'd gone clockwise tae yer work. Varies. Some places is anti-. Ithers, like this, is clockwise.'

We arrived in the glass dome, seventy-five feet above the top of the cliffs, and 300 feet above the ocean. 'That's where the clockwurk used tae be.' He pointed to a large chamber below us which was occupied by a minuscule grey electrical box. 'Nae atmosphere.'

The 'light' consisted of a stack of four, long rectangular boxes. Each box was painted black, contained a face of bulbs and was set at a different angle to its neighbour. At night the lights never went out. The stack revolved and constantly shone four beams, which because of the system of blinkers, appeared to the mariner as four separate flashes.

'Canadian locomotive headlights, that's what they are.' He showed me a box of spares. 'Bloody train bulbs.'

A ship trudged past far out to sea. 'Will the day come when lighthouses become obsolete? They've got such sophisticated satellite navigation systems now.'

'No, they'll always need lights. You canna jist rely on the one system. Whit if the machine goes kaput? No, they'll always need these lights, jist tae be sure.' He lifted his binoculars. 'Now, that ship oot there, see? It doesnae get this service fer nothin'. Depends on its tonnage. It'll pay aboot twenty thousand a year in light dues. A wee ten-metre fishing boat'll pay about two hundred. Jist commercial boats pay. They yachties get it fer nothin'.'

I camped that night a few miles south of Cape Wrath, with the Atlantic tearing at the cliffs somewhere far below the ends of my guylines. The attack sounded ferocious even though the wind was moderate. Bloody train bulbs scanned the darkness, 204,000 candles of light every thirty seconds – flash, flash, flash, flash – and I pictured them in a different role, riding the Canadian-Pacific through the Rockies. But not for them the grand views or a place in the good old days when the light endowed a proud life of scrubbing, cleaning, polishing and topping up.

21

Assynt Hills

Flowering gorse inflamed the verges with a yellow so bright it hurt the eyes. In places between Nedd and Lochinver it crowded the road with such bullyish behaviour that it looked impenetrable. The single track of asphalt rollercoastered its way through the hills in the severest inclines I'd encountered, forcing cartographers to mess their maps with a blitz of double chevrons (1:5 or steeper). The downs were giddy plummets which sent the bicycle into a paroxysm of rattles, while the ups transformed it to concrete, stiffening the pedals until I was forced to dismount.

In the distance I could see the home of Scotland's gods, Assynt's regal panoply of mountains – Quinag, Canisp, Suilven, Cul Mor – each standing tall and disdainful of its neighbours, like sulking children forced to be friends. Suilven, the 'Sugar Loaf', always drew the eye first with a deep saddle between its two peaks, one a lofty, hand-turned dome of rock. And there, toiling up to that saddle, was a ten-year-old child.

'Is it far to go?'

'No, not now,' my father replied. 'PATCH – get into heel . . . H-E-E-L.' The family dog, torn between obedience and sheep, trotted back reluctantly.

'Oh dear! Jane's gone over her boots,' exclaimed my mother. My sister had sunk to her knees in a bog.

'I'm soaking.'

'I'm tired.'

'Almost there,' came the cheery voice of our leader. 'Look! . . . deer.'

Brown shapes scattered over the dull heather in an uncertainty of indignation and panic, heads tilted up on stiff necks, legs strutting in effortless slow motion. Then we reached the top where we became a happy family again over chicken and bacon sandwiches, mugs of Tang and a view that endowed the child with a wonder he would never forget.

Suilven held him as high as he imagined an eagle flew, and below, for miles in every direction, were blue lochs and lesser puddles, thousands upon thousands of them, so many you couldn't count them, and all around were more mountains with rocky, red tops, and Stac 'Polly' (*Pollaidh*) was just like a castle with all the dents where soldiers would stand, and far out to sea you could make out a dark misty country called Lewis . . . And on that day, or another just like it, an incipient love of mountains and the outdoors began to grow.

Now, thirty years and sixty-odd countries later, I looked towards that same view with different eyes. I could still see its beauty with that same raw sense of wonder. But now I realised I was looking at three hundred years of neglect and degeneration, at a feudal system of land control and management – unique in Europe – which allowed, and continues to allow, a few individuals to exhaust the land to an extreme of biological degradation. Those accursed incubuses of the Highlands, the sporting and the absentee landlords, who profess such a love of Scotland they are even prepared to live in it for three weeks a year, still own and mismanage the largest portion of every view.

Their whims and temperaments still exact the tightest hold over the lives of those who may truly call the land their home, and yet who are made to feel so foreign in it.

Who owns this landscape
Has owning anything to do with love
For it and I have a love-affair, so nearly
human we even have quarrels.
Who owns this landscape?
The millionaire who bought it or
the poacher staggering downhill in the early morning
with a deer on his back
. . . or I who am possessed by it.

Norman MacCaig, 'A Man in Assynt'

22

Alan Macrae of the Assynt Crofters

The mechanical, monotonous nature of cycling encourages the mind to drift, and not until I spotted a car sticker proclaiming 'SUPPORT THE ASSYNT CROFTERS' did I realise that Alan Macrae lived somewhere in this area. The Assynt Crofters had recently made headlines, and history, by buying out their landlord. Alan was secretary of the Trust they had formed, and an old but lost acquaintance. A few enquiries led me to his home.

A croft, contrary to many people's understanding, is not a small self-sufficient farm. Small it certainly is, an average of between three and five acres, but self-sufficiency was never intended – in fact, quite the opposite: crofts were designed as an expediency to accommodate a displaced population, provide a rent from the poorest or unworked land, and to allow tenants to partially – not wholly – produce their own food, thus making them dependent on another source of employment. That employment was originally in their landlords' short-lived kelp industries.

By popular definition a croft is a plot of land surrounded by regulations. Today there are 17,000 registered crofts (and under current legislation new ones cannot be created), grouped into communities with an adjoining area of common grazing, and constituting an area of 2 million acres. It has taken crofters almost two centuries to have short-comings in the system addressed; now they have security of tenure and a guaranteed low rent, they can sell or pass on the title to their croft, or buy the property outright and extremely cheaply (but with disadvantages regarding eligibility for certain grants) and, as of 1992, they can even retain ownership of the trees they plant – prior to this they became the property of the landlord, which is one reason for the scarcity of trees in most crofting communities. Croft land which has not been bought by crofters remains the legal property of the landlord, but he can do nothing on that land.

It is paradoxical, and not unjust, that a system designed to hold a people on the margins of land they once held in common may now be the very means of returning that land to them. Alan Macrae and the Assynt Crofters had, against expectations, shown it was possible.

Piece by piece he carried back stones as and when he found them and fitted them into the home he was building by hand. Until it was nearer to completion it was used to house three pigs, and Alan himself lived in a caravan. I had first met him when we both ran for Lochaber Athletic Club and competed in hill races. The year he won the Ben Nevis Race, Alan was a contract fencer, and after a day's work he would train by running up Canisp or Suilven with coils of wire over each shoulder to make it harder. That's what was said, anyway, and Alan made the tales believable.

He was approaching 50, short and stocky, and had all the qualities of an Exocet; straight, unstoppable, resolute and explosive. When he spoke his lip twisted as if his teeth were clenched, and he often looked down shyly, hiding eyes that were burning and unyielding.

'The ingredients were all there, boy, waiting for an opportunity. History had stood still for too long. Yes, for far too long.' For a Highland accent his words came with unusual harshness.

'For many years the Vestey family had been very

unpopular and things were bad here. Then Vestey sold the North Lochinver Estate, which we're on, to some Scandinavian consortium. And three years later it went into liquidation. The liquidators proposed splitting up the estate into eight portions to sell separately. Well, that was the final straw, boy. People are never seen as part of the land, and that's all wrong.'

If the division had gone ahead the Assynt crofters' common grazing would have been owned by eight different people and its administration would have become impracticably complex. The crofters formed a trust, secured the support of a skilled lawyer and offered to buy the whole estate, 22,000 acres, for £200,000, a price based on an assessment of the value of the land, its rents, fishing and stalking. The offer was refused. The liquidators were looking for more than double that figure.

'There were other parties interested in buying, but we made in clear that if any came forward, we would . . . . well, be very unforgiving.' Of the total land area, almost half was held in crofting tenure. 'An outside buyer would have paid the full price and then risked losing half the land to us for a pittance. We had the right to buy our croft and an apportionment of the common grazing. So we warned everyone that if we had to take the land back piece by piece through the Land Court, then so be it – but take it we would.'

The crofters' trust received financial support from many organisations, and donations came in from all over the world. 'And we did it. We frightened off the others, upped our offer to three hundred thousand, and it was accepted. But we were lucky. We were dealing with liquidators who had to accept the best offer. A landlord might have refused to sell to us.'

The Assynt Crofters were now in the unusual position of being both crofter and, through their trust, landlord. 'We've got to stop thinking like landlords. We can't see the land purely in terms of economic benefit. This is about community growing in many ways, in entirely new ways. We've got to go slowly and carefully. Change is going to be slow.'

Representing a model which many organisations were keen to see succeed, the Trust was receiving advice and help from across the country. It had moved into forestry, released land for much-needed housing, and was looking into developing trout fishing for local people and tourists, eel farming, and harvesting water-lilies (for garden ponds) as a sustainable resource. 'Suddenly we've wakened up to a whole new dimension of looking at things. It's brought home to me how important the land is to the people. As long as the people of the Highlands have land, they have a future. Many things change but the land remains. There was nothing radical about what we did, boy . . . no, nothing radical at all. Just natural. We've been so conditioned that we've lost sight of what's rightfully ours.'

Alan Macrae alone was not responsible for the success of the Trust, but his resolve had carried it through a time when defeat had seemed inevitable.

What had this meant to him personally, I asked.

He looked down for a moment and said nothing. When he looked up the hard man of Assynt had softened his eyes. 'Often I wondered why I stayed in Assynt . . . now, I've a sort of feeling I've justified myself.'

On a journey of this nature, pedalling slowly round a large fragmented land, it would have been impossible to be in the right place at the right time for many of the 'events' I wanted to record. The Invercharron Games, Hawick Common Riding, Camanachd Cup Final, and Aberdeen Crematorium's first open day, for example, were chronologically too close and geographically too distant to conveniently fit in by bicycle. Wherever the occasion arose I would interrupt my journey and strike off across country by train, bus or thumb, to fulfil my chosen agenda.

Such was my interest in land ownership and management, and their crucial effect on Highland life, that I deviated from Assynt to Inverness, to attend a forum entitled 'The People and the Land'.

23

Highland Forum on Land Management

The opening speaker was Andy Wightman, a writer and researcher on land issues.

'Fifty per cent of Scotland is owned by fewer than six hundred people, and eighty per cent of all private land is controlled by four thousand people. This is the most concentrated pattern of private land ownership in Europe. Currently landowners *are* Scotland's rural planners.'

He went on to say that this same archaic system and shape of land ownership had survived through centuries of change in other aspects of Scottish life, but it now offered great potential and in some ways had been advantageous. The land had been grossly neglected but not destroyed; in effect it had been held in limbo. Now that we were more knowledgeable and environmentally aware we were in a position to formulate a superior programme of development than was possible a century ago. Essential to any development, he believed, was community involvement, but the possibilities had to be explored in a sensible, practical and calm manner.

After the lecture I put a question to him that had been bothering me for some time. How, I asked, would he counter the argument of a large Highland estate owner who contends that he brings employment to ten families (keepers, stalkers, gillies, etc.) and that if he sells or gives his estate away they will lose their means of income; the land is otherwise useless; without the like of his London-derived income the estate could not be an employer.

'Such landowners hold basic assumptions I simply do not agree with. They say that because nothing else is happening on the land, nothing else *can* happen. But the absence of evidence is *not* evidence of absence. In fact their argument is quite easy to destroy.

'The Highlands and Islands' resources are degraded. We have lost much of our forest, fisheries and wild-life. The focus of most Highland landowners has been mono-culture, if you can apply the word "culture" to selfish acts of destruction. It has been all sheep, all deer. Now, it's obvious that this region will never be as fertile as the Lothians, but it was once forested, and its agricultural capacity was once much, much greater than today. Farmland and pasture have been allowed to revert to heather. The productive capacity of the Highlands and Islands is now a fraction of what it once was.

'Even today, landowners and stalkers will point to a few birch and alders in a gully and say that this is the only place trees'll grow, the only shelter. But trees are growing there only because it is one of the few places they can avoid being grazed by sheep and deer! It's an ecological disaster area! Look at an extreme example – Inverewe. Things *do* grow here.'

'Yes, the land needs money to correct the years of neglect. But at the moment the landowner's money goes into subsidising a lifestyle and economy that's out of date and inefficient. It doesn't go into improving the land, it merely preserves the status quo of neglect. Currently there are plenty of people, communities and organisations, willing to enter land ownership and management, either with money or with access to funding. The problem is the availability of land.

'Land ultimately should *not* have to have money spent on it when it's been restored to its full potential. It should produce income, aside from the very important non-monetary human benefits. We are dealing with an unknown . . . *the alternatives have never been tried* . . . so who can say how many jobs would arise from more creative and responsible management? At the moment the only option is what the landowner approves. If you release the energy and entrepreneurial abilities of people in the local community and allow them access to land resources, they could hardly make a worse job. Indeed, where it's happening there are tangible signs of improvement.

'Look at Assynt, look at what's happening there where nothing was happening before. Look at the will, energy and vision of Laggan Community Association. We should be making it easier for far more people to have access to actual resources. A healthy economy and environment depend on diversity. And that's what the current system and pattern of land ownership conspicuously lack.'

Through this forum I learned of the will, energy and vision of many individuals and communities. Their achievements were too numerous and diverse to be dismissed as isolated examples; they were the genesis of fundamental change, a natural change, as Alan Macrae had stressed. As my journey unfolded and introduced me to Hamish Moore, the Duke of Buccleuch and the wolf man, among others, I was to realise how deep and widespread was the perception of dispossession, and that it affected not just the land, but politics, language, music and dance.

⚭

24

Klondykers in Ullapool

Ullapool occupies a spur of land jutting into Loch Broom and has a turnover of milk, meat, fruit, vegetables and Ladas out of all proportion to its small size. As an image of Scotland it cuts a fine figure in the scrapbooks and on the mantelpieces of many a home in Eastern Europe. The seafront of white houses, the neat gridwork of streets – for Ullapool did not simply happen, it was carefully designed by the British Fisheries Society who, in 1788, had a good eye for herring – the pier, flotilla of moored boats, tea rooms and craft shops ('The Captain's Cabin'), a population stereotyped by guest houses, ice creams and oilskins . . . it all makes a pretty picture. Washed, like the rest of the west coast, by that offshoot of the Gulf Stream called the North Atlantic Drift, which scientists (who have obviously never dipped their hurdies into it) claim is 'warm', Ullapool grows palm trees *alfresco*. By training the eye to frame a select portion of the scene, including a palm tree, white walls and the sea, on a bright day when a whiff of Balkan tobacco invades the air, a determined onlooker can readily convert Ullapool into a Mediterranean fantasy.

'TVs,' John MacLeod said, 'they used to be enormous. Hundreds and hundreds of them we went through. Not now. Gas heaters, they had a good long run too. Now it's Ladas, that's the current rage. Only car they can easily get spares for back home. I don't think there's a second-hand Lada available in the whole of the north of Scotland.'

Manager of a local store, he stood beside two pallets of groceries on the pier and the 'they' he referred to were the crews of the klondykers, huge hulks of grey paint and corrosion lying at anchor in the loch. Currently there were seven. The previous week there had been sixty, and at the peak of the season ninety-seven. Ninety-seven ships with an average crew of 40, being supplied fish by 50 trawlers with an average crew of 6, this represented a seasonal influx of over 4,000 hungry men that Ullapool had to feed, let alone supply with denims, gas heaters and Ladas. Klondyking was big business and it brought an estimated £15 million into the local economy each year.

'This year was poor,' John added. 'Bad weather, few fish. Normally the ships are here for two months but this year it's only been three weeks. And can you believe it? . . . this year the Bulgarians trucked most of their food overland here, from bloody Bulgaria to Ullapool.'

The crews arrived for their shopping trips aboard lifeboats, elongated shells of orange fibreglass with spluttering engines. Aged between twentyish and fortyish, they were always overdressed in denim, usually bearded, and they shambled about in bored, lethargic groups. Russian, Ukrainian, Lithuanian and Bulgarian conversation passed between them and frequently fooled tourists who were struck by the charm and prevalence of Gaelic.

Klondykers were dual purpose factory-fishing ships and Ullapool had been on their agenda since the 1970s. They had fished these waters prior to the extension of the fishing limit to 200 miles, and subsequently became floating factories, buying fish from the British fleet and regularly offloading their produce onto transport ships which returned to the Eastern bloc and fed a nation.

After the fall of communism, hard currency not food, became the priority and the klondykers, still state-owned, offered their services to the West. Now the majority are under contract to British companies who employ them complete with staff. The companies contract fishing boats, mainly from east Scotland and north England, to supply the klondykers and then sell the produce wherever they can, which is currently Nigeria. Fishing boats and klondykers follow the seasonal migration of the shoals. Ullapool's fishing grounds used to be ten miles away but this year they were 200 miles away.

I met Captain Ivan Zaharinov when he was waiting for sixteen pigs.

'Where my pigs? I need pigs.'

'Your pigs are coming at one, *ud-yeen*,' replied Mrs Denison of Allan & Ker, Shipping Agents. She was efficient, experienced and delightfully blunt.

'Everyday problem,' he continued, shrugging. 'Machines break, no fish, too much fish, bad weather, pigs don't come . . .'

'PISS OFF.'

The Captain and I repaired to the Caledonian Bar where we were the only ones in a room built to take half the klondyker fleet. A succession of vodkas and coke, and eleven cigarettes, revived his spirits. 'She very good,' he confided. 'She get the pigs, no problem.'

At 29 Ivan had been the youngest captain in the fleet and now, twenty years later, he was one of the most experienced. 'Ullapool my second home,' he laughed. This was his seventeenth season here. His first home was in Bulgaria, near Burgas on the Black Sea. 'In Bulgaria we know very good Scotland.'

'You do? What do you know?'

'Bulgarians, we know Glasgow Rangers.'

He looked severely under the weather. His bleary eyes struggled to remain above their horizons of dark, hanging wrinkles. He wore jeans and a black leather jacket which, it seemed, held him together and was buttoned to the underside of a black-grey beard. I had seen him in better days a long time ago, as Captain Haddock in Hergé's adventures of Tintin. Now, Captain Mackerel would have been more apt.

'No, it not easy. I have wife and two daughter who I not see, maybe, six month. But . . .' he shrugged, 'no problem, I have four month then in Burgas. It's a life.' Ivan shrugged often, but most things were 'no problem', even bad weather, failing machinery and no pigs.

'Black Sea is dead sea . . . no fish. Here OK, fish, no problem. My ship, *Aktinia*, twenty years old, not so good. Maybe three more years then finish. My company once have thirty ship but now ten.' He believed klondykers would still be coming to Ullapool in ten years but in much reduced numbers. Salaries, fuel, repairs, food, flights; it was becoming too expensive and the profit margin too slim. He would find another job, no problem, but the men . . . ? 'Big problem. In Bulgaria now we have everything. Cars, television, no difference here – but expensive. Little work.' Ivan grinned. '*Perestroika*. Not easy.'

Aktinia never went back to Bulgaria, and crews were flown in and out at the nearest airport. She started her year in May, in South Iceland fishing for red fish. In July she moved to Norway for mackerel and from there she followed the great blue-black shoals: to Lerwick in September, to Ullapool in January, to Killybegs, County Donegal, in March, to Falmouth in April. And sometimes she went to Portugal for repairs.

'*Ud-yeen*. Pigs.'

The sixteen pigs were, in fact, thirty-two half pigs, sliced along their length. They were delivered to the slipway, where Ivan's lifeboat was tethered, by a lorry driver in immaculate European Union white. He gently lowered each pig from his gloved hands onto the oil-skinned shoulders of *Aktinia*'s crew, whereupon it was thrown ten feet into the open bilge of the boat and settled in a marinade of seawater, diesel, decaying mackerel and fag ends.

I sat on the grisly cargo as we bucked on a choppy sea and Ivan alternately appeared and disappeared in a blue murk of exhaust. When we reached *Aktinia* ('a small bird, seabird – I never seen one') we scrambled up the trawl ramp at the stern, and the crew followed with the pigs.

Aktinia was a panorama of rust and piles of nets. She conveyed an impression of contagious corrosion, that anything or anyone who hung around too long would seize up, oxidise and become fused to the deck. The company was wringing every last bit of revenue out of its investment.

Each week 7,000 tons of mackerel arrived at Ullapool, each trawler bringing in 200 or 300 tons at a time. *Aktinia* took on 50-ton instalments and her crew would process them in twenty-four hours. We descended into the works and the universal trawler smell of pungent fish and sickly-sweet diesel.

'Forty-six men here, small. *Vostosk*, Russian ship, is very big. Eight hundred crew, half are women.' He raised his eyebrows appreciatively. On *Aktinia* there were no women, he said, and neither was there enough alcohol. Twelve hours' work, twelve hours' boredom was their day, every day for six months, for a salary of US$1,000 and the rest in 'useless roubles'. Although his vocabulary lacked the word he couldn't have conveyed 'drudgery' more explicitly.

Conveyor belts set a fiendish pace in a process which converted 50 tons of mackerel into 10-kilogram slabs, frozen, bagged, boxed and renamed макрéл. The air was perishingly cold but some of the men were sweating. Ivan shrugged. *It's a life. No problem*. We retreated to his cabin for coffee.

'You must have a good cook, to keep all the men happy?' I suggested, fishing for some cheer.

Ivan considered this. 'No, the cook is not so good.

The food is not so good.' He particularly liked 'special' fish, he said. But he never got special fish. And he hated mackerel.

I sat below a dismal painting of a grey day on the Black Sea. It looked as if it must have come out of the state shop and been intended as an antidote to homesickness. Those state shops, how I remembered them, with their shelves bare except for a jar of pickled this and that, but always tinned fish, an abundance of the stuff stacked high into pyramids, yellow labels, макрéл, mackerel, from Ullapool . . .

Ivan's wife and daughters smiled at us from the wall. I felt I was prying and excused myself. Ivan gathered a skeleton crew and we set off for the far shore which was where I wanted to go. The lifeboat nosed into the shallows and I waded the last five yards. As they puttered back to *Aktinia* they waved and shouted.

'God Bye, see you, OK, no problem!'

'Glasgow Rangers!'

'Dos veedanniya!'

I carried Loch Broom uphill in my boots and squelched gratitude and discomfort through the laceholes. Behind me drudgery, profiteering and exploitation on a massive international scale maintained the acceptable face of post-card Ullapool, or a grey day by the fish-less Black Sea.

25

❦

Scoraig

Buncha hippies . . . whole lotta dropouts . . . green-welly-wearing English twits . . . were the descriptions I was given of the inhabitants of Scoraig. The community ran for two miles along a remote peninsula sandwiched between Loch Broom and its southern neighbour, Little Loch Broom, and was cut off from greater Scotland by mountain, bog, ignorance and suspicion. To get there you had to walk the last four miles, or go by boat.

Everything came by boat. Old Dundonnell Hall had come by boat, dismantled piece by piece by Topher and then rebuilt in Scoraig as his boat workshop. Two grand pianos went by boat, and Robin, Annette and Tree had taken their tractor over on a boat scarcely bigger than the machine itself and almost lost it overboard in a squall. Sideboards, windmills, Jersey cows, computers and a world of 'scored' items had all made the journey. 'It's unbelievable what people throw away. We scored that at Ullapool dump,' said Annette, pointing to half a ton of Rayburn stove which looked fresh out of a showroom. 'But we did have to push it half a mile uphill from the shore, on rollers . . . by the way, d'you mind Earl Grey tea?'

Green-welly-wearing English twits . . . ?

'Yeah, I've heard that one too,' said Chai, who was 28, the secondary-school teacher, and permanently in green wellies. 'It really rankles. I'm a Glaswegian . . . but what's it matter where you come from? We're all incomers here. And green wellies, quite simply, are the most comfortable wellies on the market.'

Thirty years ago the crofting community of Scoraig almost died. In 1964 a few people/visionaries/seekers/hippies (*delete according to personal prejudice*) moved in, and bought the tenancies of the crofts. Others arrived, crofts were legally subdivided, portions were hived off in paperless, verbal agreements and Scoraig, the complete antithesis of Ullapool, evolved.

Sixty-five adults and thirty-five children lived here. They made honey, and cheese which EU regulations forbade them to sell. Topher built boats with machinery powered by a wind-generator and old BT batteries. Bev's violins had won an award, someone made pots, others fished. They got by. With grants and three thousand hours of carefully logged community labour they had built their secondary school and turned a ruin into a Restoration Award. It was the smallest secondary school in the country and the only one with a wind-powered photocopier.

Everyone was well-versed in invertors and wind-generator speak. Every house had its own whirling set of blades which powered 12-volt systems (stereos, televisions but not washing machines). Mains electricity and planning permission had not reached Scoraig yet. Their homes had also just evolved; Topher and his wife slept in a bed suspended from the inside of a ferro-cement dome covered in turf and a shimmer of harebells; the others were more conventional but no less unique examples of simplicity and craftsmanship: natural stone, natural (scored) pine, driftwood doorhandles, hanging clusters of dried flowers and homemade pasta, and shelves of glass jars containing cloudy colours and belching the gases of fermenting wine; in each home I expected to experience a battery of clicks and flashes and, months later, find myself the only misfit on the cover of *House and Garden*.

'It seems too good to be true . . .' I remarked to Chai. Trees grew in profusion around their houses, their gardens bulged with vegetables and some had cloned their herbaceous borders from Dobbie's catalogues. Scoraig had come back from the dead. It had put green patches all along the peninsula. People smiled, and even waved at strangers. Even its half-witted hens looked in love with Life.

'It's no utopia. By virtue of being here you've got to be a strong character, and strong characters tend not to mix too well. We've got haves and have-nots, givers and bludgers just like any society. I don't know if it'll survive, but at the moment it's good. We pull together when we have to. And we've even got some second generation Scoraigers making their home here. That'll be the true test.'

'Why the outside resentment against Scoraig?'

'It's only a minority who feel that way. I dunno. Ignorance. Perhaps because we get on and *do* things.'

This was exactly the reason. Scoraig had done things. Scoraig was an achiever. But by being successful it had committed that most heinous of Scottish sins, of bettering yourself, of showing your erstwhile peers up, of forgetting that your station is among the humdrum and the suppressed.

'We kent his faither' was the usual put-down, the frigid remark which extinguished qualities and achievements, and returned a person to their ancestral roots and the more tolerable traits of mediocrity or failure.

Scoraig? Oh aye, we kent Scoraig's faither . . . green-welly-wearing English twit.

I unfurled my sleeping bag on Chai's floor, blew out the candle and fell asleep with the soulful sounds of a saxophone drifting in on the night air.

26

✺

Stornoway, Western Isles

Stornoway has arranged itself into a geographical and domestic pie of three equal portions. The eastern portion is all water, a bay nearly as vacant as the Bermuda Triangle which the town claims as 'Stornoway Harbour'; the Lews Castle portion with miles of grass, trees and rhododendrons, where leisure, walking, courting and under-age drinking takes place; and, divided from the last by a river, the buildings portion where people live, work, shop, drink, and discuss their council's spectacularly unsuccessful dabblings in usury.

My last visit to Stornoway, two years earlier, had left me with the memory of waking up one morning face to face with a dead seagull. Whether the seagull knew that the youth of Stornoway made a ritual of emptying and smashing bottles in the grounds of the castle, I can't say, but it came as a surprise to me to find my bedroll spread over a fakir's ordeal of glass and myself spreadeagled next to my desiccated companion.

I had arrived with ten others shortly before dawn aboard a replica 16th-century *birlinn* or Highland Galley, a slightly higher-tech version of a Viking longboat. Exhausted after rowing through the night, we had collapsed like the unfortunate seagull in the castle grounds, concluding a voyage that had begun in West Ireland.

That day we were fêted by Comhairle nan Eilean, the Western Isles Council, in a way that would never have happened had we arrived a week later. The bubble was about to burst on the Department of Finance. As we were rowing up the coast of Lewis, the Director of Finance was depositing another couple of million pounds, borrowed cheaply from the Government and being invested at a premium rate in the Bank of Credit and Commerce International. And as the Director of Finance was welcoming us at a special dinner, the Abu Dhabi bank was going under and taking Comhairle nan Eilean's entire investment with it. By the time we'd finished our sweet, its £23.5 million had gone. (I now find it very hard to enjoy trifle.)

I had expected Stornoway to have become a ghost town. That ridiculous but impressive castle, which matched Queen Victoria for age, austerity and ponderous bulk, would have lost one of its ornamental towers; the shops would all be TO LET or FOR SALE; Rathad Mhic A Ghobhainn ('Smith Avenue') would have lost its paint; shellfish, that abundant but shunned food of the Western Isles through its association with poverty, would once again be the last resort of a hungry people; and seagulls, deprived of what little fat there ever was on the land, would surely all be halfway between emaciation and the eternal leisure of the park.

But Stornoway had not gone into decline. True, the Hat Shop had gone out of business, but to specialise in anything other than sou'westers and galeproof bonnets was a risky venture out here. Knit'n'Sew was doing brisk trade, selling off Lewis's sheep in 20-metre lengths of traditional and faddish colours. Stornoway had all the charm of a tourist town without the tourists themselves and without sacrificing itself to the things they buy.

The harbour, the real harbour, occupied the river estuary and boats could, with an extra length of line, have moored themselves to the door handles of Boots, Woolies and the

other occupants of the high street. But this was a token fleet
of small trawlers and lobster potters. When drift-netting
for pelagic fish (surface and mid-water species such as
herring and mackerel) set the standard, Stornoway had
drift-netted with the best of them. When, around 1965,
purse-seining arrived from Norway, the Western Isles
and most of West Scotland were reluctant to change,
and understandably so, for such sophisticated technology
was expensive and way outside the means of traditional
family enterprise. But purse-seining showed itself to be
deadly effective and it stole the market. The initiative
was lost, and in a home industry excessively squeezed
by competition and insufficient investment – the current
cost of a new white fish trawler is about £2 million, and
that of a large purse-seiner, £9 million – that loss has
had severe repercussions. Today a valuable resource lies
usurped on this seaboard: of the total fish caught in the
Minch and off West Scotland, less than 5 per cent is caught
by local fleets.

Stornoway Harbour was a natural Sea World Centre
with jellyfish like pulsating lampshades with long tassels,
and seals staring wide-eyed at shoppers, five fishermen
and one tourist. Lochinver had smelt of fish and so
did Stornoway, but Lochinver's smell was raw while
Stornoway's came with chips. If any smell characterised
this town it was of beer from its twenty-one bars.

By day I felt Stornoway was waiting; waiting for an
oil boom, waiting for a thumper of a contract for its
fabrication yard, waiting for the return of the drifting,
waiting for anything really. It looked a cheat of a town
for its youngsters. They had come from all over the islands
because it was the biggest thing around, but because it
didn't have any rivals it had turned introvert and stolidly
inactive.

But by night I watched Stornoway slip away over the
Atlantic. Lews Castle turned into Central Park with furtive
groups in the shadows hanging around – it seemed – for

a pleasant evening of bottle smashing and mugging. And the streets which had been quiet by day became impossible to cross with endless successions of slow-moving cars, and not just cars but Audis, BMWs, Opels and their socio-economic peers. People shouted, horns honked. On this island without a city, Stornoway's youth had contrived to make a miniature New York by taking their limited population and passing it endlessly through the streets creating an impression of the bustle, lights, and the anonymity of numbers it seemed to crave. Drinking and kerb-crawling in a town where you knew everyone and everyone knew you had its limitations. Here they had created a pretence of population, traffic, activity and surprise.

In Cromwell Street, downtown Stornoway, is a gargantuan store selling carpets, furniture, ironmongery, kitchenware; everything for the home. 'JAMES MACKENZIE: BUTH SHEUMAIS [James' shop],' says its sign. More correctly, it should read: AHMED NAZIR: BUTH AHMED. Everyone knows the owner as Nazir. Spruce in a three-piece suit, he stands out in Stornoway by his dark skin. His hair is combed neatly back and gold-rimmed glasses sit on a buzzard-ish nose. He operates a professional smile and is disarmingly blunt with his customers.

'Your order will be ready tomorrow. Bring lots of money.' 'You'd like a bed? Oh yes, beds are going very well, very cheap. Try this. Lie down. Headboards are extra. I've a hundred in stock.' 'This will be the best deal you've ever had.' 'I'm always ready to help, if you've got the cash.'

This was the self-assurance of a man who loved the repartee of the bazaar, was a legend in Lewis and, now, the world. 'I don't know why you're asking these things. My story has been in *The Times*, *The Scotsman* and the *Daily Mail*.'

'I'm writing a book.'

'Is it a good book? I don't want to be in a bad book.'

Having missed the relevant copies of *The Times*, *Scotsman* and *Daily Mail*, I had to piece Nazir's life together from the bits of the kit he gave me; my Nazir model is missing an arm and a leg but is still standing.

He was born in East Punjab in 1932. A Moslem. At the time of partition his family moved to West Punjab and what became Pakistan. In 1957 he came to Britain. 'We always believed that life was good in Britain. In Britain one could work and make a good living.'

'But in those days Lewis couldn't have been well known in Pakistan.'

'Oh yes, in our house it was. You see, my uncle he was coming out in 1928. He thought he could do well in isolated communities by bringing them things they couldn't easily get at good prices, so he went to Islay, Tiree, Barra and all the islands, selling drapery. It was Depression then and things very hard but they got better, and the more north he went they better they got.'

So Nazir made the second great trek of his life, from Pakistan to Stornoway. He had very little. He sold drapery from door to door. It built up. He worked hard. In 1964 he went back to Pakistan 'to get a wife'. He made her sound like an unusual headboard for which there would be a surcharge and a two-week delay. Now he owned this house-furnishings empire, a clothes shop and a shoe shop ('Smith's') which his brother ran.

'This must be the largest shop in Stornoway?'

'Actually, it's the second largest shop in Britain that is privately owned by an individual.'

'Do you feel any racial prejudice here?'

'None. No. Never. These are the most accepting people in the world.'

I expressed surprise and mentioned the anti-incomer feelings on other islands.

'Ah, I have my own theory. Incomers from Scotland or England usually think themselves superior and try to dominate their host community. Maybe they accept us here as they don't see us as superior, as threatening them. We try to harmonise with them. For example, at home we speak Punjabi, but my sons also have Gaelic and regard themselves as Lewismen.'

Nazir was called away to offer the purchase of a lifetime to a customer ('And just for you, madam, I can make it even cheaper'), and I went to chat to his wife who was modelling a sari and oriental headsquare by the cash till.

'No, I have never heard of Lewis when I am leaving Pakistan. It was not easy for me. My English it is poor. I come from the heat.' That first winter she was miserable. The cold, the wet, the long hours of darkness: everything about Scotland was alien to her. Worst of all was the lone-liness. 'It was the social quiet, oh yes, the *social quiet . . .*' Her voice intoned the words with the malevolence of a pogrom or a plague, and I felt the anguish of those winter months so far from the equator and her kin. I could imagine how she had sunk her energy into helping Nazir with his work, and having children. 'And Sundays they were hard, so strange. The children were not allowed to play outside then. Now is different. Now more families from Pakistan.' Her mother had come to visit, intending to stay for a couple of months, but had fled home after a fortnight. Even the Indus with its floods was more her cup of tea than Lewis with its interminable winter rain and darkness.

'Very well, madam. Give me the money and the table's yours.' Nazir returned smiling, the customer left, smil-ing.

'What about religion, how do you manage, being Moslem in the heart of Free Church country?'

'For us it is very big problem. Now we are about fifty in the Pakistani community here, and the nearest mosque is Glasgow. Two hundred and fifty miles! That's like from Karachi to Sukkur.' I contemplated this leg of Pakistan I'd never seen and inserted a mosque every ten miles for good measure. No wonder Lewis felt like a spiritual desert with no official places to align your mat on Mecca. 'It's hard to keep our faith going among the young. They see their friends go to church, and they have no place to go. The people here have their places of worship, but we have none.' He lowered his voice. 'Maybe soon we try to build a small mosque here . . .' His eyebrows travelled an inch up his forehead. '. . . maybe that will cause a bit of an uproar.'

A bit of an uproar? I could already see the minority zealots of the established churches throwing themselves before the bulldozers. And Donald MacKenzie would be in the fray, gnashing his teeth, revelling in ashes and sackcloth and self-flagellation – at least if his letter in that week's *Stornoway Gazette* was anything to go by. This was his epistle on the controversy over whether ferries should be allowed to start a Sunday service to Stornoway.

Sir,
Until recent years, people of the Western Isles enjoyed a worldwide and well earned reputation of being honest, hard working, intelligent folk . . .

Nowadays, Lewis people are infamous as drunkards, incapable of running their own little economy, grant-reliant spongers who fiddle claim forms rather than earn money by honest sweat.

Blame what you like, the truth is Highlanders brought a curse on themselves and on the land when they turned their back on the Gospel. And when Lewis ferries are allowed to run on the Sabbath Day, that curse will increase to an extent that will make the hardest soul weep.

Boy, am I glad there is a place of eternal pain and misery because a good thumping just isn't enough.

On second thoughts I don't think Donald MacKenzie would risk leaving his den of self-righteousness and sullying himself over a bit of good thumping. And even if he did, I'd back the new Lewisman who arrived with a suitcase and turned it into a mega-store.

Lews Castle College was a jumble of prefabricated Elizabethan (1970s) units tucked into the shadow of the castle, and they made Queen Victoria and all she stood for look stylish and desirable. At the college office I was given a pile of brochures, one of which had been printed in 1956 and covered the Queen's visit that same year. This visit had 'set the seal' on the college by giving it an 'important place in the royal programme'. The Queen had spent a whole hour there.

Quite why the college continued to promote as an accolade this hour of patronage by the Queen, almost forty years after the event, was a mystery. Perhaps by inference it was drawing attention to the fact that subsequent progress had been achieved despite rather than because of fleeting royal interest. Since that momentous occasion, the college had come places. Physically, it had travelled 200 yards to new premises because the old castle was threatening to collapse, and academically it had increased its roll to 1,800 students. Courses embraced an astonishing diversity of subjects from the usual Computing Skills, 'Mig and Tig Welding' and 'Abrasive Wheels Regulations' to the more novel 'Sheepdog Handling Skills' and 'New Ideas for Sweets and Puddings'. The importance of the college rested as much in its cosmopolitan curriculum as it did in its endeavours to halt youth emigration from the islands by promoting skills in cottage industries.

The exodus of young people from the islands had long been endemic. At the college I picked up a report on the subject, 'The Western Isles School Leaver', which produced few new facts but did put figures against the ones most people knew.

With limited white collar opportunities locally, the better qualified incline towards Higher Education, and the lesser qualified tend to enter Further Education rather than face unemployment. In a survey of 1,358 school leavers over the last forty years, 48% entered full time education after leaving school, and 36% entered employment.

Few who leave the islands to study tend to return. The number returning decreases as qualifications increase. Of those questioned 54% were still resident in the Western Isles; therefore 46% had left the islands and all of them 'emigrated' on leaving school. The islands lose a greater proportion of females (52%) than males. Those who stayed gave their main reasons for doing so as: peace, and safe for children. Those who left disliked: weather, and poor social life ('It tends to revolve around churches and pubs.')

For a long period there had been an attitude in the WI that to 'get on' you had to 'get out'. The view that self-improvement is linked with migration still exists to some extent. The local economy has always been an unreliable one, dependent on the fishing and Harris tweed industries. The project has shown that there is a long way to go if the WI is to reduce or reverse its sustained out migration of young people.

Two hundred yards away I entered the former holiday home of Sir James Matheson who, with Jardine & Co, made his mint in Hong Kong, and bought the whole of Lewis in 1843. The place was now in dire need of Sir James' deep purse. Plaster was losing its grip on the walls, windows were cracked, floorboards broken and generally it looked doomed, already blindfolded with its head on the block. Why, I asked myself, did they not wheel in 'Mig and Tig Welding' from next door, and 'City and Guilds Advanced Craft Certificate in Carpentry and Joinery'? But instead they seemed to have indulged trainees in 'Chainsaw and Stihlsaw Operations' in running amok. Notices advised me that dry rot had been discovered and it was unsafe to proceed outwith a designated route. The place had the air of a deathtrap and looked uninhabitable, but a series of arrows led me to the top of the building, and the precarious office of 'Emergency Planning'.

'We had to move out a year ago as the floor was caving in, but they've fixed that now. The Council would love to be shot of the liability of this place but it's a listed building and they have to maintain it. But it's running away with them. It needs seven million pounds to put it right, and the Council's credibility for borrowing is . . . none too good.'

Murdo MacLeod was Stornoway's doomsday man. He was employed to foresee every possible emergency and have ready a plan of action and a system of services on stand-by. Behind his back a crack wide enough to hold a pencil made a lazy representation of a bolt of lightning running from the ceiling to the floor. He had sellotaped a piece of paper over the crack, drawn two vertical lines on it and written: 'When the crack gets this wide – RUN!'

'Yes, I think it's a test. The joker who put us here obviously reckons that if we can cope with this place, we can cope with anything.'

Every council in the country, Murdo explained, had to have an Emergency Planning Officer. What if the gas depot blew up? What if a ferry turned turtle, a plane crashed, the *Braer* had run aground here? For every 'What If', Murdo had to be able to arrange, within the hour, an emergency mortuary, enough hospital beds, doctors, nurses, fire-fighters and telephone lines for up to 600 (respectively) bodies, survivors or reporters.

'Look,' he pressed buttons and different maps filled the computer screen. 'Here's every fish farm in these outer isles. I can log in a reported oil slick, the tides, wind direction and speed, and calculate which farms and when that slick will hit. Here's the shipping routes in the Minch. This is my biggest worry.' He zoomed the picture in on the Shiant Isles. 'Tankers aren't meant to use the Minch but many do. They're meant to use the deep water channel to the west of Lewis, but even that comes within four miles of our shores. Our nearest large tug is at Lerwick or the Clyde – so forget it. We want the tankers to be forced to go further out to sea, ten miles beyond St Kilda. But no, they save time and money by using the Minch. Look, the passage off Skye for northbound ships is just one-and-a-half miles wide.' *At best, only three-quarters of a mile of safe water existed on either side of the ship.*

It was the Fair Isle scenario all over again. The Western Isles, like Shetland, were just too far away to matter.

'Depressing, isn't it?' Murdo smiled. 'But we have to learn to live with imperfection.' And he turned and checked his crack. I left him running over his preparations for a war strike, and felt reassured for the community (not the Minch) that someone of Murdo MacLeod's ability was watching over them. They well could have used him, his plans and his powercut-immune computer that night many years ago, exactly 115 minutes into the New Year of 1919.

⤫

27

Iolaire

H.M. Yacht *Iolaire* steamed out of Kyle of Lochalsh at about midnight on Hogmanay 1918. No record of the passengers was taken but it is believed that 280 people were on board, far more than the boat was equipped to take safely, but this was a special occasion. The passengers were in high spirits and sang Gaelic songs, for not only were they celebrating the New Year but also their first homecoming after four years in a fleet at war or in the slaughter at Flanders and the Somme. It was a black moonless night and blowing a storm, but the lights of Rona and Arnish were clearly visible. For reasons that were never established beyond 'failing to exercise sufficient prudence', the *Iolaire* struck a reef called the Beasts of Holm. At the entrance to the harbour, within sight of the paraffin and gas lights of Stornoway's houses, she rolled to starboard, exposing her deck to the storm, and sank twenty yards from the shore. Two hundred and five men drowned.

28

√

Lewis and Scalpay

The morning of my departure from Stornoway brought a Force 6 (the Beaufort scale definition being, 'strong breeze; 22–27 knots; large branches in motion, whistling in telegraph wires, difficulty with umbrellas'), a fairly normal day for Lewis. Wind-driven beer cans rattled through Stornoway's streets. I followed their general direction and was blown north-west to the Atlantic coastline across a flat region the texture and colour of toadskin, tattooed with the rectangles and curves of the quest for black mud. Lewis is Scotland's peat capital with an estimated 85 million tons going free for the effort of digging it. Odd pairs of figures were stooping and dissecting Lewis into chunks, throwing them onto banks, and dragging last year's takings home in those modern, disposable (and free) creels, fish-farm food sacks. Old folk with wry smiles would say there was more heat in the cutting, curing and collecting of peat than there was in the burning of it.

A shy sun peeped through holes in the cloud and raised the colour temperature of the land several degrees. It is easy to love Lewis at its best, washed in fresh sea air and flaunting the colours that gave the world tweed. But when normal, or worse, I think you have to have been born here to feel immune to its overwhelming sense of dull deflation.

At nine o'clock, when the population of Lewis had mass-migrated into Stornoway, only a skeleton crew manned the countryside. They stayed largely hidden on a coastline which cleaved a green passage along the edge of the great peat toad, a swath of pasture whose myriad enclosures turned crofting and history into eloquent patterns. To the north and south the view was a lesson in lines and perspective, the linking of 10,000 fenceposts; and it was also a lesson in fairness, for the plots looked scrupulously equal and had each been allocated one house and one ruin.

The people of Ness were said (by the flowery and frequently certifiable writer of the tourist brochure) to show signs of their Viking ancestry. I looked hard for blond hair, square jaws and horns in the teashop owner; but, none. He had come from Lancashire ten years ago, roughly 870 years after Magnus Barelegs and his philanderers had got dressed and gone home.

But medical research has shown that, outside Ness Tea Shop (whose coffee more than makes up for any implicit deficiency in the genes), Hebridean blood groups *do* show strong similarities to those found in West Norway.

I looked too for the traditional houses: the converted blackhouses (thatched cottages, without chimneys, whose interiors became blackened by peat smoke), the two-up-two-downs with steeply pitched slate roofs and dormer or storm windows, but they were almost as rare as Vikings and signs of life. It was perhaps wrong to have hoped for anything else but it has been shown that comfort and modernisation can be achieved at no extra expense within the lines of traditional architecture. The villages of Highland Scotland are airlifted sections of kithouse Culloden, Cumbernauld, Corstorphine – kithouse suburbia given a rural setting and space. The typical bungalows of some universal Smith Avenue –

beams, bricks and Tudor windows, all neatly boxed – are, through an overlooked side-effect of a benign but blinkered Housing Improvement Policy, the only choices on offer at a reasonable price.

A black mound of peat, trapped inside a fishing net heavily weighted with stones, stood at the back door of each house. These saved kithouse Lewis from anonymity, as did the occasional wheelbarrow full of tweed parked at road junctions, awaiting collection by the 'mill' van. Tweed was still a cottage industry here. About 400 weavers on the Long Island worked to orders procured by one of the few remaining companies. Clack, clack, clack, clack, clack . . . This was the characteristic sound of rural Lewis, only marginally more common than that of the corncrake, and it stuttered its way out of huts and garages. Through open doors I saw men, only men, sitting in semi-darkness at colossal Imperial typewriters, terrifying Dickensian machines with a flying shuttle and chomping teeth, their feet pumping pedals with an effort that would have converted to 20 miles an hour on my bicycle.

Nowadays, Lewis people are . . . 'grant-reliant spongers who fiddle claim forms rather than earn money by honest sweat'.

While cycling along I considered the view expressed by Donald MacKenzie (who, incidentally, gave a Glasgow address). It was a commonly expressed allegation that the people of the Highlands and Islands were a lazy people. I saw people cutting peat. I saw people pedalling miles of tweed. I saw people as daytime accountants and evening crofters. I saw the hills and bogs scarred by a gigantic comb, evidence of the ironically named 'lazy beds' formed by raking the land's thin covering of soil into long strips where potatoes might grow when fed endless rotas of seaweed. Laziness was not in the biology of a people who succeeded in clawing an existence from nature's harshness, and who, when they went abroad, became the dynamic forces of the New World. Only those with a comprehension of this region's history, of the composition of its ageing population, of its conception of time in which work was a steady toil throughout the waking hours rather than an intensive nine-to-five burst, have a right to judge 'laziness'. I knew I was not looking at laziness but at the listlessness of people too long without work, of people too long without incentive or encouragement. That energy which built lazy beds and the New World was not extinct but latent, awaiting only a catalyst; Lewis was Shetland with a different faith, less fish and no oil.

I felt that energy in the land too. I camped in a fank near the Standing Stones of Callanish whose builders, 4,000 years ago, are believed to have measured the 18.61–year cycle of the moon and been aware of the 9-minute wobble in its arc. But I picked up none of their vibrations, just those of dozens of galvanised pipes. They were pan pipes to the wind and that night, all night, Lewis tongued, trilled, spat and whispered notes as if bursting into life. It was a remarkable act, pure soul, jazz, blues. Lewis turned Louisville.

At its southern end Lewis becomes mountainous and at some unmarked point among those bald stony upheavals, for no apparent reason at all, it becomes Harris. Harris lives in the shadow of its neighbour. It has no towns, no major industry and an even older population. Harris, in the Aegean Sea, could have transformed the finest beach in Europe into a lucrative *Veriensresort* for rich fat Germans, a colony for nudists, or a Costa del Lager for Brits, and thereby have created employment for its youth. 'New Ideas for Sweets and Puddings' could have earned a wage here. But Harris in a low of the North Atlantic can make nothing out of Luskentyre beyond the dues of those who are enjoying it, belatedly, in a large graveyard.

Scarp, an island on the west coast, had died and, like

St Kilda before it, had been evacuated. But Scalpay on the east coast was a glowing exception: a success. It had stuck with The Fishing and this afforded it sufficient prosperity to support a population of 400. At a sponsored Shave-a-thon for Leukaemia Research, Scalpay's school children raised £800 in an afternoon. Scalpay sent clothes (Harris tweed and the homeknits Harrods couldn't cope with) to Bosnia. They were a God- or Sabbath-fearing people who adhered to a scriptural view of things, and this, according to one Scalpaich, had preserved the island as the untried ground of feminism.

'Germaine Greer would have a field-day here. The concept of a good wife is still one who keeps a clean, tidy house, bakes well, and has her husband's meal ready on the table. I'll say, "What a lovely day for the beach, or a walk", they'll say, "It's a good day for drying." And funeral processions are still segregated. First the family, then all the men, then the women. It's stone-age stuff. Most women here are brain-dead.'

Mairi was in her thirties and her words clashed with her appearance. She looked an undercover version of one of 'them', wearing a headsquare, loose top and an ankle-length dress. She was lifting the peats and had resolved not to go home till the work was done. I lent a hand.

'Five years ago you'd never see a man hanging out the washing or pushing a pram. Men had to act macho. But now it's changing. God, what a life it used to be for women! Who was that First World War poet who described the terrible waiting in the trenches . . . ohh . . . I forget his name but he wrote something like, "We can cope with grief, it's dullness which is unbearable." I can really identify with that.'

Mairi was an avid reader and only watched televison selectively. Had I, she wondered, seen the recent *Horizon* programme on transvestites in Brazil? Squatting in a Harris bog as I was at that moment, it took me some time to remember what a transvestite was. No, I replied, I hadn't.

'My mother and mother-in-law would never watch such things – it would be "shocking", "indecent". I don't mean to be crude or anything but that generation would never talk about sex. It was something you had to do in the dark, with the lights out, dutiful like.' Again, this was a surprising revelation from one who was dressed like a Hutterite. Mairi continued her dissemination of island life.

'There's no tradition of debate or friendly argument here. Disagreement is taken personally and is seen as an act of aggression. There's all sorts of feuds go on and they last for years.' It was all part of the boredom complex, she believed. Scalpay was proud of being dry but drinking still went on; it simply became a secretive, guilt-laden pursuit. There were no dances or *ceilidhs* on the island. All spare energy turned outwards into feuds, or inwards into turning houses into shrines to be cleaned and polished.

'I blame it all on the Church. You know how the St Kildans used to love music, singing and dancing until the Church stopped it all? I think it must have been the same here. It's so long ago now, we've forgotten how to enjoy simple, non-alcoholic communual fun.' Of the 400 Scalpaichs, 320 of them would be at church every Sunday. Mairi saw this as being a substitute for the banned parties, the only chance the islanders had of looking their best and meeting everyone socially. 'The Church has suppressed individuality and personality, and removed incentive to help ourselves. Fatalism and a sense of inferiority make such suitable prey for Calvinism.'

'Does an inferiority complex still apply?'

'Does it ever! I'll give you two examples. My parents never spoke to me in Gaelic because for so long people had gone away and had the language rubbished wherever they went. So it's ingrained in them that English equals

Education equals Culture equals Best, and therefore they've always felt disadvantaged. And there's also a deep fear of failure here. A friend's husband once thought of sitting his skipper's ticket, which he could have passed easily, but he didn't dare. If he'd failed, he said, he'd never be able to come back and live here. Johnson, or maybe it was Boswell, wrote, "Their fear of failure is greater than their desire for success." That's still true today.'

'Why on earth do you live here? It seems all gloom.'

'Because I see Scalpay for what it is, enjoying the good and shutting off from the bad. The good is fantastic and the bad is found everywhere. I lead my own life.'

Mairi surveyed fifty yards of unlifted peats. 'Sod it. I'll finish the peats tomorrow.' She picked up her empty Thermos and piece bag. '*That*'s what I love about Scalpay.'

In small communities where everyone knows everyone else, it is easy for a stranger to betray the trust of those who speak freely. Mairi talked to me in the full knowledge that I was writing this book but, I believed, in the tacit agreement that Scalpaichs should be left in doubt about her identity.

I left the island with other doubts: those of my trade. Scalpay had been portrayed as one person's view of its flaws, whereas it deserves to be championed as the pulsating example of success in the Western Isles. No other community can match the stability of its population or the vitality of its economy. So much of Lewis and Harris is dying while Scalpay, even with an additional obstacle of isolation, is thriving.

Despite the accuracy of a writer's reportage, the narrow paths of personal experience do not always cross the wider plains of fairness.

29

❦

Incomers

In an area of caravans lashed to South Harris for security
from winter storms I encountered Ugly Incomers again. In
prejudice and rancour they were no different from the Ugly
Local – had the year and allocation of power been different,
both were of the type to light a fire under a witch, or throttle
the last auk (Scalpay, 1821) – but the Ugly Incomers
always seemed more conspicuous on the landscape. Their
strident accents clear-felled the soft voices of the Gael,
their moaning dirges were more suited to the pulpit than
the village shop, and their brash attitudes were Dover chalk
to the subtle courteous Highland cheese.

This Mr and Mrs Ugly ran true to type: they had
escaped their race in Birmingham and now ran a Bed
and Breakfast in which they hung symbols of an England
they had never known: brass trappings, ships' battles in the
days of Drake, *The Haywain*, and on their mantelpiece sat
the Cotswolds in porcelain. Mr Ugly had fallen out of a
fire-engine and been pensioned off . . . I could scarcely
believe this story any more, this improbable spate of faulty
catches, this endemic streak of lemming behaviour among
English firemen; it no longer carried a hint of conviction.
However, Mr Ugly assured me he genuinely had made an
unexpected departure from his fire-engine. He'd fought the

council and won a disability allowance for a spine injury which had brought his working life to an end, officially, and precipitated a new career as renovator and proprietor of a Western Isles' Bed and Breakfast.

He was cocky and delighted in misery, courting misfortune with a pirate's eye for plunder. His game was grants and compensation. His house had barely cost him a thing. Bills for advance annual payments he paid in monthly instalments to avoid the possibility of an overpayment should he die suddenly. For two hours he boasted of his achievements against 'the system'; how he'd fought the AA on their 24-hour Anywhere in the UK Repair clause; how he'd done the same with Volvo HQ, and his insurance company. How he'd insisted Volvo send a specialist to his house; how he'd got the Firemen's Union to take up his case; how he'd claimed 'a few extras' of the insurance and got away with it. 'Ye got to fight fer yer rights, mate.'

And how he was fighting, not just for his rights, for anyone's and anything else he could get hold of. Each week he wrote letters demanding grants, compensation and pounds of flesh, using the exclusivity of a West Highland address to extort his 'rights'. He did nothing for the community. Mr Ugly, Avarice, Greed, Selfishness, Boredom: he had many pseudonyms. The only wonder was that the name plate didn't read 'Ye Olde Crofte', 'Dunrovin', or 'Upyores'.

I once spent a winter writing in a cottage in Wales, on the Lleyn peninsula. Near Abersoch and Llanbedrog were the English enclaves; the smart ghettos of holiday homes each with their boat neatly parked outside and, as often as not, a tractor beside it; a tractor that was used twice a year to pull the boat to and from the water, a distance of half a mile. Up in the hills by Carn Fadryn were farmers who couldn't afford a tractor. I understood then – without in any way condoning – the anger that led to acts of vandalism.

Nazir was right. Complexes of superiority and inferiority were at the heart of the problem, and also a fear of the unknown. The 'issues' were as old as population mobility itself. In *Scottish Journey* (1935) Edwin Muir wrote:

> but when they [English people] are in a foreign country some of them have a strange and exasperating habit of filling it with the local atmosphere of some provincial or suburban district of their own land. When they appear in a foreign hotel or public room, it is as if they were preceded by an invisible vacuum-cleaner which removes all trace of local associations, so that they may comfortably settle in with the customary aura of their existence quite complete and inviolate round them like a vast cushion. So I found Maidenhead all round me in Dunkeld, Brixton in Ullapool, and Tunbridge Wells in Scourie. It is not merely that English people of this kind carry England about with them, as a Frenchman carries France; they carry about the street they live in, their back gardens, the views from their windows, their local politics, the churches and shops they patronise, their private jokes, everything that makes them a part of a specific locality . . . it seems to me to come from that deep instinct for security . . . By behaving as if they were still in Maidenhead or Brixton they abolish the strangeness, possibly hostile, of the places they have temporarily decided to live in.

Logically, there is no argument against incomers. The Scots themselves, after all, are incomers from Ireland. I, as a Longitude 3° W Scot was an incomer living on Longitude 6° W (Skye). I would also have been considered an incomer (but a more acceptable one) had I 'belonged' to a glen ten miles away. Incomers therefore are stigmatised according to the distance travelled from their forsaken roots, and their nationality, with some allowance for ethnic circumstance. But if home Scots, whoever and wherever, are unwilling to accept others in their midst, why should others – England in particular – accept the Scots? In reality we are all either Those Who Have Moved or Those Who May Yet Have To Move.

The contention is therefore not one of origins but of personality, attitude and sensitivity. Mr Ugly must be judged on these qualities, or his lack of them, and not on the typecast 'Incomer'. No one will deny that the people of Birmingham have a right to their identity, pride and culture, just as the people of Harris have to theirs. There must be respect and sensitivity by one when on the hallowed ground of the other.

The issue is all the more inflammable in the Highlands for this region is not 'just Scotland'; to the Gael, it is all that is left of Scotland, where language and culture are at stake as much as mere pride.

We were all *on* Harris, but what mattered was which of us was *of* Harris. Mr Ugly, unfortunately, was not.

My encounters with English incomers who had made permanent homes in the north were astonishingly frequent. On my journey from Thurso to Ullapool it seemed that every third house *in the country and by the sea* – these qualifications are necessary – was home to an immigrant with an alien accent. To be sure of finding a local Scot you had to look for an old croft (no renovations), old car and a flock of sheep (not goats).

I mentioned this to Alan MacRae.

'There are three families here who are local. You have to understand, that without the incomers we have no shop, no services, no community. Oh no, we've nothing against incomers here.' Then the man who had done so much for the Assynt Crofters lowered a voice that sounded wholly Highland and gave a smile that was half English. 'My mother's from London. Victoria. Yes, boy, one of the finest and purest Cockneys.'

❦

30

Church and the Sabbath, Leverburgh

It was the Sabbath. I pulled out my best trousers and shirt from my pannier bags, slipped into them and arrived at Leverburgh's Free Presbyterian church with a conspicuous monopoly of the congregation's unintended creases. The church was a blow-up version of the kithouses which littered the landscape, a vast hall with no ecclesiastical features other than a cross on one gable. A reception committee kindly ignored my sub-standard attire and welcomed me with a brace of books.

'The minister this evening is from Affrea'acha.'

I nodded politely at this intimation and walked on, wondering if I might have passed through it the previous day. Somewhere between Geocrab and Flodabay, possibly? I sat next to a man wearing a flamboyant yellow tie whose children sat in diminishing order along the pew and reminded me of a family of eider ducks I had seen that morning. The congregation, as in most churches nowadays, was predominantly elderly and female; yet it is an anomaly peculiar to the churches of the north-western seaboard that their elective bodies consist almost entirely of men. Women elders are rare, and ministers non-existent.

* * *

Out of the complex web of Scottish church history the Free Presbyterian Church has emerged as one of the severest and most conservative disciplines, even regarding the hard-line Free Church, the sobriqueted 'Wee Frees', as lax.

The web had begun quite simply with the vigorous missionaries of Celtic monasticism whose influence extended as far as Iceland and the Apennines. Around the ninth century, the Culdees, a group of monks devoted to strict aesthetic ideals, broke away and tried to reform the rude and declining Scotic Church. Its loose structure was no match for the assault from the south by the cohesive and solid Latin Church, and by the twelfth century the long sway of Roman Catholicism had begun. The Reformation in the sixteenth century sent out two major strands, the Presbyterian Church whose ministers were intended to be chosen by the people, and the Episcopalian Church which favoured control by bishops. The two vied for supremacy, with the Presbyterians winning in 1690 and becoming the established Church of Scotland.

The Scottish Episcopal Church has maintained its separate identity to this day, and far from being the erroneously labelled 'English' Church, its claims to descent from the Columban Church are as legitimate as those of any other sect. (The vast majority of Jacobite clansmen were Episcopalian, not Catholic.)

In a simpler world Scotland would have been left with Catholics, Episcopalians and its majority of Presbyterians. But the Presbyterians were unhappy about state intervention, patronage and such things as whether the bread and wine should be raised for consecration or left on the altar. So there followed years of secession, sub-secession and sub-sub-seccession (Burghers, Anti-Burghers, Auld Lichts, New Lichts, Lifters, Anti-Lifters), and then mergers.

The major disruption occurred in 1843 when one-third of the established Presbyterian Church ministers walked

out. Those left behind were the Moderates. Those who
walked out, the Evangelicals (opposed to the patronage
of ministers by landlords), formed the Free Church. In
1900 they picked up most of the previous secession-
ists and became the United Free Church which, in
1929, made up their differences and returned to the
fold of the Moderates in the established Presbyterian
Church. *But* a hard-core from these various components
remain as separate entities: Free Church, United Free
Church (Continuing), Original Secession Church (rare),
Reformed Presbyterian Church (endangered, possibly
extinct) and the Free Presbyterians (in whose church I
was then sitting).

The Free Presbyterians were holding a brave face over
their own recent schism. A Church principal had attended
mass at a friend's funeral and the ensuing outrage had
split congregations, resulting in a new breakaway sect, the
Associated Presbyterian Church. However (and I'd like
to be clear about this), I was amongst Free Presbyterians
who split from the Free Church (slack confessional
standards) in 1892 and were enjoying prolonged cen-
tennial celebrations – hence this special minister from
Affrea'acha.

The church was almost full. Bare white walls supported
an acre of pine-panelled ceiling. The elders sat on benches
around the pulpit which consisted of two tiers. The lower
tier was a raised box occupied by the precentor who
led the singing; no instrumental accompaniment was
permitted. The upper tier was the main pulpit up to
which Aaron Entebele was climbing. He looked old and
tired although he could only have been in his fifties, a tall
broad-shouldered man, and very, very black.

'Excuse me . . . where does the minister come from?'
'Zimbabwe.'
Aaron Entebele read the first psalm right through in
English, then the precentor launched into the opening

notes with sufficient force to rock Jericho and the congregation joined in, singing in Gaelic. A prayer followed in which the Reverend Entebele thanked God for so many blessings and asked for us to be spared so many sins that he seemed to cover every contingency. Not a chink was left to allow the devil a look-in. We sang another psalm and then came the sermon.

He took his theme from Ezekiel, 37. '*Again he said unto me, Prophesy upon these bones, and say unto them,* Ooooooh Yeeee Dryyyyyy BOWW-NUSSS . . . *hear the word of the Lord. Thus saith the Lord GOD unto these bones; Behold, I will cause breath to enter into you,* Aaaaand Yeeeee Shall LIVVVVE*', he boomed, hanging onto each word as if it were too valuable to release.

'DRY...DEAD...BOWNUS brought back to LIFE by the LORD.' For an hour he worked on this theme of God's ability to work miracles but always in the context of these DRY DEAD BOWNUS. I wondered how many more times he could bring himself to repeat the words, but they invigorated him. These dry dead bones were taking years off his life. The congregation looked numb. At times his English was so hard to understand I wondered if he had changed to Gaelic. My head nodded.

'. . . drrRRRRyy deeEAAdd booOWWNus . . .' The Reverend Entebele had hit on a variation and was now singing the words, incorporating a crescendo into each. The bones had by now been clothed in flesh and sinew and his vociferation was the breath of life being pumped into them. In his more heated moments, it seemed, they were not just inflated and alive but bulging at the dangerous level of 80 psi. The dead hope of Israel had been revived, but the miracle was as good as lost on me, benignly but ruthlessly reduced to cant.

I lay low that Sabbath and in the current issue of the *West Highland Free Press* I read of the Do's and Don'ts of Sabbath behaviour.

Here are a few of the traditional rules, though some
of them now belong to a past age:

 1 *Ashes may be lifted but not taken outside.*
 2 *Potatoes may be peeled when boiled but not when*
   raw.
 3 *Clothes or beard may be brushed but not shoes.*
 4 *No wheeled vehicle may be used unless motor-*
   driven.
 5 *No walks.*
 6 *No whistling, no singing except psalms.*
 7 *A knife may be used to cut tobacco but not to cut*
   string, a stick or even a vegetable for the broth.
 8 *One may (and should) wash one's face but not shave*
   or cut one's nails.
 9 *Horses may be taken to water but water may not be*
   taken to the horses.
 10 *No reading except leabhraichean math, 'good' (ie*
   spiritual) books.

. . . Clearly in an economy based on cattle and sub-
sequently on sheep), . . . it was impossible to ignore them
altogether on a Sunday.

What was possible for some people was to pen or tether
their cattle and to employ others to do their herding and
milking for them. This raises the issue of social status;
if you could pay someone else to do essential work for
you, you could keep the Sabbath; if you accepted paid
work on the Sabbath, you and not your employer could
be judged guilty of breaking it. It was only if the work
as a whole were judged non-essential that the employer
was guilty of the sin.

. . . It is well-known that the sin of Sabbath-breaking
is the greater when committed in public.

31

Superquarry, Harris

The map of Harris is the last word in cartography; 'map Harris and die', they might say. Here is the most intense concentration of crags, lochans and puddles in the British Isles, each large enough to merit its own borders and small enough to fragment the land into a mosaic of spectacular penmanship.

Behind Leverburgh rose a dark hill called Roineabhal which was one of the few places the cartographer could relax over a solid section. I followed a minor road which undulated moodily round the hill for several miles until I came to Lingerabay's four crofts and twelve permanent inhabitants.

The rocky shoulder of Roineabhal on which they and their homes happened to find themselves, also happened to be 600 million tonnes of a hard white stone called anorthosite. Looking ahead to a world shortage of hardcore for road-building, Redland Aggregates of Reigate, Surrey, were proposing to operate a superquarry here which would create a hole large enough – the newspapers said – to be visible from the moon and to hold eighty Great Pyramids. Then they proposed knocking the sea wall down and turning it into a marina.

The MacDonalds occupied the croft closest to the proposed site.

'At first we were against it,' Mrs MacDonald explained. Her husband had been dozing on the sofa and was struggling to regain consciousness. Mary, their 18-year-old daughter was doing a crossword at the table. Huddled by the stove was her father-in-law, seven years off his century. She nodded in his direction. 'He'd been quite upset at first. He's been here all his life, and his father before him. The croft's been in the family for generations.'

'What changed your minds?'

'We felt we were being selfish. They say it'll bring ninety jobs here. They say there'll be a trust fund for the community too, though Redland haven't made a very good offer yet. There's nothing for the young here. Ninety jobs is a lot.'

'But will you have any guarantees that the jobs will be given to local people?'

'Aye, that's the problem.' Mr MacDonald had revived. 'We're told that some jobs would be specialised and people here don't have the skills. They'd have to give us assurances that local people would get the jobs. But we've got good lawyers working for us.'

The community was split over the issue. The question of Sunday working had been a major obstacle, but Redlands had agreed that 'only maintenance and essential safety work' would take place on the Sabbath. The royalty payments offered for the Trust Fund had been deemed 'paltry' and Redland Aggregates had lost much credibility in being seen to be miserly. There were also the unresolved questions about dust, noise, vibration and the potential pollution of shellfish and farmed salmon through the dumping of ballast water.

'You'll get good compensation for your house and land, though?' I prompted.

'We hope so.' He allowed a measure of a smile, but his eyes flashed pounds. It was easy to see what had won them over, and who could blame them? 'They'll build us a house in Rodel and pay us for our lost land. But the amount was meant to be settled before the Council agreed to grant planning permission.' Permission had since been granted and the compensation agreement postponed. No one could tell them what was going on.

I asked Mr MacDonald, and Mary, if they would accept jobs in the quarry.

'Why not?' he replied.

'No, I won't stay in Harris,' said Mary. 'There's nothing to do here. What difference will the quarry make? I'm going to university.'

'It's true,' her mother agreed. 'There's nothing for the young here. Scouts and Brownies gave up. Sometimes there's a dance in Tarbert, but not often. And sometimes one of the hotels in Stornoway shows a film, but there's no cinema there.'

So Mary would join the 50 per cent emigrating. She'd already got her place at Glasgow University. Her parents would leave their ancestral ground and move to Rodel where they hoped to receive sufficient compensation and a job. The old man would see his life's work going into the gnashers and being shipped away. Leverburgh would hope the pollution wouldn't wreck its environment and its fish. The Church would hope the Sabbath wouldn't be too badly violated. It was a classic dilemma; a multi-national company offering the possibility of ninety jobs in an area of no work, on an island whose population had halved in the last thirty years and the majority of which were now over retirement age. Past versus present, tradition versus commercialism, values versus money.

32

⁓

Dutch Visitor

What had begun at the Butt of Lewis ended at Leverburgh
as the Long Island dissolved into the Sound of Harris
and -ays: Ensay, Orasay, Pabbay, Gilsay, Sursay, Groay,
Tahay, Grotay, Sarstay, Opsay. The Norse suffix for
'island' made poetry of the names. I could hear them
as a mantra echoing in the hollow shrine of Buddhists,
being muttered over a cauldron of eye of newt, or being
crooned by a mother into her pram:

Ensay, Gilsay, Groay, Grotay,
Sursay, Sarstay, Orasay, Opsay

Whether by gloom or the brilliance of sunlight everything about the Hebrides was seed to the fertile imagination.

Marieke Goller felt this too. During the crossing from
Harris to North Uist she sat on the bow of the *Endeavour
of Berneray* breathing deeply and in a hypnotic state of
wonder.

She was a middle-aged remedial teacher on her fourth
holiday in the Outer Hebrides, and two weeks earlier she
had suddenly found her legs wouldn't work.

'My ankles they become swollen and my legs they won't

go for long. Two hundred metres. That's all I can walk. So I buy this . . .' She pointed to a bicycle with a motor rigged to the rear wheel. '. . . but the air here is so good and now my legs they can go for a whole hour. *An hour*! And for two weeks, nothing! The Hebry-dees make my legs go, make my mind go. I like very much the way of life, so slow. The people they live still with nature, the life here it flows with the wind and the tide.' She took a deep snort of vaporised ocean and seaweed, and lowered her voice. 'Here it recharges my soul.'

'Why don't you come and live here?'

She recoiled in shock, as if my words were a code offering shares in Redland Aggregates.

'O no, no. For me that would be very, very dangerous. You see, in Holland, our poisoned, dirty, overcrowded land, I try to lead a life that is good for the planet. I try to save fuel. I make compost. I think pollution and the changing climate. If I live here, I think I become lazy in these things, I get used to the purity and freshness. Also, I like concerts and my friends. Here I would be alone. But when I visit here and go home, I know what I'm living for. When my friends with very much stress come to talk, I know how to let them talk and talk. I know how to share the peace I find here.'

She saw herself as a missionary. The Hebrides were the Bibleland of nature, purity and tranquillity; a Garden of Eden lacking only concerts and friends. She couldn't live here but she could carry back to pagan Holland the Hebridean creed and spread the sound and effect of the tidal life.

Unfortunately for the Hebrides their most marketable asset was of the most delicate and least commercial nature. There was, as yet, no royalty payable on peace.

But Marieke was right on every other count. As I helped to haul her heavy machine up a full flight of pier steps, the deckhand, a Berneray man, muttered under his peching and panting, 'Aye, low tide, of course. It's always the same. They always have tae bring these things along at *low* tide.'

33

❦

Lochmaddy and Ministers

The Tourist Information board in Lochmaddy was hard pushed to find anything to promote. 'Red deer, peat cuts and the CalMac ferry' were listed as its 'visitor attractions'. I always feel drawn to places which are at a loss to know why anyone should bother to visit them.

The Tourist Board had hit on the key factor behind Lochmaddy's lack of tourists with its ironical mention of the CalMac ferry. The ferry service should indeed have been a tourist attraction but the truth was that the service was so appalling and expensive that it actually scared them off. Had Scotland's island communities still belonged to Norway, they would have enjoyed an excellent interconnecting daily service; for Norway – despite having a coastline at least five times longer than Scotland's, with at least five times as many inhabited islands, and a smaller population – has made its ferry infrastructure a priority expenditure of oil revenues. The pertinent difference was the value placed by Norway's government on preserving isolated communities.

In Lochmaddy's youth hostel I came upon a few other travellers sheltering from the rain, and among them an elderly ornithologist. He had been an accountant earning a preposterous salary, but had taken early retirement and now lived half the year out of a backpack and plastic bags. He snored for half the night and spent the other half rustling bags as he packed and repacked his luggage.

You should never go to youth hostels for sleep. They are designed to have squeaky doors, squeaky springs, an apparently organised rota of late-revellers, water systems with Earth-creation sound effects and guests whose entire baggage consists of plastic bags in which the desired article is permanently lost. No, you go to youth hostels to escape the weather, dry your clothes, gather intelligence and gauge your place in the human circus.

Bleary-eyed but dry I cycled anti-clockwise round North Uist which was skirted in luxuriant machair; unique to the Hebrides this composition of sand and crushed shells is rich in calcium carbonate which neutralises the acidity of the peat and provides good grazing and fertile ground for an extraordinary variety of flowers. They imparted a honeyed fragrance to the air which softened the sharper tones of tangle and peat smoke.

At Bayhead I visited the Reverend Morrison of the Free Church. He sat as an *ay* on a mini-tractor mower in two acres of lawn, and had just switched the engine off for a tea break. His Jack Russell saw me approach and homed in for the kill.

'Ignore him,' the minister called, 'he's useless and harmless, in that order.'

I approached the manse in a vortex of gravel and growling and joined the minister for tea in his study. In size the manse looked like the Palace of Versailles on the North Uist landscape.

'And what faith, may I ask, do you belong to?'

I hesitated. Our need to reduce the lives of others to the simplicity of an amoeba in order to achieve comprehension and context demanded neat labels, black on white. Age, sex, ethnic origin, marital status, education, occupation and religion (PLEASE USE BLOCK CAPITALS) were all you needed to know to plop people in pigeonholes and classify them. You were not allowed to be part Catholic, part Taoist, part Baha'i and part Buddhist. In the Western Isles I wasn't even sure if you were allowed to be non-Christian.

'I used to attend the Episcopal Church but am now unattached.' The Reverend Morrison let his eyes drop in what I took to be a gesture of double disapproval. If he could have read my mind at that moment he would have seen me back at prep school in Aberdeenshire. The school was far from any town but a Church of Scotland was active within walking distance and most of the pupils attended it. I was one of a dozen who didn't.

'OK, you pesky-palians, your bus is here,' a senior boy would shout at 10.15 each Sunday, and off we would troop in our kilts to be driven seven miles to the Episcopalian Church in Huntly. I could have no more explained the difference between Episcopacy and Protestantism than I could have split the atom in Colonel Collard's science class. Church was simply something adult, remote and mind-numbingly boring that you had to endure and it didn't make any difference in which building you did it.

The church was small and painted lime green. The altar was set beyond a lancet arch above which was written (and you had to cock your head to the left, then right, to read it) *Come Unto Me All Ye Who Are Weary . . . And I Will Give You Rest*. The words had been painted in beautiful shadow writing. They made me think of the organist who always looked weary. She soldiered valiantly and I sat there willing her on in the weekly struggle for rhythm and breath, but the keys and stops bled an anguish of rogue notes and gaps which the organ's collapsing lungs filled with a rude hissing. The Reverend Thomas, meek, dumpy and dull, then conducted a service of what may have been an hour of wisdom and benevolence but to an 11-year-old it bore the emotional small print of a damp squib. In 1965 Episcopacy was the study of shadow writing.

'I see,' said the Reverend Morrison. 'And why did you become "unattached"?'

'Because I'm searching.' The conversation was veering alarmingly out of control. I'd come to put questions about the Church to him, not to be put through the Third Degree myself. But he looked less grave at this and I quickly took the offensive. 'What I'd like to know is how you foresee the future of the Free Church here?'

'I take three services each Sunday, each in a different church and each is almost full. There are three Sunday School groups taking place in the manse as well, and they have a good attendance. My congregations have increased over the last five years, not decreased.'

'Are your congregations mainly elderly?'

'Yes, but there are many young couples too. I'm very confident about the future. I think the young are attracted to the strength of the Free Church's reputation and the quality of the sermons.'

'It seems to me to be such an austere faith, all about threat and punishment.'

'Once, yes, but I don't think any more. For example, if I give a sermon on Eternal Damnation . . . Hell,' he elucidated for my benefit, 'then the next one will be on Eternal Life. I believe you have to balance the positive with the negative.'

'Is there any chance that ecumenism will bring the Churches together here?' Bayhead had about sixty houses and three active churches.

'One problem is that people get very attached to their buildings – wrongly, but they do. That makes it harder to unite. I think it's possible that the Free Presbyterian Church might combine with the Free Church. Combination with the Church of Scotland would be more difficult. *Some* of their ministers no longer hold Christ as central, and are into all these other ideas, these –isms as well. But really, the Free Church has such a strong hold here, we've no need of ecumenism.'

He was the rearguard of the Free Church, the only minister of this faith in the Uists. To the south the suzerainty of Catholicism began. The Reverend Morrison put the weakening of the moral fabric in North Uist down to two causes: television and causeways. The causeways had linked this former island to Catholic South Uist whose pubs opened on Sundays and drew his parishioners into sin. He saw no possibility of Catholicism uniting with Protestantism. And after talking with the Reverend Morrison, nor did I. 'I find it an oppressive faith. The way they instil the need to be Catholic from the earliest age is wrong, so oppressive. They see the Free Church as being bigots but, in my opinion, we're not half as bigoted as they are.'

When I left, with his useless mut snapping at my heels, he said, 'May you find your Faith, may you find *my* Faith, and save your soul.'

Suddenly the journey seemed that much more dangerous.

Further down the road, at Carinish, I risked conversion again in the Church of Scotland manse. The Reverend Alex Muir had come a long way from the Gorbals. I couldn't think of a more extreme definition of contrast. He had changed the view out of his window from (in those days) the seediest blocks of tenements in the country to an empty vista of blanket bog and, possibly a more poignant reminder of his work ahead, North Uist's highest hill which rejoiced in the name of Eaval.

'I'm ecumenical in outlook but not where it compromises my faith. We simply couldn't cope here if the different churches united. There wouldn't be a building big enough. There are three churches in Bayhead because three are needed . . . well, perhaps not the Free Presbyterians. There's not so many of them now.' Of the 600 people in the area, he estimated that 100 attended the Free Church and 150 came to his. I detected once again that smug feeling of self-satisfaction. Here in the Light of the Valley of Eaval, we're all right, Jack. Aeneas Sage, evidently, had thrown the only spanner in the works. I pulled a blank face at the name.

'He was minister at Lochcarron between seventeen-fifteen and forty-five. Quite a guy. Beat the local strongman at wrestling and won a lot of converts! He considered the local population so bad he stopped communion unless you could show evidence of your worthiness. Now there's a lingering hangover from that. People attend church but few *join* as they feel unworthy. Few members, few elders. That's my worry.'

He was in his forties and played guitar. Introducing guitar into the children's part of the service had been a long slow affair and had only been achieved after protracted discussions with the older members of the congregation. I could imagine the Reverend Morrison wincing at the thought. But Alex Muir was pinning his hopes for the Churches at large on charismatic revivals. He'd written a booklet on the subject. The biggest one had occurred in 1859 when 300,000 people joined the Church in that year alone, when Scotland's total population was only 3 million. The last one had been in these very islands in 1949. It was, he believed, these 'Classic Awakenings' which had built the strength of the Church in the Western Isles.

'That "strength" has also been a weakness,' I argued, 'in that it's exerted such a tight hold: music, dance, enterprise, creativity have all been stifled. It seems to stand for a monumental negative. You shouldn't, you can't.'

'That, if I may say so, is the typical media view. The Free Church and Presbyterians do a good job among their people, but the media lampoon them for keeping the Sabbath and their good work is ignored. Great injustices go on elsewhere . . . violence on TV gets little press but someone who holds the Sabbath is attacked. Soft targets, of course.'

'But the Sabbath aside, it's the aura of suppression . . . ?'

I can't remember where or how the discussion ended but we did not exchange or share labels.

What I did remember was a young man I'd met in Leverburgh who played guitar. He found it hard to find other musicians to play with, and generally found little spark in his generation, no get-up-and-go. He put it down to a stifling home life, nowhere for the young to go to express themselves and explore their potential, and the ever-watching eyes of a disapproving Church. He knew the talent was here, but it was not ignited here.

34

Eriskay Pub

In South Uist the wind turned against me. For mile after mile I toiled with what felt like a hand pressing against my chest. ('Force 8: fresh gale; 34–40 knots; twigs break off trees, progress impeded.') Once, my concentration wandered and a deviation of a few degrees allowed the blast sufficient purchase to knock me into the ditch. But of the two of us I seemed to have the better deal; with obvious agony the wind shredded itself relentlessly in the fences and telephone wires. Its shrieking had cleared the land of people. To my right extended empty machair and croftland, with buttercups and daisies recording the fury in violent quivers, and to my left, in strict accordance to the fifty-fifty split down the length of the land, were uninhabited mountains. Some blue-necked sheep lay with their backs to the storm which was now strafing us with rain. Nearby a tractor had expired. It lay on the ground in exact mimicry of the shatter-diagrams you find in engine manuals. I understood at once how its demise had occurred, and feared I might be found in the same state. A roadside madonna brought some consolation.

The ferry to Eriskay didn't run that afternoon, but it did the following morning by which time the wind had expired. Sun turned the sea into a lazy pool of semi-precious aquamarine. The air felt soothing and balmy. Shoppers and gossipers were about, looking timeless and unflappable. Flymos were buzzing. Life had returned as miraculously as it had disappeared and everything seemed deceptively normal.

The secret of survival in this fickle climate was to become immune to the weather. You always wore the same volume of clothes 'just in case' and you were rarely overdressed. You had to learn the art of emerging from Hurricane Force 12 into the village shop, dabbing a tissue over your face and saying, 'A bit wild today', and *believing* that this was nothing more than a minor inconvenience, as indeed it was, relative to the imminent collapse of The Fishing, your Council's loss of all your money and the trickier business of saving your soul. Master the weather and you were halfway into the pink. I convinced myself that yesterday's tempest was a figment of foreign, heathen imagination.

Eriskay was only two miles long and half as wide but it would have scooped the tidiest sum from peace'n'beauty royalties. The most isolated of the inhabited Western Isles because of its erratic ferry link, this island was the best of all the others compressed into one convenient visitor unit, the Readers' Digest condensed Hebrides; a lumpy idyll of grass and heather, crofts and beaches.

I picked up a sheepdog immediately on arrival, which accompanied me to the far end of the road and ran a further five Eriskays in the pursuit of rabbits. My quest was for a rare flower, a convolvulus, said to be found only at Coilleag a' Phrionnsa (Prince's beach) and to have been planted by Prince Charles Edward Stuart, for this was the first Scottish soil he touched. But the rabbits must have found them an exotic delicacy and replaced them with their droppings. With dog to heel I returned to look for the bar. As the Reverend Morrison had also noted, the frequency of bars had increased in proportion to the degree of Catholicism. At the first house in the village a man was standing by the gate with a bowl in his hand.

'Aye, well, so you've had a good run, have you, Scott?'

'He's had a damn good run. Is he yours?'

'Aye. He won't go with locals at all but he likes visitors. Every day he meets the ferry and finds one. He's had a postcard from Sweden, he has. Come on, Scott, you'd better have the rest of the tin, you'll be needing it.'

The girl behind the counter of Am Politician Bar was watching the World Surfing Championships in Hawaii on Sky TV. 'I'd *love* to try that,' Sandra remarked wistfully, 'but I can't swim. We never got the chance to go to a pool to learn when I grew up here.' She was no more than nineteen. 'Only boys learned in the sea. It wasn't done for girls to go in.' The screen showed bronzed figures rocketing in and out of monstrous waves. 'We only got to paddle.'

Among the gantries of spirits behind her were two corked bottles, one of which might have contained whisky while the other looked three-quarters full of mud. These, a Jamaican ten shilling note pinned to the wall and the porthole built into the side of the bar were salvage from the *SS Politician* which inspired Compton's MacKenzie's *Whisky Galore*. Carrying 24,000 cases of whisky, cigarettes, perfume, silks, fur coats and Raleigh bicycle parts, the *SS Politician* had the misfortune to hit one of the last rocks between Britain and Jamaica, where she was bound with all the essentials for making the Royal Family a comfortable retreat should Britain lose the war. His Majesty's dream of cycling through Kingston, fag and dram to hand, fur coat floating in his slipstream, ended on 5 February 1941 and for the next four months the ship sat on the rocks just 400 yards off Eriskay.

'I was sixteen at the time but I mind taking bottles of whisky about the place and hiding them in the peat. I bet there's still a fair few bottles lying hidden. One bog looks much the same as another at night.' Donald had broken off from a conversation with two others at the counter and joined me. He smelt strongly of sheep dip. 'And I mind when yon film came we were right excited to see it. But the fellow that brought it laid the reels and projector down on the rocks, I can't think why, and the tide swamped them. It was years before a replacement came. Ach, but it was rubbish. There was none of that policemen chasing bottle-runners through the night. Rubbish!'

'How much whisky was smuggled ashore?'

'Maybe a few hundred cases . . . not much, really. The rest was officially salvaged. And a few men went to prison for their part in it. The film never showed that.' He had his glass refilled. 'You know the truest thing Compton MacKenzie ever wrote?' I shook my head. 'That the Black-Faced Sheep has the devil in it.' And with that he turned and rejoined his companions. It must have been a hard day at the fank.

Through the hubbub of noise I caught snippets of conversation concerning the Barra Condom Affair. Condoms had been on sale in Castlebay's main store for a year, but a poster campaign on contraception and AIDS in the school had brought the issue out into heated debate. The local council was to meet the following week to decide whether the sale of condoms should be banned. Barra, like Eriskay, was Catholic.

'Where do you belong to?' a new companion asked.

'Skye, now.'

'A bheil Gaidhlig agad?'

'Chan eil.'

'I don't see why they should need them,' said a voice in the background. 'After all, we never had them.'

'But we never had AIDS either,' came the reply.

Callum was small and wiry. A former Scottish Cross Country Champion, he taught Science, English and Gaelic at Eriskay school, and had done for fifteen years. He had lost interest in teaching Gaelic.

'The curriculum has become pop-ized Gaelic. All talk

of pop music and discos. It's Gaelic with a mid-Atlantic theme. They don't learn proverbs any more. It's Gaelic without its richness. There's more to a culture than speaking the rudiments of its language. *Chan eil an Loch-nam-madadh ach beurl 'is acras* runs a proverb. *There is nothing in Lochmaddy but English and hunger.* Well, we've got the English everywhere now.'

'And hunger?'

'No, people here are reasonably well-off and have good houses. Jobs are scarce, though, and getting scarcer. Eilean na h-oige, that's Eriskay's name in Gaelic. Isle of Youth. Huh! Ironical! There's not much to hold them here. Yet life in the cities is much harder. Urban poverty, now *there's* poverty.'

'AIDS is punishment for their sinful ways.'

'Condoms just makes them promissious, if you ask me.'

'What about visitors? Maybe they need them.'

'Then they can bring theirs with them.'

It was an evening of broken conversations on topics that might have been the hidden inventory of the *Politician*.

It ended with Iain, a former merchant seaman from Barra who had swarthy skin, broken teeth and hands like grappling irons. He was into perfume.

'The wife was doing B&Bs and one night we had this scientist staying. Well, he told us perfume was pretty easy to make. So I got hold of this French book, and that was it.' He handed me his card. *The Hebridean Perfume Co. (Barra) Ltd.* His voice was gruff, almost coarse, and the words flowery, leathery, woody, tweedy and mossy sounded like heavy components of a greasy engine. Soon he was into full flow, back in his garage among beakers, funnels and pipettes.

'First I thocht I'd use flowers but you get bugger all out of them. No, chemicals is the way to go. Yer needin' a base, a fixer and top notes . . . . I'll give yer nan-allergy, Alastair.

It's like music. Yer given the notes but ye've to make the melody. The base is yer foundation scent. The fixer blends yer top notes. Yer top notes are the minor accents which make a distinctive perfume.'

He handed me his leaflet. Legend, Moonglow and Mylady had been taken out of production, but this left him with Dark Glen, Plaid ('A soft warm and tweedy perfume. Woody and tweedy base with natural floral top notes.'), Tangle, Caluna and Love Lilt.

'So how's things going?'

Iain turned down his mouth and shook his head. 'Tae be honest, Alastair, I'm thinkin' of movin' intae taxis.'

It was another Sabbath. The good people of Barra had attended mass. There was to be a football match that afternoon. The bars were open (though you couldn't buy a condom for love nor money). A general levity rubbed shoulders with humour. There didn't seem to be a dark cloud for exactly 33 miles. Even the ferry sailed.

Reluctantly, I boarded it. I had arranged a meeting on Skye with the author of 'the most fiercely impassioned poetry of this century' (*The Times*).

∽

35

Somhairle MacGill-Eain (Sorley MacLean)

> Beyond the lochs of the blood of the children of men,
> beyond the frailty of plain and the labour of the
>   mountain,
> beyond poverty, consumption, fever, agony,
> beyond hardship, wrong, tyranny, distress,
> beyond misery, despair, hatred, treachery,
> beyond guilt and defilement; watchful,
> heroic, the Cuillin is seen
> rising on the other side of sorrow.
>
> From 'the long poem', *The Cuillin*, 1939

The day was cold, filled with squalls of wetness enveloping the landscape and the narrow road that runs below the escarpments of Braes. Braes was not a place as such but a collection of places and Somhairle MacGill-Eain, or Sorley MacLean, lived at the far end within sight of the rising Cuillin and the ferry to Raasay.

The greatest Scots-Gaelic poet of the century and the 'father of the Gaelic Renaissance', was of short stature, looking dapper in a tie, light jersey and tweed jacket. His hair was brushed in a curve over his forehead and was as white as his cropped moustache. From a round fleshy face shone alertness and a penetrating scrutiny that would have been the envy of any intimidating teacher. He exercised a full arsenal of facial expressions. He frowned, smouldered, threatened, invited, cajoled and laughed with expression alone. It took some time to learn this facial semaphore and place a remark in the context of *his* meaning. I think this was his way of adding to English an undertone of subtlety, even a dichotomy of meaning, that is an inherent richness of Gaelic.

Behind those expressions lay the playfulness and pained sincerity of an exceptional intellect. When he frowned he looked the tormented poet, when he laughed he became the universal grandfather.

We sat in a pine-panelled living room with Sorley turning his right ear, his only good ear, to me. At 82 he still had another decade in hand to look his age.

'I was born in Raasay. Our MacLeans have been in Raasay for eight or nine generations. My father was a highly intelligent man. He went to Portree High School but, ach, he got fed up. He was a tailor, crofter, fisherman.'

Sorley was the second of seven children, all of whom became either teachers, lecturers or doctors. At the age of six he had almost no English; by the age of twenty-two he had a first-class honours in the language. He trained to be a teacher, 'for economic reasons. There was no prospect of a job in Gaelic.'

'Those were depressing years, the thirties. I was a pessimist. Everywhere I looked I could see the miseries of the Industrial Revolution, the Clearances, the rise of the Nazis and Fascists. I was obsessed with politics. Even at school I supported the General Strike. I nearly went to the Spanish Civil War. Jack Stuart wanted me to go but, well, for family reasons, I didn't.'

'Do you regret that?'

'I'd probably just have got killed.'

He talked in a very precise manner, in lovely rounded sounds as if he had explored the sensuousness of words, and delivered them intimately and intact. Long pauses came between sentences, at times so long I thought the answer was lost and the question forgotten but they never were. He lay back and spoke with his eyes shut for minutes at a time, and then he'd open them and transfix his gaze on a point on the wall, moving his head but holding his eyes rigorously on the spot. Everything was sacrificed to the exact weighing and measuring of words.

'I tried to get into the Army in September 1939. Tried to get into the infantry, the Camerons, damn fool that I was, but *education* meant Signals so they put me in the Signals. Then I was sent to Egypt and was attached to . . .,' he paused, changing to the voice and face of Empire, 'the Royal Horse Artillery. Gad, sir!'

In the Battle of Gazala-Birhacheim a shell fragment cut his upper leg while he was with an anti-tank battery. He bled badly but was patched up and remained off the casualty lists. But his worst injury came on the last effective day of the Battle of El Alamein. A land mine exploded below his vehicle and although the skin of his feet was unbroken, the shock waves shattered the bones. He lay for twenty minutes before being brought morphine by stretcher-bearers of the Tenth Hussars ('Hooooosaaahs'), beginning a nine month recuperation in hospitals and hospital ships.

He never forgot his respect and admiration for his colleagues in the RHA. In *Heroes* he recalled one, a pathetic little Englishman with knock knees, a pimply face, and an ugly high-pitched voice . . . *but garment of the bravest spirit*. Dying in the bullet showers, *he kept his guns to the tanks . . . a great warrior of England . . . and he took a little weeping to my eyes*.

Sorley recovered and with 'probably the flattest feet in Scotland' became a teacher in Boroughmuir and then in Plockton.

'Did you never want to be a full-time writer?'

'No, I'm an occasional poet. My work spans sixty years

but there are long gaps in my writing. Those long grinding years of teaching didn't help, nor did my addiction to an impossible lyric ideal. But full-time? No, it was never right for me.' He considered his most satisfying poems to be *Hallaig* and *The Woods of Raasay*. 'I think for the Gael the fascination of poetry lies more in its sound than in its visual form or colour. Our poetry does not normally have consonantal rhyme but it very often has vowel assonance. And, of course, that is lost through translation into English.'

I asked his opinion on what was special about Gaelic as a language.

He thought for a long time. 'I'd put it like this . . . Every language has its own qualities and defects – yes, qualities and defects. Gaelic has a very big range of sounds because fundamentally it is a mid-European language having some of the qualities of Nordic and also of the Greco-Roman languages. Also, Gaelic has a *wonderful* faculty for indicating degrees and positions of emphasis. It is especially good at this. It has a big flexibility of syntax . . . natural inversions, particles and things like that.'

His concern for the language had come to a watershed in the 1960s. At that time in almost every secondary school, Gaelic was available only to children who were native speakers. Sorley, along with a Lewisman (Gaels are precise about placing other Gaels in their rightful island and genealogy), Donald Morrison, began a campaign of 'open agitation' for learners' courses and exam grades. In 1968 they were successful and within a few years the number of learners had quadrupled or quintupled.

'Now I am optimistic . . .' No, that wasn't quite right. He closed his eyes and wiped the slate clean with a hand movement. 'Now I am *less pessimistic* than I used to be about the future of Gaelic. The great things now are the Gaelic-medium primary schools, and of course more Gaelic on radio and televison.'

'And in general, are you less or more pessimistic?'

'More, oh yes, much more fearful, things are getting worse. The world is in a dreadful state . . . the nuclear bomb created a different world. It's awfully, awfully difficult.'

I changed subject. 'What book would you take to your desert island?' I immediately wished I hadn't asked. *Up to now you've done all right, but that question . . . oh dear . . . tiresome journalist.* He squirmed. 'I would have to take a very large suitcase.'

I was a persistent, tiresome journalist. 'Then which book would you put in first?'

He squirmed again, this time luxuriating in the choice. 'The best collection of Gaelic songs.'

For a while we talked books, then the conversation returned to the war. Sorley leaned towards me conspiratorially. 'This is a joke, you understand? Yes, a joke. An NCO of the Royal Horse Artillery once told me that I should feel very honoured to be serving on the right wing of the British Army. Very honoured indeed.' He raised his eyebrows and the semaphore said, *Note that!* 'And do you know what I told him?' His smile evaporated. *This is serious.* 'I told him the MacLeans once fought on the right wing of a better army.' His explosion of laughter showed the story had lost none of its pleasure in the half century of its telling.

'If I have time to do it,' Sorley MacLean wrote in his introduction to *From Wood To Ridge* (Collected Poems), 'I brood over something until a rhythm comes, as a more or less tight rope to cross the abyss of silence. I go on it, as far as I can see, unconsciously.'

36

❦

Dr James Hunter, Skye

Judging from the vehicle registration plates I seemed to have strayed wildly off my route that morning and was somewhere between The Hague, Milan and Barcelona. Skye's prawns passed me on their way to Spain in a lorry with 'Langostinos' splashed along its side. In a bakery a smidgin of Gaelic was crushed under a preponderance of Midlands, German, Dutch and Italian accents, and the dismayed mumblings of a French family prodding a loaf of Mother's Pride. Only the scenery proved I was unmistakably in my adopted home.

Skye was famous. For mist. For its views and its lack of them. For a coastline so indented that the sea cut deep into its glens. Its character played on variety; sometimes gentle, neatly patterned in pasture, sometimes bleak and foreboding, and often overwhelmed by those outrageously soaring mountains spilling banks of scree. Skye had a plain but well-promoted castle. It had remnants of the world's tallest non-pathological giant, Angus MacAskill. And it was the land of the Fairy Flag and the ceaselessly polished romance of Bonnie Prince Charlie and Flora MacDonald.

Flora MacDonald was a South Uist girl whose affection for the Prince was never expressed as anything more than a one-night sit in a very wet boat, a chaperoned encounter quickly fictionalised into a love epic of Romeo and Juliet proportions; at her death, Flora's body was enshrouded with the bedsheet used by the Prince at Kingsburgh. And now Skye was about to unite the two again in Portree's main square where they would re-enact their departure permanently in bronze. Tourism was the economy of Skye – assisted by prawns, fish farms and the public sector – and bringing a little prosperity and some good to the island was the least Prince Charles Edward Stuart could do after his disastrous visit.

The roads were familiar to me but at eight miles an hour they took on all the surprise and depth of new discovery. The needles and spires of the Quirang badlands, dislocated from that remarkable shelf of rock which distinguishes north Skye, seemed taller and more ready to collapse than ever before. Sheepdogs saw me off from whitewashed and harled houses with barking scaremongery as I glided past crofts and fields in their summer colours. Then through the central no-man's land of rugged mountain, the Red Cuillin and the distant Black Cuillin where Sorley MacLean often walked on a tightrope over its deep abyss of silence. Then back into croftland again, only here more dereliction had crept in and the land looked less loved than in the north.

In order to try and understand the state and future of crofting, I had fixed a meeting with the recognised authority on the subject, Skye-based historian Dr James Hunter. His definitive work, *The Making of the Crofting Community*, was part of my luggage.

'Crofting today is stronger, and its future looking rosier, than ever before. The idea of combining some income from the land with that from other means is now seen as an attractive proposition. With computer modems and faxes people find they can run businesses from remote areas. It's even *fashionable* to be a crofter now! . . . You'll find lawyers proudly admitting they're crofters, whereas once the crofter was bottom of the heap. And demand for crofts far outstrips supply. Assignations can change hands for up to forty thousand pounds, or more.'

We were talking in a hotel lounge padded with tartan and chintz. Two Wallace Arnold coaches from the Borders had just disgorged another cash crop of stiff bodies and they lumbered in to create mayhem around the coffeepots. I had made the point about the black-faced sheep having the devil in it and asked what would happen if the sheep subsidy were removed.

'Without the subsidy, sheep here are not even remotely viable. It's a little-known fact that sheep farms in the Highlands, since the 1870s, never have been profitable. Sheep today provide a very small proportion of a crofter's income, but they are easily the most widespread element of the working croft. Without the subsidy, sheep, quite simply, would disappear.'

Sheep had long been the easy option. They were hardy and the subsidy was reasonably generous. Yet, ecologically, they were considerably more destructive than cattle, and for decades environmentalists like Fraser Darling, and others before him, had advocated a return to cattle production. I mentioned that the collapse of the sheep subsidy might have this desirable effect.

'Yes, but the reality is we're subject to European rules. "Sheep meat", to use the in-term, is not in surplus . . . *yet*. Beef is. So it would be hard to present a case for more cattle in the Highlands, however small our contribution would be.'

Dr Hunter was in his mid-forties, a fresh-faced energetic man who looked capable of devouring government green papers over a bowl of muesli and yoghurt. He wore gold-rimmed glasses and spoke with a quiet smile of confidence. When I put it to him that some crofters seemed to pocket their subsidy and neglect the sheep for which that subsidy was being paid, and suggested that crofting had ceased to be a system of production and become an adjunct of the welfare system . . . he even smiled when annoyed.

'I find it intensely irritating when focus is always placed on crofting grants and subsidies. The sheep subsidy is open to all farmers in the UK. Yes, there is something to be said for a "lambing" subsidy which would reward good management rather than the indiscriminate act of owning breedable ewes, but that's a national issue not a crofting one.' There were two forms of grant unique to crofting, he explained. Housing, and the Crofting Commission Agricultural Grant Scheme. If one took the combined value of these two sources of grants then it totalled £4–5 million per annum. If one took the aid given to other farmers then it totalled billions. 'So if people want to moan about the degree of subsidies then don't pick on the crofters, start in East Anglia or East Lothian.'

East Lothian shuffled, tinkled and rattled crockery in the background.

'I don't believe the current level of subsidies in agriculture can possibly be maintained. Agriculture will be moved into free competition and, of course, that could spell the end of crofting agriculture as we know it. But something else must come along to take its place, and crofting, not being a full-time agricultural system, would survive such a change better. For too long the grant system has encouraged the model croft to aspire to the status of a small farm. That attitude is now changing. Look at crofting forestry, for example – assisting crofters to plant and maintain woods is a welcome change of direction.'

Since 1976 no more crofts had been allowed to be created but Dr Hunter didn't see why that decision should not be reversed. 'I'm strongly in favour of populations moving back into previously populated areas. In this respect I'm frequently at odds with conservationists who consider these areas "untouchable wilderness", though I fail to see how anyone can call previous centres of occupation in man-made landscapes "wilderness". They'd prefer to keep them as wet deserts.' He paused to let my pencil catch up.

'The current trend shows clearly that people *are* moving back into remote crofting areas in large numbers. And this is unrelated to any degree of subsidy, which is an overplayed issue in my opinion. The key to a better crofting future is to provide adequate and remunerative employment opportunities outwith crofting agriculture itself.'

I asked if he himself was a crofter?

'No. But there's a story connected with that. When my book *The Making of the Crofting Community* came out, I gave a talk in Portree. At the end a crofter came up to me and said he'd really enjoyed my book. I was trying to look suitably modest, when he added, "You must be the first person who ever made any money out of crofting."'

37

~

Midges

In the Wallace Arnold prospectus there had been no mention of *Culicoides impunctatus*, but they were becoming troublesome. Schoolgirls wearing skirts and short socks were slapping bare legs as they waited for the bus at Teangue, demonstrating how ill-conceived their uniforms were for the Highlands. And camping was becoming an ordeal for me: whenever the sun sank low or the air was damp or the breeze dropped below a scientifically measured 5.5 mph, the west coast piranhas began their feeding frenzies. Of Scotland's 34 species of midges, only four or five enjoy humans and the most indulgent by far is *C. impunctatus*, the Highland midge. Only 1.4 mm long and requiring a modest one ten-millionth of a litre of blood, *meanbh chuileag* (the tiny fly) might be tolerable if it didn't come in such thick swarms: concentrations of larvae have been estimated to reach 10 million per acre.

For forty weeks of the year, on average, midges are not a problem. They are elusive worms buried in the top one inch of regions where the rainfall exceeds 50 inches a year. Then the hordes emerge. Their acute sensors react to the carbon dioxide left in trails of exhaled breath, and enable them to home in on their meals, mainly sheep, cattle, deer, rabbits, cats, dogs and humans. Given a choice, they show a preference for their victims to be dressed in dark colours.

According to George Hendry's *Midges in Scotland*, which makes enlightening but prurient reading,

the critical step for the females is to secure a supply of fresh blood . . . without it egg development is arrested and, given the short life-span of twenty, perhaps thirty, days for the adult, this is the point on which all future generations depend absolutely . . . But blood meals are none too common in the Highlands. The Highland midge, unlike many other species, has partly solved this problem. It appears to have evolved a way of maturing and laying at least some of its first batch of eggs without a blood meal. Whether it sacrifices part of its flight-muscle, which carries a similar nutrient to blood, in order to mature the eggs is not known for certain. This process of maturing even a few eggs in the absence of a blood meal (known as autogeny) is perhaps central to the success of the Highland midge.

A sharp-eyed palaeontologist spotted the oldest known midge, a minute fossil dated at 60 million years Before Present. Three monks wrote about swatting midges in the fourteenth century. But the most intriguing evidence, negative evidence, is for the period 1750–1850. Neither Boswell nor Johnson (who seized every opportunity to complain) mentions midges. Neither does Pennant (1772), nor Wordsworth (1803) nor the entomologist H.T. Stainton (1850) who went to Arran specifically to look at its insect life. Not a single artist, naturalist or layman mentions midges.

Yet midges were written about immediately prior to and immediately after this period. In 1746, John O'Sulivan, who was a fugitive with Prince Charles Edward Stuart, wrote, 'the Prince was in a terrible condition, his legs &

thy's cut all over from the bryers; the mitches or flys wch are terrible in yt contry, devored him, & made him scratch those scars, wch made him appear as if he was cover'd with ulsers'.

So why this period of silence two hundred years ago? Undoubtedly the answer lies in the fact that midges were absent in many areas and scarce to the point of being insignificant in others. The climate is believed to have been colder (the snow-line dropped by as much as 1,200 feet) and windier. Possibly improved drainage of the bogland was partly responsible. And possibly there is a cyclical factor in the populations of the midge, which would explain why it is only recorded in Gaelic proverbs for its small size and not for its bite.

Whatever the reasons, 60 million years on in The Year Of My Journey, *Culicoides impunctatus* had made a dramatic comeback and was ravenously hungry.

38

❧

Sabhal Mor Ostaig

I had one more port of call in Skye before leaving for Rum and the rest of Scotland, and this was to a barn. The Big Barn of Ostaig was situated in the foot of Skye where it almost treads on the mainland, a region sharply contrasting to the rest of the island through its magnificent stands of deciduous trees. The animals which the barn formerly housed were privileged in having an Italianesque tower built on their home, at a time when the people round about were without food and living in hovels. The barn was the whimsical creation of the Lord MacDonald of 1776 who had just returned from a trip to Italy in the company of Adam Smith. Today Sabhal Mor Ostaig, with its £1.5-million extension, is the only Gaelic-medium college in the country.

I entered a gravel courtyard enclosed by buildings of natural stone. A student sat on some steps filling in his lunch hour with a penny whistle and I expected at any moment the stones to open and the lost children of Gaeldom to emerge in crocodile lines. A smell of curry from the canteen nullified that image.

Norman Gillies occupied what little of the Director's office was not taken up with boxes, files and piles of paper. He was cut off at the chest by what appeared to be three years' worth of correspondence, a professorial-looking man, just right for the role, with a trimmed silver-grey beard.

'Sabhal Mor Ostaig became a reality because the time was right for it. We opened in 1982 with eight students. The building wasn't even finished. People said our location was wrong and that teaching in Gaelic would never work. But they were wrong. Here we are with twenty-seven students, employing forty people and talking of more expansion.'

He extricated himself from his desk and pointed to a wall map which highlighted what was considered the Highland/Crofting/Gaelic region. 'If you exclude Orkney and Shetland, then Sabhal Mor is roughly the centre of the Highlands. We're talking about rural communities, we're trying to prepare people to make a living in rural communities – so where better could we be? With today's technology, distance is no deterrent to learning.'

The college was set up with the aim of training students of the Highlands for meaningful employment in their home areas. 'This was a totally new concept. If we'd simply been running Gaelic courses that would have been the easy option. But we're striving for something beyond the superficial language, a practical place for that language. We teach mainly business and computing studies, and ninety per cent of our graduates have remained in the Highland region.'

Currently it was a boom period of employment for Gaelic speakers. The Government's injection of cash into Gaelic television and radio was of great (but belated) significance, and schools were crying out for Gaelic teachers with posts going unfilled. If the Highland University came to fruition, a university based on the cottage industry principle with thirteen centres spread across the Highlands, Sabhal Mor Ostaig being one, this would be a further leap forward for a language whose written form predates written English by at least 1,000 years.

Yes, he felt a degree of optimism, but he was also worried. The 1981 Census gave a figure of 84,000 Gaelic speakers. The 1991 figure was down to 66,000. At the current rate of development this number could only be at best maintained, not increased. The situation, he explained, was like an inverted pyramid: many elderly speakers at the top, very few young ones below. 'It's very hard to make it the language of the community again. And to be a healthy language it has to be the everyday language of *feeling*. People have this erroneous perception that Gaelic is only a language of the fireside, that it is not a real living language. That perception must change.'

Others were cryptically pessimistic. From the Personal Column of the *West Highland Free Press* a few months later:

'ANOTHER RARE SIGHTING in Loch Caroy, mature broken mouthed Gaelic wader, searching for gnashers at low tide.'

39

Rum

All around me Rum's frayed and scabrous mountains played cat's cradle with strands of cloud. The air smelled of goat and there were strange shufflings, always out of sight round a corner, dislodging rocks into steaming corries. It looked a mythical landscape, not long in creation, where you might reasonably expect to find living proof of dragons. The eruption which had hurled Canna, Eigg and Muck as fragments of the volcano that Rum once was might still have been warm and smoking.

'The interior [of Rum] is one heap of rude mountains, scarcely possessing an acre of level land. It is the wildest and most repulsive of all the islands,' wrote one John MacCulloch in 1824.

To me it meant quite the opposite. It had a savage Icelandic beauty and a fascination which I had found irresistible ever since my first visit as a teenager. I was with a school camp at the time and we made long hikes around the island, visiting the pitch-pine shooting lodge on little Loch Papadil which was cupped in the hills but spilled its water over cliffs directly into the sea. Harris Bay was another of our explorations and here we came across a bizarre Greek temple, a mausoleum containing three sarcophagi: 'Sir George Bullough, Baronet, of Rhum,

1870–1937' was engraved on one. We ran fingers through the letters and fantasised on the lives of the monstrously rich. For we had heard all about Sir George by then.

Now I looked down the sweep of Ruinsival to Papadil and tried to discern the lodge, but I heard later it had been burned to the ground by careless climbers. Out towards Eigg a trawler was plumbing the depths of a sea that was dappled with shadow and shimmered like tinsel. I carried on to Ainshval with the light fading. On the western horizon Mingulay, Vatersay and Barra turned as black as coal and the sky above them to an intensity of fiery colours that I have never seen duplicated anywhere else in the world except Hawaii. In the gloaming the comparison lodged peacefully.

I had left my walk purposefully late, to be alone on the ridge by moonlight but darkness hugged the crags and scree-filled crenellations. Even with a torch it was hard to find a safe route that would not end abruptly and my anxiety mounted. By then I was on Askival which was the highest (2,664 feet) and the most treacherous. Suddenly I heard a cough and made out two hinds twenty-five yards away, bending their sinewy necks and staring at me. In four bounds they had disappeared. I couldn't see any way out of the crags but made my way to where the deer had been. This brought me to the edge of another impossible precipice and I stared blindly at the void.

The cough came again. This time higher up and I found a narrow gap in the rocks which had looked impenetrable. A scuffed path led me on to the next dead end. *Dead end*. The words tolled ominously in my mind. Then a nearby shuffle alerted me to the deer who were once more indicating the least likely direction. This uncanny act of guidance went on for twenty minutes. When the deer leaped out of sight for the last time, I found myself on the safe ground of Hallival.

A crossbow bolt whizzed over my head, then others. My nerves were fraught enough without adding manx shearwaters to the night but here they were, not long in from Brazil. The stones underfoot had given way to turf fed by the guano of the world's largest shearwater colony: 120,000 breeding pairs, representing one-fifth of the species' known population.

Deer, goats, shearwaters, golden and sea eagles (re-introduced 1975), reafforestation, geology and isolation are the rudiments behind Rum's triple accolade; this heap of 'rude mountains' is a National Scenic Area, National Nature Reserve and Biosphere Reserve (UNESCO). 'It is owned by the Nation and set aside by Act of Parliament for the purposes of conservation, research and education.' Just what Lady Monica wanted for the Forbidden Island.

Today the vast factory in Accrington which once supported life on Rum has been reduced to a carpark with a modest business centre on its fringe. The story starts with Sir George's grandfather, James Bullough. He never went to school and began working at a loom in a Lancashire textile mill at the age of seven. His first invention was a form of 'fuse' using locks of his sister's hair. If tension in the loom increased the hair broke before the weft and this device saved hours of lost productivity. He rose up the ranks and devised dozens of improvements which culminated in the loom that was to be the basic workhorse of the industry for decades. In 1856 he went into partnership with an engineer and founded Howard & Bullough, The Globe Works. His son, John, proved to be not only a gifted inventor in the same mould but a businessman of clairvoyant foresight. By purchasing the patent of a ground-breaking spindle, in conjunction with his own innovations, he turned The Globe Works into a truly global exporter with over 2,000 employees. Within two generations the Bulloughs became one of the richest families in Britain.

John bought Meggernie estate in Perthshire and added Rum in 1887. (Under a previous owner its population of

325 in 1772 had been cleared and reduced to fifty in 1828.) He had just four years to enjoy it. He took a new young wife who was closer in age to his son, George. It is rumoured that George and Alexandra became lovers but, if so, John can never have found out as he was certainly not of a forgiving nature. In 1891 John died and George ended the apprenticeship in Howard & Bullough which he so disliked. He tunnelled into a rock at Harris, lined the cave with monogrammed ceramics and put his father's coffin inside, but when a friend saw it and remarked that it looked like a public lavatory, George was aghast. He removed his father, dynamited the cave and built a Greek temple nearby.

Now free and with an annual income of £300,000, he embarked on a world tour for almost three years amassing a priceless collection of souvenirs and photographs. On his return he wasted no time in purchasing his own luxury steam yacht, the 221-foot SY *Rhouma*, and establishing an annual custom of holding a ball in Madeira on her deck. In 1901 he was knighted for lending *Rhouma* to the British government for a year as a hospital ship in the Boer War. A less charitable – and unfounded – story attributes the honour as secret recompense for taking one of the royal mistresses off Edward VII's hands. The woman in question was Monica Charrington, a scandalous society belle and divorcee who claimed descent from Napoleon. George married her in 1903. They had one daughter, Hermione, a pale and sickly child who nevertheless endured as the Countess of Durham and lived into her eighties.

It was still the heyday of the nouveau riche and although George Bullough would always remain trade – like Jesse Boot the Cash Chemist and Clark of Clark's Thread – and never be admitted to the highest class of blood aristocracy, he was powerful enough to play god within his own estates. Of all the extravagant follies built in Scotland – and there were many –

none surpassed what George created on the island he called Rhum.

He imported workers from Uddingston and Accrington to build a castle, dressed them in his own Rhum tartan kilts and when the midges became intolerable he averted a threatened strike by paying a tobacco allowance of 2d a week. At least, so it is said. The plans for Kinloch Castle were drawn up in London. Red sandstone was quarried 170 miles away in Arran and transported to Rum, and it was rumoured that 250,000 tons of soil were shipped in from Ayrshire for the ornamental gardens.

Kinloch Castle, a mere shooting lodge, was built by chance close to the oldest known remains of man in Scotland, a mesolithic site occupied 8,500 years ago. Sir George represented the extreme opposite of the mesolithic lifestyle. A nine-hole golf course and a walled garden with an avenue of 100 metres under glass were laid out. One section contained a heated pool in which alligators and turtles were kept as pets, while hummingbirds flew freely in the Camellia House.

Inside the castle no expense was spared. Rum's mansion was among the earliest in Scotland to boast electricity. Fans in the billiard room changed the air every twenty minutes. The double-glazed windows were unique in that they opened outwards in parallel and channelled a breeze into the castle during summer. The combination shower-baths were also pure innovation. Each bath had a 'sentry box' built-in to one end and an array of taps enabled jets of water to be aimed up, down, sideways in any combination or in an all-on blitz. The dining room's chairs came from *Rhouma* and swivelled to allow ladies in chiffon dresses to park themselves at their place with decorum.

The early years of the century were heady days for the Bulloughs. Sir George's dogs were frequent champions at Crufts and his race horses won every honour including the Grand National. By then the island's resident population was around sixty (including two maids who were sequestered on their own to run the laundry, six miles out of sight of the guests) and this doubled during his annual visits which usually amounted to no more than a few weeks. But the game book shows other guests made regular use of the castle. At first mainly army officers but increasingly those with impressive titles. Not appearing in ink but recorded in hearsay are the groups of Gaiety Girls who travelled from London to Oban by train and from there were delivered by *Rhouma* to the resident orchestra and sprung, oak floor of Kinloch's ballroom. Is this true? In a story where many of the wildest images have been verified, it might be rash to dismiss this one. After all, Sir George's half-brother did marry a Gaiety Girl and the laird's antics in his bachelor days travelled as far as the gossip columns of New Zealand's newspapers.

In 1914 Sir George taught his fourteen gardeners to ride ponies and sent them to enlist. Only two returned. Sir George and Lady Monica never lost their enthusiasm for Rum but the golden age of Edwardian high-living had also been a fatality of the Great War. Kinloch Castle became a shadow of its former self. The garden and golf course were resumed by wood and weeds. Rum faded into obscurity. Outsiders had never been welcomed and few came. The mystique of the 'Forbidden Island' remained inviolate.

Sir George died suddenly, aged 69, on a golf course in France in 1939. Lady Monica survived another thirty years, bequeathing the island, castle and all its contents to the nation in 1957, ten years before her death at the grand age of 98.

Today Kinloch Castle is a hotel. Dinner, bed, breakfast and revolutionary showers cost £72, inc VAT.

I camped.

It was as if the Bulloughs had only just nipped out for a pint of Accrington bitter. Pull open a drawer and there was a bridge scorecard from the 1920s. Sir George's large knee-boots (he was six feet five inches tall) stood beside his bed.

'Careful!' warned Iain MacArthur, the manager, just in time as I almost lodged my foot in the gaping jaws of a lion lying steamrollered on the floor.

'This is rather special . . . probably what everyone remembers about the place. It was built for Queen Victoria so the Germans made a particularly nice job of it. She died before delivery, so Sir George was able to pick it up for a song. Oh! . . . for *a song*! . . .unintended pun, but really rather good. Now what shall we try?' He fumbled among scrolls of perforated paper entitled, 'Belle of New York', 'Geisha', 'Bohemian Girl', 'Die Meistersinger' . . . and fed 'William Tell' into the orchestrion. Behind glass doors an assembly of organ pipes, percussion and simulated wind instruments burst into vocal life.

We went through the 'Empire Room' where Lady Monica's Napoleonic genes were celebrated, passed below two enormous tarpon, the stuffed His and Hers remnants of a pleasant (for the Bulloughs, at least) afternoon's fishing off Florida – Hers was only half a tarpon because a shark had eaten the tail end while it was being played – and entered the billiard room where the air was still changed every twenty minutes.

'Oh dear, Ellen *always* gets them the wrong way round,' Mr MacArthur sighed, swapping the positions of the green and yellow.

The tour of opulence continued. The castle was the treasury of Sir George's World Tour souvenirs. We passed under the beak of an eagle weighing five tons which must have thrilled the coolies who had to deliver it to the steamer. Sadly the life-sized ivory eagle for which Sir George had outbid the Emperor of Japan at the 1895 Kyoto Exhibition was absent. Considered too valuable it had been relocated to the National Museum in Edinburgh. Then came a pair of gigantic *cloisonné* vases from China. They stood on slender bases, rose up to chest height, bulged, contracted into thin necks and then flowered into wide mouths. As we passed the second of these priceless creations, Mr MacArthur, deep in a soliloquy on the castle's history, screwed up a piece of litter he'd found and casually tossed it into the vase.

'Sorry to interrupt . . . but did you just . . . ?'

'What . . . ?'

'I thought I saw you throw some litter into that vase?'

He looked about him perplexed, unaware of the vase, let alone the litter. 'Did I really? Oh well, we empty them about every ten years.'

Mr MacArthur had to break off the tour to attend to the day's guests who were about to arrive. I browsed through Sir George's bound photograph albums: Ceylon, India (six volumes), China, Japan, New Caledonia, Australia, South Africa, Natives of the World . . . He had recorded beheadings in the Boxer Revolution, the crucifixion of dacoits in Burma, views of Calcutta and Rangoon with streets so clean the cities were unrecognisable to a modern traveller, Chinese in the goldfields of New Zealand, colonial life in Tasmania, a John Dunn in Zululand with some of his reputed forty wives . . .

'If you're wanting the ferry, it's about to leave.'

As I left this preposterous castle – squashed into arches and towers, pink and so utterly incongruous it was magnificent – I met the new arrivals. If they didn't realise it, they were playing the part to perfection. To a man they wore plus-fours that had never seen active service and carried cromags not long out of wrapping paper. It looked as if they'd received the entire outfits for Christmas. Probably from Harrods. After all, that was where Sir George and Lady Monica had shopped. Their order books still exist. Delivery address: Rhum, North Britain.

40

Mrs C-H, Inverailort Castle

Max MacLeod writes incomprehensible cartoon scripts for the *Glasgow Herald* and lives for the after-dinner story; he has met the bulk of Scotland's eccentric and authoritative figures and knows many a tale about them; incisively probing, his wit cuts through the hardest of façades and, triumphantly clutching the rib of truth, he reconstructs an effigy that parodies faults to their extreme or elevates qualities into expressions of almost painful beauty; his is the art of story-telling *par excellence*.

Max was a friend of many years' standing. We were the same age and of a similar restlessness. Max had interrupted my journey to ask if I would take the photographs for an article he was doing for the *Herald* on stalking. We had met some miles to the south of where the ferry from Rum tied up, and endured a sodden day at the killing.

'You've met Mrs C-H, of course, haven't you, Scottie?' It was a nickname I'd last been branded with at the age of ten, but Max could call you a bastard and make it sound a compliment. He was always coming out with things like this. 'Mrs Cameron-Head? Inverailort Castle? No? Good God, you can't die without meeting her.'

The country did not possess five square miles where

Max did not know of at least one Salt of the Earth. So we diverted to Inverailort Castle.

'I'll quickly fill you in. You're about to experience the last bastion of Highland hospitality, the last truly open house. Always thronging with guests. Mrs C-H . . . everyone calls her that . . . doesn't really give a damn about the castle or money. Sees herself as a temporary custodian of something worth sharing. 'Course, it's still feudalism, *but* feudalism with a conscience. There's not a soul who knows her who believes she would ever let them down. She's created a feeling in the community that the house and the land are, somehow . . . common to everyone.'

He caught my quizzical look in a glance between bends in the road, and continued. 'Personally, I *loathe* the estate system because it's so abused by power-hungry idiots who come up from the south and try to buy into being a laird, try to buy into the respect Mrs C-H has earned. The tragedy is that so few new lairds have the wit or application to fulfil their responsibilities. Many in the Highlands would prefer living under a good laird to any other system, but there's too few Mrs C-Hs, Lochiels of Lochaber and John Lorne Campbells of Canna.' Look at Eigg, Knoydart and Morvern, he said, where there was no longer a single landlord of substance in an area the size of the Isle of Wight. Look at Skye, he added, where 400 people were said to have no homes other than caravans, while as many holiday cottages lay empty. 'Look at it all, and weep. You know, you and I . . . we're writing Scotland's obituary.'

We drove a long way in silence, each lost in his own thoughts. Suddenly Max said: 'I'd better warn you. When we get there, don't inhale too deeply.'

'What d'you mean?'

'Cats' piss.'

We drove between two tall gateposts whose rusty gates had fallen from their pivots and stood slumped alongside.

Rhododendrons flanked us as we negotiated a pothole 200 yards long, and reached the gravel bay of a three-storey house that was undistinguished except for being very large. Rain drummed the roof of the car with the ferocity of hail. We dashed for the main doors which were of a siege-resistant variety, unfurnished with bell or knocker but unlocked, and entered a porch whose lead-lined windows bulged outwards. A light cough would have wreaked havoc. Two outboard engines were clamped to the base of a hat-stand.

'You do know these people reasonably well, don't you?'

I was already phrasing an apology for our trespass.

Max ignored this and led the way into a great hall from which a staircase with a balustrade of slender twists of wood led up into walls of portraits. In the stairwell a stuffed fox wore a stack of three hats, the day's tally of redundant headgear. The hall was generously furnished. Old noble furniture. Chairs of the epoch when comfort meant comfort. Carpets stained with history. Buckets set out to catch leaks. Kinloch Castle was an art gallery, was *trade*. Inverailort Castle was a home, aristocracy. Everything was tired and faded. The air reeked of cats' piss.

A door on my left stated in large gold letters, 'COMMAN-DER'. Others, 'WRNS', and 'INSTRUCTOR COMMANDER'. 'This was the Headquarters of the Special Operations Executive in the war,' Max explained. 'Mrs C-H was posted here. The laird proposed to her on an island in Loch Eilt. He was twenty-five years older than her. Died years ago.' *Splotch* said a bucket. 'Isn't this marvellous. I often think Mrs C-H could make a fortune letting it to Rentokil for training weeks.'

He flicked through a fat book lying on a table. 'Visitors' book. Fascinating stuff. You'll find the names of cabinet ministers, social workers, foreign students, literati, the handicapped, all life's elevated and put-down, all mixed in together. And they all left better people for having been here.' *Plitsch. Splotch.*

Two greyhounds came sprinting along a corridor followed by a sheepdog. Max peered down the dimly lit passage as though expecting more. 'That's funny. There always used to be a resident sheep.'

'Who's that?' called a voice, and without waiting for an answer, added, 'You're just in time for dinner.' Barbara appeared. She was Mrs C-H's factotum, and Max's cousin, it turned out. 'Oh it's you, Max! How nice to see you!'

At the far end of the passage was the sign: POST OFFICE. I asked if that was a relic of the war days too. 'No, that's actually Lochailort's current post office,' Barbara replied. She was postmistress. 'Used to be at the station and then the school but they both closed. When no other suitable place came up, Mrs C-H offered her morning room.'

We went into the kitchen which was a shambles of food, packets, dishes and cats. Gingers, tortoiseshells, tigers, tabbies, toms . . . eyes peered from dark cavities in laden shelves and balls of fluff slumbered on the plate rack above the Rayburn. The place had not seen paint since the army moved in, or out.

'These are the touches I love,' Max remarked, pointing to a piece of paper pinned to a cupboard. 'Here we are in a house full of superb furniture turning into mould and they're collecting vouchers to get forty pence off jars of coffee.'

Mrs C-H was in poor health. She would be down for dinner soon, Barbara said, so why didn't we join the other guests in the drawing room? There was a Dr and Mrs So-and-So, old Colonel Whats-his-name and an awfully nice couple whose name she'd forgotten . . . 'Help yourselves to sherry.' After thirty years of working here, Barbara was used to the steady drift of anonymous guests and had become an extension of Mrs C-H's attitudes and extraordinary generosity.

The Colonel, the So-and-Sos and the Awfully Nices were not in the drawing room so we had the blazing fire to ourselves. It was the only hint of warmth in the place apart from in the kitchen. Max was absorbed into a chair and mused, 'Ahh, Scottie, what lies have been told here!'

I stood in the doorway looking into the hall and gazed at Mrs Cameron-Head who stared back down at me from within her frame of canvas.

'She was a very out-spoken councillor in her day, always striving to improve the area,' Max reminisced. 'She can be tough . . . but heart of gold. She'll turn up on her tenants' doorstep with a replacement washing machine if she hears theirs has broken. That's what this run-down castle is all about – given her money away.' The C-Hs never charged for stalking, and each year they opened their house to city kids for a holiday. 'Inverailort's hospitality is a part of Celtic legend now. They say Mrs C-H once served afternoon tea to a couple who thought the place was a hotel, and they didn't discover their mistake till they asked for the bill and were told there wasn't one.'

On canvas Mrs C-H looked extremely tall, easily over six feet. Her dark hair was pulled back behind her ears, accentuating a prominent nose and somewhat masculine features. If the artist had swapped her tweeds and stout leather shoes for something more flamboyant and ragged, and given her a basket to carry, Mrs C-H could have passed for a shrewd, street-wise gypsy.

'Did they have children?'

'No. No heirs. A few nephews, though. I don't know what they'll do with this place. Probably tear it down and build a hotel. No, Scottie, this place represents the last hurrah of a complex system of land management that has worked well in many parts of the Highlands since before Somerled. I'm not saying that feudalism is the answer. What I'm saying is that there's something right in this house, something that ties in with Schumacher's notion of his idealised forty-person community. Something that sings back to days of great halls and the great traditions of the clans, and I tell you, I love it truly.'

The dinner gong went. We went through to the dining room and found the others already seated. I realised at once that I was a few years too late to meet the real Mrs C-H. She sat at the head of table, dressed in the same immaculate tweeds, but she was a shadow of her portrait. Introductions were made and we sat down to smoked salmon.

'I can't do much talking but I love listening to others,' Mrs C-H said, before being seized by a fit of breathlessness. Her voice was strong but the tone was that of Oates about to go out into the blizzard. The Colonel and the others looked subdued and starched. Stern ancestors scrutinised us from dark backgrounds – an illegible Cameron, Coll MacDonnell, Alexander MacDonnell, 3rd of Barrisdale and Mallaig – there was time to study and memorise their names. Max bravely provided anecdotes and cheer.

Wine was served. Beef stew and vegetables were followed by a delectable Financial Times. 'No, I don't know why it's called that. It's just always been called FT,' Mrs C-H assured me. '*Do* have some more to eat everybody. Eat as much as you can.'

Later, as we made our way upstairs to our rooms (*splotch, plitsch, splotch*) I looked again at the portrait and this time I could see the softness behind that hard edge. And I could imagine this legend in uniform, strong and blustery, striding through the officers in 1943 announcing, 'Come on, you must eat up, we've got a war to win, *do* have some more,' and then secretly opening the back door to let the lambs and ewes in because the weather was being unusually inclement.

I felt drunk but it wasn't the two glasses of wine at fault. It was the furniture with its crooked legs, the warped walls and the floorboards angled askew. The house's distorted verticals didn't give balance a chance. But they didn't seem to affect the greyhounds. At intervals throughout the night I heard them racing through the corridors, from the Post Office to 'COMMANDER', up the stairs, past me, past the Colonel and the Awfully Nices, on and on to the Catholic chapel at the far end.

The following day Max and I returned to our separate lives. I to my bicycle and the road south, Max to a stranded sperm whale and another piece for the *Herald*.

Exactly ten days later I read of the death of Mrs Cameron-Head, aged 76. The news depressed me, as much for her passing as for what went with her. Her obituary – factual, humorous, poignant, absurd, and abounding with *largesse* – did her proud. It was written by Max.

41

❧

Ardtoe Fish Research Unit

Knoydart, Morar, Moidart, Sunart, Ardgour. Big bold names running down my map. In Ordnance Survey Sheet 40 Scotland is at its most crumpled. Its contours gather in the tightest concentrations and form a square yard of swirling brown eddies. They yield nothing to the level or the mundane and even when land turns to sea or loch they produce the deepest bodies of water in the country, deeper even than Loch Ness. This is Scotland's forgotten corner, where the fewest people visit, where the weather is at its filthiest and where the land is so maddeningly beautiful it's enough to drive anyone into maudlin decline.

I was able to cope, though, with ten gears, two legs and my defences up. The gears and the legs took care of the mobility side of things and as the land tilted this way, then more, and more, and then, weeeaaaahhhooooosh, the other, I found myself making steady progress along a road that had been constructed largely as a result of Mrs C-H's lobbying and had revitalised a dozen communities. And sheer determination kept sentimentality in rein as I cruised through a dozen postcards, two calendars and a shortbread tin lid.

The copper mile of shoreside bladder wrack was undeniably attractive even though the shaggy bundles of horned cattle chewing it looked stage-managed. The crusty mountains muscling their way over the moor were not *that* unusual, nor were the fingers of mist coddling their gullies, and nor were their veins of cascading burns. But I couldn't help feeling a thrill when oaks and beeches crowded the road and threw great umbrellas of foliage over my head, frequently parting to reveal glades of ferns and trapped sunlight. Old drystane dykes frequented the scene too, only moss and lichens had turned them into green abstractions of padded velvet. But it was Castle Tioram which was my undoing. It appeared through a gap in the trees, its ruined walls standing forlorn yet rudely proud on an island amidst all this crashing grandeur. At any moment I expected a megaphone to boom: 'CUT...CAN WE HAVE MORE MIST UP THERE, PLEASE, AND A FEW MORE CATTLE LEFT OF CENTRE...OK, READY EVERYONE...CAMERAS ROLLING...' Mentally, I was just no match for this countryside.

Ardtoe. The name rang a bell but I couldn't place it. The map showed it to be on the sort of road I always tried to take, a wiggly runt of a specimen leading to nothing of obvious interest, so I took it. When I came to what looked like a fish farm and saw a sign, I remembered more about the bell. His name, I think, was Herbert and he was definitely a halibut. I had read about him in the paper, falling, in cliché fashion, off the back of a lorry while *en route* from a trawler to Ardtoe. Instead of ending up as a god-sent supper to the following motorist, Herbert was rescued and delivered intact. Ardtoe Marine Farming Unit was a government-sponsored research centre looking into ways of turning all sorts of sea creatures into factory production lines, and I chanced on its annual open day.

'Lobsters,' said the guide, 'have a cutting claw and a crushing claw.' He pointed a bandaged finger to the appropriate appendages behind the glass. The lobster sat like a redundant pile of mechanics' tools gaily painted blue, black and yellow. It blew a bubble, and miniature feelers by its mouth continued conducting a silent symphony.

'We pay local fishermen a premium to supply us with females with roe. We've found that by rearing the young in warmer water and feeding them well, then releasing them into the sea, we can get a lobster to marketable size in five years instead of seven. This is, unfortunately, not yet a practical solution but we're still working on it.'

I asked about his finger. 'Occupational hazard, I'm afraid. We're honour-bound not to damage the creatures in our care so if we get seized, we have to soothe the lobster into letting go.'

'How do you soothe a lobster?'

'I don't know. I'm still working on that one too.'

I moved on to the halibut department. I was most excited about this but unfortunately I discovered that halibut are extremely sensitive about light, temperature and vibration; especially during spawning, and they were spawning at that moment. Their lids remained on their tanks and I was diverted to see an audio-visual entitled 'Halibut Behaviour in Cages'. This was a sea-sick inducing piece of camerawork in which a diver jerked his way along endless netting looking for fish. He had only found one by the time I walked out after ten minutes, and it had wisely shot out of frame. Unlike 'A Fish Called Wanda', 'Halibut Behaviour in Cages' seemed to be missing its main star.

Disappointed at having been cheated of a halibut sighting, I tracked down a bespectacled scientist in nursing white who held a few miniatures in a beaker.

'Halibut may live for forty years and grow enormous. Up to eight feet long and seven hundred pounds in weight. Farming them will only be viable if the price stays above five or six pounds sterling per pound weight. The problem we've got to beat is a good food supply for the halibut larvae. If we could devise a dried food . . . wonderful, but at present we have to breed live food for them. They're very pernickety . . .' He hesitated after the word as if wanting to add '. . . little bastards'. Their pernicketiness had clearly cost him years and hair.

'Have a look here.' I put my eye to a microscope and saw brine shrimps cavorting in spasms. '*Artemia*. Not bad as food, but need huge amounts of them. Better is the plankton *calanoid copepod*. Lots of nutrition but again we can't get enough.'

Young halibut began life looking like a normal fish. They ate *artemia* and *copepod* and grew. They progressed to becoming mid-water fish, only to suffer one of the worst kinds of middle-aged crisis: their faces slipped and their eyes moved round to the right side of their head until they could see nothing below them. Their bodies flattened and they became bottom dwellers.

Ardtoe was keeping ahead of the Norwegians. They swapped information, but Ardtoe had maintained the lead. I wondered if it was something to do with the whisky bottles which lined the walls on shelves, large bottles of the size you only see in raffles and collecting coins for charity on bar counters. No, the scientist assured me, wearily, that they were just convenient containers. They were growing *copepod* cultures.

'You can see *copepod* in this microscope,' he remarked.

I looked at another transparent organism that was waving two transparent sausages. 'Are those waving bits its food?'

The scientist bent to the eyepiece. 'Oh! Where did they come from? Oh Lord! . . . parasites. I haven't seen this type before . . .'

The interview was terminated. As I left the laboratory I heard the scientist say to a colleague, 'I think we're about to have a population crash here. New parasite. I'd better give Norway a ring.'

Modern story, old theme.

42

∞

Prince Charles Edward Stuart –
The 1745 Association

That this was perfect fugitive country was immediately apparent to one whose eye naturally tended to assess a landscape in terms of its ability to hide, shelter and sustain life, my own life. It was a trick, an exercise in perception practised by such masters of survival as the Innuit, in which the mind ceased to regard distance and nature as an adversary but as a supplier of all one's needs. The 'hiding' aspect was my own personal slant, a relic of a childish game in which I looked for places to go when my world collapsed, or when my ship came in and I didn't want to take it. Moidart, I decided, would be high on my list.

Just how perfect it was for a fugitive was made doubly obvious by the cairns, caves and signs dedicated to the memory of the region's most famous fugitive. I had first encountered a monument to 'H.R.H. Prince Charles Edward Stuart' near Stornoway, a cairn built two miles out of harm's way and the public eye, recording the fact that he spent a few days milling around the fabrication yard. On Eriskay the first dozen stones of a proposed cairn had been gathered and an appeal launched by the island's children for visitors to bring more, for the Prince had landed inconsiderately on a beach remarkably bereft of loose rock. But around Moidart and Glenfinnan the Charliefication of the landscape had peaked.

In a shop I bought a booklet entitled *The Bonnie Prince Charlie Country* (1971).

'Though the [Jacobite] Rising failed,' said the text, 'its failure in God's Providence sent Highland men and women to many parts of the World. In the illustrious annals of Scotland and England, of Canada, Australia, New Zealand, the USA and elsewhere, Highland men and women and their descendants hold an honoured place and they have made great contributions to the growth and greatness of these countries. Their descendants in their thousands return yearly to the land of their ancestors to be inspired and encouraged by the ever-fresh memory of their gallant exploits in that fair and lovely land which has changed so little since Bonnie Prince Charlie left it for ever. That land of loch and ben and silver sea seems aye to sing: Will ye no come back again?'

Had this been written in 1871, or as the closing scene for a Broadway musical with smoke wafting across a backlit Charlie holding out his white cockade at half-mast while the New York State Choir thundered out '*BETTER LOVED YE CANNA BE*', then I could have understood the sentiment, but in 1971? Do they write up the London Plague of 1665 as a jolly good spring clean and knees-up?

It was of course the factor's writ more than 'God's Providence' which sent Highlanders abroad, and that they benefited other countries so ably cost Scotland dearly. And now they may return yearly to be inspired, but at a cost of suffering Scotland's plethora of tawdry souvenir shops selling Korean knick-knacks, our disintegrated transport network, our slapstick restaurants with surly, harassed staff who shut shop at seven; they marvel at our discourtesy and lack of service. The land may have changed very little if you disregard the eradication of its people and its neglect by irresponsible landlords, but that is a sad and empty admission rather than a boast. And as for inviting Charlie back again . . . well, yes, we probably would but on the tight contract offered to ice skaters and boxers for the endorsement of a product, the tourist industry.

The organisation responsible for the most subtle and tasteful of Moidart's testimonials was a reclusive group of non-commercial twentieth-century Jacobites called The 1745 Association. My image of fiery cross-wielding Ku-Klux-Klan lookalikes faded when I got hold of their manifesto. The Association presented the phlegmatic face of a School Examination Board.

Prince Charles Edward Stuart's fan club mystified me. Quite why we should wish to deify a half-Polish Scot whose utter selfishness cost thousands of lives and precipitated, if not wholly caused, half a century of reprisal and repression, has never been clear to me. Here, briefly, are some of the lesser known facts.

Charles Edward Louis Phillipe Casimir Stuart was born in Rome on 20 December, 1720. His mother was Princess Maria Clementina Sobieska of Poland, and his father, James, 'the Old Pretender' and son of the exiled King James VII of Scotland (and II of England). The ambition to restore his family to the throne was instilled in him from birth. He was raised a Catholic but had both Catholic and Protestant tutors. He is said to have 'distinguished himself' at the battle of Gaeta in 1734, even though only 14 years old at the time.

His first invasion attempt, a direct assault on England, failed before it left Dunkirk, for a gale wrecked the French fleet on loan to him as it lay in port. For his second attempt he decided to go via the back door, but by then French support had diminished and he arrived in Scotland with two brigs and seven companions, the Seven Men of Moidart (one of whom was English). Had the Macdonalds of Clanranald and Keppoch, and the Camerons, not turned out to offer support, that would have been the end of the affair. It was a poor showing but Charles was nothing if not an optimist.

The reasons why these Highlanders risked fire and sword to uphold the cause of Jacobitism were complex but romanticism played no part. They fought because they were honour-bound to obey their chiefs, to protect their Episcopalian and Catholic faiths, to assert their rights against increasing marginalisation, and for the compulsive need to oppose the powerful Campbells who always sided with whoever was in power. Theirs was no blind loyalty to an ethic.

By the time the Prince reached Edinburgh, so confident was he of success that he had banknotes printed for use after his victory. He won no support from Glasgow and was only dissuaded from ransacking the place by a hasty donation of £10,000 and 6,000 pairs of boots. He marched south. The day the Prince and his army reached Derby, just 125 miles from London, became known as 'Black Friday' and it threw the capital into consternation. Depositors made a rush to withdraw funds from the Bank of England which paid out in sixpences to win time, and George II is alleged to have begun preparations to flee. But at Derby the squabblesome Jacobite leaders decided to retreat.

That the Prince, after Culloden, did not go the way of Wallace and Montrose and suffer betrayal was possibly a matter of time. Nevertheless it is still a source of wonder to both historians and romantics that he managed to remain a fugitive for five months with a reward of £30,000 (over £1 million in today's terms) on his head, and make good his escape to France.

The last forty years of the Prince's life, spent in Italy,

are neither bonnie nor mentioned by his PR industry. In 1750 he is believed to have made a secret visit to England in disguise. When renewed attempts to elicit support for another invasion met with no success he had a medal struck showing his profile above the legend to which his vanity clung: *Amor et Spes Britanniae* (the Love and Hope of Britain). His frustration drove him to despair, drink and women. His father died in 1766, and he assumed the title of King. In 1772 he married Louise, Princess of Stolberg. They had no children. Brandy bloated his body. He beat his wife. His last years were lonely, nursed by his 25-year-old illegitimate daughter, Charlotte.

He died of a paralytic stroke in Florence on 31 January 1788, aged 68, and was buried by his younger and only brother, Henry, Cardinal Duke of York, at his cathedral in Frescati (near Rome). Henry, last of the direct line of the Stuart dynasty and an avowed celibate, acknowledged George III as the rightful heir to the Stuarts before his death in 1807. The bodies, in urns marked James III, Charles III and Henry IX, were later taken to the crypt of St Peter's, and Pope Pius VII commissioned Canova to sculpture a monument for their grave. The Prince Regent (later George IV) contributed £50 to its cost.

On the surface, the Young Pretender's failure was slight – against vastly superior odds he failed to secure his father's just claim to the throne – but it is on the consequences of that failure and the destructive forces it unleashed that he should be judged. Yet this is overlooked as a minor crack in the image. His current fame rests on the fact that he *almost* succeeded, and in a country desperately short of major home victories we have to create heroes where we can.

The secretary of the 1745 Association lived in Ardgour, conveniently close to my route, and I went to see what all this Charliefication was about.

'We're a non-political historical association whose objectives are three-fold,' explained Miss Ainslie. 'To study the Jacobite period, to record and preserve the memory of those who actively participated in, or who had connections with the Forty-Five, and to mark the appropriate sites. We were founded in 1948.'

'But it was all a disaster. Why does the Forty-Five continue to hold such an obsession for people?'

'I was afraid for one moment you were going to say "rebellion". It wasn't a rebellion. The Stuarts were the rightful heirs. Ooh, it does annoy me when people refer to it as a "rebellion". It was a "rising". Anyway, there was much that was noble and courageous in it – we believe those attributes should be recognised and we're keen to establish the truth when so much has been turned to romantic and commercial myth. This was a turning-point in our history. History is important. It's what we share in common, it bonds us together.'

'Did Bonnie Prince Charlie—'

'That does annoy me too. Of course, I understand why people call him that, but I'm a purist. Prince Charles Edward Stuart is correct. Charlie is undoubtedly a corruption of Tearlach which would have been the Gaelic name used by the Highlanders. And he was good-looking too. Clever, witty, and, my goodness, athletic! What stamina and fitness he had! If there'd been Olympics in those days, mark my words, he would have represented us at them. By the way, we generally refer to him as The Prince.'

Miss Ainslie was an authority on The Rising. She was a retired lecturer in agriculture and had come to this area precisely because of The Prince's connections. She was in her sixties and looked uncomfortably clamped in the jaws of a deckchair, wearing a dress of green polka dots and a white mushroom of a straw hat which cast a mesh of shadows over her face. We sat in her garden, drinking tea and inhaling a heavy fragrance of pollen, without molestation by the *mitches* which had so plagued The Prince.

'I wanted to be where I could feel HIS presence' – (I imagined she would have used capitals) – and this was the fourth cottage I looked at. I just knew it was right. Immediately I saw it, the Prince's words came back to me. "I have come home."' She adored eighteenth century history. 'I read it, think it, live it. It was a time of great music, building and happenings.'

'If the Stuarts' claim to the throne was legitimate, why were they given the name "Pretenders"?'

'This is a completely spurious name. The Stuarts, as I've already said, had the most legitimate claim. James the Eighth, as we call him, was the son of James the Seventh. His nickname "the Old Pretender" comes from the French verb *prétendre* which means "to claim" *not* "to pretend". Very similar French and English words but completely different meanings.' She sighed. 'Oh dear. There's so much that's been distorted. Take Glenfinnan . . . the monument is supposed to mark the exact spot of the Raising of the Standard. The National Trust have even put up one of their hideous centres beside it. But it's quite clearly in the wrong place. No one would hear a thing on that flat land. Then some twenty years ago the heather went on fire near the priest's house – he used to drink a bit – and a Latin inscription carved on a smooth rock face was revealed. It said that the standard was raised there. But it's a steep knoll. Tullibardine was an old man. Could barely walk. He'd never have made it up to that knoll.' Miss Ainslie knew all the characters, their virtues and ailments. She thought it much more likely that the real spot was somewhere below this knoll.

'You don't approve of the National Trust's commemoration of the Prince?'

'Pure commercialism. Have you seen what they've done to Culloden? It's a disgrace. Restaurant, bookshop . . . after all, this is a battlefield, this is a cemetery. Blood was shed there.'

Two hundred and fifty years on, Culloden was still

a source of violated sensibilities. But in The 1745 Association Miss Ainslie had found her own Jacobite army of 300 strong. They produced three magazines a year and met for an annual dinner.

'Our members come from all over.' Miss Ainslie added proudly. 'One is a priest in Africa.'

Jacobitism had spread its roots wide. It was safe for the next quarter millennium. Sprigs of white heather would continue to appear mysteriously on Canova's sculptures in the crypt of St Peter's.

43

❧

Glensanda Superquarry

In the summer of 1980 a yacht sailed along Loch Linnhe and dropped two men off at a ruined castle on an uninhabited stretch of the north shore. One of them was English, the other American and they were both in their twenties. For eight days they posed as hiker-campers and lived off whisky and Spam. Each day they walked the slopes of Beinn Mheadhoin above Glensanda, one of them hacking off pieces of rock and the other loading them into his backpack and carrying them down to the castle where they were hidden in numbered bags. The 'donkeyman' made three trips a day, carrying sixty pounds of rocks each time. On the eighth day the pick-up yacht was late so one of them walked six miles to the nearest house at Kingairloch to phone. There he met a tall woman in her seventies with a sheathknife strapped to her waist, being towed along by two straining black labradors. She said he could use her phone, later admitting that she thought the man was a shipwrecked American. The pick-up was successful.

The yacht was owned by Yeoman, senior, whose company, Foster Yeoman Limited, ran Europe's largest quarry in Somerset. Having read a government report on the predicted world shortage of aggregates, he decided to take his yacht up the west coast to prospect for promising sites. He invited his son, who was attending a mining college in the USA, to choose a friend and collect samples from the Glensanda area where the Strontian Granite Complex, the largest granite mass in the UK, met the sea in conveniently deep water.

As a result of the samples which Yeoman junior and Kurt collected, Yeoman senior began negotiations with the sheathknife-wearing landowner. Mrs Strutt, aware that 'for too long Morvern's only export has been people', agreed to sell part of her estate.

Anyone looking to Morvern from the south will not see anything of the quarry itself because it is 2,000 feet above sea level and two miles away into the hills, but they will see a massive red wound by the sea. This is the 'space' that has been cleared to store the quarry's produce awaiting shipment. Five million tonnes of crushed granite leave here each year, soon to rise to 15 million tonnes. Some of these now serve as ballast for the Chunnel railtrack but the predominant use of current output is to support the motorways of Europe (a mile of motorway uses 40,000 tonnes of aggregates). The 'milk run' to Amsterdam is a six-day round trip for one of Foster Yeoman's 'dedicated, self-unloading ships'.

The process of reducing 450 million tonnes of mountain to a gigantic hole and transporting the excavate to the sea is ingenious. Foster Yeoman burrowed horizontally for two miles into solid granite. They were then 1,000 feet directly below the site of their intended quarry. A Canadian company was called in to create a vertical shaft; using a mechanical mole they started at the *bottom* and worked upwards, the mole gnawing at the rock, excreting it below, jacking itself up and gnawing once again. With Biblical exactitude it broke the surface on the fortieth day. All 450 million tonnes of rock will be crushed and poured into this hole, the Glory Hole, and travel by conveyor belt along the tunnel to the sea. As long as the hole is kept full, apparently, it won't clog. One day the Glory Hole will cease to exist, as the rock around it is removed and the quarry floor descends to meet the horizontal tunnel.

'I dislike the term "superquarry"', Kurt explained as we drove up into the clouds and a light confetti of snow. 'Like superman, supermarkets and such like, there's an impression of something abnormal and bullyish about the term. This is the only *large* coastal quarry in the country. Actually, we don't consider ourselves to be simply a "quarry", we're a fully integrated materials handling, marketing and distribution concept.'

Kurt had clearly done well at college. I could see at once why Yeoman senior had put him in charge of this entire operation and made him a director of the company. Even though he was still in his early thirties, he had come a long way since being a shipwrecked American. His manner was typically West Atlantic: warm, deceptively casual and, you felt, Harvard-efficient. 'KEEP OUT' signs didn't exist, walkers were welcome. Red deer loved the place. They always know a safe haven. I saw more deer around the plant than humans. Kurt employed 150 people here. None of them came from Morvern but from Oban and Fort William. The quarry picked them up by boat for each shift.

I peered into the Glory Hole but there was nothing discernible but a small pile of rocks. It was full; a stationary tornado 1,000 feet deep. The quarry itself was quiet for maintenance. I tried to transplant it to Rodel and see how it sat. In a virtual white-out it looked fine, and £24 million spent on wages so far looked even better.

'When we finish each section here we'll leave a stepped wall which we'll be patty-caking with peat, heather and wild grasses. You'll hardly know anything ever went on here.'

Kurt was a master of his profession. Aggregates Maketh Man was his creed. I didn't have to ask who had written the opening lines of the Glensanda leaflet: 'A reliable source of aggregates has enabled our civilisation to advance beyond our forefathers' expectations.' Forget steam, electricity, antibiotics, cars, planes, science, philosophy . . . it was plain simple rocks that had allowed mankind to progress and become such marvellously clever apes. This wasn't a quarry, it was a fully integrated materials handling, marketing and distribution concept whose aim was the philanthropic advancement of our species. One day we'd all live happily in a giant hole, a patty-caked paradise of heather and wild grass.

The whole story wasn't believable but the most important half was. Foster Yeoman had found a site four miles from the nearest road or house. They were out of earshot and out of sight of their nearest communities. They were under contract to restore natural vegetation as they quarried, and make a complete restitution when they had finished. But most importantly they would provide 150 people with an income for the next thirty years.

With planning restraints effectively making it impossible to open new quarry workings in England, development is focusing on Scotland. Glensanda, it seems to me, should not be representative of an acceptable trend, but should stand as an isolated, acceptable example.

∽

44

Lawrence Edwards, Strontian

Within ten miles of Glensanda was the much older mining area of Strontian. The mineral first discovered here, to which the village gave its name, is non-radioactive but a derivative of it, Strontium-90, is a hazardous by-product of nuclear reactors and explosions. The despised York Building Company, extreme practitioners of asset stripping and convenient bankruptcy in the post-Culloden era of cheap sales and forfeited estates, ran mines here for almost a century. Mining-town Strontian became notorious as a hotbed of prostitution, drunkenness and crime. Even the Church was not exempt from the influence of the place: one of its ministers, Daniel MacLachlan, was defrocked by the Church of Scotland in the late eighteenth century for publishing his 'Essay upon Improving and Adding to the Strength of Great Britain and Ireland by Fornication'.

Modern Strontian was in retirement from its heady past. When the price was right a mining company dabbled in barytes, drillers' 'mud' for the oil industry, otherwise the inhabitants appeared to be occupied in nothing more licentious than collecting their papers and pensions, walking dogs, tending roses and beating off an advancing jungle of rhododrendrons.

One of those tending his roses was Lawrence Edwards, a retired mathematics teacher from the Rudolf Steiner School in Edinburgh. None of his garden work was conventional and he spent most of his time meticulously measuring buds. A chance conversation led me to his house. He was, my conversant informed me, a Chaos Theoretician. I had no idea what this was so I went to find out. It sounded almost as exciting as the late Daniel MacLachlan's interests.

'Chaos Research is what you're referring to. It's a product of the computer age. Computers, you see, are capable of performing millions of computations a second and when you get them to break something down into its smallest parts, using our neat mathematical formulae, the results they are throwing up are *not* those we would expect. Even the simplest thing is infinitesimally complex. The end result is extraordinarily chaotic. But I'm not deeply involved in that field. I'm a projective geometrist, and my theories have produced rather different results. If you've got time, I'll explain . . .'

He was in his eighties and a fervent disciple of scientist and philosopher Rudolf Steiner (1861–1925). His white beard, pointed face and small stature presented an impression of a leprechaun. His voice was soft and serious, and he had that rare gift of being able to flense the complex and present it in the bones of simplicity.

'You did a little geometry at school? . . . Yes? . . . Good! Well those are my basic tools, only I project my drawings from the page and extend them into the air, into space, to infinity. Do you see?'

I nodded, vaguely. Geometry on the blackboard had been hard enough. Off the blackboard it was unimaginable.

'I'll concentrate on *what* I found rather than the details of *how*. My research began about forty years ago. I was interested in the shapes and forms of nature and in measuring how mathematically exact these aspects were. There are fundamentally three realms of form, and the simplest of these is the egg or cone shape. I set about measuring all sorts of them. Using a scanner I was able to transfer their exact outlines onto a computer and compare them with their mathematically 'perfect' versions.'

He began with hens' eggs. He found them to be so nearly perfect that the actual deviation of one hundredth part of an inch was almost imperceptible when laid against the theoretical image. Duck eggs produced similar results and, even more startling, the inside of the shells revealed spiral markings or striations which also conformed to near flawless geometrical exactitude. He moved on to the fir cones of Scots pine and larch and again found an exceptionally neat precision of outline and whorls. Of two hundred species of flower buds analysed, ninety-five per cent proved to be mathematically precise. This inspired him to examine the form of the human heart. With the help of medical photographs he was able to study the ventricles of a living heart. At the instant of maximum contraction – systole – the ventricle tightened almost to the point of pain, and assumed a conical form which he measured and found to be identical to that of a wild rose bud.

'When I set out on this research, I had no idea what to expect. I wasn't looking to prove anything. I was simply measuring, recording and analysing. But I believe I've found something different from Chaos Researchers: that in all of nature there's a governing order which fits mathematical exactness. This order is a miracle, quite beyond wonder. There's no possible way that life's forms are a product of chance or coincidence. I'm afraid Neo-Darwinism is not credible. There's too much wonder left unaccounted for . . . But I haven't told you the whole story yet.'

It was important to realise, he stressed, that all these objects – eggs, fir cones, buds – were nascent Life, about to break out. He next directed his research to the buds of deciduous trees. Around midsummer, next year's leaves begin to form as buds which, according to current belief, lie dormant throughout the winter months. Lawrence made careful daily measurements of oak buds during winter and found that they were certainly *not* dormant. They twisted and turned. His voice became excited.

'Not only that, they were changing shape. I measured their lambda parameter . . . I'm sorry, I'll keep it simple . . . their degree of sharpness, or bluntness, and found that *every fourteen days* they became less pointed, as if trying to open, and bulging with the effort. Possibly they were testing the conditions and then deciding that the time wasn't right and reverting to their more pointed form. I drew graphs and found a startling regularity. Now, a fourteen-day cycle can suggest a lunar one, so I examined the planetary calendar and found the oak buds' fourteen-day cycle occurred when Mars was in line with the Moon.'

He tried other species. Beech had a thirteen-and-a-half-day cycle and followed the movements of Saturn. Elm was linked to Mercury, and cherry to the Moon. He found a beech which only vaguely conformed to Saturn's rhythm but it was stunted and grew under 33,000 volt power cables. He began to doubt his facts and started again with a new approach. Exactly the same results emerged. He returned to flower buds and began a regime of daily measurements and discovered the same cycles. Geraniums appeared to be a Mars plant, stitchwort looked to Saturn and primrose matched the movements of the Sun.

'I believe, as Steiner believed, that each little part of us mirrors the whole. In us are the wonders of the universe.'

Here he paused and seemed uncertain as to how to proceed. 'For you to fully understand I think I must define the essential qualities of a living organism. Firstly, all its parts are completely and intimately inter-related. What happens to one part affects all. Secondly, every little part has stamped on it the qualities of the whole. There's nothing new in this philosophy. It goes back to Hermes and ancient Egypt; "As Above, so Below; the smallest part of the universe, the Microcosm, shows forth the nature of the whole, the Macrocosm". So I find it utterly plausible that the planets can exert an effect on life here.'

'May I ask why your findings haven't caused a stir among scientists?'

Lawrence smiled and sighed. 'I'm not the first to begin this work, but I think I've taken it a little further and got more evidence in this particular realm than anyone else. Over the last nine years I've measured some 40,000 buds. I know my facts are correct, and that there's no explanation for my findings in modern science. But you're up against it when you start trying to introduce *cosmic* elements into the *earthly* sciences. No one wants to know. I don't hold with these so-called pure sciences. I see mathematics as much as an art as a science. No, modern science has proved very little, all mostly theory.'

'You must write a book on this.'

'I have. "The Vortex of Life". It's only just come out. It gives a summary of my research and findings. You see, all I can really say with any justification is that these are the results I've found here in my little patch of west Scotland. I can't proclaim them as universal facts because no one else has duplicated my work in any detail elsewhere. A colleague has done a little work in Aberdeenshire and produced identical trends. But what about New Zealand? Africa?'

I rose in preparation to leave, assuming his explanation had come to an end. His voice cut me short. 'I haven't got to the most important bit, the most remarkable bit.' He waited for me to sit down.

'I've explained my evidence and my conviction that the rhythms of the heavens, the planets, and the plant garment on Earth, all mirror one another. When I examined my findings in more detail, I found that it was all more complex than I'd first thought. The plants mirror the planets, yes, . . . *but not quite*. The plants tend to hurry ahead a little bit. Their cycle is a little bit out of synch with that of the planets, a little bit faster. Now, we all know that the planets are immersed in mathematical formulae but what few people realise is that their cycles never exactly fit the formulae. There's always something left over, a precise imprecision, you could say. Thus the universe's movements are *not* clockwork, and it's this irregularity, this little gap in mechanical efficiency, which enables change to take place, the universe to progress.'

'But if the plants are mirroring the planets, with their regular but slightly imperfect rhythms, how can they be going on a faster rhythm? Surely this means effect is coming before the cause.'

'Precisely!' It was a triumphant shout. '*Effect overtakes its Cause*. This is one mystery. But the biggest was yet to come.' He leaned forward, his eyes alive with excitement. 'I didn't want this result. I wasn't looking for it. It's just what I found. Every *seven years* the cycles of the planets and their plants come back together again – they once more coincide. Oak synchronises with Mars, beech with Saturn, and all the others on their different cycles.'

'But why? Why seven years?' I asked.

For the first time he lost his patience and retorted angrily. 'I'm simply trying to tell you *what* happens. I have no idea of the *why*.'

He sat silently for a few moments, suddenly looking very old and frail. 'Seven – the mystical number. It comes up again and again. No, I don't know why. You know, I've been a teacher all my life, and now, at eighty-two, my education is just beginning.'

45

❦

Travelling People

The precarious nature of my own place in the universal order of things was made frighteningly clear on the road to Oban. Frankly, I didn't count. My journey south was one long *corrida* with motorists intent on goring me with their wing mirrors. They resented the three feet of tarmac I deprived them of and shaved past my loaded bicycle with only inches separating victim from manslaughter. In their inherent arrogance was a blind faith that I had a firm grip on gravity and balance, and most presumptuous of all, a good road beneath me.

In this last belief they were often mistaken. Even roadmenders appeared to have conspired against cyclists. They've pulled the road surface free of wrinkles for the motorist but left handfuls of gatherings on the edge for the lowest caste of road user. Ruts, cracks, lumps, potholes, asphalt fragments, broken glass, escaped bolts, all the highway's flotsam and jetsam, and drains with mouths aligned to snag wheels as effectively as cattlegrids, are all to be found in the first eighteen inches of roadside. While motorists demanded of me a true, steady line and the matey precision of the Red Arrows, my finger-thin tyres demanded motherly protection and a wobbly course through the hazards.

It was a delicate business, this living on the truculent fringe.

Yet danger aside, I loved the fluidity of this life. Jump onto this simple geometry of metal bars, snuggle into the seat, crank up some momentum and glide silently, miraculously over distance. In time the physical effort of providing power diminished to insignificant proportions, and the bicycle too slipped into the general subconscious of being. We became one, the merging of man and Michelin rubber tubes with French valves. This wasn't mere common or garden cycling.

Or so it seemed some of the time. Of course, it was never quite as pure and simple as that. The wheels occasionally turned fractious and lapsed into argumentative squeaks. The chain joined in with irritating groans. My saddle creaked like a rope under excessive tension. This concerted protest was never constant but it tended to favour the times of peace and the places of scarcest lubrication. And a soul rolling along on air must expect the humiliation of tacks. To date I'd been let down on six occasions, once in a spectacular gunpowdery bang. But these were minute inconveniences compared to what others had endured in this area.

At the far end of the Ballachulish bridge I passed below a knoll. Had my journey been taking place 241 years earlier I could have looked up and seen the skeleton of James Stewart, 'James of the Glen', who was part of the story Robert Louis Stevenson turned into *Kidnapped*. James was wrongfully hanged for the murder of a particularly unpleasant factor called Colin Campbell. After execution his body was chained to the gallows in public view as a warning to the neighbourhood, and for two years a guard of fifteen soldiers ensured it remained there. When a gale blew the remains down in its third year of decay, the Lord Justice Clerk ordered the bones to be wired together and replaced on the gibbet. For eleven years they hung and swayed above Cnoc a' Chaolais until, bone by bone, they fell to the ground and were secretly gathered and taken to the grave of James' wife in Keil Churchyard.

The story was all the more alive and menacing in the half-light of a busy road where my own survival was seriously in question. Six miles on, many imagined deaths later and my vision a blur of white lines and drains, I pulled into a tinker's community to camp.

'Aye, ye'll be safe here. Camp where ye like. If ye want yer water het up, jist gie's a knock,' said a man in his fifties whose appearance gave no clues to his background. I put my tent up in the corner of this neat enclosure, sheltered housing for nomads who had been squeezed out of space and gone semi-urban. This was an official council-run 'camp' of back-to-back bungalows each with bathroom, kitchen and two bedrooms, and they shared a communal laundry. Outside each was a parking space filled by a modern caravan and an assortment of cars, vans and trucks which looked glad to have found repose. Stilty dogs barked from kennels; even Travelling Dogs now had fixed abodes.

I knocked.

'The said-entry life's nae really fer me but, ach, it's nae bad here.' Jimmy's father, but not his accent, had come from Skye. He'd been a traveller all his life until recently. In the background his family spilled off two armchairs and a sofa and had transmigrated into the screen of a Cockney Whodunnit. The air smelled of cigarettes and a fry-up. 'It's nae easy findin' places where yer tolerated ony mair. Them New Age Travellers hivny helped. They aye make a mess o' ther camps. Course ther's folk like that tae among oor people, but nae much. Now see's yer pan an we'll het it up.'

Dogs barked, children bawled, Cockney klaxons blared, and cars with throaty exhausts came and went. Sleep took time to come but when it did I slept well, secure in the common honour of vagabonds past and present.

*   *   *

By chance, or maybe design – after my talk with Lawrence Edwards, the parameters of coincidence had shrunk – a party of New Age Travellers had come to roost in a place they called Raspberry Lay-by, six miles from the Old Age settlement. I turned in and came to a halt near a smart car, and inadvertently found myself in a family argument.

'I don't need your money.'

'If you've run out of gas, we'd like to buy you some.'

'I can get gas myself. I don't need your charity.'

'Donald, we're only trying to help.'

'Look, I'm O-KAY. Why can't you leave me alone? . . .'

Donald was in his thirties, so thin his grimy clothes looked empty. He wore a ginger beard and his hair in a pigtail, and his words hissed through missing teeth. The owners of the car were a well-dressed couple in their mid-fifties. While Donald and the man changed subject and maintained an uneasy conversation, the woman drew away and turned to me, aware that the argument had been heard.

'Donald's our son. He lives here . . . unfortunately.'

'You don't approve then?'

She shook her head with hardened emotion. 'But we've forced ourselves to accept it.' And then, unbidden, she outlined the family history. They belonged to Glasgow. Donald was their second son. Their first, she said, had been 'a doer', 'an achiever', whom Donald had idolised and emulated, but he had been killed at the age of fifteen. Donald had 'gone to pieces'. He gave up school, 'got into bad company', left home and had been with the Travelling People ever since. Now he owned an old truck and lived with his girlfriend and their baby daughter in a caravan with a broken window. His parents had driven all over Britain to visit him and their only grandchild.

'If he likes the lifestyle, is that not what's important?' I suggested.

'We try to tell ourselves that . . . but we live in hope he'll give it up and come back.'

We were approached by one of Donald's friends, a blond-haired man with FULLISHIT branded darkly on his T-shirt. Peter's left arm was a hooked stump severed below the elbow. He invited us to his tent, a 'humpy', for tea. The others declined.

'How did you lose your arm?'

'Bomb. I was a nurse in the RMC in Northern Ireland.'

'Is that why you became a Traveller?'

'Yeah. Twen'y years ago now. Got sort of disillusioned after that. You know, fighting for Queen and Country an' all that shit and coming away with half an arm and bugger all. Fuck 'em. Fuck the system.'

'What d'you do now?'

'Aaa . . . I've got me pension, and I collect the brew, some whelks . . . odd jobs. Take it easy . . .' Peter was English. England was fucked, he said. Scotland was getting that way but still OK. He felt the press gave Travellers a bad name. Sure, they smoked a bit, and drank a bit but that was harmless. They had their share of problems and 'marital unbliss'. But they gave their kids a good education. 'Christ, the number of degrees we've got here. You wouldn't believe it, mate. Half of fuckin' Oxford's here.'

His humpy was a tarpaulin draped over curved poles. It was palatial compared to my mobile home. By the entrance were about fifty empty bottles stuck upside-down in the ground.

I explained about the Tinkers down the road saying how messy the New Age Travellers were. 'Yeah. They would say that. They look down on us. You gotta be six generations a traveller to be one of 'em. But you tell me . . . who're the real travellers now? Them or us? They've jacked it in. Six weeks, that's all they're allowed or they lose their houses. And *mess* . . . how the hell are we meant to be tidy when the council won't collect our rubbish?' He pointed his stump at a skip. 'You see that? Seven years we were here before we got that. Seven fuckin' years.'

'But you don't pay your taxes.'

'Taxes! Why the fuck should we? We don't use nothing. We aren't a drain on the council.'

'Well what about the mess here?' I said, pointing to the bottles.

Peter was relishing the argument. 'That happens to be my garden.'

We sat down to tea and turned to the safe ground of prison and police. French private prisons were the best, Peter reckoned. He'd just spent two years in one after being caught with some 'really nice stuff' he'd bought in Amsterdam. Last week he'd been caught driving over the limit by the local policeman. The last policeman had been a good guy and had come and drunk tea with them. But this new guy was uppity. 'You know, a nerd.'

'It's pretty serious for a Traveller, isn't it, losing your licence?'

'Nah. S'long as I don't get caught again.'

He'd be moving on to the Letham music festival soon. Sometime he'd track down his girlfriend who had left him during his unplanned detention in France and gone off with their two kids – but not this summer. This was *his* time and he was going to enjoy it.

I mentally swapped my bicycle for Peter's humpy. I fitted reasonably happily into it, only I wasn't into 'nice stuff' or glass gardens. Nor could I be reasonably sure that having such close neighbours wouldn't mean the obligatory intrusion of those forces which caused missing teeth and broken windows. Naturally I would have to find a way of disposing of my Protestant ethics and current nemeses – Deadline, Duty, Guilt – and that would be the hardest part. Perhaps the answer was to try it tentatively, along the lines of a package holiday.

I returned to my bicycle. Donald's parents were about to leave. I caught the end of his father's words.

'. . . especially with those dogs, you all look so . . . so *frightening*.'

'It's only your prejudice that makes you afraid.'

Another heavy silence. Clearly they were on old, familiar, irreconcilable ground; Bohemian versus bourgeois.

'I hope you'll be warm enough this winter . . . if we can . . . well . . . you know it's no trouble,' his father stuttered. Donald said nothing. He had turned to ice.

It was his mother's turn. 'I . . . I just . . . oh dear . . . goodbye, Donald . . . we'll see you again sometime, then . . . you will phone . . . just once in a while, won't you? . . . to let us know you're all right?'

She hugged her son. He remained rigid and unresponsive. Her chin rested on his shoulder. Her eyes were closed. Sunlight glistened in the tracks of her tears.

46

❦

McTavish's Kitchen, Oban

I'm in Oban. It's rich and prissy, but I confess I quite like it – and to express a liking for Oban is in the nature of a confession for it is unadulterated tourism, a J. Arthur Dixon postcard come alive in all its obsequious tints. It's not flashy and electric like Las Vegas; its brightness comes from a tarting-up of paint and the subtle one-upmanship of guest houses which congest from harbour to hilltop. Neither does the holiday spirit run rampant in Oban but, at the citizens' discretion, it's allowed a late key and a small can of red, washable paint. You can read the philosophy of the town in the faces of the bedanbreakfast proprietors who scurry back from the bakery each morning with fresh rolls for their visitors, in their expressions of that rubbery rectitude more commonly associated with Edinburgh's Morningside: 'We don't normally *do* that sort of a thing here, but, well, the visitors seem to like it, you see.' Oban is a holiday camp whose entertainment never arrived, Butlin's with a bad limp. No, it's certainly not a Las Vegas, but it replicates that resort's confidence of thinking itself wonderful, and that's why I like it.

I've spent a pleasant hour watching ducks in the town river vibrate their beaks through the mud around stranded cans of Carlsberg Special, and, one of Scotland's natural wonders, the six o'clock return of the masses from Iona. Now I'm sitting in McTavish's Kitchen with 300 others waiting for the daily TRADITIONAL SCOTTISH SHOW to begin.

Our host is Harry Lauder without his curly stick. Not the real one, of course, but in style and content Fred Bruce is a kilted chip off the Lauder block. He sings 'The Northern Lights', 'The Road to the Isles' and 'The Uist Tramping Song'. It's wonderful stuff and helps to suppress the leathery fish that McTavish's is expecting us to digest.

Fred is now walking among the tables, exercising a manic smile and his mobile mike, shouting out countries and waiting for their citizens to raise their hands. This party game never fails to delight and we anxiously await our turn to wave our national flags. I'm still waiting with my hand poised when Fred asks: 'Any other countries?'

'CZECH REPUBLIC,' shout the occupants of the table next to mine. And the game ends. They win. Only somewhere really freakish like Estonia or Southern Mississippi could out-trump the Czech Republic in Oban.

Fred introduces a piper who plays for a young girl dancer. She's nervous but bravely leaps through the choreographed explosions of the Sean Trews, Sword Dance and Highland Fling. She's followed by an accordionist and two teenagers on fiddles who play a medley of our eternal favourites. The teenagers have already played for three hours, busking in the street. Surely McTavish can afford to pay them a decent fee from their £3,000-odd takings this evening?

The piper returns and plays jigs at breathtaking speed but we're not interested in *taorluaths*, slurs or fancy fingering. We're right in there clapping and stamping our feet. Never mind the notes even, just give us a good beat. We can relate to that.

Lampshades like illuminated jellyfish have turned

Fred sunset pink as he goes through 'The Banks of Loch Lomond', 'The Dark Island' and 'Wild Mountain Thyme'. Even the Czechs know these ones and they're raa-raaing the tune. This is what we came to hear. This is Scotland, Scotch Kulcha . . .

We seem unaware that in village halls across the country a musical revolution is taking place. Celtic, ballad, border folk is breaking from the traditional into world music and adopting an eclectic identity. Shouldn't McTavish's be giving this an airing too? Shouldn't Hamish Moore or Cauld Blast Orchestra be here? But of course kitsch is safe and cheap. Do people really want a Traditional Scottish Show or is this all they're offered? Judging from those around me, I'm afraid that this is all they expect. This, the tired old formula of a resuscitated Lauder, is the perceived depth of our cultural expression.

Someone is spelling out the riddle of kilts and 'true' Scotsmen to the Czechs. Of course they know that one too. We're just a tired old joke. Soon we'll be up there holding hands and singing 'Auld Lang Syne'. I don't suppose Fred will let an evening of toxic bonhomie pass without that ritual.

And we can even buy a cassette tape of this genuine Scottish extravanganza to thrill the folks back home in Mlada Boleslav and Jackson. All that's missing is a leathery old fish to go with it.

47

❦

Cave Artist Julie Brook, Jura

Out of Jura's darkness came a deep vibrating bass, a yawning clockwork groan. Others followed, but more distant, and my night's sleep foundered on stags winding themselves up for the rut. Stranger happenings were about too. *Wwwwhirrreeeeep. Wwwwhirrreeeeep.* The sounds moved around my tent at speed, ghostly and elusive, and I was never able to pinpoint where they began or ended. *Wwwwhirrreeeeep.* Cocooned in my sleeping bag, I ran through the possibilities and ruled out frogs, insects, bats and James of the Glen, before realising this was the unseasonal 'drumming' of snipe.

Jura was similar to Rum in that it was another major island largely inaccessible by vehicle, mountainous, swampy, and whose population of deer outnumbered humans at the ratio of twenty to one. Thirty miles long and squeezed in between Islay and the whirlpool of Corryvreckan, which almost prematurely ended *1984* and the life of George Orwell, Jura is a showcase of raised beaches and caves. One particular cave was the home of an artist, and I had come to Jura to try and find her.

'Julie Brook? Yes, I know where to find her, but who are you? You a friend of hers? She know you're coming?'

'Julie? Haven't a clue. *Mad*, she's quite *mad*.'

Everyone in Craighouse knew her but very few people knew where her cave was, and those who did regarded the information as classified. Jura either thought its cave girl soft in the head or was extremely possessive of her.

My admission that she didn't know me, hadn't invited me and wasn't expecting me closed several lines of enquiry but eventually I found some informants. The *about theres* that were stubbed onto my map by their fingers spanned a generous portion of Jura's coastline, but I set off in the general direction and camped halfway for the night.

The deer had merged into miles of moorland grass by dawn, vacating the place for goats which scrambled on magnetic hooves among veins of crags slanting down to the sea. A burn of black water which frothed and had periodic bouts of indigestion led me to a bay of dunes, machair and sculptured cliffs. I checked all the caves. A dead deer here, empty ones there, then the most promising with a fishbox seat and remains of a fire, but no signs of life or permanent habitation. Summer was coming to an end and if the storm-mashed lobster pots were anything to go by, Julie had wisely cleared out.

The coastline angled sharply to the sea, sometimes chunks had been bitten out leaving precipitous coves which forced me to climb high around them. I looked down to the shingle beaches below for the Julie Brook who was no more than a name I'd been given, but whose image had emerged clearly enough in a haunted night: middle-aged, sinewy, suspicious, saturnine, with long, clarted hair and wild eyes. 'Mad, she's quite mad,' they'd said. The more the words deranged the image, the more I hoped Julie remained a secret.

An hour later I was looking down at the umpteenth expanse of shingle when my eyes discerned the outline of a cairn among the stones. It was vague but, yes, unmistakably of human construction.

Miiiaaaau.

I leapt with fright. A domestic cat stood a few feet from my ear on moss-capped rock. Then I saw a figure under the cliffs. My enthusiasm had gone. I was prepared to creep away unannounced.

Until I got a better view.

'HALLO! ARE YOU JULIE?'

The figure started, stared at me and then indicated a magnetic goat's track down to her beach. From behind she was a bundle of driftwood with long tanned legs ending in deck shoes. From the front she was white shorts and grey pullover, a strongly built young woman with very sweet, rounded features, a cherub with gold earrings. Sun had blanched all but a hint of blondness from her short hair. Dwarfed and equipped with wings, Julie would have looked the part spouting water at a fountain or holding plaster grapes at the Odeon.

'Brilliant! Absolutely brilliant! You can help me collect wood. I'm on firestacks at the moment.' She accepted my sudden arrival as eagerly as my offer to help in any way. It soon became clear that most things, at least anything good, was 'brilliant' and anything bad was 'not so brilliant'. I had expected eccentricity but I had no idea how much. *Firestacks*?

'I thought you were an artist, not a wrecker?'

'I'm an artist and a sculptor, and I'm into fire at the moment. It's brilliant.'

I had to collect wood, and more wood, while Julie built the stack. She could only do this at low tide and she became a dervish collecting rocks with such energy that I felt shamed into collecting more wood. My pile grew, her drystane tower rocketed. It was solid and beautifully crafted. She had built many of them but they only lasted half a dozen tides and then the sea undermined them. Ideally, I gathered, they were to equal the height of the sea at full tide.

With time to spare before the tide was right, we repaired

to her cave. A natural arch of colossal size curved out of the cliffs like a flying buttress and under it was enough space for a modest house. Julie had walled off part of the gap with a windbreak of driftwood and created a two-roomed flat; an open-air kitchen and a bedroom in a tent of suspended sackcloth. A porpoise skull was stuck on a pole as a centrepiece while a three-legged cat slept underneath. She lit a fire and brewed Lapsang Souchong tea sent 'direct' from one of the best houses in London. Direct to the Jura distillery. A fisherman brought her supplies on an irregular basis.

'*Why* are you here?' The question had been longing to escape.

Her smile was, truly, brilliant. 'I came to Jura three years ago to walk and fell in love with it. The landowner wasn't too happy about the cave idea at first but in the end he relented. Every artist has to find her or his own way to self-expression. This is currently mine.'

She was thirty-one and had been born into the Navy which, she said, meant she came from nowhere in particular. England had been her home but now it was Scotland. Glasgow and a Jura cave. At first she had been afraid of the nights, the sounds and the occasional stranger who stumbled on her home. But now she was used to it, the noises, smells, sights; it felt like home. She was five months into her second summer here. Like Gavin Maxwell in *Ring of Bright Water*, she found the sea provided all her needs in driftwood form.

Around us, on easels and stacked against the wall, were her canvases of mountain scenery; bold impressionist splashes in oil covering sixteen, twenty-four square feet at a time. Most were streaked with rain. A life spent without hangovers among tall walls was, I felt, the criterion for peaceful co-existence with Julie's exuberant work. Her wood rubbings I really liked. She had taken them from the broken ribs of a boat, and into each she had incised a question or phrase in exquisite italics: *how old is the*

*tree? . . . what seas has the ship sailed? . . . the storms
that broke them . . . green light in the copper nail . . .*

'I had an exhibition in Craighouse recently as a sort of
thank you to the people who've been so kind. Just to show
them the sort of things I'm doing here. Most didn't like
my work but at least they felt sufficiently comfortable to
say so.' But enough people in the rest of the country did
like her work. Her largest pictures fetched over £2,000.
She made me feel words were a mug's game.

'What I love here is how the seed of an idea grows.
It grows in a way you can never predict and out of it
comes all sorts of other seeds. That's how I got into
firestacks.'

I still didn't understand firestacks if they weren't for
good old-fashioned pillage, but it was time to go and
Julie was explaining my role. She had made a raft from
wood and flotsam and odds and ends. She would paddle
out to the stack, load it with wood, throw on turps
and ignite it. I was to hold the raft's rope, counteract
the westerly Gulf Stream, and haul her in when she
gave the word. I had horrible premonitions about all
this. I could see another Julie in years to come with
a fragment of this Julie's raft, carving: . . . *what seas has
she sailed?* . . .

'OK?' she asked.

'Go easy with the turps.'

We trooped out on our secret mission. It was still
too secret for my liking. 'What are these firestacks all
about?'

'I want to create fire on the surface of the sea, to explore
their relationship.'

Fire. Sea. Relationship. I thought I understood. She
was surely looking for what the *National Geographic*
Picture Desk calls 'moments'. ('We need *moments*, you
understand? Gesture, action, emotion but real moments,
as they happen . . .') They were Gasp or Nod Factors.
Then I knew I didn't understand. I couldn't see the point

of building cairns for the sea to knock down and bonfires for waves to extinguish.

'The point is that if something has no function it can be appreciated *solely* for what it is. For example, a kiln is a brilliant creation. The fire is often more beautiful than the pottery it produces, but it's neglected and regarded only for its function. The firestack has no function. We can therefore see it with uncluttered vision for its true worth.' She climbed onto the raft. 'You got the other end of the rope? OK, give me a shove.'

She paddled out towards America. The wind was rising. Five minutes later flames leapt up from the firestack.

'PULL.'

I pulled, thinking how absurd it all was, one of my more bizarre experiences, hauling on a rope in the dark, pulling in a woman who was no more than a bobbing headlight on a homemade raft adrift in a choppy Atlantic with a piece of fishbox for a paddle.

Smudges of cloud crept along the horizon's glow, a lurid red except where Colonsay's blackness lay stretched out like a resting lizard. Julie walked out of the ocean, rummaged in a bag, produced a couple of stemmed glasses and poured liberal measures of Isle of Jura 10-Year-Old Single Malt. We drank to firestacks and looked out to sea.

'Brilliant!'

I saw a bonfire on a pile of stones. I think Julie saw creation. But it was, without question, a moment.

48

❧

Argyll and The Gap

The bicycle traveller finds it harder to become as emotionally attached to his means of transport as, say, the boat traveller. A boat doubles as a home. It offers womb-like security in an element through which the traveller cannot otherwise go. Unlike machine travel by land, boat travel is a commitment, a marriage bond you can't walk out on when the going gets rough. A bicycle is soulless, and lacks the lavish mobility of the car and the spirited character of sled dog or horse; but you don't need to find a mooring for it in winter, and when it doesn't get up in the morning you don't need a vet or an income of £25 an hour to get it repaired. Depend on anything for long enough though, and it becomes precious and companionable.

We were somewhere in Argyll at the time when my friend's pedal fell off. I should have been either distressed or outraged at having to push its dead weight for two miles over the hills until I found a farmer with a suitable wrench and hammer but I was going through grief of another kind. Of all Scotland's many physical, social and psychological divisions – north/south; east/west; island/mainland; *Gaidhealtachd*/Lallans; Glasgow/Edinburgh; central versus the rest – I was about to cross one of its Great Divides: Highland/Lowland.

The boundaries were fudged, the transition took the form of slow seepage and always there would be patches of this or that among the other, but Argyll undoubtedly marked for me a valediction from the essence of Highland.

The Forestry Commission and some devious-sounding syndicate called Economic Forestry Group had tried to smother Argyll in pine, but her loveliness was not to be outdone and merely made their attempts look mean and boorish. Argyll was a slightly softer Moidart under trees. She had a better mix of farmland, looked better cared for (except where the FC and EFG had rampaged), was more estate-agent friendly with her pockets of marinas and timeshares, and was blatantly a favourite with the Druids who had erected standing stones willy-nilly. But as I cycled through Argyll and her tail end, the Mull of Kintyre, I began to notice more strongly the Lowland character: more cattle than sheep, more grass than bracken or heather, a rounding and mollifying, a whiff of greater affluence.

In a downpour at Keil Point, the extremity of where Scotland reaches out and tries to touch Ireland, I stared at the spot where Columba is said to have first set foot on our country. He landed with such impact that he left a clear impression of his right foot in a rock by the cemetery: size 10 (40 continental) in his socks.

Drenched, I toiled up four sheep-littered miles (it had turned Highland again) to The Gap, one of the finest look-outs in the country, but the weather was so poor I didn't see the view until I was inside the Southend Hotel, four miles away, talking to a monkeyish little man called Hugh. He was the odd one out in a bar full of pouting masculinity, youths in a slow parade of macho poses round the pool table, their chests held inflated in their T-shirts, running assassin's eyes along the geometry of balls.

'On a clear day,' said Hugh, his face almost lost in stubble, 'you can see Ireland from The Gap.'

'And not just see it,' added a bystander, 'you can make out traffic moving.'

'That's what I was going to say,' returned Hugh, miffed that his lead had been taken. 'On a *really* clear day you can see them working in the fields – you can't actually make out what they're doing, like, but you can see them working.'

'What they're probably doing,' retorted the other, 'is looking over here wondering what the hell that lazy bugger is doing staring at them.' Hugh ignored this. The other continued, 'I mind one evening, clear as a bell it was, I could see the loom of Carlisle from The Gap.'

'Oh aye,' said Hugh dismissively. 'On a *really, really* clear day, with a morning frost, if you look early, like, you can see the lights of Man, and that's sixty miles away.'

It was some view from The Gap. I looked out of the bar window and couldn't even see my bicycle parked fifty yards away. Rain was hammering down and exploding on a shallow river that, an hour ago, had been my road. I was lent a greenhouse for the night and slept among baby tomatoes, rhododendrons and palm trees.

I used Arran as a stepping stone between Mull and the Clyde coast. Arran was used to being stepped on. Even though much of its former doon-the-watter appeal to Glaswegians had shrunk, 130,000 tourists still stepped on it each year, bringing with them degrees of fortune and frustration for the population of 3,400. Much of that population had originally come as tourists. 'Little Yorkshire' was Whiting Bay's alternative name.

As a native stranger looking at home, I had a feeling that Scotland, echt Scotland, was about to begin. You wouldn't find 'Little Yorkshire' as a suburb of Glasgow.

49

Ardrossan to Glasgow

The Ardrossan hairdresser lived for her holidays in the sun. She'd been to Spain endless times, Turkey was old hat and this year she was thinking of taking a package to The Gambia. 'It's just opening up,' she said, as if it were a new and long-awaited superstore rather than another dismal refurbishment of Africa into a white ghetto of Western indulgence. While overlooking a grey deserted beach I learned The Gambia's monsoon dates and to view the country as Ardrossan with sun.

In the days of low mobility Ardrossan had been just the place. With miles of beaches and the odd façade of pseudo-Greek pillars on either side of very ordinary doors, the town carried off a pretence of the exotic – indeed it was a foreign corner to those from a black world of shipyards and tenements. Now Ardrossan was too close to home, too expensive, too old-fashioned, too dull, and its weather too bloody awful. Forsaken by the masses for the likes of Benidorm and Banjul (The Gambia), Ardrossan had kept something aside for the day-ooters, and made the easy transition from the tourist to the retirement industry.

Fairlie was hanging in there, so was Largs, though the frequency of FOR SALE signs indicated a bit of rot and a buyers' market, Wemyss Bay looked comatose and stable, doubtless feeding off the fat yacht city of Inverkip where Glasgow's rich kept boats and toys, but Gourock was buoyant: LUXURY FLATS. RETIREMENT HOMES. NEW DEVELOPMENT.

This was Scotland's middle-class Gold Coast. Savings had gone into nice lampshades and a piece of sea visible from the window. The town planners had easily accommodated the low demands of the new residents: a car bay, good streetlights and smooth pavements were all they needed to see out their lives in peace. It was a very private world, each flat a keep of bolted doors out of which few escaped, mainly dog-walkers being pulled through the street's floodlighting, stottering objects with arm extended. They seemed a joyless species, these dog-walkers, tholing a sentence of care and perfunctory walks.

Bishopton led into Erskine led into a field of Friesians led into Renfrew, Paisley and Glasgow proper. With my safety helmet (purchased in Oban) tightly strapped I pedalled through the greatest concentration of cars, people and buildings I had seen for months (and the largest coloured population since Stornoway). Nervously, I made my way through congested suburbs which had long ago lost their boundaries, to Stepps, and to Glasgow's only campsite. Craigendmuir was a small housing estate being won over by vandals. To reach it I had to pass through a mile of swamp and refuse where it was easy to imagine how Craig had met his end. The campsite had made a gesture of security by erecting netting on two sides of a square. The open half looked over a mile of Craig's deathbed to Easterhouse.

'I'd stay in the bus, sir, if I were you. There's high unemployment in Easterhouse. People hang around the street. They know everyone and, well . . . strangers aren't welcome,' advised the young tourist information officer, wearing his GLASGOW'S ALIVE AND KICKING badge. Someone, it appeared, had got the slogan just right. He added that fire engines were unwilling to go to Easterhouse any more as false alarms and stone-throwing were common. '*Do* stay in the bus . . .'

I might have been back in Rio de Janeiro again, seeing the two youths eyeing me, feeling my camera case being seized, reliving the tug-of-war, the disguised gun being held to my face, the struggle, my flight – intact but spiritually bruised. But that was Brazil . . . this was Scotland. Nevertheless, I stayed in the bus.

The days of Glasgow's population being packed into slums at the peak rate of 583 people per acre have gone. The physical slums have gone too, with the massive gung-ho of demolition in the sixties in which the good and bad of tenement life – the core of Glasgow community – was swept away to be replaced by the spiritual slums of the high rises. Easterhouse had entered the next phase of urban planning: the compromise housing estate. The new Glaswegian statistic, albeit misleading as it included large acreages of empty warehouses and derelict industry, was closer to conurbation heaven with an average of 14 souls per acre.

Easterhouse looked unworthy of its sinister reputation. Like any other concentration of blockish houses it had a fair share of grass, garden fences, and even a few flowers. It had rediscovered some pride. Admittedly a teenaged youth felt moved to restore some of the bias by hurling a stone at us. It made a solid clunk below a window. 'Aye, happens all the time,' the driver said, without malice. He might have been talking about nothing more harmless than a rude belch. In the couthiness of Glasgow the gesture was seen for what it was, nothing personal, but a frustrated reaction against the absence of opportunity.

Ashamed of my cowardice, I decided to walk central Glasgow's streets by night. George Square was a very different Glasgow, a polished and sand-blasted remnant of wealth and power but, like Easterhouse, a symbol of the New Image and revitalisation. Here in her physical heart Glasgow was only half-alive for she had been commandeered by the offices of her professionals and by eight o'clock at night, her lights were out and she had been largely abandoned.

On the Square's central column Sir Walter Scott looked baffled by the daytime crowd's dispersal. That Glasgow should have put one of Edinburgh's sons in pride of civic place was a warning of the extreme to which the city would go to humiliate those who behaved treacherously – as George III had done. As a result of legislation which he introduced, the American War of Independence erupted, the colony was lost and with it went Glasgow's tobacco monopoly on which the city's wealth was founded. 'George the Third should never have occurred' was the prevalent feeling, and so the column built for his statue was used for Scott instead.

Surrounding Scott were other statues of borrowed or home-grown sons, and a slim Queen Victoria who was tolerated because she had presided over the great days of Empire when Glasgow had been its main workshop. She arrived in 1848, well-briefed and wearing galoshes, spent two hours here and, as Glaswegians say, 'liked it so much she hurried back thirty-nine years later'.

Architecturally Glasgow could boast examples equal to the best of her flirtatious east-coast sister, but she lacked Edinburgh's concentration of them. So much in this city was dispersed and all but lost in a reputation of grime and poverty. Somewhere five minutes away from the opulent City Chambers (used by film-makers as a dummy set for the Kremlin and Vatican), in a canyon-like street of tobacco mansion and decay, I fell in – and in Glasgow you can't walk without constantly falling in – with a citizen.

'How's it goin', Jimmy? Y'all right? I'm Shaun. I'm Catholic.'

There was nothing pretentious about Glaswegians. You were what you were and you laid it down on the table. Christian name. Religion. It was a natural introduction between strangers. This is what you're dealing with, take it or leave it. In his book *Scottish Journey* (1935) Edwin

Muir wrote, '[As a] difference between a Glasgow man and an Edinburgh man, one might say that every Edinburgh man considers himself a little better than his neighbour, and every Glasgow man just as good as his neighbour.'

Shaun was going to the Scotia Bar and I joined him. In Adelphi Street we passed Nazir's mosque, the nearest one to Stornoway, and the largest outside London. By the time we reached the Scotia we had exchanged lives and knew each other well enough to drop in for tea anytime. Shaun uttered a 'God bless you', and disappeared into the distant crush to evoke the signs of the cross over a dominoes contest.

The Scotia, one of a dozen bars claiming to be the oldest in the city, was the haunt of bevviers, singers (*ceilidh*-oke) and writers. The bar staff sweated. The clientele (2,000 to the acre) stuck together in one lump. I caught the attention of a barman operating three beer taps simultaneously, and retreated to a less crushed side room with a pint and a copy of the pub magazine. According to the editorial, my one pound, the magazine's cover price, went to help Clydeside's 20,000 former shipyard workers suffering from asbestos-related diseases.

On page twelve Danny Kyle wrote about the music halls.

The Glasgow audiences were famous for two things: if you were good, they let you live; if you were bad, they gave you fruit, ashtrays, and anything else they could throw, but sometimes 'the act' got its own back, as in the case of Florrie Forde, one of the biggest stars of the music hall. Florrie was in the Metropole one Friday night, second hoose, and giving it doaky with 'After The Ball Was Over'. As she got into the song, the bears, full of the Joie de Vivre and Scotia bevvy, were giving her stick. 'BOO-HISS-SHITE-GERRAFF-YERROTTEN', and other such quaint colloquialisms, when from among the melee came a voice abune them aw. 'FUR FUCKS SAKE, SHUTUP AND GIE THE

AULD COW A CHANCE!', and Florrie Forde, to her eternal credit, stopped in mid-song, drew herself up and in grand manner replied, 'THANK YOU. I'M GLAD TO SEE THERE'S ONE GENTLEMAN IN THE AUDIENCE.'

There were no Florrie Fordes around but a Rob Roy was playing guitar and a 70-year-old man called Rikki was on harmonica ('It's *nae* a mouthie – ah kin change key, pal.')

'Mind if I join you?'

'Can ye sing?' Rikki asked.

'Badly.'

'Then piss off.'

This meant 'yes'. I sat in a social melting-pot typical of the city, between the bar simpleton and one of Glasgow's leading planning and development consultants.

'Where were we before we were sae rudely interrupted,' Rikki continued, to Rob Roy. 'Oh aye, intae a wee bit o' blues. Let's hae anither i' the same idiom.'

Tom Wilkie read my name, religion and interest. 'The bottom line in Glasgow is its lack of wealth. Seventy-nine per cent of those in rented accommodation are on Income Support. Glasgow's unique in Europe. It's a city without a middle class.' Tom was an exception, a rare example of that missing class, a middle-aged entrepreneur with a loosened tie and a social conscience. 'It's one of the obscenities here that our middle class live outside in these so-called centres of excellence. They come in to work, take their income, and then they go outside to spend it.'

Tom Wilkie had Glasgow's measure exactly. In Edinburgh, he explained, existed middle-class thinking and values, an economic balance. It had never been an industrial city and had retained its city-centre population. But in Glasgow the industrialists had built tenements, 'middens', close to their factories along the river and filled the valley with one class, their workers. They withdrew to the hills to distance themselves from the 'stench'. Dennistoun, he said, was a fine example of this. Then they moved out completely.

'Our middle class went to the New Towns. You ask anyone working in the city centre. None of them *live* there. They live in East Kilbride, Bearsden and Milngavie. These places drew out the enterprising, the academic, the cream of the commercial and cultural world. They take everything and give nothing back. Oh yes . . . they think they're wonderful. All their kids wear blazers and Brylcreem.'

It was changing, he believed, slowly. Yes, he admitted, the Workers' City Group (with author James Kelman as one of its most vociferous supporters) had a valid point in criticising city centre repopulation as being excessively biased towards the monied class and the creation of a glitzy image, but at least it was a start. At least people were returning to live in the city centre. And while some saw this as a form of 'political infiltration' to the city's core, Tom believed Glasgow's politics to be too profoundly Labour to be threatened. Attitudes and politics, he pointed out, were conditioned by environment. 'You simply can't be a rampant Conservative in Glasgow because you continually have to pass poverty. In Edinburgh you're allowed to shut your mind to it. Let me give you an example. If I go down to the Babbity Bowster at five-thirty pm on a Friday, eighty per cent of my peers there will be radically left of centre. In Edinburgh it would be sixty per cent. At the Lamb in Bloomsbury, twenty. Each has a different perception of life, a different exposure to poverty.'

'Why isn't Glasgow burgeoning from its working-class roots?'

'It is. Don't get me wrong. But along with our middle classes we're lacking their access to finance. Our class structure is both our weakness and our strength. Weakness because of the imbalance and without a middle class we don't have the same support of banks and financial institutions. And strength because there's tremendous human energy and spirit here.'

There was a further handicap, however, which he illustrated through his wife's work. She was a teacher in the depressed area of Newarthill. A young American girl had moved into one of the classes and almost at once dominated the lessons. She would answer all the questions and the other pupils withdrew into silence. 'We've still got the death-rattle of de-Scotification in this country. Those kids know all the answers but they shrink into themselves, become self-effacing because of what they perceive as their less articulate accents. *They're ashamed of the way they speak.* Can you imagine that? Can you imagine what that does to a kid's confidence? Radio and TV are helping, but it's all so slow. As if these kids haven't enough obstacles . . .'

It was late when I was among the final stragglers to be turfed out of the Scotia. Rikki was leaving too. He went up to two strangers, a girl wrapped around her boyfriend, and tapped the girl on the shoulder. 'GET YER HANDS AFF HIS WALLET,' he shouted. His insults always ended with a roar of laughter, revealing a poor legacy of isolated teeth.

He turned to me. 'Cracka ova night, eh, pal?', and he checked his wallet for confirmation. He'd come in with eighty pounds that evening, and was down to his last few singles. 'Aye, cracka.'

He asked me where I was staying. 'Christ! Campin! Oot there! Yer aff yer heid. Ye'll be mugged.'

The last bus to Stepps had left an hour earlier, so Rikki and I shared a taxi. He lived in the same direction, in a flat in Red Balornock. The blocks were built in the sixties and were the highest in Europe at the time. He'd lived alone in a highrise for thirty years.

'What's it like there?'

'It's hame tae me, pal.' He pulled out his harmonica and played *Moon River* in a way which gave a hint of what thirty years in Red Balornock had been like.

∽

50

Glasgow: Gallery, Bingo, Rangers vs Celtic

Art Gallery, Bingo, Rangers vs Celtic: it was the kind of shopping list I liked.

The Kelvingrove Art Gallery was built with its grandiose entrance facing the university. Its access road, unfortunately, was built to the rear. This was possibly to be expected in a city where energy frequently outstripped planning, and so was the solution. Rather than reroute the road, a new 'front' was built onto the gallery's rear.

I gatecrashed a guided tour being led by a man whose great age, white hair, abnormally large hearing aid, and ability to talk through wandering eyes and bored expressions suggested lecturer, doctorates, pearls, swine. The group was just leaving Rembrandt's *Carcass of an Ox* which, three hundred years on, still looked succulent enough to order for steaks.

Now we stood before one of the largest canvases. 'This,' he declared, putting the word through a roller-coaster of emphasis, 'was the pride and joy of its previous owner, and for over a century now since its donation to the gallery, this has been considered its most valuable possession. You are looking at the work of a Venetian master, Giorgione's *The Adulteress*

Brought Before Christ. Notice how Giorgione has painted the most important figure in the scene, Christ, with his head in shadow. Now . . .'

He pointed to the adjacent picture, a head and shoulders portrait of a man.

'. . . look at the blue sky in this little picture. Do you see? It's the same background as the big one. Yes, this head was once part of the large picture – look, you can still see the end of his shoulder here.

'When this picture was intact, it was once owned by Queen Christina of Sweden. A hard ruler. Another Mrs Thatcher, I'm afraid, with an iron fist and hatchet policies. Apparently, she showed this picture to a cardinal and pointed out, as one would, how charming it was that the disciple on the right was none other than a self-portrait of Giorgione. Far from being impressed, the cardinal expostulated that this was brazen sacrilege, that the artist should attempt to upstage Christ by putting Him in shadow and his own face in the light. The Queen concurred, and lopped off the right-hand figure.' He paused to adjust his hearing aid which had begun to whistle. I used the distraction to scan the walls for Faed's *The Last of the Clan*.

'So you are looking at a Giorgione masterpiece . . . but, alas, I fear you are not . . .'

I turned round at once, thinking my inattention had been noticed, only to realise he was not directing his remark to me; a pearl was about to be cast.

'Earlier this year Glasgow lent the painting to an exhibition in France. It was returned with a thirteen-page document refuting all evidence of Giorgione and asserting that this was a Titian. And I have to agree. The style is simply not that of Giorgione.

'This is a disaster for the gallery and Glasgow. Giorgione died at the age of thirty-three and produced very few works. Titian was a contemporary and lived until he was ninety. Every gallery in the world should have a Titian, but how rare to have a Giorgione.'

Our guide smiled before delivering his last body kick. 'This is just a Titian, and a rather average, early Titian at that.'

Bingo began at eight. Stewards in black and white looked out into the street through a row of six glass doors and watched a figure trying them all without hitting the right combination. That set the tone for the evening.

'It's this one, hen. Ye hae tae pull it.' A granny with her handbag clamped in the crook of her elbow rescued me.

'That's the way tae the Ladies . . . this way, hen.'

The girl at the ticket desk talked of Flyers, Nationals, Fours and Sixes. I looked blank.

'First time, is it?' I nodded. She looked incredulous that someone of my age could have lived for so long in ignorance of The Game. She gave me Flyers and Nationals because they were where the big winnings were, and Fours which were simplified versions for beginners and those not quite the full shilling. I paid £6.20 and left with a colourful handful of recycled paper worth £52,000.

Two tennis courts would have fitted into the hall which was furbished in the style of a transport café with carpets. Trays of pints n'chasers n'fish n'chips n'pie n'beans travelled briskly from serveries to tables of four, equipped with a built-in electronic bingo card and a slot machine. Outwith the Main Session – Fliers, Nationals, Sixes – we had the option of dropping twenty pences in our slots and playing 'quickies' which seldom lasted more than a minute. A LARGE PRINT scoreboard tallied the number of players each time and the prize on offer was a proportion of the takings: 11 pence to the house, 9 pence into the prize kitty. Unless someone spilt their pint down the slot and fused the table, Mecca couldn't lose.

Billy Bunter stood on a central podium, his shirt

arresting a cascade of fat as it fell over the rail which contained him, and talked incessantly into a microphone. I had expected him to catch numbered ping-pong balls bouncing inside a Perspex dome, but that archaic system had given way to computerised random selection. Billy retrieved his numbers from a VDU, and in between games he hypnotised us with a jingle which he sang in the two-tone style of a parrot:

Are you playing too-ooo, Are you playing too-ooo
Keep yer Top Red cov'aird, Top Red cov'aird
Are you playing too-ooo, Put yer money in then
Are you playing too-ooo, And here we go-ohhhhhh . . .

I studied my companions. The split was roughly two-thirds over fifty, and four-fifths women. One group was playing cards, several women were knitting and almost everyone was smoking. A blue pall descended to the level of Billy's belly button. The Main Session was announced.

'Here . . . ye canna use a pencil fer this. Here's a felt-tip fer ye.' A man from the nearest table had already spotted the credentials of a novice. He handed me a customised pen which covered a Mecca square in a single dab. 'It's yer Flyer noo – no, that's yer National, Jimmy – yer grey Flyer . . .' Even though things were colour-coded I had difficulty in separating these unknown species.

'A4, Atey-for, A4, Sex-Aw, Sex-Tay, Sex-Aw . . .'

Understanding Billy was a specialised field in itself. He had a numbers voice which dropped in tone, discarded leading letters and syllables that might be helpful, and squeezed what was left through pursed lips. It took me some time to realise he was repeating each number three times. They all sounded different to me. 'Wan, Bi-sel, wan . . .'

Somebody shouted. The game ended.

'How d'ye go?'

'Not very well.' I showed him my blank card. He took it, stood up, waved it and shouted across the hall, 'GIE'S A NUMBER CHECK, JASON – GUY HERE MISSED HIS NUMBERS.'

Everyone turned and stared at me. I smiled weakly at a cross-section of Drumoyne and 300 grannies with perms in metallic tints who obviously considered me retarded. Fortunately Jason ignored the request.

Just as I was getting the hang of it we changed games to a form of noughts and crosses. Only after struggling with two of these did I realise you didn't have to scan through twenty-five random numbers each call. The word BINGO was written across the top of the columns and each call began with the column's letter. It occurred to me that this would make an excellent aptitude test for, say, spacemen, pilots or the SAS; throw them into a session of Bingo and see how long they take to decipher the language and crack the codes.

I won nothing. The electronic screens hurt my eyes. The smoke suffocated me. Numbers reverberated in my mind like the clackety-clack of train wheels. I had a headache. Magic At Mecca was not for me; I was bingoed-out in my first session. As *Are you playing tooooo, Are you playing tooooo* came swirling, taunting, hounding, out of the murk, I fled into the comforting din of traffic.

It was in Govan that I tried hardest to belong. Privileged, middle-class, well-fed, posh-spoken, on temporary parole from comfort and security, I didn't stand a chance. The way I looked and the way I walked gave me away even before I opened my mouth. Backgrounds are stubbornly tenacious. I shed mine once with reasonable success. Unwashed, unshaven, hungry, without money, and with nothing besides a dirtied set of mismatch clothes from the Salvation Army, I spent three wretched days as a beggar and scrounger in London to gain personal insight for an article on homelessness. It felt like three lifetimes.

In Govan I didn't even try to disguise myself. In time I might have won acceptance, in the way any incomer has to earn it, but here in the short-term there was US and THEM, and I was THEM. The reason I wanted to belong to Govan was because here I felt most strongly my own lack of roots, the fellowship of gang and close that was a gap in my development. Yet it was an attraction laced with fear, for although I was envious of this sense of community and, even more so, the achievement of survival here, it was a society from which I had been shielded for most of my life (the wynds and sub-culture of Elgin's Bishopmill could hardly compare) and an environment which held an image of penitential retribution. No matter how many mountains I climbed or seas I sailed, I knew my own personal testing ground, my opportunities for greatest development, would be won or lost in places like Govan.

Given that I couldn't instantly change Govan into a place of privilege, good-feeding, comfort and security, I walked its streets assessing the hot and cold of my approach-avoidance dilemma. As a fantasy it was all the less sincere considering I had recently abandoned my campsite in Stepps for reasons of unfounded scaremongery, and moved in with friends in Dumbreck. Dumbreck happened to be Govan's neighbour, and its opposite: a conserve of old-stone houses, walled gardens, trees and respectability. Glasgow's many worlds had thin dividing lines; in this case, a hundred yards of arterial motorway.

Neptune Street's warren of houses were suitably run-down – patched, shabby and gloomy – for an indulgent act of penance, but instead I turned it into art and photographed abstract patterns of windows and hanging washing. I wasn't even trying to blend in.

'Hey, Big Man!' It was the standard greeting for strangers. It might herald an invitation to talk, to drink, supply a loan, or accept a mugging.

'Hey, Big Man! . . . You Press?'

'Take ma photie, Mister.'

I took their photie. 'Closer together. OK. Shout Gers.'

'GERRRRRRRS.'

I was on safe ground here. Anything to do with Rangers was the right password among ten-year-olds. I walked on. The street was empty except for a few children and a mother walking with her toddler on the other pavement. She crossed over.

''Scuse me. Ah couldnae help overhearin' ye. Y' are'nae frae here, are ye? This is'nae a good place. There's drugs an ah here. We've hid murders tae.' She broke off with a warning nod and disappeared into a house.

I reached Govan Cross and hit a low of cold. Beyond a GENTS, whose machine sold Jiffi Condoms to BS3704 in Lemon, Strawberry, Mint, Orange and Banana flavours, my ultimate test appeared. A street of loiterers, doorway dealings and cutting stares. Of the sixty-two companies which once built ships on the Clyde, only Kvaerner (Swedish-owned) was still in business, and its two-year contract was held in monolithic sheds at the end of the street. But more of Govan's steel went into shop fronts than ships; the rows of shutters ran on unbroken except in one place, a sole expanse of glass without protection, the only shop with nothing worth stealing. The Job Centre.

SEWING MACHINE OPERATOR, £54 p/WEEK. EXPERI- ENCED CANVASSERS FOR BLINDS & WINDOWS, COM- MISSION ONLY. BACK-SHIFT TAXI DRIVER, £2 p/HOUR + TIPS. SATURDAY SUPERMARKET STACKER, £1.99 p/HOUR. WE MAY HAVE MORE OPPORTUNITIES INSIDE. PLEASE COME IN.

I retraced my steps. The streets were filling up fast. Two hundred and fifty lemon-coloured policemen had flooded in along with twenty-four on horseback, the remnants of Strathclyde's cavalry. 'PARKING, £2' signs had suddenly materialised in every backyard and empty bay, 'patches' claimed by enterprising youths who had no other title to them than might. Here was a model of Thatcherite enterprise. Govan and Ibrox were on their bikes, earning.

'Watch yer car fer a quid, Mista?' came the calls from running gangs of youngsters. The rule seemed to be the first who touched the car had the right to protect it, or rather, the duty to vandalise it if the fee wasn't paid.

'Do you pay up?' I asked one motorist.

'Oh, aye. If yer car's OK when ye git back, ye pie.'

'And if you tried to drive off without paying?'

'Yer nae pie'in to hae yer car watched while yer away. Yer pie'in not to hae it vandalised when ye return. They've all got minders up the street. If ye dinnae pie, ye'll likely get a stone through the windae. Oh, aye, ye pie all right.'

'Hey, Big Man . . .' I was hailed by a boy still too young to claim his own patch for extortion. He was a scruff of stains and frays and holes. 'Big Man, see thaat . . .' and he pulled up his jersey, proudly revealing the shimmering blue 'Home' strip of Rangers which cost £24.99 at the club shop. 'Here, Big Man,' he beckoned me closer. 'If ye bend doon like this . . . lower, Mista, lower . . .' – I crouched down and held my head at his height – '. . . and ye look between they buildins, jist above the height av'that lamppost . . . ye kin see the lights av'Ibrox. It's *maaagic*.'

There was deep emotion in that word. Even a glimpse of the distant hallowed light lit up the heart of this Govan waif.

Later I rang the PR office of Rangers and spoke to John Greig. This legend, a player for eighteen years and manager for five, had been put out to grass in the Goodwill and Complaints department. I asked what chance that boy would ever have of seeing his team play.

'Precious little. Wer matches are pretty well pre-sold at

the start o'each season. We've thirty-one thoosand season-ticket holders.' Season tickets cost £220.

'So what do you do for fans in these deprived areas?'

'We've just appointed a full-time coach to go round wer eighteen local schools, and each week we hae a rota o' knock-out competitions for them. But we've nae spare tickets. Ye hae to mind that this is a business tae.'

And it was some business. With an average attendance of 44,000 at each match, 600 supporter clubs worldwide, and a multi-million-pound turnover of Rangers romper suits, Little Miss Gers dresses for two-year-olds (£25.99), videos, cassettes ('You'll Know Us By Our Noise – backing vocals by the 1st team squad'), aftershave . . . the business of cult and image.

The Old Firm game was loaded. The stands were filled with blue. Not a hint of green anywhere among the 47,000. Celtic, Rangers alleged, had not paid a bill for 8,000 pounds' worth of damages caused by their supporters during the last Old Firm fixture, and accordingly, they had been banned from attending this one. It was 47,011 versus eleven.

Hotdogs, hamburgers and chips, served in special Rangers styropaks, were in brisk demand and helping Glasgow along in its role of 'Sick Man of Europe'. At the outbreak of the First World War 40 per cent of Glasgow's adult males of army age were unfit for war service of any kind, so poor was the standard of health and nutrition. A recent report into schoolchildren's diets had revealed that an alarming proportion ate no fruit or vegetables, and ate chips for thirteen out of fourteen weekly meals. This city is still the heart-attack capital of the world; only Finnish men have a higher general rate of heart failures. 'High fat, low fibre, and an appalling level of exercise,' are given as the reasons. Unfortunately, watching sport doesn't count.

Rangers ran on to the pitch. The crowd rose to its feet and roared. When Celtic appeared, the whistles and jeers were equally deafening. I sat beside a man who I guessed was a second-hand car salesman, and not a very good one. He turned out to be a stockbroker. He helped me spot the big names.

'That's Durie. He always fouls someone early in the piece. He's utterly unhindered by brains. Nine's Ally McCoist, and ten's the other striker, Mark Hateley . . .' He was the current idol, tall, with thinning black hair dropping to his shoulders, and a long gaunt face like an Easter Island statue. Advanced sales of his video had hit 25,000, a British record. He ran around casually, frequently stopping to brush back his hair.

'You won't believe it when things get going,' said Allan. 'This is pure bigotry, unadulterated hate. It's hard to believe grown men can behave like this. It's historical and inherited war.'

The whistle went. Rangers earned roaring approval for every move that maintained possession, and mistakes were glossed over with a muttering rebuke. Celtic only had to touch the ball to be verbally murdered. Their moments of genius earned a stunned silence. When I looked at the faces behind me watching Celtic excel, I saw the expressions of an appalled jury.

Celtic scored from a free kick. The crowd shrieked in protest. 'AWNAW!' lit up on the scoreboard. A lone Celtic supporter, spotted waving a scarf at one end, sent the crowd into a boiling frenzy of threats and abuse. A group behind me leapt to their feet swearing to skin him alive even though he was quarter of a mile away and rapidly being carried away by the police. The air rang blue. Anger and hate vibrated in palpable fanaticism.

Rangers equalled in the closing minutes. I feared I might be seized and thrown into the air in the all-consuming jubilation.

'Poor game,' remarked Allan. 'It's not the same without the Celtic boys. Crowd was really subdued.'

*　　*　　*

I felt confused as I walked back to my lodgings. Glasgow was such a mixture of extremes. I loved its bluntness, energy and warmth. But it frightened and depressed me. It was taking time to add substance to the outstanding success of the image-makers. I passed yet another expansive void, a scene of neglect and dereliction. It seemed familiar.

'Was this the site of the Garden Festival?'

'That's right, pal. Nae much of it left, eh?'

There was nothing of it left. The National Trust for Scotland's display had been sold to a private buyer who carted it off in eighteen articulated lorry-loads to his home in Bedfordshire. The rest of the exhibits had also been removed to take root elsewhere. The site was a mess of weeds, litter and bulldozings.

'Aye, it was jist a short-term paradise. That's Glasgie fer ye.'

Down in the abandoned River Clyde, a heron was stabbing at the shallows.

51

Lanimers, Lanark

Strathclyde's fragmented roads, the worst in Scotland, carried me, jerkily, south-east towards Lanark which was holding its annual field day. I paused long enough in Blantyre to consume a bunch of bananas and two Mars bars, and learn that its famous son, David Livingstone, in thirty years as a missionary in Africa only converted one man to Christianity (a chief whose son he healed) and even this unsuccessfully, as the man later recanted.

The Hamilton Mausoleum would have made a cheerful diversion with its fifteen-second echoes, but it was closed and its builder, the 10th Duke of Hamilton, 'The Very Duke of Very Dukes', '*El Magnifico*', had been removed to another repository where he lay embalmed and wrapped in foil inside the sarcophagus of an Egyptian princess. This extraordinary barmpot, who was as ridiculously rich as he was wayward in his illusions of grandeur, had the sarcophagus enlarged to accommodate him and during his latter years he used to periodically try it for size. His palace, in whose grounds he once employed, as an oddity, a hermit whom he forbade to shave more than once a year, had disappeared seventy years ago; demolished, it is said – though not factually, but close enough to make it pointless ruining a good story – as a result of subsidence caused by the mines which made the family fortune.

After Hamilton, conurbation petered out and I entered the secret delights of the Upper Clyde Valley. The Clyde had ceased to be a torpid carrier of great ships many miles back, and here it was a real river again, a narrow, shallow affair with rapids, falls and rocky pools where spume spun in eddies and dippers dived. The road also adopted a meandering lifestyle as it coped with hills and the fruit and tomatoes Glaswegians should have been eating. The last four miles to Lanark contained over half of Scotland's orchards and its tomato belt in a valley under glass.

Lanark, or rather its smaller offshoot, New Lanark, won an international reputation in 1800 when Robert Owen became general manager of its mill, and for twenty-five years ran it on principles of safety, co-operation and social reform which were so ahead of their time that many of his codes of practice have endured into modern legislation. Like most of the small towns hereabout, Lanark had lost its industry now, but not its civic pride. On Lanimer ('land march') Day it was host to Scotland's largest street procession.

Crowds were already filling the street at 9 am. I stood alongside Mr Gunning in the central reservation of the main street waiting for the parade. Pudgy and balding, Mr Gunning was a piece-by-piece reassembly of the car boot sale, a walking trophy of bargains. 'Shoes, thirty pee,' he announced smugly. 'Fifty pee off the trousers. Torn.' He showed me the tear Mrs Gunning had mended. By ten past nine I had calculated that Mr Gunning had equipped himself for life at an outlay of £9.80, including his Praktica camera and Leningrad 4 lightmeter.

He pointed to a metal collar in the chain which ran along the central reservation. For the last sixty-five years Mr Gunning hadn't missed a single Lanimers, except during the war years when they were cancelled, and for as many as he could remember the tree that formerly grew through that collar had been his back rest during the parade. 'They cut it down. It was a scandal. There was quite a kick-up about it.'

The place was filling up rapidly. We watched souvenir flag sellers at work; old men, at least they looked old, with florid, alcoholic faces, and limps. One hid his face behind his flags when Mr Gunning raised his Praktica, probably to protect his UB40. Our gaze turned down the street to the statue of Scotland's unrivalled hero, William Wallace, and we discovered a common interest in history.

'Terrible death he suffered,' I remarked. 'Barbaric.'

'Oh aye. That hangin', drawin' n' quarterin',' he replied nonchalantly. 'But it was just par for the course in they days.'

Par for the course. The form of execution Wallace suffered had been newly devised to inflict the maximum amount of agony: he was kept conscious through semi-strangulation, castration, and the removal of his intestines and liver, and allowed to die during dismemberment. Mr Gunning was of the type to believe par for the course should be brought back.

'See all the police here today, son. You never see them during the rest of the year. Everything's going to the dogs. Take the bells for example. Taped music! Bloody scandal.' The bellringer had died years ago and no replacement had been found. The carillon which launched the parade was now taped over loudspeakers.

'And they're late again this year. It's a scandal. There'll be a kick-up about this,' he promised. Mr Gunning and Lanimerians didn't like change. There had been a major kick-up a few years back when the festival date had been changed because of a European parliamentary election. 'In future,' he assured me, 'it'll be the European Parliament that'll have to change. Aye, the council's seeing to it.'

A policeman approached and asked everyone to move behind the chain. Mr Gunning stood his ground. 'Nooooo.

We've aye stood here. No, no. We're allowed here.'
The policeman looked inflexible, so Mr Gunning pulled
Lanimer rank on him. 'You must be new here, son . . .'

I thought there was going to be a serious kick-up but
the policeman saw he was beaten and wandered off. When
the parade began, first with the dignitaries on horseback,
Mr Gunning found a new role. 'WATCH YER FEET ON
THE SHIT!' he yelled, amiably but firmly, to everyone
who followed. And they followed for an hour.

I remember Lanimers for a kick-up which almost but
not quite happened, children in extravagant fancy dress,
floats covered in tens of thousands of paper flowers, and
the neighbourliness of Mr Gunning.

'WATCH YER FEET ON THE SHIT!'

52

෴

A Missed Opportunity

In a council house in Lesmahagow we discussed missed opportunities. Robert MacLaren remembered one of his. For over thirty years it had plagued him. 'Ah was just a lad at the time, a bar waiter at some grand hotel in Dunoon. Lady Montague-Stewart took a private suite for two weeks every year. She was an auld wifie by then. One afternoon the bell rang and ah was summoned to her suite. And there was Lady Montague-Stewart sitting with two poodles on her lap. She ignored me and spoke to the poodles. "Ask the kind young man if he'll get you some water," says she, and that was all she said. So ah went off and got it, and . . . ach, ah regret it tae this day . . . ah just wish ah'd had the courage tae bend doon tae they poodles and say: "Ask the auld bag if there's onything else she wants."'

࿇

53

Robert Burns

On the back roads between Lesmahagow and Ayr, I entered deep into the land of anecdote, song, verse and penicillin (Darvel, Fleming's birthplace). Here the face of Scotland was benign and bucolic with a thin population who mostly drove tractors and applied suction cups to udders. Their smallholdings were dotted about the rounded hills and had names like Unthank, Coldwakning, Foulpapple, Hungryhill and Shacklehill which seemed strangely at odds with the impression of hymnal pleasantness. Their cows and sheep mowed the scene with healthy obsession, while their fields were the source of vegetables, grains and poetry.

'This marks the spot of the eerie encounter in "Death and Mr Hornbrook"; Raised by the Bachelor Club,' an almost invisible sign whispered in the verge near Tarbolton.

Robert Burns would have seen little change in his stomping-ground over the years since his death in 1796. The shape of the fields and hedges would be much the same, and the narrow lanes, now asphalted. The stone houses looked solid enough to have endured two centuries but they were deceptive, for thatched cottages had been the norm then. The large parcels wrapped in black plastic and lying about the fields would be alien to him, as would fences, farm machinery and the tall grain silos which looked equally alien to me. Ayrshire, it seemed, had turned Islamic and was studded with the minarets of its mosques.

At Mauchline I parked my bike behind Poosie Nansies, the howff in Burns' 'The Jolly Beggars'. The proprietor, W.R. Blake, wore a handlebar moustache that would have looked good framed in the canopy of a Spitfire, and admittedly looked manly and dashing in a bar designed for damage minimalisation during a brawl. It was a stark den of false beams, wholesale furniture and a machine which flashed and talked to itself. So this was where Burns observed, drank, socialised, recited and played Space Invaders. Two customers stood mute at the bar.

'Is this all that's left of the original bar?'

Sergeant-Major Blake poured my pint without responding. Forty years here had apparently bored him witless. He nodded for me to follow, and led me out of the bar to a door on the far side of the corridor. He unlocked it. 'All original.' It was a neuk room, small and cosy, furnished with a dresser full of ashets, a grandfather clock, a table and chairs and a fire with a swee.

In North America, Argentina and Australia I had passed many hours on the roadside waiting for cars to give me a lift, memorising 'Tam O'Shanter' from a grubby and creased photocopy. It warmed me to think that in this very room Burns might have recited it himself.

It warmed me briefly because the door was quickly closed and locked again. We returned to the howff's main den where it was hard to imagine a poet coming up with anything except two black eyes. 'Death and Sergeant-Major Blake', perhaps.

'Big boozer, they say, that Burns,' said one of the drinkers. 'And a randy bugger tae.'

Burns was far from abstemious, but equally far from being a 'big boozer' in an age when heavy drinking was the norm (William Pitt managed five bottles of port a day while Prime Minister). Despite Burns' playful tendency in both verse and letter to posture as a great drinker, frequently 'bousing at the nappy, an' getting fou and unco happy', the facts of his life show otherwise. He drank irregularly, only socially and moderately, and expressed an intense dislike of drunken behaviour. Jean Armour, Burns' wife, testified 'with tears in her eyes that in all her knowledge of her husband either before marriage or after, she never once saw him intoxicated'. Gilbert, his brother and farming partner, made the same testimony.

As James Mackay, one of the most recent and comprehensive of Burns' 900 biographers, put it (in *Burns – A Biography*): 'the man who ran a 170-acre farm, rode two hundred miles a week on Excise duties and kept four sets of Excise records, and still found time to compose such masterpieces as 'Tam O'Shanter', besides conducting a voluminous correspondence and writing songs for two publishers simultaneously, was a workaholic, not an alcoholic.'

And neither was Robert Burns unusual for his time – one in which no form of contraception was available – in his sexual adventures. Fornicators were regularly summoned to appear before the Kirk Session. For this sin, resulting in Jean Armour's set of twins, Burns was ordered to make three public acts of penance in church. Sinners were normally required to mount the penance stool, the 'creepy chair' as Burns called it, but he was allowed to stand in shame at his pew. On his last appearance he was joined by three others, that particular week's quota of fornicators, and the minister absolved them from scandal. He had to absolve Burns again on another occasion, also on account of Jean (another set of twins) before Robert and Jean were married. (Burns would have married Jean on the first occasion but for the hostility of Jean's father – indeed, Burns considered himself the wronged party.) In all, Burns had nine children by his wife, and three, possibly four, by other women. One of these illegitimate daughters, Elizabeth, was raised by Jean along with her own children. 'Our Rab should have had twa wives,' was Jean's saintly view of her husband.

Robert Burnes (he changed the spelling later), the eldest of seven children, was born at Alloway in 1759. His father, William, a solid hard-working type of above-average education, was a market gardener who changed to farming, choosing ill-judged farms which never repaid his labours and sank him into debt; a trend his sons were to duplicate. His mother was a charming, barely literate woman, a domestic servant who had been jilted and resigned herself to spinsterhood.

Burns was born into a household where books, exceptionally hard to come by, were greatly valued. Despite his limited means, William subscribed to a private library in Ayr and, in the absence of a local school, hired a tutor (sixpence per day plus board) for his children and those of his neighbours. In all, Burns received two years of formal education, disjointed and spread over ten years, but these were intense periods of learning under a gifted teacher who encouraged discussion and his pupils to think for themselves.

By the age of seven, Burns was an avid reader. His powers of retention were phenomenal and his appetite for learning insatiable. At the age of thirteen he was introduced to French, and borrowed a dictionary. Within 'a little while' he was able to read and understand any French author. He took to debating early and when one dominie tried to ridicule Burns' inquisitive mind in front of the class, the boy challenged his teacher to a debate. The subject was, 'Whether is a great general or a respectable merchant the most valuable member of society?' The dominie took the side of the general, but he was no match for the argument of his pupil and at the end, 'His hand was observed to shake; then his voice trembled;

and he dissolved the school in a state of vexation pitiable to behold.'

But William Burnes was forced to exploit his sons almost relentlessly on the farm. It was to relieve a life of 'the cheerless gloom of a hermit with the unceasing moil of a galley-slave' that Robert began dabbling in 'the sin of RHYME'. On top of strenuous labour, Burns had to contend with poor health. 'At this time,' his brother recollected, 'he was almost constantly afflicted in the evenings with a dull headache, which, at a future period of his life, was exchanged for a palpitation of the heart and threatening of fainting and suffocation . . .' He suffered at least one nervous breakdown, for which the doctor's remedy was to induce 'a good vomiting and purging'.

In 1786, depressed, rejected by Jean and threatened by a writ issued by her father, Burns decided to emigrate to Jamaica. Doubts remain as to how serious an intention this was but he paid nine guineas for his passage aboard the *Nancy* (later transferring to the *Bell*), and had been offered a post as book-keeper at a relatively meagre salary of £30 per annum on a plantation at Port Antonio. Shortly before he was to leave – he claimed his trunk was already packed and on the road – his first attempt at publishing his poems proved so successful he was persuaded to abandon his plans of emigration. The Kilmarnock edition's 600 copies were snapped up by private subscribers.

The following year he borrowed a pony and travelled to Edinburgh to publish a new edition of his poems. Fame came overnight. For months he was the toast of society. His electrifying powers of conversation, his wit and charm were sought by all the literati and socialites. The 15-year-old Walter Scott met him. Years later Scott was to write, 'the eye alone, I think, indicated the poetical character. It was large and dark and glowed (I say literally glowed) when he spoke with feeling and interest. I never saw such an eye in a human head, though I have seen the most distinguished men in my time.'

Burns made several brief tours, but returned to a life of toil. He made about £400 from the Edinburgh edition but was unfortunate in having a publisher who, if not downright dishonest, was criminally negligent in paying his dues. Burns gave away half his earnings to help his brother's farming debts. The Irish and American editions of his works were pirated and he made nothing from them. Fiercely proud, and utterly disdainful of the commercial aspect of writing, Burns asked for nothing more from the second Edinburgh edition than twenty free copies to give to friends. His publisher didn't even bother to inform him of the publication date.

Posterity has forgotten his other achievements: his government award for improving flax; his expertise with cattle and the introduction of Ayrshires to Nithsdale; his nomination for the first Professorship of Agriculture at Edinburgh University; his influential role as a religious reformer.

Farming and excise duties took the largest part of his time and energy. January 1795 saw him in the saddle for up to fifteen hours a day in one of the worst winters on record. Snow drifted to depths of 100 feet in hollows in the Campsies, and houses buried up to their windows were commonplace. His health fell into serious decline. Daily sea-bathing up to his armpits in the gelid Solway Firth was his doctor's recommendation, a treatment wholly inappropriate for one suffering from what is now believed to have been rheumatic heart disease and bacterial endocarditis. Burns' last decade had been devoted to collecting and writing songs. He was still writing within days of his death.

He died in Dumfries in 1796. His brother Gilbert was the only family member to attend the funeral. At the time the cortège was making its way down the high street, followed by 10,000 mourners, Jean Burns was giving birth to their ninth child. The funeral expenses were modest: 2s 6d for the grave, 3s for the mortcloth and 5s for the tolling of the town's bells. Burns left behind £15 in drafts, a library valued at £90 and a note of credit for £185 (in today's terms, an estate of £40,000). His debts came to less than £15, including an unpaid bill for £2 3s from Dr Brown, the misguided prescriber of cold baths.

Robert Burns died aged 37. His life and writings are the subject of over 3,500 books of critical analysis. In his 22 years of creativity, he wrote 28,000 lines of verse and maintained a prodigious correspondence of which 700 letters are extant. Over 2,000 editions of his works have been published, in almost fifty languages. Samuel Mashak's Russian translation sold over one million copies in thirty years, and sales of a recent Chinese translation ran to 100,000 in its first printing.

Statues of Burns vastly outnumber those erected to Shakespeare or any other British poet; even without the 3,460 busts which were obligatory furnishings in every Carnegie Library in the USA until the 1950s, Burns still stands in bronze or stone in 180 locations around the world. Only Christopher Columbus and Lenin outnumber him.

Not least amongst the virtues of the man were his grit and spirit which refused to allow a life of hardship and disappointment to crush his art, in the same way he refused to let a literature and education experienced entirely in English deflect him from his native Scots. Poetry and song were deep within him and, armed with a diamond stylus, he became a frequent literary vandal, inscribing panes of glass wherever his satire was wickedly roused. His genius was his incisive understanding of human character and all its quirks and foibles, and to express them in a way that made a popular cult of literary greatness. The 'Bard of Humanity' earned his title.

54

∽

Mull of Galloway Diary

'Whit brengs y'ere?'

It was rich, fluid, poetic, concise. How stilted and bland and pompous it became in the Queen's English.

'Fer why've yek um?'

I was savouring the Mull of Galloway farmer's words for so long and running through in my mind the phonetics that would reproduce them, that he had to repeat his question again before I realised a reply was required.

Idle curiosity sounded a lame lifestyle to a man with a milk quota to fill. And it seemed lame to me too at that stage, after seventy miles in the rain. What was it all about? I was cold, wet, tired, lonely and feeling low. And two hours' backlog of diary still to write from a handful of scrawled notes. The farmer let me sleep in the dairy. For once I was not sitting cross-legged on the ground trying to reconstruct the day's gleanings by candlelight. Here in the dairy I had bucket seat and electric light, a tricky birth calf-extractor, five gallons of SLAYMOR rat and mouse poison, and a large tub of LACTROSE udder disinfectant. What more could a writer want?

~~Wha' brings yer ear?~~ Whit brengs y'ere?

Fer why've yek um? Lovely poetic dialect.

Wrote till 12.15 pm in milking parlour; T-gadget, Slaymor rat/mouse poison (5 gls), Lactrose anti-infection for udders.

If this journey ever gets into a book, I suppose everyone will think it was a cruise. So damn easy. You can't write about how pissed off you are with the rain; how four gears have packed in; how half the time all you can think of is how bloody miserable you feel after eight hours on a bike with shoes, socks and feet that have been wet for three days. Avoid self-pity. They won't tolerate it.

Or will they? In small doses?

55

౬

Signs, and Alexander Murray

Wayside notices and posters conferred knowledge and a twentieth century guide to living on the cyclist in a clandestine exchange denied to the motorist. They formed a communications network of endlessly interesting facts, not just where to buy your honey, eggs and wrought iron candlesticks. Some were clues to unexpected hazards. No one travelling at 60 mph could have read, 'BEWARE OF DOWN COMING CARS' among the rhododendrons of a private drive, or, elsewhere, 'BEWARE OF WILD ANIMALS AND CHILDREN', 'AMERICAN WRESTLING – Starring: UNDERTAKER, BARBARIAN, HANGMAN, CORPORAL PUNISHMENT. It's a fight to the finish – only one man can survive. Newton Stewart Hall, 23 Oct.'

'FERAL GOAT RESERVE', stated another, which would have been more useful had it appeared before my chapter on Rum's goats (or Orkney's gots). 'Goats were tolerated throughout the ages here because it was believed they killed adders, kept sheep off rocky crags, and ate ergots of ryegrass which can induce abortion in sheep. You can age a goat by counting the rings on the horn.'

But it was the sign which led me to a monument and the story of Alexander Murray which was the prize collection of the day. The monument was a tall granite obelisk, set close to the road to New Galloway, among forested hills and names invented for unlikely fiction: Glen of Trool, Rig of the Jarkness, Murder Hole, Clatteringshaws Loch. Had I seen a sign, 'BEWARE OF THE JARKNESS', I wouldn't have been surprised, but there was nothing fictitious about Alexander Murray, DD (1775–1813).

His father, Robert, was employed as shepherd to a Mr Laidlaw of Clatteringshaws in exchange for the keep of up to sixty sheep and four muirland cows. At the age of 69 Robert married his second wife, who gave birth to Alexander and, two years later, to a daughter. Alexander's eyesight was so hopelessly myopic that he drove his father to exasperation by being unable to differentiate between sheep and boulders. His talents lay elsewhere.

Spread over a period of eight years, in New Galloway and Minnigaff, he received a total of sixty weeks' schooling. He studied to become a Doctor of Divinity – as was the practice for anyone who wished to advance their learning – and was appointed Minister of Urr. Here he began collecting Bibles, in every language he could acquire. For hours every day and night he ran his finger over the unintelligible words and deciphered them with his English version open at the same passage.

His knowledge of languages became so proficient and well known that in 1811, one anecdote runs, he was contacted by the Foreign Secretary, the Marquess of Wellesley, and asked if he could help with a letter addressed to George III which had been received from the shadows of the colonies. None of the royal advisers could make head nor tail of it. Murray duly sent back a translation with a covering letter in which he wrote, 'I'm not surprised your advisors had difficulties as the letter was in a little-known dialect of Abyssinian.'

In 1812 he was appointed Professor of Oriental Languages at Edinburgh University, but he died the following year, leaving his analysis of Sanskrit and a *History of the European Languages* unfinished.

Like Burns, he died at the age of 37.

࿇

56

Dick Brown, Cargenbridge

In Dumfries, Radio West Sound seemed the place to look for contacts. 'Who would be some of your more unusual local characters?'

A man, wearing a tie disguised as sweet peas, crumpled his face into thoughtfulness. 'Ah! . . . now let me see . . . there's Ed Iglehart who blows glass mushrooms . . . Mavis Patterson, former housewife, trans-America cyclist . . . Andy Goldsworthy, snow and ice sculptor . . . Mungo Bryson, he organises the Alternative Highland Games . . . hang on, I'll get you the complete list . . .' He ducked below the counter and surfaced with the Dumfries and Galloway telephone directory. Under 'B' I chose Brown, Dick.

Brown, 'Handsome' Dick, lived a few miles away at Cargenbridge, a village which dealt in windows, patios and conservatories. He was indeed handsome, an unrepentant heavy drinker in his early fifties.

On 14 November 1981 he was bosun on a bulk carrier (phosphates) crossing the Bay of Biscay in a storm. Massive waves broke over the ship and it began to sink so rapidly the crew didn't have time to release the lifeboats. The first inflatable was unserviceable and the second only floated for a short time.

'I remember grabbing a bottle of whisky, Ballantines, it was, and thinking, "If I'm going to die, I'm dying with this inside me."' He remembered little else. He was in the sea for eight hours before a Sea King helicopter, about to call off the search, spotted him. When rescuers pulled him out he was still clutching the empty bottle. He was flown to a unit which specialised in hypothermia, one of three survivors from a crew of 38.

'Did you drink the whole bottle?' he was asked.

'No, unfortunately I spilled some,' he replied.

He was asked how he survived? What kept him going?

'I kept on thinking that those bastards, the shipping company, owed me six months' pay.'

Dick gave up the sea. Horses had always been a part of his life. 'There's a latent cowboy in all of us,' he believed. He gave riding lessons, and did stunt riding in films. In the days when sponsorship was still a novel concept of fundraising he decided to celebrate the 800th anniversary of the founding of Dumfries with a sponsored ride from Glasgow to Dumfries in a suit of armour. The distance was 78 miles; the suit of armour, hired from Robert White, the Queen's armourer, weighed seven stone.

'I notified Glasgow police. The head guy, Elphinstone Dalgleish – how could you forget that name, eh? – offered me a two-horse escort out of the city. I thanked him but said it was unnecessary. "Listen, pal," Elphinstone told me, "in the areas you're passing through, they'll pull you off for your scrap value."'

His horse shied at the crowds in George Square and threw him. 'Geesus! You could have heard the clatter in Dumfries!' It was a 'hellish' journey. He couldn't drink beer because it went straight through. 'No zip fly. You know, that's a serious design flaw in armour.' His friends would open his visor and toss down shorts and know that he was somewhere inside and would get them. His horse lost a shoe. With difficulty he dismounted at a phone box to call his farrier. A passing *Daily Mail* photographer scooped a picture of him in a call box, in armour, holding the receiver in one hand and, through the open door, his horse in the other. He reached Dumfries sixteen years ahead of the anniversary. He'd been given the wrong date, but local charities were £15,000 richer.

Dick's ride entered the *Guinness Book of Records*. A few years later it was beaten. He won it back. It was beaten again. Winning it back for the last time almost killed him. His health was poor. He had angina, and liver and kidney problems (aside from having had open-heart surgery the year before his ship went down), but he did it: 208 miles in three days (£60,000).

Recently Dick was arrested at the end of his annual Hogmanay ride around fifteen pubs in Dumfries. He admitted that he was drunk on a public highway but maintained that Big Ben, his horse, had no need of him, was in control and walking in a straight line. He offered to demonstrate this special relationship but the judge fined him fifty pounds. (It was paid by one of the tabloids.)

Handsome Dick Brown is, currently, the last person in Britain to have been convicted of being drunk in charge of a horse.

57

Gretna Green

I felt more depressed than ever by the thought that I was on the shortest road to Gretna Green.

Charles Dickens, *The Holly Tree.*

Countries should never be judged by their border towns as these are always a tasteless excess of what is scarce or illegal among their foreign neighbours. Gretna Green stands alone as a sordid example of frontier Scotland, trafficking in legal marriages at the rate of three to four thousand a year. Gretna Green ('We accept MASTERCHARGE, VISA, EUROCHEQUES, etc.') did not simply promise romance, it force-fed it. In establishments with names dredged from the bottom of the barrel, 'Royal Stewart', 'Bonnie Prince Charlie's Cottage', 'Last Hoose' and 'Lovers' Leap Motel' (which came closest to capturing the mood of the place), Gretna Green plied its trade of kick-starting marriage.

Gretna Green offered nothing that was not equally available in any other Scottish village, but it had the right name and was the first place in Scotland on the main road north. The first rush of runaway marriages occurred in 1773 when England tightened up its laws and made marriage the prerogative of the Church. Scots'

Law allowed anyone to preside over a wedding as long as the couple's verbal agreement was made in front of two witnesses. In Gretna Green it became customary for the blacksmith to assume the role of 'Anvil Priest' and 'forge' these symbolic bonds. These 'irregular marriages', as they were known in England, were legally recognised in every country.

In order to give jilted lovers and angry parents some chance of preventing runaways from marrying, Lord Brougham's Act was passed in 1857, requiring one of the nuptial pair to have been resident in Scotland for twenty-one days before the ceremony could take place. (Lord Brougham, eccentric lawyer and ex-statesman, showed a high degree of brassiness in promoting this piece of legislation considering he himself had been through an 'irregular marriage' in Coldstream thirty years earlier.) Despite this proviso, the town's runaway trade flourished.

Gretna Green should have died in 1940 when the last Anvil Priest (a Mr Rennison, who offered as his credentials his name read backwards) had his office removed by law. Henceforth all marriages had to be conducted by the Church or registrar. What saved the village was its legendary *romanz* and the difference between the minimum legal ages for marriage without parental consent: eighteen in England, sixteen in Scotland.

ScotRail has recently reopened Gretna Station which Beeching axed in 1964, and the Registrar's Office has expanded its staff and moved to new premises, a red-brick building shared by 'Rents and Rates' and a dentist. Inside the signs probably read: COUNCIL TAX, Straight Ahead; TOOTHACHE, Right; MARRIAGE, Left. This little palace in the heart of Scotland's wedding Mecca stands slap opposite the KINGSLAND TAKE-AWAY fish 'n' chip bar.

'This is the real reason they come,' Jim Jackson said, 'to be photographed here.' He was the current owner and *ex officio* Anvil Priest of the Old Blacksmith Shop.

Thin and bearded, he posed for hours every day in full Highland dress. In every photograph of himself on display, his glasses maddeningly reflected the flash. This was Scotland's ninth most visited tourist attraction, 300,000 visitors a year at 50 pence a look. Jim Jackson's smile was deceptively genuine.

'Excuse me, please.' He had business with a happy couple from Durham. A flash, clicks from a battery of twin Nikons. It was hard to tell where the flash had come from, but Mr Jackson outshone everyone.

Under 'S': Smith, Mrs Pat, Gretna. Cheerful below a white perm, Mrs Smith exhibited all the charm the Green lacked. Now retired after forty years as the registrar of over ten thousand marriages, she had recently swapped roles and become a bride herself.

'One of my strangest cases concerned an old woman who had to be helped from the car by her intended groom and his two helpers. She was dripping in jewels. The groom could have been her son and I fancied I could see pounds shining in the eyes of the young men.' As long as the parties had complied with the law and produced the necessary documents, the registrar was required to marry them. 'The groom produced his divorce papers, and the old woman her second husband's death certificate. I felt so sorry for her. There was no apparent tenderness but, of course, I had to marry them.'

That evening Pat received a telephone call from a woman who asked if she had married an old lady under one of several names. Pat confirmed that she had. The caller explained that the groom was her former husband, and the old lady was her mother; *she*, the old lady, was the scheming partner in the affair and had been trying to marry her former son-in-law all over the country. 'At that time this was an illegal alliance so I had to annul the marriage and put the matter in the hands of the police. And there I was feeling sorry for her.'

But an even stranger case began with a knock on the door of her home late at night. 'I opened it and there was a small, round, fat Russian aristocrat with his valet in attendance. Well! . . . talk about surprise! He clicked his heels together, bowed slightly and said, "You will marry my daughter, *now*, please."' Pat explained about the twenty-one-day residency rule. He didn't understand. An interpreter was summoned from Dumfries. The Russian agreed to come back on condition that the ceremony was performed the very moment the statutory period was over, which happened to be at two minutes past midnight. Pat agreed.

'He appeared at the appointed time and, according to Russian custom, chocolates, champagne and oranges were spread over the table. Well, I married the couple and that was it. Then . . . ooooh, it must have been about eighteen months or two years later, there was a knock at the door. A small round man clicked his heels and bowed. "You will divorce my daughter, *now*, please." I had to get the interpreter back to explain to him that I couldn't do divorces.' She shook her head wistfully. 'So that was one of my failures.'

On cycling out of Gretna Green I saw a sign pointing to the left: 'INDUSTRIAL ESTATE'. It took me by surprise. I was under the impression I had just been in one.

58

❦

Samye Ling

Sounding like the frantic activity of rusty bedsprings, pheasants took to the air, startled by my sudden appearance among their roadside patches of bracken. For mile after mile their russet and chestnut plumages glided down to the River Esk which snaked lazily through a deep valley of fields and trees. Dew glistened on the ground and made the air smell of damp grass, and a light breeze caused leaves to dance on the road as shadows. The message was clear. 'We apologise for any inconvenience five days of rain may have caused. Have a nice day.' I intended to. Gretna Green was behind me. I was warm, dry, cheerful and on my way to Tibet.

Years earlier, returning from cycling in Eastern Europe, I had passed this way and been astonished to see, among some trees, dozens of colourful prayer flags and a sign stating: 'Kagyu Samye Ling Tibetan Centre'. This time I turned into the driveway and found myself in front of the largest Buddhist temple in Europe. It was inaugurated on the propitious date of 8.8.88, the Tenth Day of the Sixth Month Male Earth Dragon Year Seventeenth Cycle. I removed my shoes and entered a world I had last experienced in Ladakh. With a huge, serene, golden Buddha and thousands of miniatures occupying an entire wall, murals, motifs, thangkas, drums, prayer wheels and bald monks in crimson robes, this was an exact replica – only it had electricity, heat and a striking lack of dust, age and swarthy skin.

I made an appointment to see Lama Yeshe Losal, the spiritual leader of the centre, and joined a queue of others for his daily surgery. We waited a long time. (*Never make an appointment with a thief or a lama – neither will keep it*. Old Tibetan saying.) The girl sitting next to me had suffered a lapse from her teachings.

'I did a week's course here once to learn tolerance. I came away at the end feeling good, clean, kind and forgiving. When I got home it lasted twenty minutes, until someone jumped me in the taxi queue at Surbiton station.'

Eventually the queue diminished and it was my turn to pass through the curtained doorway into a study the approximate size of four confession boxes. The room's most noticeable feature was Lama Yeshe's smile.

He sat compressed between a wall and an upright desk, a small squat man with tonsured head and ochreous brown skin. The folds of his robe gathered round him in deep wrinkles but parted at the chest to give an impression of mole-like strength. And his smile was the complete opposite of Jim Jackson's: it came from within, the gentle glow of contentment. Lama Yeshe might just have seen his drive from the tee take a perfect line.

'The name Samye Ling mean a place which defy the imagination. We are a community living by Buddhist principles, to learn compassion, to teach compassion to everyone.'

'And how do you do this?'

'We have one course which lasts twenty-four hours, every day.' His smile widened to a mischievous grin. 'This is a place of healing – not with big 'H' but with little one. We run short courses, things like T'ai Chi, aromatherapy, art therapy. We practise meditation.

We run retreats. It is all about letting go. Letting go of fear.'

He was born in 1944 in Tibet, and at the age of three was given to a monastery to be trained as a lama. In 1959 he and his family fled to India where he was adopted and went to school. 'Then I became a Western hippy. I had led such a closed narrow life. I went wild: drink, drugs, women.' He went to America and soon came to his senses.

'I had a sponsor. He was a millionaire and a very sad man. I saw how the West had imprisoned itself in its wealth. I realised how wrong this life was.'

At Woodstock he went into a solitary retreat for five years, not even seeing the people who delivered his meals. He had since spent a further seven years in retreat, in meditation, and would have continued had his brother not asked for his help. His brother, a reincarnate lama of high rebirth, Dr Akong Rinpoche, had been approached by a neo-Buddhist group in Eskdalemuir to open a centre, and Samye Ling was founded in 1968. It was the first Tibetan Buddhist centre to be opened in the West, and Dr Rinpoche asked his brother to come out of retreat and be its spiritual leader. 'I have no ambition now. I am here to serve, to help others. It is easier because I understand their problems. I have seen both sides.'

'Have you been back to Tibet?'

'To Lhasa only. It is not the Tibet I remember. The temples have been pulled down, the people mixed so much with the Han. Here, in the West, is now the hope and future of the Tibetan religion and culture. I have family still in Tibet but we don't write. The world is now my family. I have learned compassion.'

Samye Ling occupied forty acres and included a vegetable garden and dairy. A permanent community of sixty to seventy lived here, and the venture was funded by fees and donations. The community had recently purchased Holy Island off Arran to turn into a much larger and more isolated retreat centre than the one currently in use at Samye Ling. Retreats lasted three years, three months and three days and cost £7,000. Eighteen hours were spent in meditation each day. Candidates were allowed, but not encouraged, to write or receive letters, and any correspondents were asked not to mention any items of local, national or world news.

Samye Ling's atmosphere formed a strange interstice between two worlds, between downtown Leh without the mock bowler hats and oriental features, and the hearty mucking-in togetherness of a youth hostel. 'Henny hwon for more soup?' in an Oxford accent, struck a discordant note as the words emerged from the dining room window and cut across a view of a peacock sitting on the roof of a Ford Escort parked in front of a little piece of Sheh palace. Little bits of many worlds seemed badly stuck together but they still spelled a clear message of tolerance and welcome.

Over soup I met John, a soft-spoken Londoner. Six months ago he and 24 others had ended a three-year retreat. 'I'm lucky,' he remarked. 'I'm just about to start another one.'

'Another three years?'

'Yes.'

'Why does that make you lucky?'

'Because I'm finding myself, the real me under all the sham.'

'Isn't it the easy option, the selfish option, shutting yourself away for three years?'

'No, it's not selfish. The whole point of retreat is to become a better person and so be of more use to society. And if you think it's easy, you should try it.'

To qualify for the hermit's life he'd had to become fluent in Tibetan, for all the mantras and texts were in that language. He'd taken 32 vows. The first seven months in retreat were spent in silence and without washing. His 'bed' was a box one-metre square which forced him to sleep upright.

'And you're going in for another three years?'

'To you that's hard to understand. You can only see retreat as physical restrictions, a closed door. I no longer feel the physical boundaries. I see only an open door to my mind.'

The room filled up with the weekend's intake for the Taming the Tiger course. I was tempted to stay on but my sick, clock-watching, money-obsessed Western instincts got the better of me. I took a brochure instead.

We have reached a paradoxical stage in our evolution. Our development is now threatening our continued survival. We are caught in the belief that if we are not happy, we must get our surroundings to change . . . But it is by learning to let go of our attachments to such judgements we are able to be at peace, no matter how the world may be . . . This is the 'new age' that we all truly aspire to. Not a new age founded upon some new set of beliefs – a new set of religious doctrines and dogmas – but an age in which our minds are free from prejudices and our hearts are free from judgement.

Physically, Samye Ling looked alien and contrived, the way anything innovative always appears to outsiders, but it felt much less foreign than other parts of inhabited Scotland. The only thing 'freakish' about the place was its dedication to the objectives of tolerance and peace. I arrived with contemporary society's initial scepticism of good intentions, and left feeling my prejudices were misplaced, even if Samye Ling's striving to free us from judgement was a philosophy to put travel writers out of work.

59

❦

Duke of Buccleuch

The distinction of the Borders landscape lies in its variety: here a swath of yellowing wheat, a pine forest, a shadowy grove of beech and chestnut, Friesians scattered as eye-catching blots of black-and-white, absorbed in the endless task of consumption like the sporadic fluffs of white Cheviots found higher up in the scene; there a mile of river, a ruined castle, a dozen princely homes, a clutter of farms, the green of pasture and random patches of heather in what ought to be a wholly fictional extravagance of purple; and everywhere those steep rounded hills, confidently obstructive and yet appearing benign and alluringly accessible compared to their more dramatic and cantankerous counterparts to the north.

The best of the Border country is a cocktail land of diversity and moderation, both productive and prettily 'wild' (by which, in Britain's wholly manipulated landscape, one can only mean 'non-commercial'). In some places, the mix comes as close to perfection as a human is capable of creating. One such place lies close to Selkirk, where the waters of the Yarrow and Ettrick meet and partially enclose Bowhill.

I made my way along a drive whose signs welcomed walkers, mountain bikers and ponytrekkers, and were otherwise noteworthy for suggesting things you might like to do rather than pronouncing the legal consequences of daring to do them. The drive brought me to the back entrance of a house which sprawled below a wooded hill and overlooked a lily-fringed loch. It was a long house – long enough for a mountain bike to appear useful, if not necessary – rising to four storeys, defying symmetry and supporting great clusters of chimneys on roofs of different levels. The architects had clearly striven for horrendous heating bills rather than elegance.

It was outwith the open season for house visitors, and an air of slumber prevailed. Beside the door was a speak-hole which said nothing but told me a great deal. Made of brass, it would have voiced aloofness but this one was of simple, housing-estate chrome. A label typed 'THEIR GRACES' was stuck beside its single button. I pressed it. I had an appointment with the largest private landowner in Britain and the second wealthiest man in Scotland.

The 9th Duke of Buccleuch (11th of Queensberry and, incidentally, Chief of Clan Scott) can still remember the sound of his spine cracking. He is 71 now but was 49 at the time. He was out riding and had just jumped a low wall for the second time when his horse fell and rolled over him. For ten minutes he lay in a ditch until his friends found him, looking up at the sky, knowing his back was broken and moving only his fingers, for the rest of his body was paralysed.

The door was answered by the Duke's secretary, who led me to the study and advised that His Grace would be with me shortly. No dingy study this, but a spacious room filled with light, it had an ornate stucco ceiling and was furnished like a drawing room. Silver and gilt spines packed shelves as high as a hand might reach, and where the books ended, paintings began. Twenty-two family portraits ringed the room; the subjects smiled, pondered, worried, sulked, growled. Some stroked pets, some were squeezed into fashionable tourniquets of tight lacing and looked dangerously explosive, others were incapacitated by the bulk of their costumes, and two long-haired youths (c1780) looked human enough to have just smashed a window and escaped undetected. At Bowhill you were never far from the eyes of Raeburn, Reynolds, Gainsborough, Landseer, Van Dyck and Canaletto. I looked around for Leonardo da Vinci's *The Madonna with the Yarnwinder*, an un-insurable masterpiece painted over 450 years ago, but I heard later that it had been moved to another of the Duke's homes, Drumlanrig Castle.

The door opened and His Grace appeared, his strong frame working a manual wheelchair. His sandy hair had gone on top, and a bold forehead, combined with a broad face and heavy glasses, gave him a studious, wise countenance. His manner was relaxed and warm, as if he were at ease within himself and even quite glad I had come, when in fact I must have been just another prying reporter.

We exchanged formalities and he indicated a sofa for me to sit in, parking his wheelchair nearby.

'I saw you looking at the paintings. I'm very proud of the collection we have here. But I believe if one is lucky enough to have lovely things, one should share them. That's why I opened up my homes to the public eighteen years ago. I was one of the first.' He had three homes, he explained, and four estates. Bowhill was his main residence, while Drumlanrig Castle (Sanquhar) and Boughton Hall (Northampton) were occasional homes. He also spent time in London, and Eildon Hall near Melrose was 'the family nursery'. Whenever a Buccleuch raised a family they moved to Eildon Hall, it seemed. His son was currently living there with the new generation. But Bowhill was the base for running the 277,000 acres of Scotland that he owned.

'But we aren't here to discuss art. I believe you want to know my views on the ownership and management of the land?' He opened a folder and searched for a sheet that was missing. 'Please excuse me one moment', and he drove his wheelchair at a wall of books, swung open a panel of false spines and disappeared through a secret door. He returned with a photocopy of a page from *The History of Sanquhar* by James Brown, published in 1891. The author had observed:

> Notices of "Trespassers will be prosecuted", "Keep to the Road", and others of a like nature, by which a selfish and exclusive landlordism would seek to deprive the general public of enjoyments which are the heritage of humanity, are nowhere to be seen. In this respect the Duke of Buccleuch, and, following his example, the other landed proprietors of the district, have allowed to all the liberty to roam wheresoever they list [sic].

The Duke waved his hand round his canvas family. 'We've had this policy for over one hundred and fifty years. You see, today, ninety-six per cent of the population live in towns . . . and *they* will ultimately decide what happens in the countryside. We landowners have to recognise this and foster understanding, bridge the gulf between town and country and demonstrate that we are the best stewards of the land.'

It was during his thirteen years as an MP of an urban constituency in Edinburgh that he became aware of how big the gulf was. When he inherited the estates in 1976 he began to actively encourage visitors rather than passively tolerate them. 'I want to show people all the work that goes on here, let them see that the country is not static but a constant activity of farming, forestry and conservation. I see my responsibilities to the land as going far beyond the simple need for profit. Do you know, we look after 5,100 miles of dykes, fences and hedges? That's enough to stretch from here to San Francisco! They bring in not a penny of revenue and constantly need repairing.'

The Duke had taken a degree in agriculture and forestry

from Oxford and made the estate his life-long thesis. His mind was a data bank of yields in tons per acre and the statistics of success and failure. He gave the impression of knowing the land intimately, and, more unusually, caring about its people. There were over a thousand of them, including 200 tenant farmers who had been sent questionnaires seeking anonymous suggestions or grievances. Only 8 per cent, he asserted, had expressed dissatisfactions and would have preferrred to be owner-occupiers. Together they and the Duke produced an annual 127,000 lambs, 14,000 cattle, 18 million litres of milk, 20,000 tons of cereals and 50,000 tons of timber.

'But do you think it's *right* that private families control so much land?' I asked.

'Right? What is *right*? I can't answer for how estates acquired their land, but all my life I've fought against any moves towards nationalisation of the land. When you see the mess the government's made of every resource it's taken over, you can't believe it would do any better with the land. It's a long-term asset, and governments have short-term policies and lives. We've built up a working relationship with our tenant farmers over centuries. We're planting hardwood trees that won't mature for another 160 years. We've maximised production, conservation and access. I am convinced that caring families are the best stewards of the land.'

'But caring families are very thin on the ground. Particularly in the Highlands.'

'Ahh, but a sporting estate is another matter. This is a difficult one. Thank God we don't have stalking here. We shoot pheasant and grouse but as a by-product of grazing. We don't have any exclusive sporting land.' I felt he was about to expand on this and express strong disapproval but he carefully changed tack. 'Of course the commonest misconception about landowners is that they are port-sodden old hermits of immense wealth. When the reality is that most own land they can't sell and which yields a negligible return. They inherit cold draughty mansions which are impossible to maintain.'

I smiled at the thought of the second richest man in Scotland pleading poverty, and ran my eyes round his canvas family. He too smiled. 'No, not here. But none of this is mine. I could no sooner sell the house than I could a painting or an acre of land. The estate was made a company the year I was born, and I'm simply chairman of that company. It's just like being chairman of the National Trust – yes, that's a valid analogy. Only, I like to think we do an even better job.'

His aim had been to make Bowhill a model of integrated land-use, and few would deny that he had succeeded. As to whether it was the best use of the land, I was not qualified to judge, but it was undoubtedly a good use. And he was undoubtedly a man of rare energy and vision, preparing for future accountability a vast estate that had been passed from father to son for thirty generations.

As he accompanied me to the hall I asked what had gone through his mind that day 22 years ago while he lay on the ground with his back broken.

His ready smile reappeared. 'Well, it's curious but rather a happy thought, actually. For many years I'd been trying to give up smoking and as I lay there it suddenly occurred to me: "Right! This is the perfect opportunity to stop." And I did. Never smoked again. And I feel much healthier for it.'

He lingered by the window and waved, a small figure when set against the enormity of Bowhill, but not when magnified by his principles, a man of stature still waving as I retreated down the drive and headed west.

I had to see a man about a wolf.

60

Alastair McIntosh and the Wolf

If I believed the Scots suffered a surfeit of myths, there were others who felt we didn't have enough. One of these was Alastair McIntosh, Director of Edinburgh University's Centre for Human Ecology. I'd heard of him at the Inverness Forum on 'The People and the Land' and resolved to look him up. He taught his own blend of theology, accountancy and ecology, was inclined to play a flute in mid-sentence, and passionately wanted to reintroduce the wolf.

He was in his late thirties, bursting with energy; his tangled fair hair and a ginger beard would have let him pass as a disciple in any classical portrayal of The Last Supper. When I found him, he was talking into the microphone of a Japanese film crew who were making a documentary on Japan's last wolf which was shot in 1905 and now holes up in the British Museum. His theme was the psycho-spiritual significance of the wolf.

'Here in Scotland we killed our last wolf in 1743. Our last wild pig was killed a few decades earlier. We had already exterminated bear and reindeer, and were about to kill off, amongst others, capercaillie, great auks and sea eagles. *What does the conscience of having killed these animals do to our psyche?*' He left the question hanging, much to the director's unease, and played hollow notes on his flute.

'It has broken our links with nature. When animals become extinct, it is an indicator that all is not well in our society. The psychology which destroys animals, exterminates the wolf, kills deer and birds for sport, also drives people off the land and protects itself with the most powerful weapons of destruction. The limit was reached with the creation of nuclear weapons – as your country knows only too well.

'So we killed our last wolf in 1743. Three years later, coincidentally, the last great battle, called Culloden, took place on our soil. Then came the long period of evictions, clearing the people from the land. And what did these cleared people, the oppressed, do in the new lands they were sent to? They in their turn became oppressors and evicted the indigenous peoples off their land.' He lanced the Japanese nation with a hard stare, and allowed it time to ruminate on this over more impromptu music.

'We killed our wolves and we still feel guilty about that, so it helps if we convince ourselves that wolves are dangerous and bad. We cleared the people because they were unproductive or dangerous. We destroy nature because it stands in the way of urbanisation which is *progressive* and *civilised*. This is psychological projection; guilt reworked into justification.' He leaned closer to the camera. 'Only what can be given a price is given a value in the market. The priceless is chipped away – nature, community, ourselves . . . God?

'My point is this. We can no longer relate to nature because we've destroyed it, the land, its animals, its forests, its mythology. We can only recover our soul, our link with God, our spirituality, *our community* . . . through music, poetry, nature and the land. Scotland has *one* per cent natural forest cover. Once it had sixty per cent. We need to reforest our land and bring back our wolves. A land movement has begun here in Scotland –

through poetry, arts and music we're rediscovering our history, rebuilding communities and re-establishing our links with nature. It has a name: geopoetics. The poetics of deep relationship with place.'

I could imagine how the piece would end. Fade in flute music under 'The poetics of . . .' Cut to wolf – full frame, low camera angle – running in muscular slow-motion through a snow-filled forest. It mounts a rise and stops on a rock. Camera pans across a wintery Rannoch Moor. Fade out flute. Wolf howl. End. It made perfect sense to me. I wondered what a Japanese audience would make of it? Or a Scottish one?

'You said a new land movement has begun in Scotland,' I began, when the Japanese crew had gone. 'Do you mean Assynt?'

'A "land awareness" would probably be more exact, and yes, Assynt is one of its most obvious manifestations.'

'When do you think it'll really take off?'

'When our one million urbanised deprived realise that they too have rights to the land, that they came from the land and were dispossessed. When they get fire in their belly, the touchpaper will have been lit.'

61

Sir Walter Scott

Clarty Hole, as locals once disparagingly dubbed the small, run-down farm on the Tweed, was a name deliciously ripe with irony for the final home of the man who was always driven to 'improve' and 'prettify' everything to his artistic vision of life. But the real name of the property which Sir Walter Scott bought, extended, rebuilt, demolished and rebuilt again, and the land into which he sank the greater part of his astonishing fortune by cultivating it, foresting it, increasing its size ten times and stocking it with a loyal band of shepherds, gamekeepers, gillies, a piper and gasman, was originally called Cartley Hole. Scott renamed it Abbotsford. Historically not too far from the truth (monks from a nearby monastery may have regularly crossed the river here), but much more importantly to the lame son of a solicitor who was considered too lowly to marry the earl's daughter he loved, Abbotsford sounded much statelier and romantic.

Abbotsford was long and narrow, a sandy-red in colour except where its windows were outlined in checks of lighter stone, and it appeared much larger than it really was. Chimneys mobbed its roof, corbie-steps decorated its gables, but what gave it away as a fantasy building was its buffoonery of turrets and towers.

The tourist season, the author's most enduring endowment, was almost over and I was the only visitor, which for once was unfortunate. Abbotsford has rather too many ghosts. They sneer at you as gargoyles, writhe in gothic embellishment and loiter with intent inside suits of armour. As an imitation chamber of horrors, Abbotsford passes admirably.

Scott's study was cramped and austerely business-like. His desk, made of wood from ships of the Spanish Armada, was restrictive enough to impose a methodic and neat work routine. Here Scott sat on a chair made from wood grown on the site of Wallace's betrayal, and wrote one, two and even three novels a year. His Journal logged his progress:

Feb. 19th, 1828: A day of hard and continued work, the result being eight pages. But then I hardly ever quitted the table save at meal times. So eight pages of my manuscript may be accounted the maximum of my literary labour. It is equal to forty printed pages of the Novels . . .

His application to a task was doggedly single-minded. In his flat in Castle Street, Edinburgh, where even more of his novels were written, a neighbour was almost driven to distraction by what he saw:

there is a confounded hand in sight of me here, which has often bothered me before, ... Since we sat down . . . I've been watching it – it fascinates my eye – it never stops – page after page is finished and thrown on that heap of MS, and still it goes on unwearied – and so it will be until the candles are brought in, and God knows how long after that. It is the same every night – I can't stand a sight of it when I am not at my books' – 'Some stupid, dogged, engrossing clerk, probably,' exclaimed myself or some other giddy youth in our society. 'No, boys,' said our host, 'I know what hand it is – 'tis Walter Scott's.'

(quoted by A.N. Wilson, *The Laird of Abbotsford*)

I moved on to the library. The largest room in the house, it glittered with the gilt spines of 9,000 volumes. Rob Roy's purse, Bonnie Prince Charlie's quaich, Napoleon's pen case, a Burns toddy glass, a thread from the cloak of Mary, Queen of Scots, a box made from Shakespeare's mulberry bush, and other tenuously heroic trinkets were encased under glass, coldly defying moth, worm and clumsy charpersons. Sir Walter himself, in spectral white marble, or plaster – I was too reverent to poke him – watched me nose through his collection. I noted that he had filed a book entitled *Scotch Haggis* under Magic and Witchcraft.

In 1819 Scott lay on a sofa in this library suffering from gallstones and jaundice. Too weak to hold a pen, he dictated to a secretary who later recalled, 'though he often turned himself on his pillow with a groan of torment, he usually continued the sentence in the same breath.' Scott dictated *The Bride of Lammermuir* from start to finish without notes in a fortnight. Later that year, still in the grip of the same illness, he dictated *Ivanhoe*.

The rest of the house unfolded as the relics of a battlefield. Scott, mesmerised by Napoleon, had rushed out to Waterloo as soon as the battle was over. Too late for Culloden, he had nevertheless bought swords pillaged from the field. The studded gate from the Old Tolbooth, the last gate the condemned passed through on their way to the gallows, was a prized item. Here were the very keys used in the escape of Mary from Loch Leven Castle, Rob Roy's sword, a cast of Robert the Bruce's skull, and odd little touches like a set of walrus tusks mounted upside down to offer symmetry alongside the head of an African antelope. More than relics, they were keys to the workings of Scott's mind and the contradictory unrealities in which he immersed his private life.

How remarkable it is, that the man who achieved fame as a *historian*, not just as a poet, historical novelist, critic and lawyer, could have been so unapologetically selective in the history he chose. Scott lived through one of the most brutal periods of Highland evictions. He can't have failed to have known about them, about the famines and poverty. Yet they are never mentioned. His Highlanders were noble picturesque warriors whose time had passed. He gave them no present. As a novelist that was his right, as an advocate of justice the omission is glaring.

The reason behind his complete blindness to the contemporary plight of the people he romanticised, and similarly, to the injustices of the young industrial revolution, lies in his paranoid fear of revolution. It challenged his order, the discipline on which he had carefully, and successfully, aligned his life. He could only write freely about things long dead and unthreatening.

And this fear also explains Abbotsford, why he chose to create not a home, but a museum to live in. Notwithstanding that he was among the first to install the latest in technological gadgets – gas lighting, air-bells, water closets – he was happiest cocooned in the past. His creative genius, and genius it was, burgeoned not amongst the simple or the mundane, but amongst the contagion of history, its bloodied and emotion-imbued relics.

Scott contracted polio at the age of one and the interference of doctors who strapped his weak legs in freshly skinned and still-bloodied sheep hides simply exacerbated his lameness. He was taken on trips to London and the Trossachs, and steered into his father's profession. He became an advocate and Sheriff-Deputy for Selkirkshire. In 1805 he published his first long narrative poem *The Lay of the Last Minstrel* which was hugely popular, and encouraged him to enter into secret partnership with his publisher, the Ballantyne brothers.

Other epic poems followed and each achieved fast and hefty sales. *The Lady of the Lake* sold 25,000 copies in eight months, and immediately pulled the plug on the Trossachs by launching a new industry of mass travel.

By 1814 Scott was concerned that his literary success might be seen to conflict with his judicial duties, and his subsequent novels were published anonymously for the next eleven years. *Waverley* was his first benchmark. He returned from a trip to Orkney to find it the most successful book ever published in English. Within a year it had run through four editions and brought £2,100 profit.

Success built on success. *Ivanhoe* shifted 10,000 copies in a fortnight. His authorship was guessed but not made public. 'I have read all W. Scott's novels at least fifty times . . . grand work,' enthused Byron. 'Scotch Fielding, as well as great English poet – wonderful man! I long to get drunk with him.'

By 1825 he had reached a peak of success. He was internationally acclaimed and respected. No other writer had earned more money through authorship. Abbotsford was completed to his utmost delight. The following year it all fell apart. Ill-health returned, his wife died, the stock market had crashed and his publishers, through gross mismanagement, went under. Scott found himself liable for a share of their debts, and that share came to £130,000.

It is a measure of Scott's pride and integrity that he resolved to pay back every penny through his writing ('My own hand shall do it') and not opt for the easier route of bankruptcy. Six years and fifteen books later he died, a little short of his target, but the debt was easily settled within a few months of his death.

Scott, generous and amongst the most genial of men, was the single greatest artistic influence of his century. When his achievements lay shattered before him, he faced personal disaster with the heroism he had written into his plots and secretly craved, in its most dashing form, in his own life had he not been crippled in childhood. Scott was never a 'full-time' writer, yet few other authors, anywhere, have matched his output in a creative spell which effectively spanned only fifteen years, and no others have done so under such duress. His writing is void of even an inch of conceit or affectation. True, in the final stage of his life he suffered bouts of madness, storming rages in which he believed himself to be King Lear, but these were short-lived, just cracks in a life of discipline as rigid as fired clay.

A.N. Wilson summed him up thus:

Had he merely been crippled since infancy, perpetually afflicted by bile and gallstones, jaundice and rheumatism, financially ruined and occupied by almost full-time activity as a judge, a businessman and a conscientious landowner, his collapse at the age of sixty would have been unsurprising. But a glance at our bookshelves shows us that this was not all. Booksellers deal in Scott by the yard, more often than in individual volumes: a four-volume collection of ballads; editions of Dryden and Swift; a poetical output the size of Shelley's; twenty-seven novels; numerous tales; a child's history of Scotland in three volumes; a nine-volume life of Napoleon, twelve large volumes of correspondence, and as many again of miscellaneous essays and reviews; a Journal which runs to over 700 pages.

Scott concluded *The Heart of Midlothian* with the words: 'The paths of virtue, though seldom those of worldly greatness, are always those of pleasantness and peace.'

Ironically, pleasantness and peace eluded the man who achieved worldly greatness through a mixture of real and contrived virtues.

62

❦

Tweeds & Tartans, Galashiels

With Scott as its unwitting but highly successful market-ing manager, and its convenient abundance of rivers, the tweed and tartan industry of the border towns flourished. Jedburgh claims it was the first to begin commercial tweed production, Galashiels says it perfected the art and made more of it, while Hawick asserts it was responsible for the name: in 1832 a clerk of Messrs Wm Watson supposedly wrote 'tweels' (a Scots word for woven fabric showing patterned lines) on an invoice in a hand that was indistinct enough to be misread as 'tweeds'. That anything so minor should have earned a place in history bodes well for the vandalised sign on the wall of a Galashiels mill. As prophecy or indict-ment, in large gold letters, were the words, 'TWEE. . . TART. .S.'

The boom years produced such a demand for twee tarts that wool was imported to the Borders from Australia, New Zealand, South Africa and Argentina. Embedded in the fleeces were the seeds of exotic plants, some of which survived the heat and acid cleaning processes and took root on the banks of mill-town rivers. Up until 1920 Galashiels was second (to Montpellier) in Europe for the number of foreign plant invaders; 348 species. Botanists found here plant species from Australia *which were yet to be discovered in Australia.*

Today the numbers of border tweed mills, which once read like fine rugby scores (Galashiels 40), now reads like a dismal soccer table: Langholm 4, Selkirk 3; Galashiels 2, Peebles 1; Jedburgh 0, Hawick 0; Walkerburn 0 . . . In Selkirk, in the shell of a mill once employing 120 looms, I found Andrew Elliot with his nine. Twenty years ago, when everyone else was bailing out of the industry in the face of diminishing orders, unable to compete against the new league of mill owners with their computerised £100,000-looms, he bought up their antiquated machinery and Andrew Elliot Ltd entered the fray.

'Visitors Welcome'. The door opened on the late nineteenth century. A murky interior of dust, cobwebs and thousands of multi-coloured bobbins in a cacophony of man-eating machinery. Oily wheels and limbs spun, waved and kicked in what looked like deathly contractions, sending miles of thread on tortuous journeys. Most of the din came from the shuttles being hammered from side to side at 45 mph.

'. . . What's that, dear . . . ?' The operator had no hesitation in turning off her loom to allow me to repeat my question. 'Dangerous, did you say? No, dear, it's not dangerous. Mind you, sometimes that shuttle shoots off course and hits you on the arm. I don't like that. No, not at all.'

Visitors were free to wander where they pleased. I made sure I had no loose edges trailing. It would have been a simple matter to have become incorporated into the sampler Andrew Elliot himself was working on; the sampler was for a Japanese designer who was trying to create a 'braille effect' textile whose patterns could be enjoyed by both the sighted and blind. I didn't want to end up an interesting tactile experience in Tokyo.

Andrew was in his fifties, and took a turn at all the machinery.

'No way could I compete against the big boys, but' – it was the *but* on which his business depended – 'no way can they compete with my versatility. They can churn out fantastic quantities with their high-speed looms, but it takes them two days to programme and set up the machines. It takes two hours on these old looms. I do all their samplers, all the small orders. I was lucky. I found a hole in the market.'

He was also a designer. He had just produced a 'Vermont Tartan' for a large store in the American state. It cost £700 to register a new tartan, and there were now over 2,000 on record although only 60 were recognised by the Lord Lyon King of Arms.

Three of my five years wandering the world were spent in a kilt. I wore it through derision and hostility as well as what amounted to tacit applause, unashamedly as a badge of identity. It is a rare privilege accorded to the Scots, and to few others, to have a national dress that is both reasonably practical and almost universally recognised – if not always accepted, as it is not, for example, in parts of Mexico and Scotland.

It was late summer, a few years prior to this journey. I had been in Edinburgh and had thumbed my way home to Skye with ease, wearing my kilt. Walking off the ferry at Kyleakin, I noticed two local boys giving me strange looks. In a voice intended for me to hear, one said to the other, 'He must be English. No one around here wears a kilt.'

While not wholly correct it was nevertheless a poignant observation on the Highland perception of what was once, in a simpler form, their own mode of dress. This garment, once regarded with derision as a sign of barbarity by Lowlanders, outlawed by the Act of Proscription (1747) in the Highlands for 38 years, revived by anglicised land-lords, Scott, George IV, Victoria and the Italian Sobieski Brothers, for reasons of snob appeal, commercialism or romanticism, has almost vacated the Highlands and become the adopted symbol of Scoto-philes (usually expatriate) and Scotland as a whole. Aside from their use as uniforms (pipe bands, pipers, competition dancers) you see few kilts at Highland Games, and even fewer at village dances. Weddings and the annual circuit of London Scots doing the balls constitute the popular kilt-airing times. *He must be English. No one around here wears a kilt.*

From *Chambers Twentieth Century Dictionary*: 'fili-beg, filabeg, fillibeg, phil(l)abeg, phil(l)ibeg, the kilt, the dress or petticoat reaching nearly to the knees, worn by the Highlanders of Scotland [Gael. *feileadhbeag – feileadh*, plait, fold; *beag*, little].' Its origins are believed to lie in the tunics of Greeks and Romans. In the Highlands it evolved into the *feileadhmor* (big wrap), an all-purpose coat, cloak and sleeping blanket, about 5 feet wide and 12 to 18 feet long. The lower, belted portion became the *feileadhbeag*.

The sporran and most definitely the jacket have no traditional authenticity in the outfit, and the facts all cock a snook at the so-called 'purists'. The kilt has evolved and is still evolving. The 'Hill Walking Kilt' has recently been introduced: 'Taking the kilt back to the great outdoors. Hard wearing 16 oz material. A kilt that doesn't need a sporran to make it complete, but instead comes with two leather-trimmed trouser pockets and (optional) a hip-sporran. A kilt that (coolly) breaks most of the rules set by the established "national dress" . . . (a Victorian concoction made for the parade-ground). We're even prepared to do away with the tartan.'

And so to the hallowed ground of tartan. The oldest known example of 'tartan' is the Falkirk sett, named after the place where it was found, and has been dated at *c*245AD. This fragment of woven white and brown (undyed) wool was discovered as the stopper for a jar of buried coins. From then through the great reach of history until the end of the eighteenth century, the association between a clan and its set patterns or colours is, for the most part, non-existent, or at best tenuous and inconsistent. What is most likely is that each locality would have a weaver who would produce simple cloth which might be distinctive to his loom and thus make the wearers identifiable by name or district.

The concept of a tartan unique and standard to a particular clan seems to have evolved during the eighteenth century. Wm Wilson & Sons of Bannockburn, supplying the army and having a virtual monopoly on the trade, were producing in 1770 and had 200 setts in their pattern books, although many were of dubious authenticity. (As Lowlanders, the Wilsons were exempt from the prohibition which banned the manufacture and the wearing of tartan in the Highlands at the time; the army, women and landed gentry were also exempt.) Thus the manufacture of tartan became a Lowland enterprise, and kilts the property of the army and the Highland Societies of the south. Although they adapted the garment to suit their purposes, they also probably saved it from extinction.

In 1815 the Highland Society of London decided to commission a comprehensive collection of the 'named tartans' it believed were in common existence. It wrote to all clan chiefs and heads of families asking each to supply an authenticated sample of their tartan. This caused some consternation. Lord Macdonald of Sleat, replying to the Society's request in October 1815, wrote, 'Being really ignorant of what is exactly the Macdonald Tartan, I request you will have the goodness to exert every Means in your power to Obtain a perfectly genuine pattern, Such as Will Warrant me in Authenticating it with my Arms . . .' A year later the Society had received 76 specimens of which about half failed to show evidence of authenticity.

In 1832 George IV provided an advertising *coup* to tartanry by appearing in Edinburgh in a kilt (with pink tights, a fashion which fortunately didn't catch on). In 1842 the suave Sobieski brothers appeared on the scene with their sensational book, *Vestiarium Scoticum*, which they claimed was the authoritative word on tartan authenticity. As few people had any notion of what their own tartan, if any, looked like, were loath to admit it and certainly had no proof to counter the Sobieskis, London's Highland Society welcomed them as its guests.

John Sobieski Stolberg Stuart Hay and his brother, Charles Edward, claimed to be the legitimate grandsons of Prince Charles Edward Stuart and his wife, through a son that history failed to record. They further claimed that their grandfather had deposited a manuscript written in 1721, listing contemporary tartans, in the Scots College of Douai, in France. They had acquired this manuscript and their book was its published form. *Vestiarium Scoticum* was in fact a work of fiction. Nevertheless it was good fiction, well-researched and incorporating elements of facts to lend credence to their inventions. What caused the darkest shadows of suspicion to fall on their integrity was their novel inclusion of Lowland clans. Not even Sir Walter Scott was so deviously romantic. 'The general proposition that the Lowlanders ever wore plaids is difficult to swallow.'

Yet many of the Sobieski Stuart patterns were adopted by Lowland families. Which is why anyone called Scott can't afford to make too much of a song and dance in a kilt.

63

Hawick Common Riding

A thick stew of mist hung over the hills and fields above Hawick, and over 'the mair' where most of the population had set up camp. I sat a mile away with a select group of men in the Hut, drinking milk and rum by the crate. To get into the Hut was as hard as getting a place in the London Marathon and we had either queued all night without sleep or resorted to insider dealing to get one of the two hundred tickets on offer. Custom-built seventy years ago for the same function as today, the Hut was a single-roomed wooden hall with tables and forms like a school dining room, and rafters barely clearing head-height. It was situated among farm buildings but it belonged to the town and was only unlocked for this annual ritual. In the Hut women were forbidden, the wearing of a tie was compulsory and drinks were delivered only by the crate.

Out of the mist came a confused but rhythmical striking of metal on stone, the sounds of 300 horses' shoes. Their riders were all male, all ages, all dressed in tweed and cling-jodhpurs and looked immaculate except those less able to hold their rum who were stained with Teviotdale mud. Led by the Cornet (Robert Pringle, butcher) holding aloft a blue and gold flag, they piled into the Hut, flung their jackets over the rafters, took their reserved places and ate curds and cream before the toasts began.

Their prowess at rugby gives the Borders folk confidence to be friendly, and fearless of strangers. After half a millennium of being in the rucks of hostile armies and reivers, they have secured their boundaries, amassed a self-satisfying number of victories, and turned their energy towards mauling the opposition on the sports field. Historically they have sometimes had to hunt hard to find those victories.

In 1513 James IV unwisely left his secure entrenchments on Flodden Hill and led the Scots to their greatest ever defeat, leaving as many as 10,000 dead on the field. After the battle, a band of English looters made their way to Hawick and plundered the town before continuing south, but they were secretly pursued by a group of youths. The looters were surprised by night at a place called Hornshole, utterly routed and their blue and gold colours carried back to Hawick. Apart from the obligatory duty of touring the municipal boundaries to prevent the Crown from resuming unclaimed land, the annual Riding of the Marches around Hawick celebrates this civic victory at Hornshole, plucked myopically from the national disaster that was Flodden.

> Ever since our flag's been carried
> Round our Muir by men unmarried –
> Emblem grand of those who won it –
> Matrimonial hands would stain it

runs one verse of the main Riding song. Quite why Hawick has taken agin' matrimony and women is not clear but 'it's aye been'; the Cornet must be a bachelor and must remain one during the three years of his official involvement.

In a tent specially erected beside the Hut was Hawick's Lord Provost, by custom one of the officiating dignitaries at the Hut and the person who had the right to choose the guest speaker. But the current provost was a woman, and had chosen Lady Jane Grosvenor as guest speaker. As both were banned from the Hut they sat alone in their tent, divorced from the proceedings.

Inside the Hut we polished off another crate of rum and milk. Hawick's Common Riding was a red letter entry in the Milk Marketing Board's diary. The local magistrate led the proceedings, resplendent in his red robe and furs of endangered species, and introduced the first speaker, a former Cornet.

His was a rousing speech, complete with the rattling of halberds and spurs. In five minutes we repulsed 480 years' worth of invaders and were urged to be vigilant against threats on both a local and global level. Villainous landlords had wrested away our lands, and right then, as he was speaking, plantations of Sitka spruce were continuing their insidious advance on little Hawick. Steve Biko and Nelson Mandela made a surprise appearance among the Sitka. 'Whit we hiv in common is we occupy a border. We hiv a heritage to protect and churish.' And hot on the mention of Martin Luther King came chilling news of the threat to the local playpark. 'WE MUST FIGHT FOR FREEDOM!' He sat down to feet-stamping, bottle-banging and riotous applause, but this, I discovered, was the standard reaction to everyone – speaker, singer, speaker, singer . . . – but if you read the lips of the exchanges within the din, you got a different story.

'Tae fuckin' political . . .'

'Mechty! We dinnae come tae the Hut fer thaat . . .'

Those of us at my table felt so vulnerable and unnerved by the dangers around us that we ordered another crate, and joined in a song to the greater glory of Hawick. During the next speech I hunted for unusual professions. They were listed at the back of the songbook against the names of previous cornets, as far back as 1703. Little had changed in the town over three centuries. The people were still predominantly merchants, artisans and farmers: the Flesher, Skinner, Cadger, Currier, and Millwright had disappeared and been replaced by Designer, Draughtsman, Frameworker, Power Knitter, Stable Lad and Insurance Agent. But they were still all 'braw Teri lads'.

The magistrate rose to his feet, and his announcement was masterfully economic with the truth. 'The guest speaker is unable to be with us today . . .'

We rose to our feet, raised our glasses in the general direction of Lady Jane Grosvenor's tent and sang 'For She's A Jolly Good Fellow . . .' with all the verve of having just heard her give a resoundingly good address. It was touching. For a moment I felt we were genuinely sorry she was unable to manage the last twenty yards to our company.

More speeches and self-congratulatory brow-beating Hawick songs followed and then we decanted from the Hut and went to try our luck at screwing the bookies at the flapping track and winning goldfish on the Mair.

The rest of the afternoon was a blur of fragmented memories. I tried to be Writer but too many crates caught up with me. My notebook nevertheless threw up some scribblings in a strange hand. The franchise holder of the beer tent at this moorland race track, who was competing with Hawick's 74 licensed premises, was recorded as expecting to get through 7,040 pints of lager and 216 bottles of whisky that day. The ping-pong-ball-in-a-jar fairground lady was noted as averaging a turnover of 200 goldfish a week at 80 pence profit each. She was sulking over a lousy season. Rain. Recession. 'If ah hidny fau-a generations ahind me, ah'd pack it in.'

I recall a bookie smugly belted into a gaberdine raincoat. Money tumbled into the Gladstone bag hanging below his blackboard of odds. A drunk, barely able to walk, approached, stumbling, with a fistful of £20 notes for the favourite, Hallowed Ground. Win. Six to one.

Two hundred pounds must have been in that hand, and I watched, with a sick feeling in my stomach, as Hallowed Ground failed to take a place.

My last memory is of leaving the mair and looking behind to see a scene like the aftermath of Flodden; a field of bodies by the hundreds, resting, singing, talking, sprawling, a blight of crushed cans and plastic cups, police breaking up a brawl, girls crying over tiffs, swearing, the body of a horse which dropped dead during the ride-out . . .

'THEN *UP* WI AULD HAWICK,' sang a group of diehards nearby. 'O' THE BORDERS SHE'S QUEEN . . .' I hummed along. I was an honorary citizen for the day, a willing but fraudulent member of the club. 'THERE'S NAE TOON AMANG THEM A', CAN WI *OOR* TOON COMPARE . . .' They left me behind. I couldn't keep up. I wasn't any good at this bogus belonging.

'Grade 'ay, wunnit?' a figure weaving across the full width of the road uttered companionably.

'Great!' I replied, feeling like a terminal case of James IV. But then auld Hawick has had considerably more experience of shaping great achievements out of apparent carnage.

64

The Debatable Lands

Between Kelso and Coldstream, leaping randomly from hilltop to hilltop at first, then developing a phobia for high ground and avoiding it, travelling northwards across OS Sheet 74 in a route so jerky it must have been determined over a case of rum and milk, came the Scottish-English border. At map reference 803364 it suddenly sidestepped Nottylees Farm, looped round, latched onto a bend in the Redden Burn and followed it down to the Tweed in an absent-minded fit of logic. The Tweed carried it north-east, mid-channel, for about twelve miles, through Coldstream (where a plaque on the Bridge advises that on 7 May 1787 Robert Burns took his first and only steps into England, and ventured as far south as Newcastle and Carlisle) until it comes within three miles of Berwick-upon-Tweed. At 947522, nowhere, a void of anything noteworthy, and *à propos* of nothing, the border abruptly quits the river and sets off on a day dream to the north.

South of the Tweed, England was consolidating its own identity in red brick and indigenous names: Wark Common, Crookham Eastfield, Etal Manor, English Strother. The river had flattened a path through the 'Debatable Lands', between the Lammermuirs and the Cheviots, and created a valley of rich farming country. Trios of tractors working in staggered tandem were making the land blush, folding over the layer of yellow stubble to reveal a rouge of light soil. It looked land well worth fighting over.

The Debatable Lands, so called because they had changed hands with every change of fortune in the medieval Scottish–English Wars, were where I perceived the greatest degree of Scottish consciousness. Yet even here, where I had expected national feeling to be most rampant, it was dressed in local colours. The precedence of belonging was always: first town or island, then region, then country. And the further people lived from the seat of government, the more deeply rooted their local allegiances became. With the exception of national displays of eating and drinking (Burns Night and Hogmanay), our country's customs and festivals, such as the Common Ridings and Highland Games, are all primarily municipal celebrations.

On deeper reflection, my initial disappointment at not finding a greater display of national awareness across the country gave way to a growing sense of reassurance, for the preservation of our smallest differences, I realised, could only add to the enduring distinction of the whole, of being a Scot. Scottish consciousness is safest with local roots.

65

Eyemouth and The Fishing

Eyemouth's fishing fleet was hurrying home ahead of a predicted gale. At regular intervals boats, trailing flocks of bickering seagulls like private snow storms, rounded some rocks marked by leaping surf and entered the narrow inlet which led to the harbour. Eyemouth is a model village, successfully blending tourism with The Fishing. Streets of good, solid houses slant down to the shopping area by the harbour. Looking clean and cared for, the renovated centre of the community retains charm in its appearance for the visitor, while losing none of the practicality of instant ice and refrigerated storage for its working fleet. Even its puddles look clean.

'Demersal fish,' Bill Speirs informed me, 'bottom dwellers. Cod, haddock, sole, saithe, and others like that. Whitefish. That's what we mostly fish here. And prawns.'

We stood watching the boxes being unloaded straight from the boat into the auction market. 'Next year, we won't be allowed in here to look at the unloading. European regulation. White overalls only. Ridicky-lous! Do the fishermen wear white overalls? No, no, but when the fish reach land . . . white overalls.'

Bill was in his late fifties. He was thin and had a thick

crop of brown hair which looked as if it ought to belong to someone half his age. His movements were slow and deliberate, a trait I put down to a lifetime cramped among the dangers of nets, hawsers, otterboards and winches. His speech had been affected too and his words came in soft, spongy tones. He said he was a 'prematurely retired' skipper, and his eyes turned watery. 'I still cry about it,' he said, and explained how he'd lost his boat on a rock the previous year, near where the 'Whisky Galore boat went down'. He visited the harbour every day. 'But . . . nah . . . it's not the same. I miss the *involvement*. I feel I'm going downhill. If I lived out of sight of the sea, I'd just pine away altogether.'

We went for a pint in The Contented Sole and then for another in The Whale. The walls of both bars were liberally hung with photographs of trawlers. I asked Bill if his was there and he pointed to one whose name I couldn't read, and I didn't like to ask. She had been a typical boat, he explained, 70-foot long, larch planking on an oak frame, with a steel cuddy over the bow. Wooden boats were still cheaper to build than steel ones, and they lasted longer. Larch, he said, was the most popular choice, but when it was scarce, iriquois was used. But fishermen distrusted this hardwood because it was too dense to float.

'Are fishermen still very superstitious?'

'Oh yes. In some places it's stronger than others but there's still many words ye mustn't use. They bring bad luck.' He lowered his voice to a whisper for fear of being overheard. 'Ye mustn't say "salmon". Ye have to call it a "pink one". "Pig" is bad too. That's "curly tail". "Rabbits" are "four-footeds". An' it's still bad luck to meet a minister on the way to a boat. Some folk, when leaving port'll only turn the boat into the sun, never away from it, and some, if they accidentally put their jersey on back-to-front, they'll leave it that way.'

I could see little incentive to put to sea. Rocks, bad

weather, a stroke of absent-mindedness where four-footeds and curly-tails were concerned . . . I understood why Bill's voice had permanently softened. The potential for incurring bad luck was immense.

Would he, I asked him, given his time again, go into The Fishing? I was thinking about the reports of excessive exploitation, dwindling stocks, the limits on days at sea.

He grinned slyly. 'I wish things were as they are now when I first joined the industry.'

'But I thought fishing was in crisis?'

No, he replied, he thought quite the opposite. The boats were finding the fish where they'd always found them. The stocks rose and fell as they'd always done. He had never seen as many shellfish as had been caught in the last few years. The government's quota system had its defects but he believed it was working. The decommissioning scheme was also proving effective and it needed to reduce the fleet still further to assure the industry of a promising future.

'If anything, we've got too much fish for the level of demand. That's really why we need fewer boats. OK, so things go up and down. If ye want security ye don't go into fishing, ye join the post office. But, if ye get yer teeth stuck in, fishing's one of the few industries where hard work and skill is always rewarded. We've come through the worst recession since the 1930s, but there's been few casualties compared to other industries.'

Eyemouth was the home port of fourteen large boats and was regularly used by over forty others. These were mainly pair trawlers (two boats pulling one much larger net, the most efficient method) and twin trawlers (single boats pulling two nets side by side). The chief threat to the industry, he believed, was the latest proposal to limit the number of days boats spent at sea. The allocation was to be assessed on the number of days a boat had worked in the base year of 1991, with an allowance made for days lost through a variety of circumstances, such as an engine failure or attendance at a funeral.

'Most fishermen would accept this if it was fair. But the system's going to favour those who were greedy in 1991, those with double crews who fished for most of the year. No, I don't think this'll ever be accepted.'

'Is your view typical of most fishermen?'

'Listen.' Again he lowered his voice. 'I've never met two fishermen who agree on anything. We're like farmers. We love to moan. And like gold-diggers in the Yukon. No one goes rushing around telling everyone what ye've caught and where ye caught it. Like I said, things go up and down, but I'll tell ye this . . .' His words became barely audible, '. . . we've never had it so good.' He turned to the picture of his boat, and added, 'At least for thems that still got their boat.'

I asked what he missed most about the sea, aside from involvement in the activity of the harbour. I thought he would describe the flight of a tern, or the banter of the crew, or the feeling of arriving home, the boat held low in the water by the weight of a full hold.

'I miss the days when we had one-way radios. It's a hi-tech industry now. Fancy radar, fancy sonar, satellite telephones. In the old days I used to speak to my wife every day over the radio. Then I had to wait till Friday to get her replies.'

66

❧

Edinburgh, and John Knox

'Welcome to Edinburgh. The burgh of Edwin, King of Northumbria in around 633. Up there,' said the guide, pointing to the castle in the sky, 'during the three-week festival when over a thousand theatre companies perform in the city, a lone figure stands on the battlements at the end of each day, piping, in a kilt fitted with lead weights.'

He could have used lead weights himself. Sitting in the top of our open bus, he frequently had to subdue his airborne kilt.

'On your left there used to be a loch where Edinburgh tried her witches. Now drained, it's occupied by Waverley Station, the finest part of the city, according to Glaswegians, because that's where the Glasgow train leaves from. Now here's Sir Walter Scott in thirty tons of Carera marble with his favourite dog, Maida. The largest memorial to any literary figure in the world. The next building is the Royal Scottish Academy and if you look up' – we, a mixed flock of Scots, English, Germans, Americans and Japanese, dutifully looked up – 'you will see a colossal statue of Queen Victoria. It was given to her by the people of London. She hated it. What to do with this unwanted present? Simple! Off-load it onto the Scots. We couldn't think what to do with it until someone thought of stuffing it on top of the gallery.' Queen Victoria was sprouting yellow ragwort.

Half the time I felt insulted by the tour. I was being treated as if I had spent all my life in Kyoto. *I was born here. I've lived a fifth of my life here*. The words shouted their protest in my mind, but they rang hollow and impotent. This was not the Edinburgh we, the Scott family, knew. The Edinburgh of Guide Friday Bus Tours was infinitely more interesting. Not since Disneyland had I experienced so much sensationalism compressed into a few miles. I hadn't realised that we lived in a natural theatre of so many distinguished (but dead) actors.

My great-grandfather was an Edinburgh lawyer who must have won many cases on the strength of his scowl. His son, my grandfather, felt he had to follow the family profession but was a rugger player at heart, winning twenty-one caps for Scotland before the age of 24, until his parents intervened and said it was time he settled down. He found life as an Edinburgh lawyer was only tolerable when combined with life as an international rugby referee. Then, hard up for money, he wrote a book, *Rugby Football, And How To Play It* which caused a ruckus over his amateur status, instantly terminated his official involvement with the game and failed to improve his bank balance.

Edinburgh was the stomping-ground of my father for the first forty years of his life, playing rugby, earning *his* cap in cricket and learning the whisky trade before his transfer to Speyside. My Edinburgh lasted six years and was a view from a pram, visits to the zoo and *my* first and only cap (purchased, nursery school). When I returned to work there years later as a trainee photographer, I saw the capital as my daily walk through five street crossings, through the Meadows, to a dark world of f-stops and reciprocity failures. I knew Edinburgh's cinemas, where it sold its fresh vegetables, cut-price clothes and second-hand books. I knew pubs with open fires, friends who, like me, all seemed to live up eight flights of common stairs which carried a maximum penalty of three months' imprisonment if you missed your turn cleaning them. I knew the places to avoid and the quickest ways out.

But now I was a tourist in a place I scarcely recognised, swivelling my head in unison with the other passengers and seeing the city with fully zoomed-in vision. We were allowed a glance at the Victorian splendour of Jenners department store and then asked to look into Princes Street Gardens, thus avoiding the architectural vandalism of prefab buildings labelled Boots, Menzies and The New Club. Edinburgh came across as being an old film star, still arrestingly beautiful but a bit hacked about and bruised in a way that was permissible through the rigours of age and the assumption of rough wooing. Where she was ugly you believed it was just a temporary blemish, a recent mishap which would be put right when the council found some money, or else you were awed by the grimy authenticity of history.

Outside the city centre, in Craigmillar, in Wester Hailes, Edinburgh is indistinguishable from Glasgow. Smaller, certainly, and always with a view of green hills, but 'FUCK YOU' is written on the walls of these areas in just as large letters and with the same degree of ire. But we did not go to Craigmillar or Wester Hailes. We went through Arthur's Seat park which Queen Victoria had landscaped as a little token of her love for Albert. We learned that Edinburgh has 500 bowling greens and 54 golf courses, that its first cobbled streets were laid by Frenchmen, that the statue of the Duke of Wellington riding his prancing horse, Copenhagen, is inaccurate, for Copenhagen is sculpted as a stallion but she was in fact a mare; furthermore, she is hollow, fills up with rain water and is periodically drained through her bronze penis.

In the time of James IV Edinburgh was known as the

'Maiden City' for the obvious pun that she had never been taken. Since that time she has been taken twice but she still exudes much of the primness and prissiness of one who has never known wooing, or certainly never enjoyed it. Whatever the past, introvert Edinburgh, not extrovert Glasgow, is the AIDS capital of the country; according to one theory, the unenviable statistics trace their origin to a boatload of Pakistani heroin which was landed at Leith in 1983 and peddled round housing estates at £3 a bag, introducing hundreds of people to the habit and the risk of HIV infection through needle-sharing.

The Edinburgh-Glasgow conflict is wearing thin, the differences becoming less marked. While Edinburgh continues to run itself down through complacency, Glasgow continues to tidy itself up and steal more and more of the cultural cake.

Yet it irritates me to hear Edinburgh's friendliness being denigrated. It is not that Edinburgh is an unfriendly place, just that Glasgow is so extraordinarily friendly. The two cities share more in common now than in the past. Yet they are still worthy of each other as counterpoints, one the physical heart of the country, the other the emotional heart, each the *bête noir* of the other's imagination.

I made my way up the Royal Mile towards the castle. It struck me forcibly that I couldn't recall having seen a single tourist shop in Glasgow's centre. Here every other shop catered for the visitor's insatiable need for tea towels, tartan, canned haggis and mist, Korean-made Highland dolls and Pakistani-made bagpipes (Pakistan boasts over 450 pipe bands). Out of some of these shops trickled accordion music, the sickly strains to which Scotland's musical heritage has been reduced through ruthless marketing. They induced in me the same suffocating sensations as the childhood memories of sitting in a dentist's chair, being gassed.

Halfway up the Royal Mile I passed John Knox's

house, where visitors are charged a very modest one pound to see a building which was never owned or occupied by John Knox, or had any association with the man who was to imprint his beliefs so deeply into the Scottish character. He was neither a great theologian nor philosopher but a great preacher, a man of courage and brutal determination. The prime mover of the Scottish Reformation which overthrew a degenerate and corrupt Church of Rome, Knox took part in murder and pulled no punches with Mary, Queen of Scots. ('Mary was historically wrong but romantic, while Knox was right but repulsive': Iain Finlayson, *The Scots*.)

'He split the Scottish mind,' wrote a poet of Knox, 'half he made cruel, half he made unkind.' And Knox's cruel repulsive side is amply illustrated in his *History of the Reformation in Scotland* in which he describes in graphic detail his part in the 'merry work' of murdering Cardinal Beaton, and a Protestant's delight in pissing in the mouth of a Catholic corpse. He spent nineteen months as a galley slave in France for his part in this murder but returned to foment the storm which brought in the first reign of Protestantism.

'The Knox Syndrome is at the root of all our major national afflictions, . . . a distrust of pleasure so profound as often to be mistaken for religious paranoia . . . Inter-marriage with Italians seems to be the only hope, at present, of a cure, but is rightly seen by many as a somewhat extreme remedy (and a shame for the Italians),' wrote Dr Anne Smith, in *The Scotsman*.

67

Homelessness

Two hundreds yards downhill from the John Knox deception and the tartan frippery market of the Royal Mile is the Cowgate, a backside of the Old Town and where most of Auld Reekie's soot has settled. A cavernous street, deep below the castle heights, it is robbed of light by tall buildings and by bridges which carry the city's more important thoroughfares. This is a shadowy world, almost deserted compared to its prestigious royal neighbour, a haunt of winos, short-cut commuters and equally transient trippers to the Burke-and-Hare spookery of the city's past. History affords Edinburgh privilege. Here, it is possible not to be shocked by dirt and poverty in a way that is unavoidable in Glasgow.

In the Cowgate I entered a gloomy building whose windows were covered in grids to prevent movement, either in or out; it wasn't clear which. Floors were painted red, walls an institutional off-green. The sultry smell of disinfectant pervaded the air and I could have guessed where I was even if a sign hadn't told me: Salvation Army Hostel for Men. I was back in 1987, a journalist dressed in cast-offs, without money, a voluntary exile among London's homeless for three days, learning gratitude for the work of the Salvation Army in a way that will never diminish.

Day 1. An old woman approaches. She's carrying a bulging plastic bag which suddenly breaks. Old magazines fall to the ground around her feet. She picks some up and dumps them in the nearest bin, then shuffles back and forth carrying a few issues at a time until the scattered pile has gone. Why has she carried this load past innumerable bins only to dump it when the bag breaks? My gaze catches her eye and she comes over with a gait that wobbles like a failing top. 'The world's falling apart, my dear,' she says. 'Falling apart, it is . . . shocking!' She turns and hobbles off. I follow her into her disintegrating world where a different perspective prevails.

At once I find I'm walking too fast. I'll have to learn to walk slowly, show no sign of pace. Pace means purpose, and the homeless have none; nowhere to go and no reason beyond boredom for going.

I feel ashamed of my appearance. My face is unshaven and intentionally dirty. My clothes are old and stained, my coat torn. The toe of one shoe is worn to a hole and the sole of the other flaps.

The old woman leads me to Regent's Park. She sits on a bench. People pass. I try to avoid their eyes but whenever I look up, they're staring at me, avidly curious, but instantly they turn away and pretend their attention is elsewhere. The rebuff is continual.

Some children are feeding ducks. After fifteen hours without food, hunger slowly churns and convulses in my stomach, and the spectacle is tormenting. I feel tired, weak, old, useless, ostracised. Joggers run by. I've run for the last twenty years but now such exertion seems unimaginable. Sport is for the well-fed, for those with energy to spare. The old woman sits on. Her boredom threshold is far out of sight, while mine has been crossed already. I leave her and go to try my hand at begging.

It takes me all my courage to beg, even though I'll repay the money to charity another day. Sitting on the pavement holding out my hand produces nothing. I change tactic, asking people directly for the price of a cup of tea or any loose change. They move out of my way or stare right through me as if I were an elusive mirage. A polite refusal would be tolerable, and even welcome, rather than this blatant shun or denial of my existence. Over an hour, I'm unsuccessful. Perhaps my own abhorrence of begging is to blame and my fraud registers, for my pride is still greater than my hunger.

I trudge the streets all day without food, and drink only tap water at a public lavatory. It's October. The days get dark early and are already wintery. I sit at Waterloo Station until 10 pm when two policemen arrive and systematically question those who do not look like travellers. They confront me, and one jerks his thumb towards the exit.

In a rubbish skip near Waterloo Bridge I find a piece of carpet and some cardboard boxes. I take them to the suburb of street-sleepers under the bridge. There must be 150 people who sleep here, side by side, a few with sleeping bags, some no more than a pair of shoes protruding from piles of paper and polythene, most carefully built into cardboard coffins. And near by, the National Theatre. Dramatic irony; a cardboard suburb of street-sleepers neighbouring a pleasure-house where a seat can cost £50 an evening.

I try to find a place to sleep but every spot is taken. Some people are drinking, playing cards, talking, arguing. I unroll my carpet on an empty patch in the shadows. Most of the people I can make out are men in their twenties and thirties, wearing suits. From their conversation they're professional dole-collectors who've signed on at several offices.

Suddenly a German guy appears and starts kicking at boxes, shouting about people stealing his gear. He stands over me and then pulls at my carpet. Fear stiffens my body, but I pretend to be asleep. Fortunately he goes away. Ten minutes later someone else comes up and points a torch in my face, then wakes the nearest sleeping figure. 'Hey, Vince. Who the fuck's that in oor place?' His accent is Glaswegian. I get up and gather my carpet and boxes. 'Ye canna sleep there, pal. It's taken. Here, I'll show you where ye kin go.'

He leads me round a corner and shows me a spot. I grunt a reply. There are more Glaswegian accents nearby: it's estimated there are 10,000 homeless Scots in London. One is explaining why he left Glasgow and talks about a 'razor job'. I feel very afraid. For once in my life I've nothing that anyone would want to steal. My destitution is my security, but here nothing is certain – anything is possible where behaviour is governed by desperation. The parameters of 'normality' have collapsed for all of us, and I fear menace in unfamiliar actions: the twitching, mumbling, shouting, the sudden outbursts of aggression . . . All through the night figures get up to piss against the wall opposite me.

Day 2. I hardly slept. The cold pressed deep into me. My back is sore, my legs stiff. By 7 am many of the young 'suited' homeless are up, shaving in bowls of cold water, combing their hair and dusting themselves off. Some of them might even be holding down jobs in an office. Society's deepest exiles take longer to emerge, limping off with their emblematic carrier bags and broken shopping baskets.

It's an odd sensation just getting up and walking off. No luggage to pack. No doors to close. I feel washed out, wrapped up in my own little world of aimless walking, hunger, and looking for a warm place to sit. These are now the sum contents of my life.

I find I frown all the time. A limp now comes easily, as does the pathetic tone of voice. What frightens me is the speed with which I'm acquiescing. The way I'm ceasing to care what people think of me, the suddenness with which everything appears so demoralising and hopeless. No wonder so many take to drink. A few hours' release is worth more than a bed.

Two days ago I had money and lazed in comfort, today I've nothing and seek what comfort can be found in dark allies amongst litter, puddles and piss-stained bricks. The only tokens of friendship come from the incoherent mumblings of the deprived and the methylated whispers of the lost. To be so suddenly and openly unloved, rejected and despised by those who, yesterday, were indifferent; to suddenly find yourself surrounded by suspicion, hostility, uncaring or unseeing eyes – the eyes of those amongst whom, only two days ago, I was one – that is what is so hard to bear.

I long to return to my former world of clean clothes, baths, excessive meals, help-yourself coffees, home, security and run-of-the-mill acceptance that tomorrow will come. I'm lucky. I have that option.

But what if I lost my memory, lost all contact with my former life? How could I fight back with nothing? How can anyone pull their lives out of an abyss this deep? It's the degradation of the self that terrorises me, the mental condition of being trapped in a world where you have nothing and believe you are nothing.

Someone gives me 50 pence. I go to a Salvation Army Hostel for Men where a plate of mince and a cup of tea cost 40 pence. I sleep under Waterloo Bridge again, in what is now *my* place. Even this little seems precious. I walk the streets the next day, and in the evening I return to the world of the 'haves'.

If I have to single out one image from those hellish days, it is of a late-middle-aged canteen worker at the Salvation Army hostel. She had become inured to the sight of filthy, abused and broken men. She didn't flinch before the restless eyes, the glazed stares, stammers and compulsive twitches. She seemed to see beyond the depths of our degradation and offered love to the unloved. Or maybe I flatter her. Maybe she felt the same revulsion as everyone else, and kindness – mere words – were her defence against the objects of her fear. Who cares why? Hers was the only emotional warmth I was given. 'Here you are, love,' she said, handing over a steaming bowl of soup with an encouraging smile. For me it was no cliché. 'This'll see you right.'

The homeless were no different in Edinburgh. Some of them were gathered outside the Captain's office in the Cowgate hostel.

'You're just in time for the morning service. Do join us, if you like.' The Captain led me upstairs to a small gathering room. He was approaching retirement age, a round snuffling man with loose jowls and a prominent hearing aid.

The service was taken by Annie, a Church of Scotland deaconess. We sang Hymn 417, 'Are you washed in the blood of the Lamb?' The Captain led in a bold tenor. Mrs Captain and a cleaner sang harmonies. Three residents and I mouthed timidly at the back. The theme was 'having fun', and 'Are you washed in the blood of the Lamb?' was a bouncy, frolicking little ditty if you judged by the music and Annie's reckless cheer, and didn't dwell too literally on the words.

Captain Bailey had spent forty-two years managing Salvation Army hostels. Fifty-eight homeless people could sleep here, paying £2.60 a night or £18.55 a week, including meals. The hostel rules were simple: no alcohol, no visitors to dormitories, no misbehaviour and strict lights-out times. Usually the hostel was full. On a typical night three-quarters of the residents would be English. Every day the composition changed, even though people were free to stay for an unlimited period; vagrancy, by custom and definition, was a migratory affliction. Tea and cakes were served in the dining room. Suddenly one of the residents hurled his tray to the ground and screamed abuse at a server. An unbroken torrent of swear words was unleashed. The Captain rushed up and placed his portly frame between the two. He looked pathetically inadequate as the scene grew uglier, but he calmed them down and returned to his lukewarm tea. A 17-year-old youth, his arms a mess of scar tissue, walked by.

'Captain . . . thanks fer yer help.' It was an admission evinced from the cold psychology of the street where gratitude represented surrender.

'Have you given up yet, Mark?'

'Aye. Awmost.'

'Almost's not good enough.'

'Ah'm gettin there.' He wandered off.

'I'm afraid he'll probably be dead in a year,' the Captain remarked. 'Tragic.'

I asked the Captain how he had endured forty-two years living among abuse, drink, drugs and broken lives? 'I just need to see one mended life every now and then. That's all. Just one, to make it worthwhile.'

They were ageless, these men, but all prematurely old, their bodies warped. Their teeth had fallen out, their mouths had turned in, their eyes sunk into hollows, and they carried the dispirited look of caged animals. Some had leather jackets and lank hair brushed back. Time had left them behind in a different era, perhaps the era when they felt they were someone, when they last had their lives in order.

It must have seemed such a short time between then and now, such a short distance between Cowgate and the fiction of the Royal Mile.

❧

68

Tam the Gun, and Democracy for Scotland

The Scots are the most accomplished purveyors of myths. Where we have not invented them ourselves others have invented them for us and we have adopted them, adapted them, cashed in on them (to our credit) and, inevitably, (not to our credit) believed in them. Myth and fact are so inextricably bound together that the Scots are capable of drifting along in almost any level of unawareness and misunderstanding and accept it as reality. Out of these dwams come our apathy, our tendency to concentrate on petty detail rather than the well-being of the whole, and, perversely, the lateral thinking that has produced an extraordinary degree of invention and profound philosophy.

It is therefore no coincidence that Scotland's capital is such an admixture of myth and questionable realities. You can walk from the New Town to the Cowgate, from Holyrood to Haymarket, crossing a zebra's back of alternating new and old, rich and poor, stately and slovenly, home and abroad; and be unable to decide where the real Edinburgh is. And in its complexity of contradictions, to my mind, lies the essence of Edinburgh's considerable charm.

'We used to keep you English out,' the ticket collector told the group in front of him. 'Now we charge you a fiver and let you in. Makes more sense.' Edinburgh Castle attracted a million visitors each year, the most popular tourist attraction in Britain after the Tower of London. At twenty to one I went to see Tam Mackay, otherwise known as Tam the Gun.

'Suxteen years ah've been here as Dustruct Gunner – that's longer than any other since this began in 1861. Dinnae you think it's easy, mind. Folk aye think all ye've tae dee is pull the trigger wunce a day an that's it. Naw, naw, ah've got tae clean and maintain that gun, organise twenty-one-gun salutes fer royalty and such like. Naw! It's nae a cushy number at all, ye ken. There's a lot tae it.'

His figure did not suggest the build of man who broke sweat often. Tam the Gun was late 40-ish, a small plump version of Lord Kitchener. His moustache ended in dapper curls. With the cooperation of the Speaking Clock and a 25-pound howitzer from 1946, it was Tam's job to administer Edinburgh's daily shock treatment, the one o'clock time signal.

'In 1861 there were several official clocks aboot the toon, all controlled electrically from a master clock on Blackford Hill, at the Observatory there. There wis one on Calton Hill. So they rigs up this cable from Calton Hill tae a clock in the castle – wis the longest cable in the wurld then – and a lanyard connected the clock tae the gun and it could be fired, remote like. Didnae last long. Ah use the Speaking Clock. Cannae go wrong.'

But things had gone wrong twice in his career, due to a mechanical or a charge failure, and the gun had failed to fire. Each occasion had made the newspapers. 'If ah cannae get it tae go off within ten seconds of one, ah dinnae bother. Nae use. It's a time signal, ye see. People set their watches on it.' Tam's moustache unfurled half an inch. 'Ah control all the business in the city.'

'What happens to the empty shell cases?'

'Nae chance, mate! They get refilled. Today's one . . .

let's see . . . 1945 it wis made and we use it again and again. Ye ken, some years ago ah begged six empties off the army to auction fer charity. Wis a hard fight but ah got them. The maist ah could raise for each was forty quid. Bloody disgrace . . . Ah weel! There's ma time signal.'

Tam rang the Speaking Clock at twelve forty-five and activated a stopwatch on the exact count. Fifteen minutes later, reading from the stopwatch, he fired the gun. 'Two years ago the wurld slowed down by a tenth of a second – all clocks had tae be adjusted, but that wis the Speaking Clock's problem, nae mine.'

He took precisely three and a half minutes to change into his uniform and comb his moustache. Loading the gun was a performance, a display of marching and a choreographed ritual of exaggerated gestures. At precisely 1 pm Tam's gun gave a single violent contraction, some of the spectators screamed and Tam was consumed by blue smoke.

I looked along the line of the barrel. 'What are you aiming at? It looks like the Scottish Office.'

'Yer dead right, pal,' Tam the Gun roared. 'Ah'm a great one fer Scotland. They bastards are nae goin' tae privatise *ma* watter.'

The Scottish Office which will disappear, should Tam the Gun ever confuse a blank with a live round, is St Andrew's House, a block of dirty sandstone in a style so distinctly Soviet that it is hard to believe it is an extension of Westminster rather than the Kremlin. It is a solid blockish building with decorative columns out of which emerge half-length busts representing Education (обче́ние), Industry, Agriculture, and other socio-economic deities around which our lives revolve.

On the other side of the road the mood is Mediterranean, the former Royal High School standing conspicuously empty and expectant, on parade in simple Greek style with fluted Doric pillars. Set aside and refurbished at

great cost for the Scottish Assembly which failed to
come about in 1979, the building is pretentious; vacuous;
impotent; as worthy of its place on Edinburgh's skyline
as it is symbolic of the nation's politics.

'It's a fine building but . . . what do we do with it?'
asked Mr Cairns. 'Any ideas?'

'Keep it for a Scottish Parliament?' I ventured.

'Oh, I think that's really why the council decided to
buy it, but we must do something with it until then.'

Mr Cairns had offered to show me round. He was about
to pack in his job with Lothian Regional Council, who
had recently purchased the building from the Scottish
Office for £1.725 million, and wasn't worrying about
such formalities as discretion. 'The asking price was
actually £2.5 million but when we measured the floor
space we found it much smaller than specified. That
was a result of the £3.5 million the Scottish Office spent
refurbishing it.'

'And they're trying to run the country!'

'It does make you wonder, I must admit.'

Our voices echoed eerily in the empty passages. The
interior was a tasteful mix of wooden panelling and white
walls. No paintings, no decorations, no furniture; just an
empty Belhaven beer barrel by a door.

The principal room, the Debating Chamber, consisted
of seats and tabletops in concentric ovals dropping in
tiers to a wrought iron bannister enclosing the floor area
where the Royal High's teachers once sat. Seating and
microphones were provided for 169 speakers in the main
chamber, and 100 viewers could be accommodated in the
gallery. 'PRESS ONLY', stated a sign on one section,
shouting optimism in the emptiness and silence.

Whatever else the Scottish Office had spent £3.5
million on, it was not on furnishings. The decor was
that of a cheap car; the tabletops and backrests looked
wood-effect veneer, and the seats were a shiny green
leather-effect something else. Most absurd of all were the

three chairs for dignitaries at the south end. With chunky wood-effect arm rests and high square backs they were art nouveau relics of the sixties.

'Hideous, isn't it?' Mr Cairns remarked.

As we passed the gatehouse, the caretaker handed Mr Cairns an envelope. It was an electricity bill from Scottish Power, a FINAL REMINDER to the Scottish Office that it still had not paid the £2,000 outstanding on the last account.

'Yes, it does make you wonder,' Mr Cairns repeated, thoughtfully.

Fifty yards from the gates of the proposed site of a Scottish Assembly and fifty yards from the doors of the Scottish Office, on the north side of the road where a wall holds back Calton Hill, stood a Portakabin with a brazier burning alongside. 'DAY 779. DEMOCRACY FOR SCOTLAND VIGIL,' read the Portakabin's ID badges. A manifesto was pinned to a wall.

> Democracy for Scotland is a new strictly non-party political organisation with the following aims:
> 1. To maintain the 'Vigil' for a Scottish Parliament and to do so until one is in place.
> 2. To campaign, using all peaceful means necessary, for the recall of the Scottish Parliament, to be elected by a fair voting system.
> 3. To promote decentralisation of the decision-making process to the regions, districts and communities of Scotland.

From inside came an intense smell of body odour and the twangs of a strummed guitar. Jim, Aleck and Chris sat inside a ghetto of unemployment. Chris looked up from his guitar, continued writhing to his own beat and gave a grin that might have accompanied either hallo or a growl. At 21 he was, he said later, an ex-Marine. Aleck was the same age, and harsh on the eye: black shoes, white socks, black trousers, white jacket, black baseball cap. He considered himself unemployable until he had passed a certain Scotvec module which he had abandoned. Yet he was an encyclopaedia on election dates, candidates, majorities and votes polled. Jim had ten years on the others, wore his black hair slicked back, and cool shades. He was their spokesman.

'We're just volunteers. Every day we have a rota of people manning the place. It began two years ago—'

'Tenth April ninety-two,' Aleck cut in.

'—aye, that's right, when the election results came out and we heard that by far the majority of Scottish voters—'

'Seventy-five per cent, it was.'

'—had voted for political parties who had included a commitment to constitutional change in their manifestos. Yet due to our unfair electoral system, the wishes of the people can be ignored. *Democracy* they call it. Huh! It's contemptuous. That's why we're here.'

Aleck nodded solemnly. Chris was on the C&W trail somewhere in Texas.

'Chris has been here since Day 67,' Aleck mentioned, as if to explain why his friend appeared AWOL.

'Off an' on, like,' Chris admitted, between mouthings of something else.

On that evening of 10th April, a group of dispirited Scots gathered on this spot and decided to hold an impromptu vigil as a protest. They were surprised by the degree of support and publicity they attracted. The vigil continued. One of the band *Hue and Cry* hired a Portakabin at his own expense to provide the Vigil with a base. Two months later it was purchased with donations. The Council had subsequently given permission for the cabin to stay on the spot. The caretaker of the 'Scottish Assembly' buildings provided them with water. For over two years people had brought more firewood than the Vigil could burn.

On its first anniversary a Declaration of Calton Hill was drawn up. 'We, the People of Scotland, demand our inalienable right to live within an accountable and democratic system of government and to determine the form that this system of government should take . . .'

'If you'd like to join us . . .'

I signed on for a shift from midnight to 6 am. Chris was my companion. He slept (but then he had been around since Day 67). The small hours passed slowly. I half-expected, and hoped, for some propitious sign to appear like a saltire in the stars, but none came and nationalism remained a fire in a drum and a pastime of the unemployed. That long night many words came back to me, and among them, those of Buccleuch and the wolf man. '. . . ninety-six per cent of the population live in towns . . . *they* will ultimately decide what happens in the countryside' . . . 'one million urbanised deprived . . . dispossessed . . . When they get fire in their belly, the touchpaper will have been lit.'

I kept the brazier well stoked.

I also think a new Scottish parliament will be squabble-some and disunited and full of people justifying themselves by denouncing others – the London parliament on a tiny scale. But it will offer hope for the future. The London parliament has stopped even pretending to do that.

Alasdair Gray, *Why Scots Should Rule Scotland.*

~~

69

Forth Bridges

I left Edinburgh on the tide of rush hour traffic. It sucked me through the city's own Corryvrecken, the double-death roundabouts of Barnton, swept me out towards the Forth bridges, and filled my imagination with the sounds of bones being crushed under wheels. At the first opportunity I took the liberty of trespassing on the Earl of Rosebery's estate, a delightful maze of leaf-littered lanes where the greatest danger was from hidden potholes and reckless rabbits.

My memories are old enough to include the gritty smoke of a steam engine entering the coach as my mother opened the train window to allow me to throw out a penny (doubtless to the hazard of those painting below) while crossing the Forth Rail Bridge. These were rare and special excursions, for fun not destinations, and we got off at the first station and returned on the next train.

Since then I've always thrilled at the sight of those three red Victorian giants holding hands (and 6,500,000 rivets and a resident population of 3,000 pigeons) over the Forth. I had tried to get permission to be an official tourist to the top of the bridge but, understandably, my request was refused. ScotRail was not wanting any more publicity, having just been branded 'cheapskates' in the press for killing the metaphor for never-ending work by removing the permanent staff of sixteen painters for a year at a saving of £600,000, and 17 tons of paint. So I had to settle for a visit to its more prosaic neighbour.

Jim was a patrolman. He started my tour in the main office beside the toll booths, demonstrating the camera coverage of the bridge. He pressed various buttons and the views on a dozen screens, panned, soared, plummeted, and zoomed in and out. There was scarcely a nook on the bridge or its approach roads that could not be scrutinised. 'You'd be surprised at some of the things those cameras pick up,' Jim said, and winked. The Forth Road Bridge and its environs were popular with lovers.

We drove out to the north tower. Jim fed me statistics, his hand motioning a dive to the sea far below.

'Suicides. We average about five a year. Hundred and fifty feet, they drop. There was one about a fortnight ago. A German sailor, he was. Jumped just as I got to him. Found his body thirteen days later, off Newcastle.'

'Have any survived the jump?'

'Two. A student, he even managed to swim ashore. And a woman. She had back injuries, but she recovered. Then she went and jumped again, six months later, and didn't get away wi' it that time.'

At one and a half miles long, this was the second longest suspension bridge in Europe. We stopped at the north tower. Ninety seconds later we were at the top, looking down from 512 feet. Below us the bridge had shrunk to a tightrope. This wasn't a bridge, but a balancing act. Everything looked terrifyingly fragile. The view had enough natural drama without Jim adding to it.

'At peak traffic flows it bounces three feet up and down in the middle.'

'Really . . . ?' I would have preferred the bridge to have kept some secrets.

'These bridges are child's play, really. The idea of them, I mean. All they've done is attach a cable to one bank and drape it over these towers and fix it to the other bank; then they feed it back again and again – it's actually one cable fifteen thousand and four hundred miles long. And then they do it again alongside so you've got two of them. And then you just hang a road from it.'

He made it sound like advanced crochet. Only this example had cost £21 million in 1964. Now, thirty years later, the bridge had only just repaid its debt.

'So there's no problems with it, then?'

'Yes, we've got worries. Global warming and congestion, they're our worries.' The bridge was designed to safely withstand winds of up to 120 mph. Recent winters had consistently produced gusts of 110–115 mph, a phenomenon linked to global warming. The Bridge Authority had just plunged into debt again, confounding any hopes of the bridge becoming toll-free, by borrowing £8 million to strengthen the towers to withstand 140 mph winds.

'Congestion's the biggest problem. We really need another bridge. Eighteen and a quarter million cars used it last year, and this is rising by four per cent annually. Every day cars break down and, if this happens at rush hour, in five minutes we've got a four-mile tailback. Often the cars are so jam-packed, we can't get in with a tow vehicle. Believe me, it's getting chronic.'

In the distance we could see the booths of the toll keepers ('There's fifty of them, in four shifts') collecting the 40-pences which would total a gross £8 million a year. From a height of 512 feet, it was a bargain.

'Do you always take visitors up the north tower?'

'Yes.'

'Why's that?'

Jim looked uncomfortable. 'Because the south tower – don't ask me why – is always covered in bird shit.'

I looked around my feet. I hadn't noticed it before. The north tower was spotlessly clean.

'Starlings won't nest here. They'll only nest on the south tower. Strange, isn't it?'

70

BP Grangemouth

'MUSEUM OPEN – PLEASE RING *ONCE* AND WAIT.' The museum at South Queensferry was practically under the end of the road bridge. I rang once and waited by the notice which was screwed to a door in a spacious hall. The hall had a further two doors and a sliding glass window where some unnamed public service was hibernating.

Ten minutes later I was still waiting, wondering if I should risk the wrath of the custodian – doubtless some grumpy relic of the trade in archaeologists – when a young couple came in and rattled on the window. Just as the window slid open, the door beside me opened. 'Do come in, please,' said a smiling woman in white lace and designer jacket.

I made a remark to the effect that it was a relief to find the museum was open after all, but she didn't seem to hear this and motioned me into her office.

'Please take a seat.'

'I'd rather stand, thanks. I've been sitting on a bicycle for too long!' She gave me a fixed stare during which her smile slowly deflated. A recent puncture had left my trousers a bit oily and whatever happened to my trousers usually tended to replicate itself liberally over the rest of me.

I was in the Museum Director's office. Warm, personal, bright, carpeted, with a single central desk of a size suited to an oil magnate or a contract for forty Waverley novels. A frilly rosette was tied round some dried flowers in a bowl. Beyond the bowl was a fine view of the distant rail bridge. The director ran a pen over two forms on her desk, checking the details of one against the other. Why, I wondered, could I not just be allowed through to look at the exhibits? Was I going to get a personal tour when she'd finished this urgent business? I studied the view.

'That's it,' she suddenly said, swivelling the sheets round to face me. 'Now, if you'd just like to sign there, please, at the crosses.'

I hesitated to take the pen she offered. 'You do understand that I'm here to visit the museum, don't you?'

She looked stunned, took a gulp of air and flushed. Then she collapsed over her papers in a gesture that was so theatrical I feared for her heart. 'Ooooo-ooooh.' She looked up with the complexion of a two-bar heater. 'What an awful mistake . . . ooooh, I feel quite weak . . . I'm just temporary here . . . but . . . I'll find out about the museum . . .'

Still ringing with apologies, she ushered me out of her office and consulted with the sliding window which informed her that the museum would be open tomorrow. ('Don't take any notice of the sign – it always says "Open".')

'So sorry,' she said, and turned to lead the young couple into her office. I stole a prolonged glance at the girl. In a building shared by a museum and a Registrar's Office, I had come within two feet and a couple of seconds of being married to her.

My next port of call, ten miles along the coast, lay fuming below a black sack of cloud. It chain-smoked day and night, employed Intelligent Pigs and Cat Crackers, and was separated from the docks by a road three miles long whose lamp-posts were all on hinges and could be collapsed flat to allow access for wide visitors. Intelligent Pigs, apparently, though small themselves (maximum waistline 108 inches), had very large friends.

Every three years Intelligent Pigs home in on the 250 acres of interwoven and convoluted pipes that give BP Grangemouth its distinctive cloud and acrid smell. Here Fluid Catalytic Crackers disassemble and reassemble chemicals, and Scotland's oil is refined. Intelligent Pigs are automatic devices sent along pipelines to clean them. From the north they start at Nigg and Aberdeen and crawl 130 miles home to clear the way for the flow of North Sea oil. From the west, at Finnart on Loch Long, Intelligent Piglets (for 12-inch pipe) burrow and clean 57 miles for the access of imported heavy crude. And finally, they are sent down the tubes for 15 miles to the Tank Farm beside the Forth Rail Bridge where excess North Sea crude is sent to await export. Such is the turbulent life of oil and pigs.

Oil, 'protozoic soup', is a complex affair and emerges from the ground in Heinzian varieties, fizzing with gas. North Sea crude is a light oil. Refinement of this oil is easier to accomplish when mixed with imported heavy crude. The first stage of the process was to mix the crudes and separate the gas. I could never understand why this gas wasn't used for anything more purposeful than sending 40-foot flames into the air. I'd seen these burn-offs at Sullum Voe and Flotta, and here they were again.

'Why,' I put it to Jack Henderson, BP PR, 'couldn't your flare stacks be heating, for example, Falkirk Old Folks' Home?'

'We'd incinerate them more likely. Flare stacks are our safety valves. They only burn off the excess and the surges. It's not worth doing anything else with it.' This seemed lame to me, not the reply to be expected of Intelligent Pig keepers.

BP had positioned themselves here not just because 80 per cent of Scotland's population was found within a

40-mile radius, but also because this area was the centre of the country's first oil strike. In 1850 oil was extracted on this spot first from cannel coal, then from shale. Over a hundred companies entered the business, producing mainly paraffin, until foreign competition squeezed them out. That competition came from Persia.

In 1902, one William Knox D'Arcy was invited out to Persia to look for oil. It took him six years to find it, dipping into the Middle East's black oasis which, today, represents 65 per cent of the world's proven reserves. D'Arcy made his strike at Masjid-i-Sulaiman, and the Anglo-Persian Oil Company was formed. By 1919 the Lothian shale industry had been reduced to six operators, whom Anglo-Persian bought out and absorbed into its new identity, British Petroleum.

Mr Henderson was immensely proud of British Petroleum. He felt at home in this steaming industrial jungle which kept half the neighbourhood employed. And the future, he believed, looked encouraging. Only half of the world had been explored for its oil-bearing potential.

'How much oil do we know is left?'

'If no more oil is found after today, the present known reserves will last the world forty-two years at our current rate of consumption.'

I climbed back onto my bike – pedal power – with all the sanctimony of a temporarily repentant sinner.

The farms of the central belt looked hamstrung by obstructions and many were giving up, turning to the new cash crop of building plots. This was urbanised countryside, slashed by motorways, A roads, B roads, lanes and railways, and squatted on by shale bings, towns and their connected tentacles of housing estates. One led into the other, Grangemouth into Polmont into Falkirk into Bonnybridge into Denny, with barely a glimpse of a cow, sheep or Less Intelligent pig. I camped in a lonely field beside the Forth and Clyde Canal. Built from funds raised in 1784 when those families whose estates had been annexed by the crown after Culloden were allowed to *buy* them back, the canal had since been truncated. Its access to the sea had gone the way of most things here: cut off, filled in and sat upon, in this case, by Glensburgh's houses.

It was late October. Scotland had lost its colour and turned winter grey. Grey sky, grey towns, grey grass. It was all as dreary as school mince. Each day darkness came a little earlier and banished me from the road that much earlier. The evenings became unbearably long and the temptation to dash home ever harder to resist. It was no time of year to be muddling through Scotland with a tent and bicycle. The country had shut up shop for the season.

The decision to pack in and go home was reached while perusing the parochial press in Falkirk library. I found I wasn't the only one still on the road.

'A bus driver who failed to notice when one of his school pupil passengers fell out was fined £150 at Stranraer Sheriff Court on Monday,' reported the *Wigtown Free Press*. *The Perthshire Advertiser* showed a picture of the visiting Aschaffenburgh Rifle Club, looking more like an anti-tank squad as they posed beside their arsenal. The *Falkirk Herald* invited me to a recital by the Neheim-Huston Fanfarencorps who, if anything, appeared more dangerous than the Aschaffenburgh crowd, but I was more drawn to Tigers on Vaseline, a band described by the *East Fife Mail* as 'doing a turbo-grunge gig in Levenmouth'. Unfortunately both dates had passed and the only social highlight I could find was the *Kilsyth Chronicle*'s announcement of Cumbernauld Racing Pigeon Club's AGM.

That night, for the fourth consecutive night in a row, the temperature dropped to minus 4°C. This was the final straw. I went home; and resumed my journey from exactly the same spot six months later. For the sake of the narrative, it was early winter when I settled into my sleeping bag in Falkirk, and early spring when I emerged.

∾

71

Blackgrange Warehouses

Spring had touched up the greens of the Ochils, brightly
where patches of bracken flourished, faintly where sheep
found grazing, and darkly – a Forestry Commission drab –
where gorse invaded the steep slopes. I knew their outline
well, having spent three years at university below them,
but this was the first time I had ever stood on top of the
area's most prominent feature, the arrow-shaped tower of
the Wallace Monument.

Below me, the River Forth had developed a bad case
of the staggers. Within a few miles it had turned from
being a host of international shipping to a twisting
muddy rivulet offering little more than minnows to
truant schoolkids. To the west was a pocket of Holland,
the flat (utterly flat) farmland of the Carse of Stirling,
while to the east Clackmannan looked torn between going
bush and lumping itself in with the Highlands or going
built-up and hanging in with the Central Belt. The latter
seemed to be winning and my gaze came to rest on an
area of regular blocks, 49 black rectangles. This was
Blackgrange, covering 250 acres, the richest acres, by
far, in the entire British Isles.

It's a moot point whether Coca Cola or Scottish whisky
can claim to have conquered more of the world. Whisky

is sold in 190 markets at an average rate of 30 bottles a second (or 995 million a year), grossing an annual £2 billion in overseas sales alone. Americans buy more than anyone else, followed, surprisingly, by the French. But consumers are fickle, and distillers contend with a particularly difficult problem in the equation of supply and demand, that of trying to match current production with the anticipated needs of the market in ten years' time.

Of the 2,000 brands available, only a hundred are considered major sellers, and the long-reigning leader is Johnnie Walker Red Label. In the money stakes the runaway leader, who has been dabbling in the industry for at least 500 years but assumed firm control in 1823, is the Exchequer, who pockets 70 per cent of the shelf price of every bottle sold on the home market. Blackgrange is the exciseman's honeypot.

'What's the value of the whisky kept here?'

Mr Carmichael twiddled his moustache and thought. He was the manager of these bonded warehouses, the centralised depot for most of United Distillers' production. 'The honest answer is, I don't know. Technically, the spirit doesn't become whisky until it's three years old. Every day about eight thousand casks come in and seven to nine thousand will go out. The casks are different sizes – butts, hogsheads, American Standard Barrels . . . so it's not easy to guess off the top of my head.'

'Have a shot . . .'

'OK.' He got out his calculator. 'We keep the spirit maturing for an average of eight years, and there's usually three million casks here at any one time. Let's call them all hogsheads, that's 160 litres at, say, a value of £20 a litre . . . spirit here is, of course, over-strength . . . ah well, it's gone right off the scale.'

Later I repeated the calculation. Blackgrange contained approximately £9,600 million's worth of potential whisky.

Mr Carmichael was a large man. I guessed the capacity of his shirt at about about 80 litres, or half a hogshead. He led me into a warehouse. It was dark, silent and smelled gloriously of damp wood, a rich earthiness worthy of billions of pounds. The casks were stacked nine high and in long rows.

'People forget the important part wood plays in the whole process. We use Bodega sherry casks, again and again, only we fill them with sherry between each filling of spirit. It goes in clear and raw and pretty bland, and comes out eight years later, mellow, and with flavour and colour.'

Mr Carmichael had been suspicious of me at first and had referred me to Head Office where I was vetted for affiliations with Santori.

'Fraud – it's a constant problem in the industry.' In the half-light of a warehouse Mr Carmichael looked maliciously Mexican, Emilio Zapata without the sombrero and ammo belt.

'Who are the main offenders?'

'The French and Belgians. They bottle coloured alcohol and sell it off as Scotch. Their governments aren't any too conscientious about prosecuting either. The Scotch Whisky Association looks after this side of things. They've usually got about a hundred prosecutions in process worldwide all the time. And India's bad too but there it's just coloured water they sell – not even an attempt to get close to whisky. But few people have tasted the real thing, so they think the muck really *is* whisky. Wrecks the market for us. Same in Russia and Eastern Europe, big new markets opening up, full of con-men.'

Running a dormitory for casks on an eight-year snooze was not as simple as it might appear, Mr Carmichael was at pains to emphasise. Blackgrange took in the produce of over thirty distilleries. Every day blenders sent in orders for so many casks of this or that – up to three dozen whiskies went into the recipe for a single blend – but it always varied and the gaps among the remaining casks always had to be refilled with new intake. Over eight years and three million comings and goings, the potential for chaos was immense.

'Bar codes,' Mr Carmichael announced proudly. 'Brilliant things. We've just gone computerised. The screen tells us which cask is next in line and where to find it.' He beamed. 'Care for a dram?'

We returned to his office, startling a hare on the way. 'Funny thing I've noticed. We never see a single rabbit here, even though they're all around us, but hares. Lots and lots of hares. And huge ones at that.'

It struck me then that a pattern was emerging. The Central Belt's wildlife was prompting several interesting areas of research: *The Geopoetics of South Tower for Starlings,* and *Blackgrange Hare Syndrome.*

The smell of whisky followed me for miles along the foot of the Ochils.

72

∞

Mary, Queen of Scots (Centre Court)

In the north-west it had been Prince Charles Edward Stuart. In the south-west, Burns. In the Borders, Mary, Queen of Scots. Around Stirling, Bruce and Wallace. In Fife I was back in Mary's country. In the course of my journey I became a keen collector of the trivial and tenuous links certain localities claimed with their avowed heroes or heroines.

'By the way,' an amateur historian had informed me in Dalbeattie, 'you may be interested to know that it's on record that Rabbie Burns once played draughts with Dalbeattie's barber.'

Jedburgh presented the following sign in a Mary, Queen of Scots exhibition which was embarrassingly short on memorabilia: 'A French watchcase unearthed by a mole at Queen's Mire, a spot passed over by the Royal party on their return from Hermitage.'

Fife had more to offer. It had one of her prisons and, at Falkland, her tennis court. In all the razzmatazz of sensationalism concerning Mary's life, history has tended to overlook how sporty she was. Her early years were spent in genteel pastimes in France but when she came to Scotland, fresh from the *eau de Cologne* of the Versailles Courts to the bad breath and body odour of the Scots, she took to sport in a big way. She once rode forty miles in a day. She enjoyed the odd round of golf, as the tabloid press of the time noted:

> A few days after the murder [of her second husband, Darnley], remaining at Holyrude House, she went to Seton openly exercising there with the pall-mall and golf, and at night plainly abusing her body with the Earl of Bothwell. (Book of Articles, December 1568.)

In Bannockburn I first met Mary the Tennis Player. As the battle exhibition was a bit thin on reportage and few of Robert the Bruce's artefacts have survived since 1314, it had been decided to beef things up with a mini pageant of later history. And there, lifesize, was a dummy of Mary, wearing bloomers and tights as pink as those of George IV, holding her racquet and looking as if she had just missed a nasty serve by Navratilova.

Tennis had been played in Scotland since the reign of Alexander III (1249–86) but always as a sport for royalty. As the court at Falkland Palace showed, Royal (or 'Real') Tennis was a strange concoction of the modern game with elements of squash included. The court had high walls, and an enclosure for spectators which jutted out into the court on two sides. The walls and the enclosure's roof were all 'in play' and the ball was allowed to perform multiple bounces on the obstructions, but only one on the ground. It was customary for a servant to make the first hit and start each game on behalf of his master or mistress, hence the derivation of 'to serve' and 'service'.

73

∽

Caddy, St Andrews

Since Alloa, which sounds like a Hawaiian greeting until
you get there, neat brown signs had informed me that I
was on the Mill Trail. In heritage centres heavy with
wistful nostalgia I learned about the area's golden age
of tartan and serge, and how, a century later in times
of no work, even the sweat shops and slave labour of
former tyrannical institutions assume that coating of
Good-Old-Days reverence.

The Mill Trail turned, unofficially, to the Beer Trail
(Alloa Breweries) and then the Farm Trail. Fife was
arable and had been ploughed into dark brown squares,
or put under plastic to boost the growth of what I
took to be infant strawberries. The land coasted by
with self-satisfied ease, showing the practised hand of
repaying handsome dividends, and saved its hills for
real hills, abrupt conical laws: Largo Law, Kellie Law,
Norman's Law, Blacklaw, Lucklaw. The map of Fife read
like a new act of privatisation.

Ever since leaving the Highlands and Islands I had
failed to recognise a collective identity that could truly
be described as a separate culture. In landscape and
dialects, Lanimers and Common Ridings, distinctive
elements were present but they didn't hold together as

a strong entity in the way that language, religion, common grazings, peat and isolation bonded the entity of 'Highland'. As a counterpoint to the north, 'Lowland' relied on strength of numbers for its corporate image rather than on the sum of its living differences. Through the Borders and up the east coast, thus far, longer histories of accessibility and industrialisation had moulded lifestyles into a general sameness.

Here and there that sameness inhabits pockets of character. Around Fife's coast are some of Scotland's most worshipped fishing villages – Dysart, Elie, Anstruther, Crail – which boast more artists on their piers than lobster pots. Like great auks, they are pretty, beautiful even, but past their best, museum pieces. Pittenweem was my favourite, less likely to appear on canvas than any of the others, but in September it died less than the others too. It had fishermen. They sat around in huddles, gossiping; old storm-beaten faces, whiskery, ruffled by wrinkles, their mouths down-turned and loose like a cod's. In their dotage and infirmity old fishermen have always the salty smells of their youth, the constancy of the sea and the credible lie of its long friendship. I envy them that solace.

St Andrews seemed to have everything for the retiree. It had the sea for old fishermen, and for landlubbers it had those rare qualities which are only found in small university towns; the frequent sounds of laughter in the streets and a high percentage of young people who, if not gainfully employed, are at least not disruptively unemployed. Its population lent the place a warm, carefree sense of abandon while its wide streets and aged buildings lent it dignity. Apart from its perishingly chill wind, St Andrews struck me as being a grand place in which to grow old. And of course it had golf.

'Some folk think ye kin buy golf, know what ah mean? – best gear an' a' that, but ye cannae. Ye got tae ler-run it,' Gordon the Caddie said. 'D'ye play much yersel?'

'No, hardly at all. Just a wee bit for fun.'

For fun. That wasn't really true. I found golf intensely frustrating. It was the devastation of losing your rattle over the side of the pram, the joy of having it returned to you, only to lose the bloody thing again. Golf balls were one pound's worth of devious bloodymindedness.

I withheld a piece of information from Gordon the Caddie. Amongst my illustrious sporting ancestors (Mary, Queen of Scots, was not one of them) I had an aunt who hit a mean golf ball. She represented Great Britain in the Curtis Cup on three occasions, was a regular in internationals and then turned professional when Slazenger put her name, Jean Donald, on their clubs. But my standard of play forced me to keep Jean a secret on a golf course. People always had unreasonable expectations that talent was unfailingly hereditary. To be a bad golfer was acceptable, but to be a bad golfer when there were birdies and eagles in the genes, was either freakish or negligent.

And besides, I suffered a pathological dislike of losing golf balls. If a round of the game didn't allow for the odd half-hour here and there to root around in the rough for my errant ball, I wasn't interested. A choice of four clubs tended to suffice for my needs, but a tour of the Golf Museum in St Andrews showed me that one more might well have lifted my game. It was described as 'ane scraper'.

What distinguished Scottish golf from the *kolf* of Holland, the museum also enlightened me, was that Scottish golf always aimed for holes. The more adventurous Dutch aimed for trees or people's front doors. The earliest reference to golf in Scotland appears in a statute in 1457, and by 1618 it was sufficiently popular for James VI to award a trade monopoly (which went unrecognised) in golf balls. Leith's five-hole course was the oldest in Scotland but somehow St Andrews stole the show and by 1650, its twenty-two holes had become recognised as the game's 'home'. Today the town has five and a half courses. In May the Old Course was already fully booked until October.

It was a Sunday, the only day the Old Course is given a rest. For six days a week, a round cost £50 per player, foursomes only, teeing off every twelve minutes from 7 am to 6 pm . . . this was serious money. Quite aside from the other four-and-a-bit courses, the Old Course alone netted £1,000 an hour.

Caddies cost £20 on top of the fee for the round. I hired one ('Pay afterwards') and was allocated Gordon. He was one of my more extravagant travel expenses.

'Wha's yer clubs then?'

'I haven't got any.'

'Ye whit . . . nae clubs . . . ?'

I explained that all I wanted to do was to walk round the Old Course with a guide and learn something about what went on. Gordon looked insulted. I fished out two ten-pound notes.

Gordon the Caddie brightened. 'Nae bother, pal.'

We set off. He began with a summary of his life's injuries and ailments. Apparently his first eighteen years had been trouble-free but his 'guarantee must hiv ren oot'. He lost half a thumb on a Normandy beach. He held up the stump. 'Shortly after, broke ma leg, bad, aye, fib *an'* tib it wis. Then . . .'

'Excuse me, but is that the Royal and Ancient Club-house?'

'Aye, that's it.' He became my guide again. 'Yon flagpole there's the mast frae the *Cutty Sark*. Now, the club house dates back to . . .' and he told me all about it.

'Can we go inside?'

'Not a hope in hell. Ah've been here thirteen year an ah've niver yet been inside. Last year I caddied fer Clint Eastwood—' he guddled in a pocket and pulled out a photograph. Proof. Credentials. Clint Eastwood and a grinning Gordon. '—an Clint says, "Ah fancy goin in there." "No way," ah says, but he goes in and a moment later he gets thrown oot.'

'How do you become a member?'

'It helps if you hiv a title, and loads a money . . . an the last thing ye do is show any interest in becoming a member. Oh aye, that's yer chances jist deid. There's aboot 1,600 o' them. There's one. There's the Major.'

He pointed to a hirpling set of plus-fours and tweed jacket approaching the main door. The Major opened it with his own key. He disappeared through another door beyond a bowl of water laid out for members' dogs. Gordon led me round to a side window where we pressed our noses against the pane. We could almost smell the antiquity of oak panelling, plush, leather and vellum. Past club captains stared back from their frames, men in red jackets looking strangely out of place, hijacked from a fox pack. The Major joined another tweed-wrapped ancient reading a newspaper and sank into an adjacent chasm of padded chair. Around the room were rows of lockers. 'Some o' they lockers hivnae been opened in a hunner an' fifty years,' Gordon whispered.

We set off up the first fairway.

'. . . ah got appendicitis. Well, they took that oot and then whit happened? . . . TB . . . tub burrk yule ohsis. Ah wis nine months ina sanatorium wi that . . .'

'What club would you advise me to use here?'

Gordon stopped to consider this unnecessary question. He turned his stout and apparently indestructible frame this way and that until he spotted a landmark. The breeze played with his white hair which stuck out in punkish quiffs. 'Ah hivnae seen ye hit anything yet so ah couldnae say whit club, but frae that stank there, it's a hunner an twenty three yards tae the hole. An see they flags, it's the right one. Ye've got tae remember here that the fairways share greens. Double greens they are. Now, ye can always tell where y'are by adding up the holes. Greens add up tae eighteen, fairways tae nineteen. So if yer on the fourteenth green that's shared wi the fourth. If yer on the fourteenth fairway, the one alongside is the fifth.'

I nodded politely at this piece of mind-boggling logic and realised that if you didn't have a caddy on the Old Course you certainly needed to pack a calculator along with your irons and scrapers.

By the time we reached the tenth, Gordon had exhausted his catalogue of calamities. My grasp on the timescale of his heart attack and quadruple heart bypass (he pulled up his jersey and shirt to reveal the scar, 'That's ma zipper') was shaky but his recent hernia and gallstones brought me bang up to date: Gordon, caddy, retired baker, van driver, steel worker, telephonist, film extra (crowd scene, *Chariots of Fire*) and civil servant, aged 69.

It wasn't my type of course at all. Rangers patrolled constantly to ensure the flow of players remained unhindered. The greens were cut twice a day and were ridiculously fast. I preferred challenging greens with rogue tufts of grass and dips and sheep droppings. On these billiard tables my putts would have ended up in the fields. And to cap it all, five minutes was the maximum allowance for a lost ball.

We reached the famous seventeenth where, Gordon said, more great reputations had been ruined than on any other hole in the world. Tommy Nakajima's was one. In the 1978 Open he was lying in joint second place when he teed off on the seventeenth. He got within putting distance of the hole in two. His putt was long and went into a bunker. He took another seven shots to get out and end the hole, but by then he was twentieth and had lost £100,000 in prize money. 'We call this bunker the Sands of Nakajima now . . . unofficial like.'

We passed the Old Course Hotel which had netting on its roof to protect its slates, a pock-marked wall, two cracked windows and a figure (paying £170 per night without breakfast) daringly having coffee in a glass conservatory. Golf at St Andrews was funded essentially by Americans (85 per cent) and Japanese (5 per cent).

'Oh aye! Gone! It's aye goin'. Somebody's stolen the eighteenth flag again.' A bare pole marked the final green. The disappearing flag was simply high jinks or souvenir hunters but St Andrews was developing a fearsome reputation for the theft of golf clubs. Warning notices were liberally posted. I felt disappointed. Crime, and my caddy's susceptibility to rupture, fracture, inflammation and arrest had badly tainted my round. Until Gordon remarked:

'Ye know, ah must hiv walked doon the eighteenth hunners of times, but when ah walk doon wi' a playin' guest, ah still feel a thrull. Fer maist folk who come here this is a once-in-a-lifetime experience. A great privilege. Some get really emotional, an it aye affects me tae.'

This was a startling revelation from a man who had just admitted to keeping a log of air crashes. His records went back to the 1920s. He listed the date, aircraft, cause of accident, number of dead and, where possible, their names. He thought he might get it published some day.

'An see that beach there?' St Andrew's sands were half a mile wide and ran to infinity. 'That's where ah wis shot in *Chariots o' Fire*.'

I nodded appreciatively and thanked him for the tour. He looked disappointed. I thought, *he's surely not expecting a tip, is he*?

'Are ye nae wantin' a photie o' me . . . ?'

∽

74

Highland Cattle Sales

My arrival in Perth coincided with that of Dosan Og 53rd of Achnacloich and Lili Ann 15th of Corriemuckloch. They both had 'good ends' and passed muster with the farmer who sat next to me in the crowded amphitheatre of the sale ring. Ben Coutts knew a good end when he saw one. Number 132 (Deidre 42nd of Rothiemurchus) caused him a flush of indignation.

'That's a shocker . . . sickle-walk, ewe-necked . . . that's a runt.' He was horrified to hear it fetch 400 guineas.

But Highland Cattle were currently in vogue. They were, according to my programme, 'living antiques', an old breed with a different digestive system not suited to 'hard' (commercial) feeding. As a result they were exceptionally cheap to maintain, needing only 'fresh air and whins', and their toughness was the stuff of legend and law. In Sweden, Highland Cattle were the only breed legally permitted to overwinter out of doors. Germans loved them. Unlike Charolais and Simmentals, breeds bolstered to grotesque levels of production by manipulation and chemicals, Highlanders were wholly green. Short on quantity but big on quality. Their fat structure was also unique and resulted in flavour pervading the meat during cooking. They had it all, even the looks.

Perth Highland Cattle Sales was one of the biggest events in any bovine's calendar. Very similar, I imagined, to that not unrelated Society event, the Perth Ball. 'My dear Martha Mhor of Aigas, how perfectly *delightful* to see you again . . . you *have* met Furan 14th of Glengorm? . . . yes, of course, and Donnag Sgairteil 42nd of Leys? And how's little Jock 1st of Auch . . . oh, how you've grown . . . my dears, *do* have a top up . . .'

It was now the turn of Capleadh 3rd of Ardanaiseig (who was given a footnote, implying the aristocracy was up to its old tricks again, 'in calf to Lord Tara of Old Greenlaw').

'Three thousan' for, three thousan' for . . . c'mon this cow speaks for hersel', one o' the better-ended cows in this yard, three thousan' for...you'll lose sleep over this one if you miss her, take her home and bull her with any bull ye like, three thousan' for, aye, it's a wretched business this money, THANK YOU, sir, three thousan' five . . .'

I asked Ben for a crash course in cow appraisal.

'You look for a good head. That's a short snout, broad mouth, strong, nicely curved horns pointing forwards and down in the males, but a female's should be less thick at the base and getting thinner evenly, curving upwards to slender points. Neck shouldn't be too long or short. Straight back. Deep ribbed. BIG backside – that's where the beef is – and a straight walk, keeping hooves aligned under its body.'

He made it sound easier to get into the Marines.

'I always look for a good head first. My son, he's on a cattle station in Australia, he always looks at the legs first. Out there, if it can't walk well, it starves. In general cattle here have bad legs, too much standing around in barns, not enough grazing.' He shook his head disdainfully. 'The art of feeding has taken over from the art of breeding.'

I put my new knowledge to the test. I thought Number 166 had few defects and guessed 1,200 guineas.

'Now here's something useful from Mr Taylor . . . four hundred, four hundred, yes, four-fifty, four-fifty, four-fifty . . .' Annag Ruadh let a long string of saliva trickle from her mouth and looked above the disinterest her form was attracting. 'C'mon everyone, there's not many left . . .'

Whenever the bids dried up, the vendor, who was usually in the ring holding the beast, would lean over to the auctioneer and whisper some information which the auctioneer would relay into the microphone to excite interest. Mr Taylor leaned over and whispered.

'Last year she was fourth in Oban Show.'

This heralded a further silence. The hammer was raised. Mr Taylor tried one last whisper.

'Her granny was twice champion of the Royal Highland Show.'

Annag Ruadh failed to out-price runt 132. Number 93 looked long in the neck to me but Brogach of Balmoral made 3,400 guineas for Her Majesty the Queen (who did not appear in the ring to hold him).

Outside the yards, judges were eating their hats. Among the farmers the consensus of opinion the previous day was that the wrong bull had been awarded 'Overall Champion'. Today they had been proved right. The champion had gone for 5,000 guineas while the reserve champion made four times that figure. He was posing for a press photographer who was calling instructions.

'Try and move his rear near corner forward a few inches . . . easy . . . easy . . . GOOD! . . . Now the off-side front corner needs to go back . . .' With all the care associated with shooting a Pirelli calendar, he was endeavouring to achieve a perfect profile. It was news to me that cows, like cars, had corners, near-sides and off-sides. The attendant following his instructions beside a murderous set of horns would go to the appropriate corner and stand on the hoof of one ton and 20,000 guineas' worth of long red hair.

'He'll be off to Germany, just as soon as these BSE restrictions are lifted,' said Bill Smith, who had bought him on behalf of a client. Bill reckoned he'd got a bargain, and had bought a few others too. In fact he'd spent 54,000 guineas that morning.

I mooched behind the scenes to see the preparations for those about to enter the ring. Traditionally Highland Cattle were black but now the majority were red and some were blond (officially 'white'). Red, black and white were all being smothered in attention in what was a beauty salon for living antiques. Cattle were being washed, soaped, scrubbed and blow-waved with industrial hair-driers. Next came brushing, combing, and teasing with liberal dollops of Safeway Hair Gel to give curls lift, body and a silky sheen. Finally, out came the bottles of Johnson's Baby Oil to add gloss to the horns.

I stood before a particularly magnificent example of the coiffeur's artistry. 'What's her name?'

'*He*. He's a bull. Fergie's Fascination of Strathmashie.'

To a novice, it seemed that the art of breeding which had given way to the art of feeding had given way to the art of tarting up.

75

Perth Prison

On the edge of South Inch park – not far from the Cattle Show – a wall of prefab slabs, embedded with dark shingle, rises twenty feet into the air and supports a horizontal tornado of barbed wire. At the centre of the fourteen acres it encloses stand two sandstone blocks in the bleak utilitarian lines of a Victorian institution: school, asylum, barrack, prison. These blocks comprise four storeys of barred windows whose smallness indicate their particular brand of retention. The main buildings of H. M. Prison Perth, Scotland's oldest, remain largely unchanged since they were opened in 1842.

I was given my starter pack: cutlery, mug, shaving pack and notes, ADMISSION INFORMATION FOR CONVICTED PRISONERS. It gave my week-day routine:

6.00 am	Staff check numbers
6.10	Prisoners are unlocked to enable them to carry out toiletries.
7.00	Lock-up
7.15	Breakfast
8.10	Move to Work Parties
11.30	Return to Halls and lock-up
11.45	Lunch

12.10–1.10	Exercise (optional)
1.10	Move to Work Parties
4.10	Work Parties return to Halls
4.20	Tea
4.50	Lock-up
5.25	Staff to tea. Halls placed on Patrol
6.10	Unlock
6.30	Recreation facilities are available for use
8.30	Supper
9.00	Lock-up – Numbers check

Having chosen from a menu of three main courses, including a vegetarian dish, we would eat our meals off a tray in our cell. We could choose to miss breakfast and lie in if we felt like it. Work was a different matter. HMP Perth could produce 600 pairs of shoes and 1,000 aprons per week (we'd just received an order for 50,000 from the Ministry of Defence). Apparently we made every pair of shoes, slippers, trainers, football boots, every shirt and every officer's uniform issued within the Scottish Prison Service. We made rocking horses and dolls' houses, and garden furniture and bunk beds (for B&Q). What the notes didn't tell me was that although I had to turn up for work (for a maximum wage of £6 per week, related to output), frequently I would be laid off – the prison employed its own sales staff, but . . . no orders, no work. A recession hit prisoners too.

'*Struggle*,' Governor Milne ordered. Tall, brawny and paunched, he resembled a hairless grizzly bear. I struggled. Pain seared through my arm. *My wrist . . . you bastard, it'll snap*, I wanted to scream, but the agony was so intense I only managed a feeble squawk. He had grabbed one of my thumbs, turned my hand in, and the next moment my arm was twisted behind my back and my wrist bent to breaking point. Mr Milne held me with one hand and was smiling. 'Effective, isn't it? I used to be an instructor. That's how we restrain any undisciplined behaviour.'

'And do you have much "undisciplined behaviour"?' I asked, exercising my fingers to see how many of them still worked.

'Hardly ever. We've a very special relationship with the prisoners here.' The official terminology kept changing. At first 'convicts' was deemed politically correct, then 'prisoners', then 'inmates' but now officialese had gravitated back to 'prisoners'. 'We've a much more open, trusting regime here. There's a lot of pride in Perth. We're seen as a model in many ways. Other prisons have got the men segregated into small units and they never mix. We've still got the old "halls" here. When we unlock the cells, we've 125 prisoners in a hall patrolled by six officers. Now with that sort of ratio, you've got to have trust.'

To cater for every possible 'incident', prisons would have to be staffed at preposterously uneconomic levels, Mr Milne explained. Perth, one of three prisons in Scotland for long-term sentencees (over four years), had gone for the minimum staffing levels and an attitude of fostering goodwill. Even on this slimmed-down scale, the prison employed 394 personnel whose salaries accounted for £9.5 million out of a total annual running cost of £11.5 million. Perth was home to 455 prisoners, including high security Category A prisoners, and was full to bursting.

'We're easily the most popular prison. We aim for quality care, quality staff, quality service.' 'Quality' was Mr Milne's buzz-word. 'Convicted long-term prisoners get to see a video and choose where to go. Perth, Shotts or Glen Ochil. More of them choose us than any other.'

I could imagine Mr Milne in the video, doing the opening piece-to-camera sequence, Mendelssohn's Hebridean Symphony fading before his prompt: 'Welcome to a life sentence of quality at Perth . . .'

He led me out of his office and down the corridor

to show me what prisoners found, if not attractive, at least preferable. 'Oh, just one thing,' he cautioned, 'I'd be grateful if you'd not mention names, crimes, lengths of sentences or nationalities in anything you write. We respect a prisoner's right to anonymity.'

'C' Hall was a walk back into school, except that prisoners didn't have to wear shorts, or even uniforms: watching eyes, bells, regulations, the warren smells of human life in concentration overlaid with the thin disguise of carbolic soap and disinfectant. Cell doors ran along both sides of the large hall, and up three storeys. A net was stretched across the first-floor level to prevent objects being dropped on those below from the upper tiers. I felt dozens of eyes running over me. I was a morsel of vague interest to paralysed lives in the gap between tea and lock-up.

'Hey, Jimmy, ye old bastard, how's it goin'? See a wee look at yer room, eh? This guy wants to experience being inside – the quick way.' A change had come over Mr Milne. His mateyness had assumed a new dimension. He had gone from office to street, slotted into colloquialisms and was now throwing in swear words with the best of them. His performance was impressive, and his rapport genuine.

I nodded at the man. We were alike in age and characteristics. It was all too easy to swap lives with him. He would have been in for drugs. Perth had all sorts: a murderer whose motiveless case had occupied the press for weeks, sexual abusers of children (the 'beasts' in prison jargon, the most despised prisoners who had to be segregated from the others for their own safety), fraudsters, and the full ambit of lawbreakers, but the vast majority of crimes concerned possession of, and dealing in, drugs.

This man lived in a candy-green room with scribblings revealing that the previous layer of paint had been yellow.

He owned a metal frame bed and a table with built-on shelves where a few paperbacks languished without support. A noticeboard was affixed to one wall. Four snapshots pinned in one corner showed a woman and two children. They looked less a cheerful reminder of things to come, more sad relics of the past. The rest of the board was a barren expanse of cork. Under the bed was a chamber pot.

'We'd like to provide each cell with a basin, shower and lavatory,' Mr Milne explained, going posh again for my benefit. 'We've got a few cells like that but most of them are like this – nothing. Slopping out. It's degrading but we'd need to reduce our capacity by a third if we're going to provide those facilities.'

We moved on. A tightness crept over my chest. Keys tinkled, a sliding door clanked, and we were outside again. Even in the fresh air I found the atmosphere oppressive. The slowly panning video cameras, the hollow noises of closing gates, the knowledge of simmering frustration, the dark uniforms of the wardens, the lack of infinity in my vision – stones, bricks, walls: all man-made, hard lines, hard surfaces.

'Each prison seems to have its own speciality subjects. Greenside in Greenock produces an amazing number of hairdressers.' He saw my quizzical expression. 'Yeah, really. One guy's won top awards. We've become known for our Braille translation unit. We've just put Perthshire's Tourist Brochure into Braille.'

We toured the deserted workshops. In one it had been a black shoe day. Soles and uppers lay in separate heaps beside sewing machines. In another, painters and decorators had been practising in a long maze of alcoves and walls on hinges; it was the cheeriest room in the whole prison, a fantasy suite of luxury decor compared to a candy-green cell, and an escapist's dream of doors and windows, but leading nowhere. 'Vocational training,' Mr Milne explained. 'At least if a prisoner can't get a job when he gets out, he can earn money doing homers. We also do bricklaying, and of course lots of clinics: Alcoholism, Anger Control, Drug Abuse, and that sort of thing.'

'How bad's the drug problem here?'

'Same as anywhere else. It's impossible to stop them coming into the prison.'

This struck me as an astounding admission. 'Why?'

'Because we've a policy of open visits. Prisoners and visitors meet in a large room. They're watched and videoed but you'll never stop the transfer of drugs. Wives hide them in their mouths and transfer them when kissing. They're hidden in Mars Bars and the wife offers the prisoner the first bite. The drugs are usually tied in a bit of a condom. They're swallowed and recovered when excreted. Or sometimes the package is just swiftly handed over and the prisoner stuffs it up his anus. We can strip search a prisoner but can't go any further. So the drugs come in.'

The worst situation, in his opinion, was the pressure put on prisoners nearing the end of their sentence to smuggle drugs back in when returning from parole. One man had almost died. He'd swallowed several condoms of heroin. One had broken in his gut. 'What the surgeon found in him was unbelievable. But it's a sick, vicious circle. That guy probably wanted to go straight and then one day three heavies probably came into his cell to tell him what they wanted. And if he refused . . . ?' Mr Milne ran through a scenario. '"You've a little five-year-old girl, haven't you? Name's Paula, isn't it? And a pretty little wife called Jenny. And every day Jenny collects Paula from school, at 3.30. You wouldn't like anything to *happen* to them, would you? . . ."'

'So what do you do about the drugs?'

'Same as they do outside. Try to help them give up. Attack it from the demand side.'

'Do these prisons achieve anything then?'

'They're the best we've got, and we're doing the best we can. But you're never going to change a prisoner unless he wants to change. Society's also at fault. Okay, some guys, a few, are bad through and through. Most are not, but when they go back to no work, to a family they've lost touch with, peer pressure to drink, drugs . . . when they see other people's kids getting presents they can't afford to give to theirs . . .'

I asked if I could speak to some prisoners in private.

'Sure. We've no secrets here. Why don't you join the Sociology class?'

There were eight takers for sociology and they sat round a table in a modern set of boxy rooms. They ranged from 18 to 55 years in age, and four to twenty in sentence.

I was welcomed: 'We're really glad you come 'cos the screws let us take off wer balls 'n' chain.'

I surveyed the faces around me, trying not to think of the crimes that might lie behind them. 'What I'd like to know,' I began boldly, deciding that pleasantries would probably be shot to pieces, 'is, *if*, before committing your offence, you knew then what you know now, would you have gone ahead with it?'

'No way,' somebody said. Two others agreed. Two didn't answer and the rest said they'd known what prison was like before their last conviction. 'No way,' repeated somebody. 'I'm finished with this waste of a life. I'm going straight after this. Get a job, settle down.'

'Get a job . . . ?' sneered another. 'So what ye gonna say at yer interview when they's ask what ye been doin' the last eight years?'

'Tell 'em I do a nice little number in slippers.'

Boredom, they agreed, was the worst aspect of prison life. And separation from their families. But they had recreated *families* here, transferring the word and symbol to their groups of closest friends. The food was all right. 'Better than we deserve,' thought one. He had learned bridge and cribbage inside, and wished there were more educational things to do.

'One of the cons' – this was their name for themselves – 'videos the films for us, an' all he tapes is violence, *Rocky, Terminator, Kungfu* – fuckin' junk.'

There weren't enough *News of the Worlds*. Three copies daily among 140 men. And two sachets of coffee per week. After that they had to buy their own. And the soap . . . they called it *white death*. Jargon came thick and fast and I needed an interpreter. *Peter* was a cell (from an early make of lock, they thought), *digger*, solitary cell; a *barm*, a dafty, heidcase; *skanker*, a scrounger; *skins*, cigarette papers; *civvies*, commercial cigarettes; *sheds*, workshops....

We talked for twenty minutes, and I found myself slipping into this club talk of peters and skankers and barms with ease. Then a bell called them away. They went back to lock-up and boredom, I went back to the open road. Seldom had the option seemed so precious.

A con was arriving at the main gate as I was let out. He was handed his starter's pack. He looked hard and defiant. As I passed through the outer gate and heard the solid pronouncement of interlocking teeth behind me, I felt the dead-weight of those left inside.

76

〜

Rab Blair, Glen Lyon

From the 3,000-year-old yew in Fortingall, near which Pontius Pilate is believed to have been born (to a Roman legionary and a local girl), to its end thirty miles away, Glen Lyon cuts the longest inland scar across Scotland. Somewhere,

> Ay free, aff han', your story tell,
> When wi' a bosom crony;
> But still keep something to yoursel
> Ye scarcely tell to ony.
> [Robert Burns, 'Epistle To A Young Friend']

in this deep and often foreboding glen lives a man from a past century, from around 1790 to be exact. To help maintain the cobwebs he cherishes, I'll call him Rab Blair.

I'd been warned that he was often crotchety and attempts to confirm his identity would immediately evoke a denial and a pseudonym. Rab was said to be kenspeckle in home-made clothes and shoes and was notorious for not suffering fools or Jehovah's Witnesses kindly.

The hunt to find his cottage proved so exasperating that when I did finally reach it, the inadvisable words were blurted out in relief.

'Hallo. You must be Rab Blair?'
'No . . . I'm his brither.'

> Conceal yoursel as weel's ye can
> Frae critical dissection:
> But keek thro' ev'ry other man
> Wi'sharpen'd, sly inspection.

(ibid)

Intense, scrutinising eyes bored through me. His expression was impermeable. 'If it's Rab yer wantin', he lives three miles thata'way.' He carefully indicated a direction I knew to be uninhabited. He elaborated on this bluff until he saw I was not to be put off easily. 'And just whit would you be wantin wi him . . . ?'

I had once lived in Glen Lyon for three months and the mention of a few common aquaintances won him over.

'Aye, it's a small world,' he said. 'Kick one arse an' a'body dirls. Well, I suppose you'd better come in then.' His brother was never mentioned again. I followed a short stout man who looked as though he had been thrown to the lions and just managed to struggle out alive and comb his hair.

He led me into the dark interior of the cottage. We sat in the living room where heat radiated from a polished stove, and a kettle sat mouthing puffs of steam. Clocks ticked relentlessly.

'I like clocks. There's eighteen in this room and thirty-two in the whole hoose. I hid tae stop the chimes itherwise I'd be even harder o' hearin than 'am noo.' He kept them on British Summer Time year round. 'Nae bugger's goin tae tell me whit time tae keep. An ivery year, whit happens? . . . aye, they change back tae *my* time.'

His voice was soft, floating like a Highlander's, but his words were pricklier, more Lallan. He lit his pipe. 'Yer not a Jehovah's Witness, are ye? No? Cos if y'are, ye kin git oot. Bissy bodies. I dinnae like 'em. They're aye chappin' here wi *Their three-mile prayers, an' hauf-mile graces.*' ['To the Rev. John McMath']

He'd sent one Jehovah's Witness on the three-miles-up-the-glen goosechase. Another, a woman in her fifties and the last one to call, was astounded by his knowledge of the Bible. '"I've read the Bible frae cover tae cover," I telt her, an it's true. "Took me three years by candlelight. An' I knew less when I'd finished than I did whin I started." An' whin I finished wi her she took off frae here, an' laddie, she would've beaten Sebastian Coe aff the blocks.'

He removed his pipe and held it ready to tap out the rhythm of his next quote. He was a natural performer. He knew it, and he did it well.

'Ye want tae know ma feelings on religion? . . .

God knows, I'm no the thing I should be,
Nor am I even the thing I could be,
But twenty times I rather would be,
An atheist clean,
Than under gospel colours hid be
Just for a screen.'

(ibid)

Despite being in his mid-seventies, he hadn't a single grey hair. It was black, swept-back and greased down. Rab Blair might have just stepped down from a polished Harley Davidson. He carried a deadpan expression on his face, what you could see of it, above ten inches of red beard. A twist of smoke emerged from this wodge of hair but his pipe, which curled down sharply from his lips, remained buried save for an inch of stem. In terms of life assurance he had to be a supremely high risk.

His clothes were indeed home-made; his kilt had frayed into great tears along its edges and was held together by a belt. He wore no sporran. Leatherwork had burnished the front of his waistcoast into a brown sheen. Kilt and waistcoat were of the same material, a light tweed like the old black and white shepherd's plaid, or perhaps the pattern more commonly found on cloth caps. His shoes were a magnificently solid set of brogues with flaps over the laces.

His wife, Peggy, had his measure. Devotion was magnified in spectacles as thick as jamjars. A slight, gentle figure, she gathered in her skirt and became absorbed in his stories, providing all the smiles and expressions that were missing from her husband's face. She would cut in with prompts or corrections, and laughed in a strange manner, like a ventriloquist's dummy with her mouth working slightly out of time with her voice, but it was a genuine laugh, as if she were hearing the stories for the first time. Then she'd leap up and pass round another plate of home baking. If you were out, you were three miles up the glen. If you were in, you were a son.

'How did your love of Burns come about?' Apart from rifles, stuffed birds, old sporrans, a sword draped with Flamenco castanets, eighteen clocks, a collection of pipes of the type used by Red Indians to smoke peace with, the room, fading into a premature dusk of peat and pipe smoke, was a gallery and a museum to Burns. Burns in print, in etching, in oil, plastic and brass. His quotes stood out in relief on every wall.

'Burns is ma Bible. Whit he didnae say wisnae worth a hen's arse. I wis raised on Burns. Ma mither wis a witch. She wis a midwife. Used herbs. Bee an' nettle stings are good for arthiritis. Did ye ken that? Tantalic acid. Aye, she was a good witch. My faither wis a slater. Loved Burns tae. I grew up wi' Burns.'

Rab had been born in the glen and lived all his life here as a stalker. Once, when he couldn't find a single pair of decent shoes in the shops, he carved a last out of a fencepost and made his own. He now had more orders for shoes than he could cope with. He'd made a size 17 pair for Skye's Giant Angus MacAskill Museum. He used to play and make fiddles. And he nurtured many pet hates: hill walkers, the Queen, Germans, the English and, doubly, English landlords:

> Ye see yon birkie, ca'd a lord,
> Wha struts, and stares, and a'that;
> Though hundreds worship at his word,
> He's but a coof for a'that.
> ['A Man's A Man For A' That']

It was quite unnecessary to ask if he was a Nationalist, but I asked all the same.

'Oh aye. Sometimes I surprise myself that I dinnae jist grab ma claymore and run tae the border.' He was a great admirer of Hadrian. 'He made jist one mistake. He didnae build that wall high enough.'

Rab Blair remains the most vivid character I met on this journey. He was that rare and precious person around whom an entire national identity, and an industry, has been built. He was the archetypal Scotsman, the personification of the myth, and completely genuine. I felt deeply privileged to have met him.

'I'll gie ye one bit of advice, laddie,' he said, as I got up to go. 'Burn yer Bible, an' read Burns!'

He poured a final couple of wee ones. We raised our glasses. Rab removed his pipe and conducted the grace.

'If the Lord made better than wis in this trough, the bugger must hae kept it tae himsel.'

By then I could no longer tell which was Rabbie Burns and which was Rabbie Blair. I suspect they may have been one and the same.

∽

77

Highland Sporting Estates

In Perthshire, and along the remainder of my route north, I was frequently among deer forests – those ironically named tracts which characteristically have no forest at all. To gauge attitudes towards the land and public access, I visited the owners of a variety of estates which catered for 'sporting interests'.

Some of these owners were titled and owned castles which they opened to the public ('We need 60,000 annual visitors to cover the extra running costs'), and ran their estates on a multiplicity of business activities. They ran a home farm, collected rent from house tenants and tenant farmers, harvested timber and let fishing, shooting and holiday cottages.

Many of the 'smaller' estates were the anachronistic playgrounds of owners who had 'other means'. These parcels of land, from two to twenty thousand acres, had been hived off larger estates, either to earn ready cash or as the arbitrary spoils of family inheritance, usually without consideration for economic viability, alternative potential, or their place in the wider landscape. The owners of these properties tended to be feistier and more intolerant. They let a bit of fishing and stalking but mostly enjoyed the sporting interests themselves.

'I detest walkers,' said the head of one family, for whom sheep subsidies constituted half the income produced on 20,000 acres. The family had been forced to abandon stalking on Saturdays because so many walkers were attracted to a Munro on their estate. 'They park their cars and caravans on the road here and hang their knickers on the trees. They leave litter and trample paths all over the place. Yes, I can understand if I lived in the city I'd want to walk these hills, but what annoys me is the way they think they've a God-given right to go where they please.' A proportion of walkers, it was acknowledged, were considerate, but they were in the minority. 'Well, *you'd* get upset, wouldn't you, if you'd paid £250 a day to go stalking and walkers came along and scared away the deer?'

'Basically, I don't want people on my land,' stated another (135,000 acres).

'Anyone is free to go anywhere here,' replied a third (100,000 acres), whose estate contained no Munros and attracted few walkers.

It had not been a vintage year for sport. Severe weather during the nesting period had devastated the grouse population across the country and the season had begun and ended on an 'inGlorious Twelfth'. The fishing had generally been poor. Stalking alone was seen as the consistent factor, even though the price of venison continued to fluctuate. Stalkers, with paying clients or otherwise, continued to achieve the target culls recommended by the Red Deer Commission. Scotland has an estimated 300,000 red deer occupying 40 per cent of the country, causing increasing concern over their destructive effect on the ecology. The Red Deer Commission, supported by Scottish Natural Heritage, is proposing to reduce the population by 100,000 animals; sporting estates are being assured that this will not affect their annual culls, for research suggests a decline in population densities results in increased fertility among hinds. Nevertheless, the owner of one large estate was endeavouring to reduce the emphasis on field sports amongst those who rented his shooting lodges.

'I used to sell weeks of intensive fishing or stalking. Now I offer different packages which can include days of golf, nature walks and bird watching. My keepers are learning to become guides, instructors and entertainers.'

The nature of managing these estates had changed, but had attitudes? 'As landowners,' I put it to them, 'you are Scotland's rural planners. How do you see your responsibilities to the land and its communities?'

The question appeared to pose a novel concept to several of those asked. The majority did not consider themselves to be under any responsibility to communities, believing that local planning authorities had sufficient control to look after public interests. Responsibilities to the land were invariably defined in terms of maximising and sustaining profit from it. Only one, another of Scotland's largest landowners, shared the Duke of Buccleuch's more enlightened perception.

'What I find is that the so-called "big issues" of the land are nothing of the sort. What you find is a few individuals on both sides who are astonishingly inflexible. What we have to learn is that in questions of land management there is no place for sweeping generalisations; each question needs to be examined in detail in each locality, with extensive enquiry and reference to local interests.'

78

∾

Hamish Moore, Birnam

Hamish Moore, former vet turned rebel-piper, is considered a virtuoso on the Highland pipes, Scottish Lowland pipes and Scottish Smallpipes. He plays them, he makes them. In Glasgow at the age of eight he first took up a chanter. By eighteen, in the slipstream of major success, he realised the *feeling* had gone out of pipe music. It was stiff, formal and overly preoccupied with correct technique. He put his pipes away and for ten years little air passed through them, abandoned for a career among Sutherland's ailing cows and sheep.

'But I always wanted to get back to the pipes. Deep down I knew we had lost so much in our music.'

Hamish sank his spare time into research, studying the rhythms of the written music with the rhythms of song, dance, poetry, language. The entire piping tradition, he realised, had been hijacked, restyled and rewritten. In Nova Scotia his suspicions were confirmed. Now in his mid-forties, Hamish Moore goes his own way, putting old life back into old tunes, putting new tunes into an old instrument and promoting it as one worthy of sharing the stage with any other. Inevitably his ideology sets him at odds with the haughty and ponderous bulk of the piping establishment. Anyone who combines bagpipes with clarinets, saxophones and didgeridoos is inevitably going to be considered wayward in purist circles, yet he retains official recognition as having been one of the prime movers in the revival of the bellows-blown pipes of Scotland.

Hamish sat in a kitchen of raw wood and dried flowers in his home in Birnam, working on the bellows of a set of Small Pipes. He had changed profession from veterinary surgeon to Maker of the Cauld Wind Pipes, musician and teacher. His schools of 'old-style' piping were established in several east and west coast American states, and in alternative Scotland – Nova Scotia – which he believed held greater claim to being the last refuge of authentic Scottish music and dance than any shire or island of the Old Country.

He placed a roll-up in a generous smile and smoked. His manner was relaxed but overlaid a high level of energy, Slow Air over Jig. 'I'll give you a potted history. It starts after Culloden. The Act of Proscription was an axe. Cultural genocide. The Hanoverians were clever. They saw the Scots were culture led. Crush the culture, crush independence. The pipes, the kilt and all that, were banned. When the British Army realised it could use the Highlanders as a fighting force, they were allowed to sign up and wear the kilt, *but* as part of a clownish outfit – white spats and long sporrans. And similarly with the pipes. The Highlander's culture was harnessed and then controlled.'

The army standardised and formalised the tunes. They slowed down the strathspeys and reels. They made competitions out of playing and because 'musicality' is subjective and too hard to judge, the principal criterion became a piper's technical ability, and tunes became technical tests. Today, technique and the quality of the sound has never been better but, Hamish asserted, the soul and spirit of music was the loser. The Mod, the annual Gaelic festival of competitions, had exerted a similar influence on the quality of singing, and the Church had also played a major role in suppressing music, song and dance in the Highlands – to extinction in some cases, such as fiddle music in the Outer Hebrides, once a tradition as deeply rooted as in Shetland.

'Traditionally, song and dance were inseparably linked. Dances were performed to *port-a-beul*, or "mouth music", and its instrumental versions on the pipes. The syllabic structure of the language as it was sung dictated how to play the tunes. As words were cut and held, so notes were cut and held. The rhythm and tempo came from step-dancing. If you couldn't dance to music, it wasn't music. So – the music had three elements: the tune itself, the syllabic structure of the "words", and the rhythms of the stepping feet. This holistic approach to playing the tunes gives us the clues to how they would have sounded in their original social context.'

Pibroch (*piobaireachd*), the 'great music' of the pipes, was also proving to be inherently linked to Gaelic song, and he touched on the research of Allan MacDonald, a piper of wide repute who had won the establishment's highest piping awards and was now rocking the traditional foundations with a thesis in which he demonstrated how pibroch had been radically transformed into a new format. Allan MacDonald and Hamish Moore were questioning the interpretation of the classics, ground that had long been held as sacrosanct.

'The infamous Highland Clearances saw some 30,000 Gaelic-speaking Scots settle in Cape Breton Island. They took with them their bagpipes, fiddles, dances and songs. They had long winter nights, when they played and danced. They were cut off from the rest of Canada by poor roads. The communities stayed remarkably intact. Right up to the middle of this century they remained isolated and without electricity – now just think of that! No radios, no gramophones! They've remained a stronghold of Scottish musical tradition from the late eighteenth century.'

Hamish's research has led him to believe that Highland pipers of the old style and repertoire often sat while playing the Highland pipes (something which is never done in modern etiquette), that they 'clogged' their feet heavily in time with the beat, and that they played eight beats to the bar in strathspeys.

In Cape Breton he met an 84-year-old piper, Alex Currie, one of the last of the old-style players. Several facts about Alex and his family were crucial in the proof that dance styles existed and flourished in Scotland prior to the military and competitive influences which were imposed on piping. Alex's grandfather came from Uist at a time when there would have been no military influences on piping in such a remote area, and arrived in Nova Scotia in 1820. The family settled in an isolated part of Cape Breton Island. Alex's playing was learned from his grandfather and mother, and he could sing literally hundreds of pipe tunes before he took up the practice chanter. Hamish noted that Alex sat while playing, wore hard-soled shoes which he clogged noisily, one foot adopting a rolling beat, as he fingered strathspeys at eight beats to the bar. And when Alex played, people were expected to, and did, dance.

They danced step-dances which the Cape Bretoners have always regarded as having originated in Scotland. A knowledge of step-dances *has* survived among the elderly in pockets of Scotland, though modestly, or shamefully, tucked at the back of memories for sixty years in the face of the highly simplified and stylised 'correct' versions of Highland Dancing competitions. Step Dancing (usually prefixed with 'Cape Breton') is now being reintroduced to Scotland and winning popular, though not yet official, approval, but the old style and repertoire of pipe music which Hamish is championing is finding the going sluggish.

'I'm not trying to say modern piping styles don't have a place. I just want to see the old style be given an equal place and for pipe music to become valued as music. What really saddens me is that when Scots look for *musical* music among the Celts, they turn to Ireland. Highland music has become synonymous with formality. Our old repertoire has been so thoroughly commandeered and reshaped that not even Scots musicians see through the deception.'

79

J.M. Barrie, Kirriemuir

If Shakespeare was indeed one of a troupe of comedians who visited Perth, Birnam and Aberdeen in 1599, as is believed (James IV had sent a request for entertainers to Elizabeth I and the troupe was led by a future partner of the playwright), then he remains refreshingly absent from the scene today. Birnam's own natural theatre of Tay, forest and knobbly hills has been spared Tudor half-timbering and a Macbeth's revenge of teashoppes.

Between Birnam and Kirriemuir, Perthshire gave way to Angus in a last fling of affluence and raspberries. Grand homes playing host to virginia creepers, farms exuding the look of those who possess the pockets bank managers like to eat out of, and a land of benign hills which readily gave itself over to rape, wheat and soft fruits. The berry fields increased until they formed a concentration around Blairgowrie, the industry's capital. Here and there were outcrops of beech and pine, remnants of Great Birnam Wood which marched twelve miles against Macbeth to Dunsinane Hill (OS Sheet 53, grid reference 214317), if Shakespeare is to be believed.

I was more interested in Kirriemuir, a small market town of red sandstone, the 'Thrums' of its most famous author.

'PETER PAN TO BE RECAST IN BRONZE,' proclaimed the *Kirriemuir Herald*, easing fears that the current fibreglass statue would be an easy target for vandals when relocated in the town centre.

His father was a linen weaver of above average means. His mother liked to tell stories and was an avid reader. J.M. Barrie was the ninth of their ten children, born in 1860 in the house which is now a museum. Here the young Barrie used to await eagerly the arrival of the children's magazine *Sunshine*, and when it failed to appear through an erratic delivery service, and encouraged by his mother, he wrote the stories himself. Here he entered the world of make-believe on which he became dependent, his tales winning his mother's love and bringing consolation in her grief on the death of her favourite son, David, in a skating accident. And here I browsed amongst the official facts of his life, and unearthed the sad personal side of the man who never grew up.

Barrie left Scotland in 1882 to pursue a career in writing, moving first to Nottingham and then to London where he built on his modest successes as a journalist, short-story writer and theatre critic. In London he concentrated on writing plays – *Walker London, The Admirable Crichton, Quality Street, Mary Rose* – out they came and in the audiences poured. *Peter Pan* almost never made it. 'Barrie has gone out of his mind . . . Barrie must be mad', was the reaction of his producer, who didn't want to touch it. Barrie found someone else who would and it caused a sensation on both sides of the Atlantic. In 1906 his net income amounted to £44,000, and his reputation was international.

'My Dear Barrie, We are pegging out in a very comfortless spot . . .' wrote Captain Robert Falcon Scott in one of his last letters, found with his body, '. . . Under these circumstances I want you to think well of me and of my end and more practically I want you to help my widow and my boy/your Godson . . . as a dying man my dear friend be good to my wife & child – Give the boy a chance in life if the State won't do it – . . . I never met a man in my life whom I admired and loved more than you but never could show you how much your friendship meant to me – you had much to give and I nothing.'

And Barrie, even though his friendship with Scott had soured for unknown reasons, did provide for his godson – Peter – in many ways: amongst them, gifting him a Life Fellowship of London Zoo which instilled an interest in animals and birds at an early age.

'The horror of my boyhood,' Barrie once wrote, 'was that I knew a time would come when I also must give up the games and how it was to be done I saw not. I felt I must continue playing in secret.' So he played in secret, and his games were played on the stage. This talented writer, considered one of the greatest of his generation, made one attempt to break out of his prolonged childhood by marrying a beautiful actress, Mary Ancell, when he was 34 and she two years younger.

A note in his diary at the time read, 'Our love has brought me nothing but misery.' Their marriage was never consummated. They went for walks with Porthos, their Saint Bernard, but otherwise led separate lives: Mary's, one of cloistered boredom and being ignored, Barrie's, the secret world of his study and the platonic flirtations with the woman whose family he would adopt and turn into *Peter Pan*. When, after over a decade of this mutual misery, Mary shocked Barrie by asking for a divorce, such luminaries as H.G. Wells and Henry James rushed to his aid and beseeched the press to treat the news with discretion and avoid what would have been a public scandal. The press complied.

One of the most revealing aspects of Barrie's character was his relationship with the Llewelyn Davies family, the Darlings of his fiction, whose five sons Barrie commandeered and among whom he openly became a child again. I read the sorry story in a scrapbook of newspaper articles in the museum. This particular article had been written by Andrew Birkin, author of *J.M. Barrie And The Lost Boys.*

Barrie met Sylvia Llewelyn Davies while walking in Kensington Gardens. Their meetings, at first irregular and coincidental, became more frequent and arranged. Barrie would enthral her three children – George, Jack and Peter, who was still in his pram – with tales of fairies and pirates. He would study their reactions and comments and then return home and write them into his notebook. Sylvia was the sort of woman Barrie felt attracted to: beautiful, unobtainable and a 'little sister' figure with whom he could be generous, entertaining and protective, without risk of revealing his asexuality and emotional immaturity.

Sylvia's husband was a young and undistinguished barrister. What he really felt about Barrie's increasing involvement with his wife and family is not known, and Barrie was certainly too insensitive in his preoccupation to have considered Arthur's feelings, but Arthur openly acknowledged that Barrie was able to provide holidays and treats for his wife and children (eventually five in all) which were outwith his meagre means. Sylvia never left a record of her true feelings about Barrie but undoubtedly she enjoyed his company, and being indulged. She even accompanied him to Paris for a week.

'There never was a simpler, happier family until the coming of Peter Pan,' Barrie wrote about the Darlings in an early draft of his play. That was to become ironically true.

Three years after the opening of *Peter Pan*, Arthur Llewelyn Davies died of cancer of the jaw. Barrie, always generous even if that generosity was at times self-serving, stepped in to support Sylvia and 'our boys'. With the exception of Jack who resented Barrie and later referred to him as 'the interfering little baronet', the boys adored their Uncle Jim who was at heart one of them. Within three years of Arthur's death, Sylvia died, also of cancer. George, Jack, Peter, Michael and Nico were now Barrie's, 'my boys'. He rented fishing lodges, took them on extravagant holidays, sent them to Eton and spared no expense in their upbringing. But the tragedy as far as Barrie was concerned was that their youth passed, they grew up, and one by one he struggled to hold onto their childhoods which were inextricably his own. He surrounded himself with their photographs and pinned their redundant school caps to his wall.

'To understand his obsession, the argument that Barrie was a repressed paedophile must be discounted,' Birkin wrote. 'The relationship was more complicated. Innocence and inhibition would have prevented Barrie from being consciously aware of any sexual overtones but he did, nonetheless, behave like the touchy and sensitive lover.'

George, who as a boy had listened to Barrie's stories in Kensington Gardens and exclaimed, 'To die will be an awfully big adventure,' words which Barrie immortalised in *Peter Pan*, was killed on the Western Front in 1915. In 1921 Barrie's favourite, Michael, was found drowned in the Thames along with the body of a close friend. The deaths were reported as a 'swimming accident' but as Michael had never learned to swim and eye-witnesses saw no sign of struggling, it was secretly believed that a homosexual suicide pact was the real cause. Barrie was shattered by the news and barely wrote again, producing only one play in the remaining sixteen years of his life, and finding it ever harder to maintain a charade over depression.

Peter, who gave his name to the play, 'that terrible masterpiece', as he called it, rued the association all his life. He wished Peter Pan had been called George, Jack, Michael, Nico, *anything*, and thus have spared him the misery of his sobriquet and the suppression of his own identity and character. When he compiled a family history (not for publication) he entitled it 'Morgue' for it seemed to him the Llewelyn Davieses had done more dying than living. And when, as a depressed publisher in 1957, he threw himself under a train in the London Underground, the press seized the opportunity and ran the headlines he himself would have predicted, and seen as justification of his despair. 'PETER PAN COMMITS SUICIDE.' 'THE BOY WHO NEVER GREW UP IS DEAD.'

Sir James Matthew Barrie died in 1937, having assigned the royalties from *Peter Pan* to the Great Ormond Street Children's Hospital. A distinguished writer, a happy man in make-believe, a desolate, naive and insular man in reality.

80

Walk to Balmoral

Glen Clova was another long glen and the finest example of glacial bulldozing in Britain. I picked up this geological fact, along with two days' worth of spaghetti, tuna, cheese and oatmeal, on my way into the glen, a cul de sac, intent on parking my bicycle at the far end and walking twenty miles over the hills to Balmoral.

The valley narrowed, its sides became steeper until most of the sheep seemed to have been shaken off and settled on the level floor where they grazed with enviable nonchalance towards the weather. A nightmarish gloom hung over the glen. Leaden clouds with black bruises had fused into a thick mass and were slowly sinking. It was quite obvious that if I wasn't going to receive an updated version of the Ten Commandments, at the very least a deluge was being held in store for me.

It began innocently enough as drizzle. This knocked two miles off the visibility and added to my feeling of compression between the narrowing jaws of the glen and the collapsing heavens, as I abandoned my wheels and set off on foot. The path climbed at an easy gradient and left the last greens of fertility behind, entering the knee-high jungle of sedge grasses, bog flowers, mosses and lichens. The colours here were spectacular in their subtlety, heavy masculines flecked with low-key feminines – jade, cinnamon, flax, russet, mustard, peach, mauve – so often overlooked by a society that likes its landscapes bold and bright, and readily writes off gentleness as blandness. In a square yard of bog Scotland holds her own to no lesser extent than in her fabled frames of the Cuillins from Elgol.

This was a generous thought considering the drizzle had turned to rain. The path oozed a peaty soup and contested its right of way with boulders like grey putty which had been dislodged from unseen heights. Yet it led me unfailingly through the murk, over a top and down into the deep trough of Loch Muick ('means *pigs*, *not* a pretty name,' in Queen Victoria's opinion), where I camped. Just before the deluge came I caught sight of a stone lodge among trees across the water. It was the 'mountain hut' which Victoria and Albert had built.

The following morning the rain switched itself on and off with childish malice; on when it saw me remove my waterproofs, off when I had laboriously sealed myself into them. The clouds remained as entrenched as the previous day and their colour hadn't improved. They forced me to use my compass to navigate round Lochnagar's great bowl of crags. Then came a sound like a gigantic tray being dragged over distant hills, rattling and grating, and the electric whiteness of lightning. I hurried off at twenty-five degrees on a long slope down to Balmoral.

The final five miles were across the royal grouse and stalking moors. Butts had been erected at regular intervals and they presided over patches of browns in three variations depending on which year the heather had been fired, the darkest being the most recent. And somewhere in the scene would be the system of trenches Albert had constructed near the favourite feeding grounds of the deer. Despised by his stalkers for his poor shooting ability and his unsporting ruthlessness (in their words, his

'German tricks'), Albert had these trenches dug to ensure he could approach his quarry undetected.

Eventually I reached the final hill, thickly covered in pine, which prevented me from seeing the castle a mile away. By approaching Balmoral via its back door, I had expected to be confronted by 'PRIVATE' and 'NO ENTRY' signs, barbed wire and even guards; had this been August when 'the Court of King James', as it is still referred to, moves to Royal Deeside, then undoubtedly things would have been different, but in June there was nothing. Not a single mention of the estate, not a single restriction. 'Please Keep Gate Closed' was the only sign I encountered, even though the estate had closed to visitors two hours earlier.

Queen Victoria's much vaunted love for Scotland got off to a slow start. She had been on the throne for five years before she troubled to visit the northern part of her kingdom in 1842 – the first reigning monarch to put in an appearance here for over 130 years. Edinburgh and Taymouth Castle, near Kenmore, enchanted her. Two years later a stay at Blair Castle induced even giddier levels of happiness; indeed, such was her rapture over the hospitality she received that she granted to the Dukes of Atholl the enduring right – unique in Britain – of retaining a private army. In 1847 it was Loch Laggan, and a bit of a let down; 'the country is very fine but the weather is most dreadful'. The following year she and Albert were recommended Balmoral, and committed themselves to a 27-year lease without even seeing the place.

Balmoral's 50,000 acres (as it later became through additional purchases) proved to be 'Dear Paradise' to the lady who liked a daily dram in her tea. 'The wildness, the solitariness of everything is so delightful, so refreshing, the people are so good and so simple.' It was all 'so pretty'. The royal couple wished to purchase the property outright, and in 1852 this became possible through an unexpected windfall: a miserly, eccentric Scot, James

Camden Neild, bequeathed his entire fortune of £250,000 to none other than the Queen herself. Balmoral was purchased for £31,400 which left ample funds for Albert to do up the castle. Under his artistic guidance, what had been a reasonably attractive and well-proportioned house was enlarged into a vulgar and pompous extravagance, a style to be called 'Albert baronial' which set a trend among imitators for the rest of the century.

A path cushioned by pine needles led me on a tour of Queen Victoria's cairns. She had an irrepressible mania for these pyramids and under her command they sprang up in honour of Albert, the purchase of Balmoral, her princesses, and wherever she felt the landscape was a bit lacking. A few more bends took me down through the thinning forest to a view of lawns and cultivated policies, and to John Brown who was standing alone among some trees. He had moved about since Victoria's death, been demoted from her personal holy trinity of statues to the obscurity of a storage shed and finally banned to a less undignified but solitary existence in a back corner of the grounds.

For thirty-four years John Brown was the Queen's favourite servant and, after Albert's death, a confidant and influential companion.

> FRIEND MORE THAN SERVANT,
> LOYAL, TRUTHFUL, BRAVE,
> SELF LESS THAN DUTY,
> EVEN TO THE GRAVE

were the sentiments suggested by Tennyson which the Queen had incised below his statue, and which so rankled her son, Edward VII. But I didn't discover this family strife until the following day.

I strolled through Balmoral's grounds, an obvious interloper with a backpack, uncontested. With the busy A93 less than 200 yards from the castle's backdoor, I wondered whether Queen Victoria would still find

Balmoral so solitary or whether she would now prefer the other property she considered, Ardverikie on Loch Laggan, despite its 'dreadful' weather.

At opening time the next morning, I joined the itinerants of Titterington's Tours from Cumbria and others of a modest armada of buses and visited Balmoral's ballroom, the only part of the castle open to the public. Large glass showcases had taken the floor, full of ponderous silver sculptures and the hideous sorts of things foreign monarchs and rulers give 'one' during travels abroad. The walls, however, gave an enlightening pictorial impression of life at the castle during Victoria's time, featuring predominantly the gillies, stalkers and servants. John Grant (gillie to QV) was given good space, so were John MacDonald (gillie to PA) and Angus MacKay (head keeper); but, not a single mention nor a single photograph of the favourite John Brown. I asked an official why he had been ignored.

She smiled and reddened. 'John Brown has been banished from Balmoral.'

She explained that when John Brown died, Queen Victoria erected a statue to him and positioned it close to one of Albert and to another of herself, forming a close triangle on the east side of the grounds. After Victoria's death, Edward VII and her seven other surviving children were so resentful of the influence that Brown had exerted over their mother that they had the statue removed and hidden in a shed. It was Edward's son (George V) who later salvaged the statue, feeling it was too fine a piece of work to be ignored, and had it re-erected, only this time in the woods well away from the effigies of his grandparents. This, at least, was the version I was given. The story seemed to be concealing more than it revealed, so, at a later date, I guddled deeper into the hushed facts of the John Brown story.

'[Brown] takes the most wonderful care of me,' the Queen wrote in a letter to her Uncle Leopold, 'combining the offices of groom, footman, page, and maid, I might almost say, as he is so handy about cloaks and shawls.'

Brown's working relationship with the Queen was extraordinarily intimate. He openly called her 'wumman' ('Hoots, wumman, canna ye hold yer head still,' he once expostulated over her fidgetiness while he was trying to rearrange her plaid), and at times treated her like a child. He was allowed to touch her royal personage – notorious for recoiling in abhorrence at any form of contact – in a way denied even her own children. For weeks on end, in her long periods of seclusion, he was her sole means of communication with the outside world. Such was the assumed importance of his influence over the Queen, and the prevalence of rumour, that government ministers feared riots if he were to be seen with her on state occasions. And the papers lampooned her as 'Mrs Brown'.

John Brown is first mentioned in Queen Victoria's diaries in 1849, when, as one of the youngest and sturdiest estate workers, he was promoted from pony herd to under-groom of Her Majesty's carriage. He possessed a magnificent physique and, according to Tom Cullen in *The Empress Brown*, the queen was 'peculiarly susceptible to masculine good looks'. But it was not until 1858 that Victoria's interest in 'Johnny Brown', as she took to calling him, took a marked turn; he was appointed to lead the Queen's pony, and his name becomes a regular entry in her diaries. He was 32, and she 39, and feeling increasingly isolated from Albert who neglected her and took to absenting himself on prolonged stalking expeditions. Brown was poised to advance, as she later recalled, 'step by step by his good conduct and intelligence' to become her personal servant.

Brown remained at Balmoral until he was invited to serve at Windsor in 1865, four years after the death of Albert (aged 42). His arrival proved to be the remedy that transported the Queen out of her long depression. For the next eighteen years he was never far from her side, and never missed a day's service until his final short illness. Latterly he suffered from painful bouts of swelling in his face and legs, and a moderate affinity to whisky turned excessive. (Queen Victoria generously recorded his drunkenness as 'being bashful' or 'confused'.) He never married, and died in 1883 of the inflammatory disease erysipelas.

The 'Brown question', the degree of intimacy in their relationship, has baffled all biographers. Some have tried to ascribe to Brown the image and role of Rasputin, but Brown was scrupulously honest and this accusation is better imputed to Brown's successor, Abdul Karim, known as 'The Munshi'. If Brown's influence on the Queen was not political, then it was emotional. Were they, or were they not, lovers?

Cullen believes a convincing case can be made that their friendship was more than Platonic. 'The fact was,' he argues, 'that Queen Victoria was a full-blooded, passionate woman widowed in her prime, and the Hanoverian heritage [the illegitimate offspring of her uncles, George IV and William IV, were prodigious] did count for something. . . . she herself speaks of "my very violent feelings of affection".' In support of this letters exist in which the Queen refers to Brown as 'darling one', and even more suggestive are the lacy valentines she sent. One, dated 1 January 1877, depicted a saucy, buxom wench with the printed inscription, 'Smile on her and smile on me, and let your answer loving be'; and hand-written below, 'To my best friend JB from his best friend, V.R.I.'

The other pointers are equally inconclusive: that the Queen's second book, *More Leaves from the Journal of a Life in the Highlands*, was dedicated to Brown; that she was intent on writing a *Life of Brown* until her advisers dissuaded her; that in a memorial prayer Brown was accorded equal place with Albert. These 'circumstances' may hold no more meaning than childishly pure infatuations in a life horribly devoid of friendship.

We shall probably never know. Scarcely had the Queen been laid to rest than Edward VII, smouldering from a lifetime of being snubbed by Brown for his mother's affection and confidence, began his purge. Busts of Brown were smashed, photographs of him were burned and his apartment at Windsor Castle was immediately converted into a billiard-room. And Princess Beatrice, Edward's youngest sister, abetted the erasure by censoring her mother's journals. She copied out the contents, omitted unseemly references to Brown and any other remarks she considered indiscreet, and then burned the originals. The extent of those omissions is indicated by the pages which survived.

The enduring ostracisation of Mr Brown is puzzling. The fact that he continues to be so zealously persecuted at Balmoral today contributes to the belief that Mrs Brown actually existed.

81

~

Aberdeen: Pub and Crematorium

Deeside regularly flies more St Andrew's flags than any other part of Scotland, although Norwegians, who furnish every house with a flagpole and set of official colours, would find even this display of national pride laughably lacking. I found it lacking too, for Deeside's flags seemed symptomatic of rank vanity, seemed to be saying less 'Up Caledonia', more 'We own a castle'. Every two miles or so flags fluttered from the phoney battlements of homes straight from the drawing board of Prince Albert.

Being the shopping place of the Royal Household, Ballater's wide streets were a gallery of 'By Appointment' signs. Only after visiting the premises of six appointed suppliers did I find someone who could explain their significance. Three 'By Appointment' crests were available, depending on whether you supplied the Queen, Queen Mother or Prince of Wales. The Prince's 'By appointment' was evidently the grail of the trade and the hardest to earn, though whether this was because he was the most selective or simply because he spent the least, no one could say. Once a trader had supplied the appropriate member of the Royal Family for at least three years, an application for enrolment could be submitted. If accepted, and this was not automatic, insignia, certificate and club membership cost around £600. *By Appointment* was awarded to an individual, not to the business, so it could not be transferred from one owner to another.

'We've almost got there,' said the new owners of a gun and tackle shop. They'd bought the business a little under three years ago. 'Confidentially, like,' they were paying the previous owner not to remove his insignia until they'd earned theirs.

Ballater's handsome streets and solid civic pride was somewhat marred for me by the similarity of its behaviour to that of its flag-waving neighbourhood. The flaunting of so many royal crests, and the existence of a black market trade in them, smacked of fragile values; it was all about one-upmanship and having the goods to prove it. These merchants, like simpering Boy Scouts with their Keeping Shop badges, advertised their glee prominently.

In choosing Deeside as her Scottish home, Queen Victoria certainly chose magnificently, and wherever she had chosen would have become an identical mecca for Titteringtons, By Appointees and anyone looking to build with 'nice' neighbours. Deeside was above any need for royal patronage and had managed to preserve solitary spots where, if chosen carefully, Queen Victoria might still sit with John Brown and fill her diary with pleasantness. Some of the best of Lowland and Highland scenery – farming, forestry and heatherland – formed an inspirited blend here, and the roads were the most litter-free I had yet encountered.

By the time the Dee reached Banchory, the first of the real 'granite towns', the hills had flagged into undulating fields. Then followed Peterculter which extended into Aberdeen as an unbroken link of executive houses.

My memories of Aberdeen were of bruised feet, 112 visits to offices asking for a job on an offshore oil installation (you had to get the terminology right), 110 rejections and two 'maybes'. That was in the boom years when house prices tripled, guest houses turned their rooms into dormitories and charged exorbitant rates per bed, and when people paid. The city was in a state of shock at that time, gripped in the nervous rush to be included and yet fearful of having arrived too late.

In the intervening years Aberdeen had settled down. Oil had peaked and troughed and settled into a more stable level of activity. Many spin-off industries had spun off completely and gone under, and the Seven Sisters (Shell, BP, Gulf, Total, Oxy, Expro and Conoco), while losing none of their enormous economic importance to the city, had lost much of their glamour. Among their workforce they were once synonymous with 'big bucks', but now they had trimmed their budgets and their favours, and their jobs were as rare and normal as anyone else's. Aberdeen had been knocked about a bit, but become street-wise.

The city is still a town bewildered by its importance. It has been landed with someone else's traffic – Houston's or Stavanger's perhaps – congesting its central streets, but within a few blocks Aberdeen becomes a fishing town again, without the fishing. The splendours of affluence and vice expected of oil-rush towns are only noticeable in token quantities. An uncommonly large but not excessive number of Porsches, scant nightlife and an insignificant degree of kerb-crawling compared to Stornoway's.

Under rain, Aberdeen's austere and matronly grey granite turns a shade more sombre than is comfortable. Under sun, a reassuring sense of permanence emanates from these majestic streets of chiselled stone, as well as a surprising intensity of radiated heat which lasts until the first intersection when a blast of sea breeze rakes your face. Aberdeen continually goes hot and cold on me, but hottest always when I turn a corner and suddenly find myself looking at the tall bow of a ship rearing high above the street. Aberdeen, to me, is its harbour. Here the mythical city of oil becomes reality, a bustling sea suburb of rig supply boats, snorting and jostling for position in an orgy of gorging and disgorging cargos.

The Ministry of Sin nightclub, controversially sited in an old church and featuring a madonna on its poster, was closed for the evening. I ended up in St Andrew's Bar (the city seemed to have a penchant for irreverence towards the sacred and sanctified), in a nook of life's assorted casualties. Unfortunately my arrival by bicycle had been spotted.

'Ewon holiday?' The question was put by Gregor, an out-of-work Aberdonian hermetically sealed into a black leather jacket.

'Yep.' I played casual and held up my pint, adding 'Slàinte' in an attempt to change subject. To fail would be to suffer the usual pattern of character assassination. '*Holidays*' meant Majorca, Greece, Turkey, Gambia . . .

'Bloody hell. Holidays, in Ayber-DEEN!'

'And on a bike. Without a motor . . . !' added a Geordie. I nodded.

'So, are ye havin' a nice wee cycle trip, then?'

Nice wee cycle trip. Gregor could not have injected more contempt into his intonation. He reduced my journey to an afternoon out on my tricycle. Fair enough, I wasn't exactly a Dervla Murphy roughing it over the ruts of Afghanistan, but I did resent the implication that my pedals were still attached to the front wheel and there were stabilisers at the back. In the eyes of Gregor and the other *nice wee trippers*, I was one of three species: too poor to afford a car, too mean to go by bus, deranged. I tolerated these judgements because they were less offensive than the general pub reaction to an admission of writing a book. In some places travel writers were particularly reviled; known to trade in subterfuge, betrayals. In Aberdeen, after Paul Theroux's dyspeptic remarks in *Kingdom by the Sea* ('it was an awful city . . . [of] tartan tightfistedness . . . the food was disgusting, the hotels overpriced and indifferent, the spit-and-sawdust pubs were full of drunken and bad-tempered men – well, who wouldn't be?') I suspected they burned travel writers at the mercat cross.

'Yes, a very nice wee trip, thanks. Where do you go for your holidays?'

'Ha! This is ma holiday, pal. Life's one long fuckin' holiday fer me.' Gregor picked up his pint and staggered off for less sober company.

'Just wait,' said the Geordie. 'He'll go to the jukebox and play "Things Can Only Get Better". Betcha.' Gregor, he said, was out of work. He tapped his pint. That was the problem. His girlfriend had walked out on him long ago. He had a 14-year-old son who hardly knew him.

'What about you? Have you got a job here?'

'Nah, nuthin' doin' here, mate. Been lookin' fowa months. I wanna work offshore, like.'

'Have you got a skill?'

'Oo-wee-aye. I'm a gardener. Got all me papers.'

Somewhere in the background a thin voice was singing 'Things Can Only Get Better'.

The issue had caused heated debate in the *Press and Journal* for weeks. It was variously described as 'insensitive', 'morbid', 'bold' and 'forward-thinking'. The *Antis* predicted no one would give up part of Sunday to attend. Yet it had gone ahead and for the first time in Scotland, a crematorium was holding an Open Day. The intention was to 'demyth' the process and to offer a tour of the works to those who were interested.

'Ah'm nae sittin' in front in case they ask fer volunteers,' wisecracked one man while we waited for everyone to take their seats. There were to be four tours and this one had attracted sixty participants, mostly middle-aged.

'Welcome to Aberdeen Crematorium,' announced our diminutive guide, Henry Spence, 'and I hope you won't be coming back for a long, long time.' It was just the softener we needed. All of us were nervously beginning to wish we were elsewhere. Henry (he said we could call him Henry) launched straight into the nuts and bolts. He pointed to the central bier which was a bed of rollers surrounded by an electrically controlled curtain.

'We call this "the catapult" but of course it's just a name. The coffin rests on this during the service and is usually open to view. During the service we close the curtain and the coffin is removed through the hatch at the back. Some places have a hydraulic system which lowers the coffin to the level below. I once worked in such a place . . .'

Henry had worked in several such places. Apart from the obvious merit of possessing a fine line to drop at parties to test social graces, I could see no appeal in owning a daily reminder of life's fragility as a profession. But Henry had experienced lighter moments.

'. . . and it took us some time to realise that if the back door of the building was open when a coffin was being lowered, a draught shot up the chute and fluttered the curtains around where the coffin had been. Ghostly! Not nice for the relatives. Couldn't happen here.'

An Aberdonian was charged £130 to be cremated, which was one-third of the cost of burial. Anyone who paid community charges outside Grampian Region paid an additional 50 per cent. 'As yet,' Henry added, 'there's no VAT on dying.'

Seventy-five per cent of Britons were now cremated, and Aberdeen could manage twenty-two each day. Time was a vital factor. Services had to run to clockwork, *but* Henry stressed, and this was clearly the message that had been highlighted in his notes, 'there's no chance of coffins being confused, no chance of the wrong ashes being given out. No chance. Take it from me.'

I was happy to take it from Henry. I was wanting out.

We were led behind the scenes. Trolleys with roller tops were neatly parked in rows as at supermarkets. Coffins were not lifted – everything happened at trolley height, and seven men in total ran the place.

I joined a breakaway group and descended to the

furnaces on the level below. Another small man worked here, making me wonder if size was written into the job description.

'Have you always been a cremator?' I asked

'No. Only been here aboot four years, mun. Wis a Cunard engineer maist o' ma life.'

I imagined him with his spanners looking down on Barbados, grabbing an evening off in the Seychelles, wearing a straw hat in Acapulco. Now Aberdeen Crematorium. The last resort.

'I got bored wi' retirement. Ach, it's nae bad here, mun. Ye get used tae it, ye ken. Maist o' the time.'

But not all the time. He had cremated his bank manager. He admitted he should never have done it. 'The manager wis guid tae me. Aye, grim. It lingered wi' me fer a week.'

Otherwise it was just a job to him. He took as much pride in the Dowson & Mason Twin Reflex Cremators as he had in the QE2's engines. He explained how you didn't want things too hot at first. Six hundred degrees ('That's Centigrade, mind') was fine for a start. If the wood didn't ignite quickly he could 'help it along' with a blast of gas and flames. He had four nozzles for selective 'helping along', but he had to be careful. Too much and that created smoke. People didn't like to see smoke, hence the special smokeless gowns undertakers used. Eight or nine hundred degrees was 'a nice temperature – gies us nice combustion'. He had a peephole to check on how it was going. The average incineration took between 60 and 100 minutes.

The engineer was matter of fact about the process. With the exception of his bank manager, he had remained detached from the personal level. He had no qualms about removing the ashes, putting them in the cremulator which reduced them to dust and fine fragments. He was just an engineer, he said. He was a shy man and admitted he was finding this Open Day an ordeal. A lifetime in the bilges of a ship hadn't prepared him for talking to the public like this. But he warmed to the subject of dust.

'We hiv tae turn on the fans sometimes, dust gets richt bad. An' course we hiv tae wear masks. Oh aye, fairly thaat. The authorities here are red hot on dust, mun.' It was a metaphor that came naturally to him and he was oblivious of having used it. He was outside that attitude of Western society which regards death as an unwholesomely sensitive subject, almost inexpressible through taboo and offence. (From an unidentified newspaper cutting I came across some weeks later: 'Crematorium staff at Stourbridge, Worcs. apologised to mourners after accidentally playing "Smoke Gets In Your Eyes" at a funeral, instead of "Every Time We Say Goodbye".')

The engineer led me back to the Twin Reflex. It was old now, he said, but still very efficient. There were newer models. He ran through names, specifications and their advanced features. I couldn't eradicate from my mind the ghoulish image of a stack of the latest cremator catalogues by his bed at home, forgetting that he simply saw them as machines and diagrams in maintenance manuals.

'Wi' the Twin Reflex,' he said proudly – and this in a city whose generosity is legendary – 'we kin channel heat frae ane cremator into the next.'

I looked at him without any comprehension whatsoever of this apparent marvel.

'Big savin' in gas. Oh aye, we dinnae want tae waste gas.'

An official of Gulf Offshore confirmed that there would be no problem over my request. If a berth was free I was welcome to have it at no charge, but my signature would be required on some paperwork. He handed me an indemnity form with a single sentence which ran for ten lines.

At the harbour I took ship for the North Sea oil fields, having agreed to reimburse Gulf for any interruption to the ship's business that might arise on my account, at a rate of £6,000 per day.

I gripped the handrail tightly.

❧

82

Oil Rig Supply Boat

'Which *bass*sturd marked the carpet?'

Harry the Chef was furious. He'd only just noticed the dirty footprints. His hands were bloody and he carried a knife.

I blushed, and was about to admit it . . .

'Some docker did it,' Dickie the Mate lied.

'I hope you leathered his arse.'

'Yeah. He won't do it again.'

Highland Pride was exactly that and not the festering rash of rust with a grubby interior of linoleum and Formica that the Klondyker was, or, for that matter, many of the world's great barnacle-carriers are. She was palatial. Set in granite in Aberdeen's Union Street she would have qualified for three of the AA's precious stars. Only two years old, she was an offspring of Norway's shipping industry, and a glowing tribute in red and white epoxy paint to massive state subsidies. The extra tens of thousands of pounds spent on the furnishings and finishings brought the ship's total cost up to the Norwegian Government's minimum to qualify for a hefty discount. Among the hundred odd supply boats working the British sector of the North Sea, *Highland Pride* was pure class.

She was the workhorse of the oil industry, the marine equivalent of a flatbed truck. Her engines never stopped. She could carry 3,000 tonnes, turn circles in her own length, cruise at 15 knots, and through extreme contortions of her twin rudders, each shaped like two segments of a tapeworm, she could stop with a jolt. As Second Engineer on board (at least I occupied the cabin of one), she provided me with underfloor heating in my private shower, and, through the medium of Harry the Chef who was volatile ('COOK? Don't youse ever call me a cook again. OK?') but highly proficient, with a daily five-course menu and unlimited access to her snacks cabinet.

I didn't make much use of it. I felt sick. *Highland Pride*'s figure was designed for rolling. She rolled on a calm day. In 9-metre waves, which we encountered on our second day, she became an earthquake in a pendulum and it was only the thought of a bill for £6,000 that persuaded me to hang on in with her.

'You think this is bad? This is nothing! You want to see . . .' I always found horror stories at sea particularly disturbing, but when they came from six foot three of bearded skipper, they came with some credentials – '. . . some of the seas we have out here. You get into twenty-, thirty-metre seas, now that's *really* big.' Captain Peter Gordon whooshed an imaginary wave over the bridge.

'And you can be thankful we haven't got pirates out here,' added John, Relief Captain. 'Not yet, anyway.' As a master mariner he'd steered a bow or two around the world. 'South China Sea's bad. So's Borneo. And Indonesia . . . wow-weeee! You know, to those Dyaks, pirating's just another form of crofting. You keep a pig and a goat and steal ocean-going ships on the side.'

At that moment pirates seemed infinitely preferable to a Force 9. Through the bridge windows the view down the length of the boat had dissolved into a fuzzy, subaquatic image.

I tried not to think of gigantic walls of ocean. Even among these 9-metre whippersnappers *Highland Pride* was being tossed high over crests and then, in some unintelligible sequence, she would lurch and crash into a trough, burying her bow in an outrage of surf while vibrations coursed along her length with a violence determined to crack her seams. Loose chunks of sea became airborne and smashed against the bridge windows in muffled explosions, then flooded down in a thick film of obscurity. Somewhere out there 18,000 men and a small proportion of women were living on an unnatural archipelago of steel and concrete islands the size of football pitches. And to some of them, cutting confidently through the obscurity on a bearing provided by SATNAV and FURUNO, *Highland Pride* was delivering ice cream.

Under contract to Marathon, *Highland Pride* made two trips a week to the installations of the Brae Field. She carried everything to sustain an offshore population: their fresh water, their drilling mud, their pipes, fuel, food, videos and laundry. An Offshore Installation (or, casting official terminology aside, a rig) with 250 people on board would require 200 visits by supply boats each year to cater for their weekly consumption of 1,500 tons of fresh water and 21 tons of food, including 2 tons of meat and fish, 1,800 pints of milk, 45 pounds of instant coffee and 40 gallons of ice cream.

Dickie the Mate ran through the manifesto. 'Just the usual stuff this trip. Last week we took two and a half thousand pounds' worth of pot plants to the East Brae. *Bluddy pot plants*! I tell you, sometimes you wonder . . .' Plotted on a map, the rigs of the British sector form gossipy groups close to the maritime border with Norway. Move that border five miles west and a remarkable proportion of British rigs would be out of work. Although technology now enables seabed drilling to take place in water 2,000 feet deep and to depths of 12,000 feet underground, the rigs in the North Sea are drilling in a maximum of 500 feet of water and to a maximum depth of 8,000 feet. At first the oil flows up through natural pressure, but, as this drops, water is pumped into the well to force the oil out. At the most, only 50 per cent of a reserve is recoverable. The rest is left behind, and the hole plugged.

My stomach eased into the juggling life. After we had polished off Veal Escalope Garni and Mandarin Baked Alaska, we watched a Star Trek video. The North Sea was full of surprises and Dickie the Mate was one of them. A fervent fan of the cult series, at 45 he had been a paid-up member of the Star Trek Fan Club for years.

'You should grow up sometime,' Archie the AB from Stornoway told him.

'Like you, you mean? No bluddy fear.'

The crew were all ex-Merchant Navy, representing an unlikely mixture of well-heeled and sole-holed addresses from the southern counties to UK unemployment black-spots: London, Hertford, South Shields, Western Isles, Cowcaddens, Easterhouse and Dean Village. They worked one month on and one month off. 'Ach, *ma-tha*, it's not bad at all,' Archie the AB said, 'fifteen grand fer six months' work.'

By teatime we had completed the 120 miles to the Brae Field, the wind speed had halved and a good-going blizzard was in play. Brae Alpha reared up tall above us like some crude anatomical model, some eviscerated creature whose skin had blown off. Six tiers of interwoven pipes and grid walkways held high above the waves on massive tubular legs.

Incontinent, Brae Alpha leaked the entire time. Bobbing about below her we received a constant shower of her cleaning and cooling water and the gardyloo contents of her other plumbing systems. By night she glowed fiercely like an octogenarian's birthday cake;

her generators were capable of supplying Perth's 50,000 inhabitants with electricity.

John the Relief was at the controls. He sat in an executive chair with windows on three sides, nudging a three-inch joystick while listening to the test match on the radio. The joystick converted each quarter-inch movement into the equivalent combination of forward-reverse screws and side-thrusters necessary to send *Highland Pride* in any direction.

No run...so England are still on sixty-six for four . . .

'Theoretically I could log-in the SATNAV and get the computer to hold this exact position, but I never would . . . thirty-five feet from the rig is a little too close for error. It's just not worth hitting it. Too much paperwork.'

The North Sea was the home of understatement. To the uninitiated the deceptive quality of expertise could appear as casual and effortless as England's collapse in cricket. John's nonchalance belied an acute concentration. His eyes were flicking from screens of flow diagrams and evanescent numbers – revolutions, temperatures, consumption rates, tons of cargo discharged – up to the crane operator who sat 200 feet above us and could have passed for a pigeon on a church steeple, down to the ABs scrambling around on deck, across to the steel cliff of pylons just ten yards from our stern which continued to buck wildly. With complete disregard for the delicacy of the situation the sea treated us like flotsam, and snow continued to rake diagonally across the deck from the general direction of Norway.

Ohhh he's gone . . . he's out, clean bowled . . .

'What happens if you need to get away fast?' The question had been bothering me for some time. We were connected to the rig by six umbilical cords, thick hoses through which water, diesel, mud, base oil, cement and bentonite were being simultaneously pumped from our tanks up into Brae Alpha's belly. We would stay connected to the rig for three hours.

'If I need to go, I go. I shut down the pumps and take off. The hoses'll snap.'

The biggest danger was from an erratic crane operator. 'Those guys have got the worst of it.' He indicated the luminous ABs on deck. 'It's quite common for waves to break over the stern and knock them off their feet. And these rubbish skips you see there. In three inches of water they float, so they can come skating across the deck. They're dealing with eleven-ton containers, a deck that might be rising and falling thirty feet, and a crane driver so high up it's hard for him to read what's happening. We once had a container swung through the bridge window. Scary. It fair put me off my dinner.'

Through binoculars I spied on the crane driver. He was peering at the numbers painted large on the containers on our deck, consulting his papers and then radioing down for the particular container he wanted. With limited space on the rig the storage sequence of supplies was meticulously organised. He lowered his hook, weighed down by a large lump of metal known in the trade as a 'headache ball', and the ABs secured it to the container. They scuttled for cover. Picking his moment as the boat rolled and heaved, he hoisted it clear, and 11 tons of drilling and eating sundries rose into the sky above us.

There were delays. A hose leaked and had to be replaced. Helicopters came and went and each time we had to cut our links with the rig and retire a safe distance. Then the rig radioed a halt to the container transfer. We were to deliver a package to Brae Bravo and then return. 'Bluddy 'ell. Moost be the manager's packed lunch,' exclaimed Dickie the Mate as he disconnected a box the size of two sandwiches from the hook. 'It'll be a coop of sugar next.' We made the delivery and burned 180 gallons of fuel in the process.

Peter had taken over in the executive's chair. He was beyond the shocks of 30-metre waves and 8-ounce cargoes. 'Drilling for oil must be the easiest thing on earth to do,' he remarked. 'When you see the chaos on rigs you know they couldn't do anything that wasn't idiotically simple.'

Yet it looked quite the opposite to me. Below the rig thirty to forty pipes dropped vertically into the water and down 500 feet to the seabed. Each one represented a hole drilled deep into the earth, for rigs did not simply sit above a single pipe tapped into an oil reserve, but above dozens of them like the roots of a plant. Directional drilling was a process beyond my comprehension but it enabled holes to be bored in curves, even *horizontally*, bending under one reservoir and penetrating a more distant one beyond. And many rigs were not even fixed to the seabed but were semi-submersibles, flooding their legs to float low in the water and being tethered precisely in position by eight gargantuan anchors. All things considered, some confusion over a lunch box was allowable.

We reconnected our lines and fed Brae Alpha her essentials once again. I joined the ABs on deck. Dickie the Mate was rummaging for valuables in the rubbish skips offloaded from the rig. 'Amazin whit ye find,' Jerry the AB (frae Coo-cuddens) explained. 'When they deecumussion a rig, they throw oot all sorts. Desks, chairs, radios. All good stuff. Just thrawn oot.'

Archie the AB, who never lost a chance to tease the Mate, nodded at the figure still ferreting away. 'Pitiful, isn't it? He's worse than the seagulls in Stornoway.'

I looked around for the North Sea's seagulls but saw none. A few stray guillemots appeared and disappeared among the waves. Had the season been different I would have seen swallows, redstarts, wheatears, flycatchers and a host of other regular and accidental migrants resting here, for rigs served as emergency refuges for exhausted birds. On some, kestrels had shown remarkable adaptation by moving in and setting up bases from which to prey on the weakened arrivals. One rig even acted host to a family of killer whales which fed off scraps.

We completed our business and turned *Highland Pride* towards Peterhead, honking goodbye to the standby boat. Insurance regulations stipulated that a standby vessel be employed to circle each rig every second of every day. The crews of these boats were crusty fishermen from Hull and their boats the lucky ones from a redundant fleet. They endured lives of unutterable boredom and the incessant rolling of a little boat in 10-, 20-, 30-metre seas. Not for them the pot plants, gymnasiums and rich scavengings of offshore life.

Soon the Brae Field was lost from view. The Second Engineer of *Highland Pride* turned his attention to Boeuf Bourguignonne and the further escapades of Star Trek. Then he thought he'd have a root through the bins.

∽

83

Peterhead and the Doric

Peterhead had all the trappings of wealth. It had swapped its industry in whales for other sea leviathans like *Highland Pride* which operated from a base on the edge of town. The Blue Toon, as it was called despite having streets of red granite, had not only kept its fishing industry but had held onto its record of being the largest whitefish port in Europe. Four hundred boats sat out the Sabbaths in its harbour.

The Blue Tooners themselves appeared to be losing the habit of cooking. Instead, they frequented a throng of chippies and carry-out joints. They kept a large number of bars in business as well as car accessory shops where youths converted haddock, ling, cod and saithe into wide wheels, spotlights and racing transfers for the essential courtship display of cruising. They fixed hardwood doors with brass handles to their homes and played golf in their time off. A canty folk who spoke the Doric.

'Aye aye mun. Fit like?'

'Nae baad. Who's yersel?'

'A'richt. Aye, fairlie that, mun.'

'Hiv ye hid yer fly?'

'Aye, we've bin richt connacht. We hid wer fly oot.'

The origins of the Doric lie a long way from its home

in the north-east. '*Doric* (dor′ik), n. a Greek dialect: any dialect imagined to resemble it, esp Scottish.' Doric was the dialect of Theocritus, a Greek poet who lived in Sicily around 310 BC. He wrote bucolic, pastoral poetry which would never find a publisher today, but at the time he did quite well for himself inscribing pedestals of the dead and famous. Through association with Theocritus, the Doric came to represent anything primitive and rustic, particularly the rural dialects found all over Britain. These gradually disappeared or were diluted until only the dialect of the north-east around Buchan and the Moray Firth was acknowledged as having retained its distinctive attributes, and Doric came to refer specifically to it.

Scotland's languages have a history of migration. In Lewis and Harris, current bastions of Gaelic, scarcely a single place name is of Gaelic origin but of Norse. In Aberdeenshire, where Gaelic is seen as being purely a language of the far west, scarcely a place name is not of Gaelic origin for in the thirteenth century Aberdeenshire's Deer Monastery was the centre of learning for Gaeldom.

Now the Dorians were making a comeback. New Pitsligo was holding a Festival of Doric Plays. A new awareness of, and pride in, their dialect was evident. Why, they asked, if Gaelic can get a £9-million injection of funding for more airplay on radio and television, shouldn't the Doric get it too? How could it survive if it didn't become the official language of the schools? And they were right. The Doric too was an essential part of our fabric.

For sixty years teachers in Alaska made children wash out their mouths with soap if they spoke their 'filthy' native languages. By the time the authorities reached a cultural awareness of the heritage they were losing and tried to reverse the situation, they had suppressed two generations of Athabascan speakers and, worst of all, had instilled a deep sense of inferiority in those who had held onto their language.

Some years ago in Galena, on the Yukon River, I had interviewed an old woman who was one of the last great teachers of Koyukon Athabascan. She did not believe the language would be heard in twenty years' time. And in *Tracks Across Alaska* I quoted the words of a missionary, Hudson Stuck (1863–1921), a man of vision and an exception among his generation of cultural bulldozers. His words bear repeating, and are as applicable to Scotland as they were (and are) to Alaska, and the wider world.

The time threatens when all the world will speak two or three great languages, when all little tongues will be extinct and all little peoples swallowed up, when all costume will be reduced to a dead level of blue jeans and shoddy and all strange customs abolished. The world will be a much less interesting world then: the spice and savour of the ends of the earth will be gone. Nor does it always appear unquestionable that the world will be the better or the happier. The advance of civilisation would be a great thing to work for if we were quite sure what we meant by it and what its goal is.

❦

84

Alex Salmond, SNP

'You don't join the Scottish National Party for an easy career!' remarked Alex Salmond, MP for Buchan and Banff and Convenor of the SNP, as we sat in his Peterhead office. His features were round and solid, housing considerable confidence and a politician's oracular knowledge of *the facts*, and his eyebrows were strikingly black. He had joined the SNP in 1973, which is when I guessed he would have been at university. He had once had an easier career, as an economist with The Royal Bank of Scotland, until he 'fell into this den of thieves', by which, he stressed, he meant Westminster.

I had come to ask him about the oil. Whose was it? Had it already been pre-sold?

'Currently the UK assignation of the Continental Shelf is demarcated into a Scottish and an English sector. The border runs along parallel fifty-five degrees, fifty minutes north, if you want to be exact. This was drawn up in 1968 to define the areas where Scots or English law would apply. Any oil and gas fields north of this line, and their revenues, would naturally belong to Scotland.' If the SNP were elected to power in an independent Scotland, it would propose that this boundary, ratified under the Continental Shelf (Jurisdictional) Order, should remain.

If England disputed this line, the matter would have to go to international arbitrators, who, Mr Salmond believed, would apply the standard principle of equidistance. 'By this measure, Scotland would be awarded ninety per cent of revenues from the Northern and Central Basins of the North Sea.'

'What sort of money are we talking about?'

'The North Sea has produced to date about 100 billion pounds' worth of oil and gas. So roughly ninety per cent of that over the same period. And to answer your other question, no, the oil and gas revenues have not been "pre-sold". They are collected on production and each licensed block is an individual accounting unit. So it would be a simple matter to allocate revenues between Scotland and England.'

'It seems to me the feasibility of independence rests too heavily on oil revenue—'

'Not true! Oil is important but Scotland has a very successful economy without it. We've a good resource base; we're strong in food and drink; we've good skills in quality engineering and textiles; we're leaders in the electronics industry and financial sector. If you look at the successful European countries in the last few decades, they're relatively small – Sweden, Norway, Denmark.'

There was evidence, he continued, to support the case that these sizes of countries, with populations ranging between a few to fifteen million inhabitants, were the optimum economic units. Scotland had everything going for it. On a par with Australia and New Zealand, we were currently the 23rd richest country in the world in terms of income per head. Mr Salmond believed we should be higher up the rankings. Scotland was *not* the recipient of substantial Treasury largesse. Quite the contrary. In his opinion Westminster had caused Scotland lost growth and lost opportunity. 'Even so, we export more per head in the manufacturing industry than either Germany or Japan.'

Independence would, of course, bring a high cost.

Inheriting the nation's divided assets meant also inheriting its liabilities. And Scotland's share of the National Debt at present would be in the region of £3 billion. Mr Salmond accepted this without concern, perceiving Scots as being no worse off with this personal debt than they were at present sharing the UK's debt of £30 billion.

'What about the disruption independence would bring?'

'Disruption? What disruption? People are always talking about a disruption but they can't explain what it'll be. There won't be one. We're in a single market. We're in the European Union. It doesn't matter if your office is in Caithness or Greece. It simply becomes a matter of paying your taxes to a different authority. So let the Scottish companies keep their head offices in London, if that's what they want, but they'll pay their dues to the Scottish Exchequer rather than the Inland Revenue. Even the Public Sector will scarcely be changed. If the Czech and Slovak Republics can achieve separation in six months, why can't Scotland? With Westminster's power waning, what's more important now is Scotland's place in *Europe* rather than our place in the UK.'

As I left his office, Mr Salmond handed me the latest statistics of SNP support. The last five years had witnessed the sustained support of one-fifth of Scottish voters. In the 1992 General Election, the figure was 21.5 per cent and three MPs were returned. In the 1994 European Election which, Mr Salmond maintained, was a much more reliable indicator of support as it was fought on Scottish issues, the SNP had won 33 per cent of the vote.

That is considerable. But why, I asked, were two-thirds of Scots *not* voting for the SNP.

'I wish I knew. Perhaps we've forgotten what freedom is, what governing is. We see only the risks, not the opportunities.'

'The only constant thing in human experience is the

constancy of change. There is no stopping the clock, and it should be no part of our or anyone's philosophy to flee into a purely imaginary unchanging past. The problem is not change but the management of change, whether to be the slaves of change or its masters. You dwell in the past only when you have no ability to see the future as your own, when the past is all you can think of as safely and unchangingly yours.

Cultures die by losing their capacity for self-transformation and self-reshaping.'

Professor Neil MacCormick,
Constitutionalism and Democracy

'We are at some kind of eleventh hour in our country's history. There is no noise of battle around us, right enough – no screams of the dying, no sound of guns. Just the rattle of a padlock on a factory gate that is closing for good, the rustle of redundancy forms. But even a nation can perish quietly. And that may be what is happening . . .'

William McIlvanney, *Stands Scotland Where It Did?*

85

Spey Gillie

The coast of the Moray Firth fragmented into coves where retired fishing villages turned their gables to the sea below crimson cliffs of puddingstone. They clung equally to the land as to the austere male-orientated faith of the Plymouth Brethren. The smells of salt air and seaweed washed through their streets. Pennan and Crovie had possibly never seen a smuggler but they had pieces-of-eight complexions and Long John Silver looks, and roads which plummeted in vertiginous zig-zags. Gardenstown was so precious it had to have an alias: it was Gamrie (a corruption of the Gaelic for 'running leap') to those in the know, reputedly the richest village in Scotland with over a dozen fishing-boat millionaires.

I cycled by with vague hopes of stealing an insight into the vice and eccentricity of wet fish tycoons but Gamrie's rich lived in ordinary harled houses and the village displayed excess only in churches (four) and the finest bakery this side of Vienna.

By the time I reached Banff, and from there throughout Moray, I was back on more familiar ground, the whisky country of my father's work and my rambling youth. This neuk was Scotland's banana belt, a microcosm of sunshine, pasture, vast arable acres, pine forest, just enough moorland to set Theocritus off on another outburst of idylls, dozens of distilleries, and RAF Lossiemouth and Kinloss whose windows I once cleaned. One of Scotland's richest rivers ran here, and at Fochabers, a village which was once relocated by a Duke of Gordon who found its situation offensively close to his castle, I fell in with a Spey gillie.

Niall had just shot a mink and tackled up his guests for the morning. They had arrived in a Range Rover and tumbled out in a torrent of Barbour greens and Stoke-on-Trent accents. They had cast their Jock Scotts into the eddies and moody pools of Norway, Iceland and Alaska, and were now thinking of giving Russia a go.

'Lydia's been to the Kola Peninsula,' announced a tall woman who looked a dab hand at killing conversation, if not fish. 'She took a helicopter from Murmansk into the wilds. It was an army one and only cost five pounds. *Five pounds*! Of course those Russians have *no* idea – the accommodation and food were dreadful. You could get appendicitis for all they care but you're still stuck there for a week. And you have to use barbless hooks and return anything you catch.' She was addressing a member of the party who was obviously unfamiliar with Russia's sharp practices.

'What'll be loik today then, Niall?' asked a man called Alan, who'd made a mint in barley.

'Ah think we'll get a few, though it's maybe a wee bit bright,' replied the gillie.

'Yeah, thou's got to learn th'excuses before thou learns t'fish.'

'Niall, did you put a Willie Gunn on?' Lydia's friend asked.

'Yes Mrs Wilcox.'

'I think I might try at the top end of the Dipple Pool.'

'Whether thou're a millionaire or what, thou're all the same on river.' Alan cast this little pearl to us in general.

A non-sequitur unless he was trying to get a dig in at Mrs Wilcox, but it didn't work because although he implied that he was an 'or what', by virtue of being there he had to have a bob or two. And besides, the accent was phoney despite his assurances that Shakespearean 'thous' and 'thees' were still common currency on the Trent.

Niall showed Mrs Wilcox the best spot on Dipple Pool, where the hidden rocks were and where the hidden holes lurked. He had the whole beat mapped out in his mind. Each winter floods jumbled up the features and the map had to be relearned. Gillies knew their rivers and took particular pride not only in returning home with fish but also with all their guests. Many a Mr and Mrs Wilcox in chest waders had hit a hole, turned turtle and ended illustrious world tours in Speymouth looking like unusual navigation buoys.

'What does a Willie Gunn look like?' I asked, as Niall and I walked back to the others.

'An orange fly. Ach, it's all the same. Red, yellow, orange. The fly's just to catch the angler.'

'N-E-E-Y-A-L . . .'

We quickly turned round, fearing that Mrs Wilcox might already be inverted in mid-rapid but she was standing in the same spot, dangling a Willie Gunn and a magnificent fankle from her £400 carbon-fibre rod. Niall went back to sort it out.

He led the others to their pools and we sat down to watch and wait.

'These people have been coming up for years. Almost all the people who come here are English, and regulars.'

'How much does it cost to fish here?'

'Now, peak season, a hundred pounds per rod per day.' With five rods to the beat, and five beats, Gordon Castle was netting £2,500 per day during its three renowned months. Most of the salmon caught in the lower Spey were taken during the late-summer and autumn run, making it, in angler parlance, a back-end river. But this year it was proving to be front-ended too.

The riparian owners had bought out the netters who used to work the river mouth, and this year, for the first time, the governments of Britain, Norway and Canada had combined to buy out the Greenland netters for a trial period of three years. The experiment seemed to be working.

'Last spring by mid-May we'd only seven fish out of the river. By the same time this year we'd had a hundred and seven.' Niall raised his eyebrows in a gesture which, had it been with his hands, would have turned a minnow into a monster.

The estates on the Spey were secretive about their catches. Information passed down the gillie grapevine but figures were never published, except when a beat came onto the market. The commercial value of the Spey's beats was calculated on a rough basis of £10,000 for each fish caught. That the Spey was one of Moray's major industries, bringing in an estimated £5 million annually, was widely appreciated; quite how much of that sum actually entered the local economy rather than underwent immediate transfer to southern bank accounts was not known but it would undoubtedly have sent Niall's hands in the opposite direction, from monster to minnow.

'N-E-E-Y-A-L . . . Sorry . . . done it again . . . J-A-W-O-R-G-E . . . I think I might gawff this after-noon.'

86

Camanachd Cup Final, Inverness

'When two false teachers shall come across the seas who will revolutionise the religion of the land, and nine bridges shall span the River Ness, the Highlands will be overrun by ministers without grace and women without shame,' predicted Coinneach Odhar, the Brahan Seer, in about 1650.

'So what'll be new?' has been the customary response to his prophecy, quite apart from the doubt as to whether Scotland's most famous exponent of the Second Sight ever really existed. The Highland evangelists, Moody and Sankey, could be deemed to have fulfilled the first part of the conditions, and the ninth bridge has long been in place at Inverness. Whatever shades of scarlet or lack of grace now exist, the Capital of the Highlands keeps them under wrappers. The chief curse of the town is the usual malaise of town-planners-gone-cubist. Disregarding the lines and proportions of fine old buildings and an abundance of churches, the natural showpiece of castle and river, they filled the town's gaps gracelessly with their enlarged versions of Lego. But in her pastiche of charm and abuse Inverness stands as a fitting symbol for the region she represents.

Inverness divides her wares between tartanry for tourists and the needs of those living in six million acres of Highlands and Islands for whom the town is the nearest shopping centre. In summer, at ten o'clock at night your shopping is restricted to cans, carry-outs and kilts.

At five past ten I passed Hector Ross' shop as the shutters were going down, his dummies trying to show, apparently, how well the kilt goes with *rigor mortis*. Fishermen were still fishing, and catching fish, in downtown River Ness. The castle had turned a jaundiced yellow under spotlights but looked imposing nonetheless, albeit mock-archaic and Prince Albertine. A German tourist sat on the river bank reading a guidebook: *Schottland*. The title struck me as derisory, even offensive, but only because it was not far off the mark. Reluctantly I had to admit that it concurred with many of my impressions. Shot maybe, but not dead, and showing flickers of revival.

With blinkered vision – contentment's essential accessory – I liked Inverness. I liked its international traffic and its parochial politics. The issue of the moment (running equal with 'FEARS OVER BLACK ISLE HOUSING BOOM THREAT') was, according to the *Inverness Courier*, 'INVERNESS CREMATORIUM SET FOR PLANNING GO-AHEAD . . . Decade-old plans to establish a crematorium for the Highlands in Inverness are expected to take a substantial step forward tomorrow.' I felt I'd had a surfeit of the crematorium in Aberdeen and my curiosity was fully spent, but the *Courier*'s story illustrated a telling difference between the two cities. In Aberdeen it was the proposal to have an 'open day' for visitors at the crematorium which was the controversial issue, while in Inverness the heated debate was over whether it was morally right to build one in the first place. Aside from the opposition of some councillors, the Free Presbyterian Church 'slams the plans as a misuse of public funds . . . In addition, Kyle Free Church minister, Rev. R. MacKenzie,

says cremation is a pagan way of disposing with the dead.'
Aberdeen is Lowland, Inverness is Highland.

A mile upstream from the town centre 2,000 people
were gathering at Bucht Park. Old gillies and gamekeepers camouflaged in tweeds and deerstalkers sat
tightly in the limited seats of the stand long before
play began. Highland accents hovered softly in the air
as friends met friends in endless calls of delight and
surprise, exchanging the mild insults that familiarity
engenders. On the field the players in the final of
shinty's most prestigious event, the Camanachd Cup,
were warming up by socking balls about in violent
exchanges of grapeshot.

Shinty's outstanding attribute is that it is a game wholly
dedicated to action. Played with a stick called a caman, the
game has often been described as 'hockey without rules';
this is inaccurate, for just sufficient rules exist to distin-
guish it from warfare, while simultaneously ensuring the
minimum interruption to play. 'Shinty, or camanachd as
it's known in the west, has been played for over 2,000
years and today there are some forty clubs. But shinty
is now at a crossroads,' the *West Highland Free Press*
reported. 'The game's dilemma is whether to promote the
ancient sport of the Gael as a modern vibrant game, or to
preserve it as a quaint aspect of Highland culture.'

'Quaint' is not an adjective which springs to mind when
watching shinty.

'C'MON KYLES . . . GIT YER FANGS OOT . . .
BITE HIM, IAIN . . .'

'NEVER MIND THE BLOOD, GIT ON WI THE
GAME . . .'

'Calm it down, boys . . . RIGHT IN THE BOLLOCKS,
MURDO . . .'

These last instructions were delivered by a man who
was having trouble with a loose set of teeth. He turned
to his neighbour and added, apologetically, 'Jist wait till
ah get ma mooth intae gear.'

A single deft strike was capable of sending the ball three-quarters of the length of the field, and the players chased it in ferocious swarms. They dribbled, juggled, body-blocked, scrummaged, swiped and hacked. The action changed ends with remarkable abruptness. Fort William in their waspish stripes were the favourites, and they muscled their way through the lighter figures of Kyles Athletic. But Kyles were nippy and their number 11 ('Peter Mobeck (25). "Pedro". Fish Farmer. Fast and skilful. Excellent moving shot. Unpredictable with sense of humour. Can score from nothing') scored from nothing.

'C'mon the Fort . . . Let's play a wee bit shinty, boys . . .'

'YAAASSSHOWERRRABASSSSHTARDS . . .' Someone had got his mouth into gear.

In 1886 the *Oban Times* reported, without exclamation marks, that a goal judge at an important match was wearing 'yellow shoes, tartan stockings, tight knee-breeches, black waistcoat, night-cap with tassel and . . . a modest display of jewelry.' The referee at this match was a dull specimen in black. He was overweight and judged the game from the centrefield, much to the disapproval of the crowd and two off-duty referees.

'Let's just say he's not having a good game,' remarked one generously.

'Mind you,' returned the other, 'a good game is when you get off the pitch in one piece.'

After ninety minutes of spectacular mayhem the final whistle went. Kyles 3, The Fort 1.

Later, in the beer tent, The Fort's supporters had sequestered a member of the pipe band to play slow airs and retreats. Two men danced to 'When The Battle's O'er', their steps doleful hops, each treating the other as an essential support. A paunched man stood slouched against a pole of the marquee and said to the glass of beer held by his companion, 'Aye . . . it wis bludgeons oot there . . .'

'Right enough,' replied the holder of the beer, '. . . bludgeons . . .'

They were already dressing the loss in bias, reshaping the memory to make it rest more comfortably in their personal archives.

Meanwhile, out in the field, the winning team had lined up for an intensive photo call. The press forced the captain to wear the tall cup as a hat. He was past caring how he looked, which was idiotic, and ecstatic. His life had just peaked.

'Next stop . . . OBLIVION!' a photographer cracked, to raise a laugh.

Everyone grinned the toothless smiles that are the battle honours of the game. It would be a photograph of happy casualties, of Elastoplast, bandages, bruises and bloodied shins.

87

ᘛᘚ

Invercharron Highland Games

... ...

I had come across them at Braemar, Strathdon, Newtonmore, Glenurquhart, Strathpeffer and a host of other
places. Their appearance on the rostrum could be relied
upon. Some, like Balconie, had bought their titles, others
had inherited them. Some had no title but had bought
all the land, and a few (with names that one might
reasonably expect to have been scuttled at Scapa Flow,
like Schellenberg and Feigenbaum) had collected entire
islands. On an appointed day each year, a proportion of
these modern 'chiefs' don their kilts, throw a tartan tablecloth over their shoulders, pin silver-mounted cairngorms
to their chests, stick a pheasant's tail in their balmorals,
and preside over such-and-such a Highland Games.

> . . . these Highland Games are, for the most part,
> merely fancy dress shows, got up for the entertainment
> of visitors who don't know the difference between a
> philabeg and a pibroch. These meetings, as at present
> constituted, do nothing to encourage the youth of the
> district in Highland Games, indeed they do not touch
> the life of the district any more intimately than does a
> travelling circus. . . . When there is a reversion to the
> old form of Games, there will go, with much else, that

which emulates the burlesque of the pantomime and music hall.' (Donaldson, 1926. Quoted by Grant Jarvie in *Highland Games, The Making of the Myth*.)

By 'old form' Donaldson is referring to the days when gamekeepers, farm hands, fishermen and all others in the community competed in the races and heavy events. The days, for example, like the one in 1886 at the Arisaig and South Morar Games, when 270 locals drank twenty gallons of tea and ten gallons of whisky, and some took part in the 'Hill Race. 1st Prize: a silver watch. 2nd Prize: 10s. (NB Gamekeepers will be handicapped in this race.)' Today the gamekeepers have to compete against national champions from as far afield as Wales and the Peak District, and a predictable troop of regulars who do the rounds of the heavy events. (Most of the heavy records at the better-known Highland Games are held by English Olympic shot putter, Geoff Capes.) But in wanting to return to the 'old form', Donaldson is on dubious ground. 'Old' must be qualified when applied to the history of our games and gatherings.

In diverse forms the key elements of the modern games – Highland dress, music, hill races, and tests of strength – can be traced back to some of the earliest written records. A hill race is said to have taken place in the eleventh century on the Braes of Mar. Pushing, tripping and wrestling were allowed during the race, and the winner arrived back naked, having shed his clothes as the only way of escaping the clutches of his main rival. These gatherings were never held as regular events and seldom for the pursuit of 'games'. Their purposes were to select the best runner for carrying messages, to hold councils or to celebrate a successful harvest.

As with so much of current Scottish 'tradition', the origins of the modern games lie in the post-Culloden period. They began as social gatherings, the first being the Inverness Northern Meeting in 1788 where 'Ladies and Gentlemen' were invited to attend a dinner and ball, and subsequently not just one ball but five consecutive nights of balls. The Braemar Highland Society, in the 1820s, adopted among its resolutions 'the preservation of the kilt, . . . language and the cultural interests of the Highlands'. Paradoxically, as Jarvie points out, it was the members of such societies, many of whom 'were initially responsible for the destruction of the distinct Highland way of life after the 1745 rebellion, who were [now] the very people who became primarily responsible for the preservation of many of the cultural artefacts and customs of a previous social order'.

Of course, it became a highly Balmoralised version of 'Highland culture'. The Braemar Highland Society was the first to introduce sporting contests in 1831. By 1850 the practice had spread under the trendy patronage of lairds who turned up to match their estate workers, specially attired in the house tartan, against those of their neighbours.

'About eighteen or nineteen started,' Queen Victoria wrote in her diary of 12 September 1850, describing the Craig Cheunnich hill race, 'and it looked a very pretty sight to see them run off in their different coloured kilts.' Less amusing, however, was the finish of the race when the winner, one of the queen's gillies, Charles Duncan, returned coughing up blood 'and has never been so strong since'. The race was never run again.

The Highland Games were the inevitable consequence of the Victorian era of romanticism and the image of the Highlands as a sporting playground. If visitors today are disappointed by the general disinterest and cynicism many Scots exhibit towards gatherings and games, the reason is buried as deep as eighteenth- and nineteenth-century history, and its lingering, ever-rankling class-consciousness.

Yet if Highland Games, whether they be Highland Highland Games or Lowland Highland Games (for naturally both are allowable when little authenticity can be found for either), were ever to disappear, I would mourn their loss as much as the cancellation of any other form of entertainment. But I have reservations about allowing our aristocracy and lairds to continue acting as figureheads for these occasions, despite their obvious flare for dressing up and making spectacles of themselves. Respectful audiences are getting harder to find:

> But when I come across one of those characters, complete with tartan plaid and eagle feather bonnet, assuring a respectful audience, in the accents of the English upper class, that he is the chief of this clan or of that, I tend to dwell a little less on such a man's descent than on the extent to which his family may well owe its present privileged position to their systematic annihilation of so many of the things this self-same nincompoop is telling us he holds so very dear.' (James Hunter, *Scottish Highlanders – A People and Their Place*.)

The solution, as I see it, is quite simple. Clan chieftainships should cease to be hereditable titles. Divorced from the influences of rank and money, they should be honorary positions bestowed on those of suitable surname and character, whom others would elect for a limited period of office. Perhaps the contest could even be decided by an annual 'no-holds-barred' hill race? To de-class what little remains of clan activity in Scotland by having a person from a traditionally devalued occupation and background as chief of Clan MacDonald or Scott, would be a step in a refreshing direction.

At Bonar Bridge's Invercharron Games (Highland Highland) a crowd of several hundred had gathered in a field below a wooded bluff. On the slopes, bell heather clamoured in patches of strident pink-purple and stole the show from the mute shades of the chieftain's kilt. I had chosen these games for being small and relatively unknown and was keen to see who would wear the feathers. Wisely, Invercharron's organisers had avoided aristocracy and chosen a celebrity: dentist-cum-singer, Alasdair Gillies. Equally wisely, he had dispensed with pheasant, eagle, cairngorm and tablecloth accoutrements.

Yet he wasn't spared other indignities. For some reason withheld from the spectators, Alasdair Gillies had to perform a ritual that looked as ancient as the pagans, but was in fact thought up in 1980: holding a plywood targe above his head, he had to face each point of the compass in turn and strike the targe once with a sword (a real one). Discreetly holding a pistol loaded with blanks and standing alongside, the master of ceremonies fired a shot which was synchronised to the impact of sword on targe. Whatever else this achieved, it sent a group of whippets into a frenzy.

The Highland air journeyed sluggishly that afternoon, holding the smells of the Games as muzzy pools of hamburgers, cut grass, the eucalyptus and wintergreen ointments of athletes contorted in the theatrics of warming up, and the perspiration which a mild day readily produces in a population evolved through winters. Children ran around with squeaky inflatable mallets and poked their noses into candyfloss. Muscular 'heavies' waddled about with self-important swaggers and the slow-moving menace of wide loads. Pipers were tuning recalcitrant reeds, and dancers were running through their steps before taking to the boards. Apart from the unusual feature of so many foreign flags, including Pakistan's, a notable aspect of these Games was the numbers of cromags being brandished by officials. Either the cromags had been designed for Africa's six-foot-six Masai, or Bonar Bridge's dignitaries had shrunk, but they were clearly objects from another time or place.

My programme provided some clues. 'These games were first held in 1888. Whilst field events, piping and Highland Dancing were part of the Gathering then, major entertainments . . . were provided by the Scots Greys and Seaforth Highlanders, who delighted the assemblage with bare-back riding, wrestling on horse-back, cutting the lemon and cleaving the Turk's head.'

The cromags must have become elongated in some hardship posting of the Empire where the Scots Greys had developed such ingenious remedies against boredom. A quick scan around today's park showed that the versatile Greys had been replaced by Bouncy Castle and Win a Goldfish.

'It is interesting to note that the heavyweight athletes of today show a great improvement over the 1901/2 records, whereas the light field (high and long jump) show a decline.'

It was equally interesting to note, under the latest regulations: 'A kilt is a requirement for taking part in the Heavy events.' 'All competitors must be prepared to be drug tested.' And the allocation of prizes. The top prize for piping went to the winner of the piobaireachd, £40. The sum of £25 could be won by dancing the Sailor's Hornpipe or Throwing the 56lb Weight Over the Bar. Tossing the Caber fetched a maximum £22, and Hopping, Stepping and Leaping the best, £15. As a poignant cultural comment, however, to earn the top prize of the day – £100 – you had to be the fastest whippet on the dog track.

In the absence of such charming pastimes as Cleaving the Turk's Head, I watched the Highland dancers. I had half-hoped I might see some signs of the revival in Scottish step-dancing, but this renaissance was still too young to be brought before judges of the accepted schools of dance. My enjoyment of the Highland Fling, though an elegant and skilful discipline in itself, was marred by the knowledge that before the Scottish Country Dance School ('I can see LIGHT between your heels') ballet-ified and formalised the dance, what now has ten or twelve movements once offered closer to eighty.

Dangerously compacted within the confines of the oval

track, which was surrounded by onlookers, the various activities of the Games were proceeding simultaneously; a heavy had transformed himself into a whirling vortex about to unleash the 22lb hammer; just out of range were the dancers and pipers on their separate platforms, and close by, high jumpers, who had to keep an eye out for the track events which cut through their approach. Occasionally in the past, events had overlapped with unfortunate results. It was not unknown for an errant hammer to collapse the dancing stage, or for a piper, disgruntled by a poor performance, to storm off the podium and be run over by the 800-metre cycle race.

By late afternoon £3,000 of prize money had been pocketed and it was all over bar the shouting of the tug-of-wars. Falkirk's eight hulks, who had tipped the scales at 132 stone, were being slowly dragged off the field by a leaner Elgin. But this was of no interest to a man who identified himself as Sandy, Agricultural Supplies.

A mainstay of the refreshment tent, he must have been personally responsible for lifting Invercharron's whisky consumption above the 1886 total of South Morar and Arisaig. He had refreshed himself into a state of good-natured acrimony. His younger brother, he asserted, had cheated him out of his inheritance. As eldest son, the croft had rightfully been Sandy's, but his father had been persuaded otherwise and left it to his brother. For twenty years Sandy had lived in England, dispossessed. He had been young and angry when he left. This was the first time he'd returned.

He smiled and raised his glass. His mouth opened but hesitated. He was going to get these words right. Through an optical effect his face appeared in upside-down miniature in his dram. His expression said, *What the hell. I'll go and see him. Let bygones be bygones. Besides, I've done all right in tractor parts* . . .

'A toast to my brother,' Sandy pronounced. He beamed happily. 'May he never shit thicker than snare wire.'

◦◦

88

Knoydart

South of Inverness, Aviemore's highrise hotel appeared as a domineering blot on the landscape and forced me to pedal harder to rid it from the view. To me it represented another lost opportunity: the chance to create a resort with a unique, truly Highland atmosphere, instead of a dismal imitation of a modern city.

South and a little west of Newtonmore, a side-road led me to Garva Bridge where my bicycle drew to a final halt. From there, with the help of two boats, I could walk the remaining ninety miles to Skye. For anyone feeling unsociable, this stretch offers Britain's best chance of a long lonely walk. I needed time to think.

For the first few miles I hobnobbed with the ghosts of drovers and the Jacobite Army. General Wade paved this cattle-route in the 1730s to facilitate the movement of government troops in suppressing the Jacobites, but, ironically, the first to use it was Prince Charles Edward Stuart leading the Jacobite Army on its march south. The ghosts soon branched off, leaving me to my westerly migration through glens that were empty save for the great sheep and scatterings of deer.

Like ermine stoles, mist draped itself luxuriously over the hills. My path disappeared in miles of waterlogged tussock coloured like straw. It sank and made rude, intestinal noises underfoot. The odd cuckoo added a musical chime to my orchestra of slurps, sucks and squelches as the miles passed in adhesive torpidity. My mind was on other things.

'It has no unity except upon the map,' was Robert Louis Stevenson's view of Scotland. 'Two languages, many dialects, innumerable forms of piety, and countless local patriotisms and prejudices, part us among ourselves more widely than the extreme east and west of that great continent of America.'

Little had changed in the intervening century. In 1935, the poet and author Edwin Muir was able to ascertain the character of Glasgow, Edinburgh or Aberdeen by observing the citizens in their main streets for an hour. He would be unable to do that today. Like any other nation, in our city centres and to an increasing extent in our rural communities, we have become a polygenetic cocktail. Yet we remain diversely idiosyncratic and it is important to hold on to these differences, even if they are now in diluted form. It is equally important to welcome the cultural differences of others, as an enrichment not as a substitute.

In the past our sense of dispossession, and our fear of it, has sharpened an awareness of our identity. Lying beneath the history often denied us at school, deeper than the superficial confusions of myth, stronger than the creeping assimilation of a sister-parent state, here in Scotland we have a rich heritage, a distinctive image more readily recognisable than any other nation's on earth, and a national consciousness that has survived almost three hundred years of integration with a politically and economically stronger partner. A partner who, too often to pass off as a slip of the tongue, defines the northern part of Britain as Newcastle, and England as Britain.

In a sense then, the threat of being absorbed into Great England has allowed us the 'luxury of some such close and sweet and *whole* national consciousness' as outsiders have enviously believed. And this feeling of wholeness is at its sweetest and most manifest when we are abroad or at war (which includes sport). What holds us together – 'unites' is too strong – is not only a perception of what we are, but also of what we are not: we are not English. Deep down we are Scottish, but firstly and amongst 'wir ane' we are Shetlanders, Orcadians, Gaels, Sgitheanachs, Lowlanders, Borderers, Glaswegians, East Coasters, Incomers, Parochial Locals, Displaced Locals, Cosmopolitan Locals; shuffle us about, and we all become native strangers. Put the Gael in Eyemouth and Gallowegian in Unst and each will feel as if in a foreign land. And this, in a country the size of ours, is a provenance to cherish.

Glen Roy opened up before me, and I tramped below its eerie tramlines, the geological phenomenon of the Parallel Roads (the shores of a former loch whose various levels were determined by a glacial dam at the end of the last Ice Age). A light rain fell, so fine it might have passed through muslin. Up, and over, and down into Glen More. Along Loch Lochy, past the Cia-Aig waterfalls, through An Mille Dorcha, 'the Dark Mile' where the road was overshadowed by ancient beech trees, to Loch Arkaig. These were dreich days of weather with occasional flashes of sunshine; like much of our weather, our history, our character.

'Do not tell me that the Creator has made anything so odd, awkward and individual [as the Scot], just to let it evaporate or fizzle out hereafter . . .' wrote the author of *Nigel Tranter's Scotland*. 'I feel that since recognisable individual human character will assuredly survive into eternity, so probably will national character.'

This 'odd, awkward and individual' character is our strength and weakness, mixing the seeds of brilliance and dissent. Of all Scotland's destinies, acquiescence is the one I fear most, the long, steady slide into anonymity. Independence is not the central issue. No one is depriving us of our 'freedom' – the majority of us have not asked for it. Acquiescence happens in a variety of ways: through apathy, through a sense of hopelessness, through a disregard for where we spend our money and whose local communities benefit from our patronage. As I see it, the 'problem' comes, as it always has, partly from without, but largely from within. Our future well-being depends on something deeper than an act of separation, though separation may prove a beneficial catalyst; and that something is self-esteem.

I repeat John Goodlad's words in the Shetland dialect.

Hoosumever, whin I look ahead, I'm braaly hoopfil at wir communities could be on da aidge o a time o economic growth an excitin new developments at wir never kent o afore. But dis'll only happen if we hae an awaarness o wir ain identity an a confidence i wir ain abilities. An forbye dat, we maun hae mair say in decisions aboot wir ain future.

I read in my journey the inchoate stages of change, a growing sense of awareness of our real identity, worth and potential, emerging from the myths and historical distortions that have cocooned us for so long. This perception, as yet fragile, is linked closely to the physical land and our place in it, and nurtured by a reawakened interest and pride in language, dialect, literature, music, song and dance; in effect, not without pain, a therapeutic process of healing, of going back and redefining who we are and what is important to us. This journey tipped me, tentatively, towards the side of optimism through a belief in the vigour of our culture.

'You ask what culture is?' Joy Hendry prompted in the 1992 Donaldson lecture, and she furnished one answer by referring to a contemporary front-page newspaper photograph of an Assynt crofter and his dog.

It was there in that man's face: a deep feeling of humanity, living experience, an accent of the mind, a relationship of a man to his community, and to his land. . . . Culture is not something for the few: it's what keeps us all going: it's not the icing on the cake, the dispensable luxury: it's who we are and what we are, and ultimately it's *that* we are at all.

Loch Arkaig, with its legend of Jacobite gold (35,000 louis-d'or) which arrived from France three weeks *after* Culloden and was hastily buried by those in flight, gave way to the serenity of empty, utterly empty, Glen Dessary. Once again Scotland was bunched into a concentration of wrinkles. The mountains' ribs poked through a thin skin of heather and matgrass. Boulders crowded the floor of the glen, and then came two lochans of crystalline water where trout darted from the approach of my shadow. A long downhill, a 2,000-foot climb and five miles in uncluttered sunshine brought me into the boundaries of Knoydart Peninsula Ltd (parent company, Titaghur) and to the hamlet of Inverie.

'JUSTICE!' read a memorial cairn set among the shoreside row of houses,

'In 1948 near this cairn the Seven Men of Knoydart staked claims to secure a place to live and work.

For over a century Highlanders had been forced to use land raids to gain a foothold where their forebears lived. Their struggle should inspire each new generation of Scots to gain such rights by just laws.

History will judge harshly the oppressive laws that have led to the virtual extinction of a unique culture from this beautiful place.'

The Seven Men were ex-servicemen, and Knoydart's landlord at the time was the pro-Nazi Lord Brockett. They failed in their attempt. The last of them now lives in an